ORACLE®

Oracle Press™

Oracle Database 12c PL/SQL Advanced Programming Techniques

ORACLE®   *Oracle Press*™

Oracle Database 12c PL/SQL Advanced Programming Techniques

Michael McLaughlin and John Harper

Mc
Graw
Hill
Education

New York   Chicago   San Francisco
Athens   London   Madrid   Mexico City
Milan   New Delhi   Singapore   Sydney   Toronto

Library of Congress Cataloging-in-Publication Data

McLaughlin, Michael (Michael J.), author.
  Oracle Database 12c PL/SQL advanced programming techniques / Michael McLaughlin and John Harper.
    pages cm
  Includes index.
  ISBN 978-0-07-183514-5 (paperback)
1. Oracle (Computer file) 2. PL/SQL (Computer program language) 3. Java (Computer program language)
4. Database design. 5. Database management. I. Harper, John M., author. II. Title.
  QA76.9.D26M44 2015
  005.75'85—dc23
                                                                                2014035554

McGraw-Hill Education books are available at special quantity discounts to use as premiums and sales promotions, or for use in corporate training programs. To contact a representative, please visit the Contact Us pages at www.mhprofessional.com.

Oracle Database 12c PL/SQL Advanced Programming Techniques

1234567890   DOC DOC   10987654

ISBN   978-0-07-183514-5
MHID   0-07-183514-8

Sponsoring Editor	**Technical Editor**	**Production Supervisor**
Paul Carlstroem	Brendan Tierney	George Anderson
Editorial Supervisor	**Copy Editor**	**Composition**
Janet Walden	Bill McManus	Cenveo Publisher Services
Project Manager	**Proofreader**	**Illustration**
Anubhooti Saxena,	Lisa McCoy	Cenveo Publisher Services
Cenveo® Publisher Services	**Indexer**	**Art Director, Cover**
Acquisitions Coordinator	Jack Lewis	Jeff Weeks
Amanda Russell		

From Michael:

To Lisa, my eternal companion, inspiration, wife, and best friend; and to Sarah, Joseph, Elise, Ian, Ariel, Callie, Nathan, Spencer, and Christianne—our terrific, heaven-sent children. Thank you for your constant support, patience, and sacrifice that made writing a tenth book possible. Ultimately, I also want to thank my grandmother, Margaret Mary Atckison, for the knowledge and personal testimony that what we do in life reflects what we receive from on high.
As with any team project, it's not possible without all the team members.
I want to thank John, Brandon, and Tyler for their hard work and support.

From John:

To Kim, Whitney, and Avery, who dealt with my countless hours of researching and writing…during which time I could not kill any spiders, read bed-time stories, or simply talk. You three are the reason I work as hard as I do. In addition, to all my work buddies and managers, who responded so enthusiastically when Mike and I discovered a new feature or set a new benchmark. We appreciate your continued support. Lastly, to Brendan, Brandon, Tyler, and the McGraw-Hill team, who kept us on track and down to earth.

About the Authors

Michael McLaughlin, D.C.S., is a professor at BYU–Idaho in the Computer Information Technology Department of the Business and Communication College. He is also the founder of McLaughlin Software, LLC, and is active in the Utah Oracle Users Group. He is the author of eight other Oracle Press books, such as *Oracle Database 12c PL/SQL Programming, Oracle Database 11g PL/SQL Programming*, and *Oracle Database 11g PL/SQL Workbook*.

Michael has been writing PL/SQL since it was an *add-on product* for Oracle 6. He also writes C, C++, Java, Perl, PHP, and Python.

Michael worked at Oracle Corporation for over eight years in consulting, development, and support. While at Oracle, he led the release engineering efforts for the direct path CRM upgrade of Oracle Applications 11*i* (11.5.8 and 11.5.9) and led PL/SQL forward compatibility testing for Oracle Applications 11*i* with Oracle Database 9*i*. He is the inventor of the ATOMS transaction architecture (U.S. Patents #7,206,805 and #7,290,056). The patents are assigned to Oracle Corporation.

Prior to his tenure at Oracle Corporation, Michael worked as an Oracle developer, systems and business analyst, and DBA beginning with Oracle 6.

Michael lives in eastern Idaho within a two-hour drive to Caribou-Targhee National Forest, Grand Teton National Park, and Yellowstone National Park. He enjoys outdoor activities with his wife and children (six of nine of whom still live at home).

Michael's blog is at http://blog.mclaughlinsoftware.com. His twitter handle is @MacLochlainn.

John Harper currently works for the Church of Jesus Christ of Latter-day Saints as a principal database engineer. He thoroughly enjoys working with data warehousing, business intelligence, and database engineers there. He has been working with databases for the past 14 years, specializing in Oracle administration, database architecture, database programming, database security, and information quality.

John's mentors include Michael McLaughlin, Robert Freeman, Danette McGilvary, and many others who have spent considerable time becoming experts in their industry. John is both awed and inspired by their abilities and feels lucky to be associated with them.

Recently, John has had the opportunity to work closely with some of the top-notch minds in database security. He hopes to produce a series of publications focused on Oracle products such as Oracle Audit Vault and Database Firewall (AVDF) and Oracle Data Redaction.

John enjoys Japanese martial arts. During his teenage years and early adulthood, he took jujitsu, karate, judo, and aikido. He loves aikido and hopes to teach it one day. He would also love to learn kyūdō if he can find any spare time. John lives with his wife of 24 years in Northern Utah County, Utah. They have one adopted daughter, whom they cherish and thoroughly spoil.

John's blog is at http://security.mclaughlinsoftware.com.

About the Contributing Authors

Brandon Hawkes is a database engineer for the Church of Jesus Christ of Latter-day Saints. He is responsible for maintaining the principal data warehouse. He enjoys developing business intelligence solutions that improve database performance.

Brandon graduated from BYU–Idaho with a degree in financial economics and a minor in computer information technology. He currently lives in Utah with his wife and three kids. During his free time, Brandon plays semi-pro football in the Rocky Mountain Football League, and he referees high-school football and basketball.

Tyler Hawkes graduated from BYU–Idaho in 2011 with a bachelor of science in financial economics. He currently lives in Salt Lake County, Utah, with his wife. He has been working with databases for the past three years, specializing in performance tuning, data modeling, data warehousing, and ETL processes. Tyler is interested in data science and predictive analytics on big data and spends some free time working with Hadoop and Apache Spark.

About the Technical Editor

Brendan Tierney, Oracle ACE Director, is an independent consultant (Oralytics) and lectures on data mining and advanced databases at the Dublin Institute of Technology in Ireland. In addition to being Oracle ACE Director, he has extensive experience working in the areas of data mining, data warehousing, data architecture, and database design. Brendan has worked on projects in Ireland, the United Kingdom, Belgium, and the United States, and has been working with the Oracle Database and tools since 1992. Brendan is the editor of the *UKOUG Oracle Scene* magazine and deputy chair of the OUG Ireland BI SIG. Brendan is a regular speaker at conferences across Europe and the United States, including Oracle Open World. In addition, Brendan has written technical articles for *OTN, Oracle Scene, IOUG SELECT Journal*, and *ODTUG Technical Journal*.

You can follow Brendan on his blog at www.oralytics.com/ and on Twitter at @brendantierney.

Contents at a Glance

Contents

PART I
Java in the Database

PART II
File I/O

PART III
Application Security

PART IV
Applied Technologies

Acknowledgments

M any thanks go to Paul Carlstroem, Amanda Russell, Anubhooti Saxena, and the production team that made this book a possibility. There are many unsung heroes and heroines in the production department because they're behind the scenes. The production department typesets, proofreads, and gives their all to make books real, and while we don't know all their names, they deserve acknowledgment for their meticulous work.

Special thanks goes to Bill McManus, the copy editor. He gave an awesome effort to keep the book consistent, well written, and well organized! Special thanks for moral and project support to Paul Carlstroem and Amanda Russell because they were critical to our success, especially as the project went beyond a year. Thanks to Sheila Cepero, who manages the Oracle Publishers Program, for her help with the Oracle Database 12c beta testing cycle, and to Lynn Snyder, who managed the Oracle Database 12c program.

Thanks to Brandon and Tyler Hawkes, who contributed Chapters 10 and 12. They also acted as supplemental technical editors for elements of the book. They have collectively great eyes for detail, and certainly contributed to the quality of the book.

We would like to thank the good people at Fusion-io. We were very impressed with their solution and were able to obtain some amazing results. Our largest object, a 148GB fact table, took only 12 seconds to fully scan. Conversely, many of the production systems we work on are IO bound, leaving the CPU largely unused. It was exciting for us to see our small, two-node RAC cluster fully utilize its CPUs, even though we could not drive Fusion-io's midrange ION Accelerator to its 20-Gbps capacity. Our only regret was that we did not have a larger RAC and more time to truly test the limits of their products.

In particular, we want to thank the Fusion-io board, a Sandisk Company, and the members of their *AccelerationLab* team: Shane Robinson, Scott D. Sandell, Forest Baskett, PhD, H. Raymond Bingham, Dana L. Evan, Edward H. Frank, Ph.D., John F. Olsen, Trip Hunter, Jonathan Flynn, Mark Johnson, Mark Lehrer, and Chris Edgar.

Thanks to the many students and lab tutors who took an interest in this project, such as Chris Hepworth. Also, thanks to Kent Jackson for reading elements of the book and providing suggestions for improvements, and to Steve Rigby, Michael's department chair, for his support in the project.

Introduction

This book shows you how to write, use, and deploy Java libraries inside Oracle Database 12c. It also shows you how to effectively use the utl_file and dbms_schedule packages, and how to use external tables, external procedures, Oracle Data Pump, Oracle Streams, and intersession communication. The book also covers application security and the In-Memory feature of the Oracle Database 12c.

The book is full of examples and techniques that can help you build robust database-centric applications. This introduction covers the following:

- The "Book Outline" section summarizes each chapter in a sentence or two, and should be worth a quick look to give you an overview of how this book is structured.

- The "Lexicon" section gives you the rationale for variable naming conventions in the book, and provides recommended time-saving techniques you can use when debugging your code.

- The "Data Model and Source Code to Download" section describes the basis for the examples and tells you where to find the code that creates and seeds the sample video store database.

Book Outline

The book has four parts: "Java in the Database," "File I/O," "Application Security," and "Applied Technologies." There's also an Oracle Database Java Primer as an appendix.

Part I, "Java in the Database," shows you how to implement Java libraries with PL/SQL wrappers—functions, procedures, packages, and object types. Part II, "File I/O," shows you how to work with the utl_file package and Java libraries that read and write files to the external file system. Part II also demonstrates a complete framework for implementing push-pull paradigms with Oracle's external tables and how to effectively use Oracle Data Pump and Streams. Part III, "Application Security," discusses database-centric development with security as a foremost consideration. Part IV, "Applied Technologies," covers intersession communication, the dbms_scheduler package, external procedures, and the new In-Memory feature of Oracle Database 12*c*.

Each of the chapters starts with a "Purpose" section, providing you with a brief description of the technology, followed by both an "Advantages" section and a "Disadvantages" section, which enable you to compare the value of the features described in that chapter. After these sections, the chapter begins with an "Overview" section.

Part I: Java in the Database

Chapter 1, "Java Functions and Procedures," explains how to write Java libraries to support PL/SQL functions and procedures. The chapter shows you how to use loadjava to upload Java class files and how to use SQL to create or replace and compile Java source programs. You learn how to pass scalar and Attribute Definition Type (ADT) parameter values from PL/SQL to Java libraries. You also learn how to troubleshoot working with Java libraries.

Chapter 2, "Object Types," introduces how to work with the SQLData interface and pass objects from PL/SQL to Java libraries and back. It also shows you how to work with Oracle's oracle.jdbc.Struct class as a parameter, including the limits on how a SQL Date data type inside a Struct casts to the Java Timestamp.

Part II: File I/O

Chapter 3, "utl_file Package," shows you how to use the package to read and write data files. The chapter also shows you how to create and work with virtual directories when using the utl_file package. You learn the limits of copying files with the utl_file package and how to leverage the package to write structured and unstructured data.

Chapter 4, "Java I/O Libraries," covers the configuration of Java permissions to read, write, and execute external files. This chapter also shows you how to use Java libraries to read and write structured and unstructured data. It covers the 4,000-byte limit when working with variable-length strings in Java libraries.

Chapter 5, "External Tables," describes how to define and use external tables, including the necessary privileges required on external virtual and physical directories. The chapter also describes an effective framework for managing the push-pull paradigm for large input files and how to combine PL/SQL and Java to create this framework.

Chapter 6, "High-Speed Data Transfer," explains various methods of transferring large amounts of data within and external to the database. It introduces various extract, transform, and load (ETL/ELT) tools and explains how to use the impdp and expdp utilities. Lastly, it illustrates how to use the dbms_datapump API.

Part III: Application Security

Chapter 7, "Database Security," uses four specific case studies to shed light on some of the vulnerabilities that database environments can have. It introduces enhanced methods of password hashing, password dictionaries, rainbow tables, and password validation. This chapter also shows how to align database security programs with programs like SANS and NIST and discusses how to obtain executive sponsorship of database security programs.

Chapter 8, "Developing Secure Applications," explains why good design patterns are essential to building maintainable database systems. It introduces auditing and Oracle Audit Vault. This chapter explains how secure application roles work and introduces an enhanced method of this technique using proxy access and after logon triggers. This chapter also discusses how to sanitize SQL and PL/SQL input parameters via bind variables and `dbms_assert`.

Part IV: Applied Technologies

Chapter 9, "dbms_scheduler Package," details Oracle's scheduler. It illustrates how to create simple jobs and shows how to create programs and job chains. This chapter also details how to create custom schedules and shows how to use `dbms_scheduler` to rebuild indexes in a fraction of the time that it takes for common scripts.

Chapter 10, "Optimizing Using PL/SQL," introduces you to performance tuning concepts and how to gather effective statistics to analyze the effectiveness of your PL/SQL programs. The chapter also introduces key performance views and different SQL queries that let you gauge the performance of your queries.

Chapter 11, "External Procedures," explains how to use external procedures, and shows you how to build them in external C libraries. This chapter also covers the Oracle heterogeneous service agent and how to configure the `listener.ora` file to support external procedures.

Chapter 12, "In-Memory Column Store," shows you how to use and implement the new In-Memory Column Store (IMCS), which becomes available in release 12.1.0.2. This chapter also shows you how to configure and work with the SGA to maximize performance.

The appendix, "Oracle Database Java Primer," covers the fundamentals of the Java programming language and discusses the Oracle JDBC connection for Oracle Database 12c. It also demonstrates how to build stand-alone Java applications that work with the database, including LOBs.

Lexicon

There are many ways to write programs, and they generally differ between programming languages. SQL and PL/SQL code share that commonality: they are different languages and require different approaches. The three subsections cover, respectively, SQL lexicon, PL/SQL stored programs, and other conventions in syntax.

SQL Lexicon

Our recommendation on SQL statements is that you align your keywords on the left. That means placing SELECT list commas and WHERE clause logical AND [NOT] or OR [NOT] syntax on the left, because it allows you to sight-read your code for errors. That recommendation is easy to follow, but our recommendations on how to write *join syntax* are more complex because you may write joins that use ANSI SQL-89 or ANSI SQL-92. Whereas ANSI SQL-89 lets you organize tables as comma-delimited lists, ANSI SQL-92 has you specify the type of join using keywords.

These are our suggestions on join syntax:

- Always use table aliases, because they ensure you won't run into an ambiguous column error when the SELECT list can return two or more columns with the same name. This can happen when you join tables that share the same column name. It's also a good practice to use aliases when you write a query from a single table, because you may subsequently add another table through a join. Appendix B of the *Oracle Database 12c PL/SQL Programming* book covers the SELECT statement and syntax that supports this recommendation.

■ When using ANSI SQL-89 and comma-delimited tables, place each table on its own line and the separating columns on the left, like SELECT list columns. This lets you sight-read your programs.

■ When using ANSI SQL-92, you put the join conditions inside the FROM clause by using either the ON subclause or the USING subclause. Two common approaches seem to work best for most developers inside the FROM clause with the ON or USING subclause. In small (two or, at maximum, three) table joins, place the ON or USING subclause after the join on the same line. In large joins (three or more), place the ON or USING subclause on the line below the joining statement. When joins involve multiple columns, left-align logical AND [NOT] or OR [NOT] syntax to allow you to sight-read your code. This is the same recommendation as I made for the WHERE clause at the beginning of the section, and it really works well generally.

■ ANSI SQL-92 lets you use fully descriptive keywords or use only required keywords. While most of us would like to type the least amount of words possible, ultimately, our code goes to support staff, and its clarity can help avoid frivolous bug reports. Therefore, consider using INNER JOIN instead of JOIN; LEFT OUTER JOIN or RIGHT OUTER JOIN instead of LEFT JOIN and RIGHT JOIN; and FULL OUTER JOIN instead of FULL JOIN. We've shortened syntax in the book solely because the page-width constraints put a 70-character limit on code lines (or require shrinking the font, which make it less readable).

With that in mind, let us share one of our experiences at *not* following syntax advice. The advice was given to Michael by his instructor at IBM's Santa Teresa Lab (now IBM's Silicon Valley Lab) when he taught him how to write SQL (actually SQL/DS, Structured Query Language/Data System) in 1985. He told Michael to put the commas on the left and save himself hours of hunting for missing commas. Michael ignored the advice and put them on the right, at the end of the line, for a couple of months before realizing he was right. The instructor repeated this maxim to Michael often that week: "Good programming follows simple principles."

A Word on Tools
This book focuses on writing SQL at the command line, because that's how it'll work inside your C++, C#, Java, or PHP programs, but CASE (Computer-Aided Software Engineering) tools are nice. They help you discover syntax and possibilities, provided you don't use them as a crutch.

The best developers aren't those business users who know how to talk a great game, use all the catchwords properly, and market themselves. The best developers are folks who learn how to solve business problems by understanding which technology truly provides the best solution.

Those who apply good engineering skills aren't members of an exclusive club unless we lock ourselves into only using what a CASE tool provides us. That's true because CASE tools generally only solve the general problems through a drag-and-drop interface. Those folks who advocate *NoSQL* solutions are typically those who never understood how to use a database or how databases help meet critical day-to-day business needs.

In short, use a tool to learn; don't become a slave to it. Always ask why something works and how it might work better. If you do, you'll find that CASE tools are a blessing for getting your job done, not a potentially career-limiting curse (as many have found over the past few years).

At school now, Michael emphasizes this advice term after term. Some students accept it and use it, and some don't. Those students who don't accept it struggle with the syntax throughout the course because they're always trying to find that missing comma or component in their SQL statement. SQL is not an easy thing to learn because it requires creating a spatial map of data, which isn't a skill all developers possess immediately. Sometimes it takes quite a while to sort through seeing the relationships between data in a relational database. It becomes easier with practice, provided you strive to maintain the clarity of your statements, the consistencies of your approach, and a consistent choice of using portable SQL syntax.

PL/SQL Stored Programs

PL/SQL is a fully fledged programming language. It allows you to write programs stored in the database that manage collections of SQL statements as a complete transaction.

Variable naming conventions can be controversial in some organizations because many developers believe variables should be semantically meaningful. The argument against naming conventions is that the conventions, such as prefixes, decrease code readability. This controversy is simply a conflict of ideas. Both sides have merit, and there are always situations in which choosing one practice over the other is logical. From our perspective, the key is finding balance between what adds stability to the company or corporate enterprise while providing meaningful variable names.

Here in the book, we've tried to be consistent and use prefixes. In some places, we've opted for semantic clarity in variable names. We believe that using prefixes increases readability in your code, and we suggest using the prefixes in Table 1.

Some advanced variable data types, known as composite variables, require both prefixes and suffixes. The suffix identifies the type of composite variable. These requirements are unique to the Oracle database. Table 2 qualifies our recommended suffixes (with a lead-in underscore) for Oracle composite data types. Table 2 shows you long and short name versions for the suffixes.

Prefix	Example	Description
cv	cv_input_var	Represents cursor parameter variables. These are pass-by-value input parameters to cursors in PL/SQL stored programs.
lv	lv_target_var	Represents local variables defined inside PL/SQL stored programs.
pv	pv_exchange_var	Represents parameters to PL/SQL stored functions and procedures. They're not exclusively input parameters because PL/SQL supports input and output parameters in both stored functions and procedures.
sv	sv_global_var	Represents session, or Oracle's *bind*, variables. They act as global variables for the duration of a client connection to the database. Oracle lets you share the values in these variables between anonymous blocks by using a colon before the variable name (:sv_global_var) inside the block; and they're called bind variables because they bind the variable to the session.

TABLE 1. *PL/SQL Variable Prefixes*

Suffix		Description
Long	**Short**	
_ATABLE _AARRAY	_ATAB _AA	_ATABLE, _AVARRAY, _ATAB, and _AA are used to describe associative arrays in PL/SQL. Our preference is the _ATABLE or _ATAB suffix because the other suffixes aren't intuitively obvious and require documentation in your code.
_CURSOR	_CUR _C	_CURSOR, _CUR, and _C are used to describe variables based on a cursor structure defined in a local declaration block or a package specification in PL/SQL. Our preference is the _CURSOR or _C suffix.
_EXCEPTION	_EXCEPT _EX _E	_EXCEPTION, _EXCEPT, _EX, and _E are used to describe user-defined exceptions in PL/SQL. Our preference is the _EXCEPTION or _E suffix.
_OBJECT	_OBJ _O	_OBJECT, _OBJ, and _O are used to describe user-defined types (UDTs) in both SQL and PL/SQL. Object types can act like PL/SQL RECORD data types, which are record data structures. They differ because they're schema-level SQL UDTs and not exclusively PL/SQL UDTs. Object types can also be instantiable objects such as C++, C#, and Java classes. Our preference is the _OBJECT or _O suffix.
_NTABLE _TABLE	_NTAB _TAB	_NTABLE, _TABLE, _NTAB, and _TAB are used to describe nested tables, which are collection types in SQL and PL/SQL. They act like lists because they have no upward limit on how many elements can be in the collection. Our preference is the _TABLE or _TAB suffix because a nested table is the collection most like a list in other programming languages.
_RECORD	_REC _R	_RECORD, _REC, and _R are used to describe UDTs exclusively in PL/SQL. They are a PL/SQL implementation of a record data structure. They can be elements of PL/SQL collections but not of SQL collections. Our preference is the _RECORD or _R suffix because they're fully descriptive or shorthand, but many developers opt for _REC.
_TYPE	_T	_TYPE and _T are used to describe UDTs, like subtypes of normal scalar data types. Either suffix works for us, but _TYPE seems more frequent in code repositories.
_VARRAY	_VARR _VA	_VARRAY, _VARR, and _VA are used to describe the VARRAY (our mnemonic for this Oracle data type is *virtual array*). The VARRAY collection is the collection most like a standard array in programming languages, because it has a maximum size and must always have sequential index values. It can be used to define SQL and PL/SQL collections. Our preference is the _VARRAY or _VA suffix because _VARR too closely resembles generic variable shorthand.

TABLE 2.   *PL/SQL Variable Suffixes*

Using suffixes for composite data types is a generally accepted practice because they are UDTs. However, it isn't a rule or requirement in the PL/SQL programming language.

PL/SQL is a strongly typed language with declaration, execution, and exception blocks. Blocked programs use keywords to start and end program units, as opposed to the use of curly braces in C++, C#, Java, and PHP. As found in the GeSHi (Generic Syntax Highlighter) libraries, PL/SQL block keywords are in uppercase letters, and we've adopted that convention throughout the book.

Other Conventions

Sometimes code blocks need clarity. Line numbers are provided throughout the PL/SQL and SQL examples for Oracle because they're a display feature of the SQL*Plus environment.

The text conventions for the book cover highlighting, italicizing, and separating syntax. They are qualified in Table 3.

Hopefully, these conventions make reading the book easier. You'll also find that sidebars appear in gray shaded boxes throughout the book.

Convention	Meaning
Boldface	Focuses attention on specific lines of code in sample programs.
Italics	Focuses attention on new words or concepts.
`Monospaced`	All code blocks are `monospaced`.
`UPPERCASE COURIER`	Denotes keywords used in SQL and PL/SQL, and SQL built-in function names.
`lowercase courier`	Denotes the names of user-defined tables, views, columns, functions, procedures, packages, and types.
[]	Designates optional syntax and appears in the prototypes.
{}	Groups lists of options, which are separated by a single pipe symbol (|).
|	Indicates a logical OR operator between option lists.
...	Indicates that content repeats or was removed for space conservation.

TABLE 3. *Text Conventions*

Data Model and Source Code to Download

The data model is a small video store. The source code to create and seed the data model for Oracle is found on the publisher's website for the book: **www.OraclePressBooks.com**

Figure 1 shows the basic, or core, tables used in the example programs. Figure 6-2 in Chapter 6 shows the ERD for the data warehouse used in a number of the security, performance, and tuning chapters.

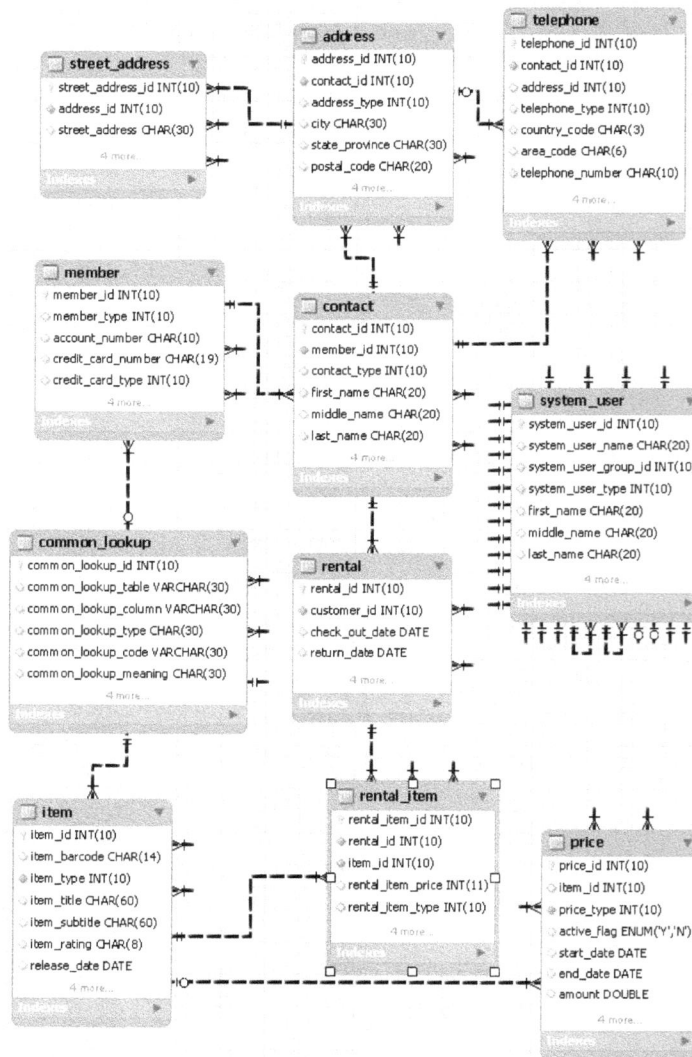

FIGURE 1. *Video store entity-relationship diagram (ERD)*

common_lookup_id	common_lookup_table	common_lookup_column	common_lookup_type	common_lookup_meaning
1	SYSTEM_USER	system_user_id	SYSTEM_ADMIN	System Administrator
2	SYSTEM_USER	system_user_id	DBA	Database Administrator
3	CONTACT	CONTACT_TYPE	EMPLOYEE	Employee
4	CONTACT	CONTACT_TYPE	CUSTOMER	Customer
5	MEMBER	MEMBER_TYPE	INDIVIDUAL	Individual Membership
6	MEMBER	MEMBER_TYPE	GROUP	Group Membership
7	MEMBER	CREDIT_CARD_TYPE	DISCOVER_CARD	Discover Card
8	MEMBER	CREDIT_CARD_TYPE	MASTER_CARD	Master Card
9	MEMBER	CREDIT_CARD_TYPE	VISA_CARD	VISA Card
10	ADDRESS	ADDRESS_TYPE	HOME	Home
11	ADDRESS	ADDRESS_TYPE	WORK	Work
12	ITEM	ITEM_TYPE	DVD_FULL_SCREEN	DVD: Full Screen
13	ITEM	ITEM_TYPE	DVD_WIDE_SCREEN	DVD: Wide Screen
14	ITEM	ITEM_TYPE	NINTENDO_GAMECUBE	Nintendo GameCube
15	ITEM	ITEM_TYPE	PLAYSTATION2	PlayStation2
16	ITEM	ITEM_TYPE	XBOX	XBOX
17	ITEM	ITEM_TYPE	VHS_SINGLE_TAPE	VHS: Single Tape
18	ITEM	ITEM_TYPE	VHS_DOUBLE_TAPE	VHS: Double Tape
19	TELEPHONE	TELEPHONE_TYPE	HOME	Home
20	TELEPHONE	TELEPHONE_TYPE	WORK	Work
21	PRICE	ACTIVE_FLAG	YES	Yes
22	PRICE	ACTIVE_FLAG	NO	NO

FIGURE 2. *The* `common_lookup` *table (table of tables)*

One table in the model may require some explanation, and that's the `common_lookup` table. The `common_lookup` table is a table of tables, as shown in Figure 2.

A set of attributes (columns) that uniquely identify rows is the natural key. It consists of the table and column names plus the type. Types are uppercase strings joined by underscores that make querying these lookup sets easier. The `common_lookup_meaning` column provides the information that you'd provide to an end user making a choice in a drop-down list box.

The primary key of the `common_lookup` table is a surrogate key column, `common_lookup_id` (following the practice of using the table name and an `_id` suffix for primary key column names). A copy of this value is stored in the table and column, such as `item` and `item_type`. With this type of design, you can change the display value of *XBOX* to *Xbox* in a single location, and all code modules and table values would be unchanged. It's a powerful modeling device because it prevents placing components like gender, race, or yes/no answers in web forms (embedded options), and it reduces management costs of your application after deployment.

Let's examine an approach to leveraging common lookup tables in a web-based application. The explanation starts with data stored in a join between two tables—the `member` and `contact` tables. The internal lookup uses the customer's name (the natural key) from the `contact` table to find the membership account information in the `member` table.

```
SELECT   m.account_number
     ,   m.member_type          -- A fk to common_lookup table.
     ,   m.credit_card_number
     ,   m.credit_card_type      -- A fk to common_lookup table.
     ,   c.first_name
     ,   c.middle_name
     ,   c.last_name
     ,   c.contact_type          -- A fk to common_lookup table.
FROM     member m INNER JOIN contact c
ON       m.member_id = c.member_id
WHERE    c.first_name = 'Harry'
AND      c.middle_name = 'James'
AND      c.last_name = 'Potter';
```

The preceding query returns the following display when you run it through the dbms_sql Method 4 code example discussed in Chapter 13 of *Oracle Database 12c PL/SQL Programming*, which displays column names on the left and column values on the right. You should note that the member_type, credit_card_type, and contact_type columns hold foreign key values based on the common_lookup_id surrogate key column.

```
       account_number: SLC-000006
          member_type: 6
   credit_card_number: 6011-0000-0000-0086
     credit_card_type: 7
           first_name: Harry
          middle_name: James
            last_name: Potter
         contact_type: 4
```

You have the option of using these values to connect the data through a join or through function calls to the common_lookup table. The common_lookup table contains values that are frequently displayed in application software forms.

The following join connects all three foreign keys to three separate rows in the common_lookup table:

```
SELECT   m.account_number
     ,   cl1.common_lookup_meaning -- Customer friendly display.
     ,   m.credit_card_number
     ,   cl2.common_lookup_meaning -- Customer friendly display.
     ,   c.first_name
     ,   c.middle_name
     ,   c.last_name
     ,   cl3.common_lookup_meaning -- Customer friendly display.
FROM     member m INNER JOIN contact c
ON       m.member_id = c.member_id JOIN common_lookup cl1
ON       cl1.common_lookup_id = m.member_type JOIN common_lookup cl2
ON       cl2.common_lookup_id = m.credit_card_type JOIN common_lookup cl3
ON       cl3.common_lookup_id = c.contact_type
WHERE    c.first_name = 'Harry'
AND      c.middle_name = 'James'
AND      c.last_name = 'Potter';
```

The preceding join yields the following meaningful business information:

```
          account_number: SLC-000006
    common_lookup_meaning: Group
       credit_card_number: 6011-0000-0000-0086
    common_lookup_meaning: Discover Card
               first_name: Harry
              middle_name: James
                last_name: Potter
    common_lookup_meaning: Customer
```

The data returned from any query is symmetrical, which means all columns return the same number of rows. The results of the preceding query are the business results from three lookup activities, and they return the previously chosen values by a business user. However, the results are not what you'd want to display in a web form that presents the ability to change values, such as the member, credit card, or contact types. The reason they're not the correct values to display is that you need the currently selected values and the list of alternative values that an end user can choose when working in an application software form (as shown in Figure 3). Queries don't deliver that capability because result sets are limited to symmetrical data, like that shown from the last query.

You need to get the current and possible values by using the foreign key as a parameter to a function call, and in this example, you actually need to make a call by using the table name, column name, and current value. In an HTML web form, the function would return a set of HTML

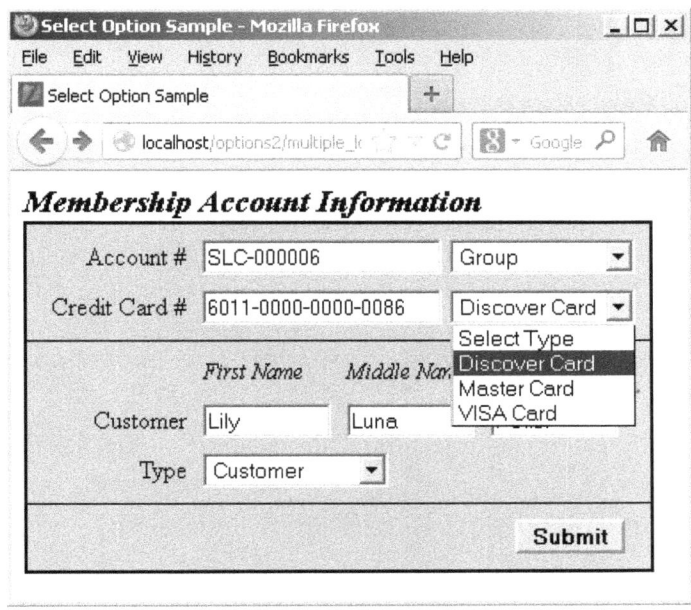

FIGURE 3. *Web form selectivity fields*

`option` tags to embed within an HTML `select` tag. The currently selected value from the lookups would be the selected HTML `option` tag, and the other possible values would be the unselected HTML `option` tags. This approach would return an asymmetrical result set like the following:

	f(x)		f(x)				f(x)
	↓		↓				↓
	Select Type		Select Type				Select Type
SLC-000006	Group	6011-0000-0000-0086	Discover card	Lily	Luna	Potter	Customer
	Individual		Master card				Employee
			Visa card				

Taking this type of approach to commonly referenced values lets your application code leverage reusable modules more readily. Naturally, this type of function would be more ideally suited to a PL/SQL result cache function in an Oracle Database 12c application.

PART

I

Java in the Database

CHAPTER

1

Java Functions and Procedures

Purpose

This chapter teaches you how to configure, deploy, and troubleshoot Java libraries. It shows you how to

- Understand the JVM architecture of Oracle Database 12c
- Use the default Java 6 SDK or override the default with the Java 7 SDK
- Compile Java source files into class files, and then load the class files into Oracle Database 12c by using the `loadjava` utility
- Create and compile Java libraries directly through the SQL*Plus Command Line Interface (CLI) utility
- Use scalar and Attribute Data Type (ADT) collections as parameters and return data types through the Oracle JDBC libraries

Some of these examples build on concepts introduced in *Oracle Database 12c PL/SQL Programming* (Oracle Press, 2014). An introduction to the Java programming language is also provided as a primer in the appendix of this book.

Advantages

Oracle Database 12c lets you extend your applications by writing stored functions, procedures, and packages. You also have the opportunity to write these stored programs in the Java programming language. There is one catch: While you can write the implementation in the Java programming language, PL/SQL is the tool that builds the gateway between the environment and the Java libraries. Therefore, you must write PL/SQL wrappers, much like you must write SQL triggers, to launch PL/SQL anonymous block trigger bodies.

A PL/SQL wrapper is a small piece of code that specifies a schema-level function or procedure, or a package. These PL/SQL wrappers point to internally stored implementations of Java libraries. They map the PL/SQL formal parameter and return data types to Java data types.

PL/SQL wrappers are much like package specifications, which define functions and procedures that you implement in Java libraries rather than package bodies. *Publishing* Java libraries is nothing more than creating PL/SQL wrappers to Java libraries.

Writing Java libraries in lieu of native PL/SQL functions, procedures, and packages is advantageous when your core development language is Java, because then application and database backend programmers speak the same language.

Also, while it's possible to unwrap PL/SQL programs to see the programming logic that was wrapped, there's no equivalent utility for getting at the source code of Java libraries when you use the `loadjava` utility. That means putting key logic into Java adds another layer of security protection to the code.

Disadvantages

Writing code in Java isn't necessary, because PL/SQL provides all the features that you need for functions, procedures, and packages. Writing PL/SQL in the database while writing Java on the middle tier of an application can make understanding the complete logic of any applications more complex.

Overview

This chapter focuses on the following:

- Oracle Database 12c JVM features
- Java architecture in Oracle
- Oracle Java connection types
- Importing Java class libraries
- Building Java class libraries
- Troubleshooting how you build, load, and use Java libraries

The chapter builds on the PL/SQL concepts covered in *Oracle Database 12c PL/SQL Programming* and introduces new material sequentially. If you feel you understand the basics of any of these sections, you should be able to jump to a section of interest for the details, though a quick browse of all the material might save you time looking for a missing piece later in the chapter.

Oracle Database 12*c* JVM Features

The Oracle Database 12c Java Virtual Machine (JVM) has matured. The following new features are available in this release of the database:

- The internal Oracle JVM is now compatible with Standard Edition of Java 6 by default, and configurable with Java 7.
- Oracle JVM enhancements include support for the `loadjava` utility, list-based operations with `dropjava`, the ability to resolve external class references by using the `ojvmmtc` utility, and increased functionality in the `ojvmjava` tool.
- Database-resident JAR files have been introduced, which means that when you load a JAR file, you now have the option of creating an object representing the JAR file transparently.
- Metadata can be shared between user-defined classes. This mimics the concept of a multithreaded process control block.
- Two-tier duration for Java session state is now possible. This lets you use Java as previously done in autonomous transactions within a connection, or as a persistent session with preserved state between transactions. You can use the `endsession` function in the `dbms_java` package to clear the previous session state on entry. This function preserves any property settings when it clears the session state. You should use the `endsession_and_related_state` function from the `dbms_java` package when you want to clear both the session state and property settings.
- Output streams can be redirected externally from the database.
- System properties can be set that are propagated on connection to the database server.
- A Java just-in-time (JIT) compiler reduces Java byte streams directly into machine-specific code, improving performance by eliminating the interpretation phase.

The Java Interactive Interface

The `ojvmjava` utility is an interactive interface to the session namespace and database instance. From Oracle Database 11g forward, you can launch executables through this tool. A new `runjava` option lets you run the `ojvmjava` shell in command mode or resident class mode. The current version of `ojvmjava` has reduced the stack trace for thrown exceptions. You also can open a new connection without leaving the current `ojvmjava` session.

Java Architecture in Oracle

The Oracle Database 12c databases provide a robust architecture for developing server-side or internal Java programming components. Java components are object-oriented (OO) structures that fit naturally into Oracle's object-relational model. The component architecture is a library stack that contains

- Platform-dependent operating systems, such as Unix, Linux, and Microsoft Windows
- Platform-dependent Oracle database management files and libraries
- Oracle database instance JVM, which is platform independent
- Java core class libraries, which are ported to various platforms
- Oracle-supported Java application programming interfaces (APIs), such as SQLJ, JDBC, and JNDI
- Oracle PL/SQL stored objects that provide an interface between SQL and PL/SQL programs, as well as server-side Java classes

The Oracle and Java libraries store and manage application programs like a ubiquitous file system. Virtual directories create ubiquitous file systems because the physical locations of the programs are operating system independent. Oracle libraries make storing, retrieving, and recovering files a standard process across many diverse platforms. The JVM provides a standard environment in which you can build and execute well-documented OO programs. Oracle PL/SQL enables the development of wrapper packages to access the Java libraries from other PL/SQL stored objects and SQL. The architecture of the Oracle JVM is shown in Figure 1-1.

Oracle JVM uses two types of namespaces: the long name and the short name. The long name is exactly as the class is named in Java, which is a case-sensitive name that may be longer than object names stored in the Oracle Database 12c data catalog. The case-sensitive Java program name must be unique in the scope of the Java namespace within the database server. Short names are those assigned by the database when you store Java libraries, and they conform to the storage requirements of the data catalog.

The short name for a Java library must be unique within the core namespaces for the Oracle Database 12c server. There are two namespaces for each schema in an Oracle database. One namespace covers all functions, libraries, procedures, packages, tables, objects, sequences, and views, which includes the short names for Java libraries. The other namespace is reserved for database triggers. Trigger names are unique within their own namespace, but that means a trigger name can duplicate any of the other object type names in a schema.

You can call stored Java programs by their native namespace. While the chapter examples are short and not placed into packages, you'll most likely put your Java programs into packages. The

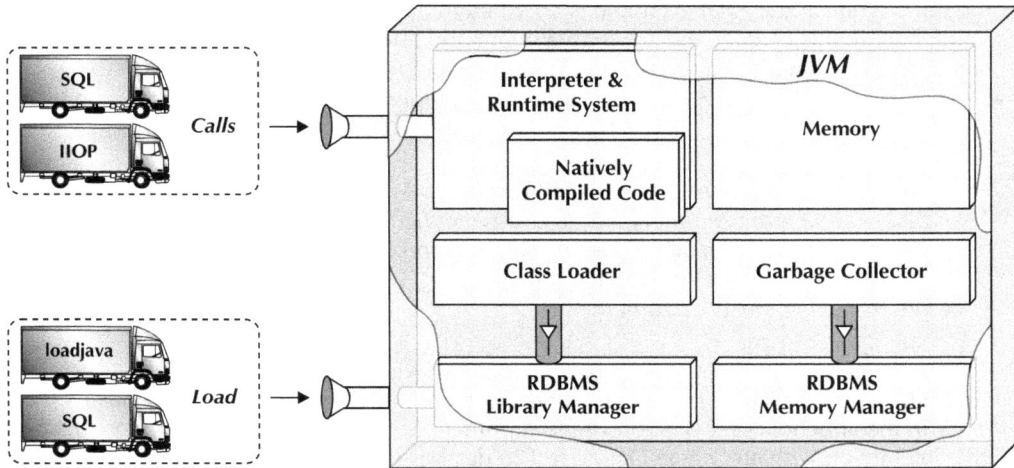

FIGURE 1-1.   *Oracle Java Virtual Machine*

namespace for Java stored code includes the entire package hierarchy. When this is larger than 30 characters, Oracle uses a hashed namespace in the data dictionary views. Use the dbms_java package and longname function to get the full namespace. You can also use the dbms_java package and shortname function to get the short name.

The JVM enjoys automated storage management, which means you do not need to allocate and free memory explicitly. Also, Java is a strongly typed programming language, like PL/SQL. The combination of strong typing and a garbage collector to manage memory provides a scalable and simplified environment like the PL/SQL runtime engine.

Both Java and PL/SQL are interpreted languages and they require JIT compilation. Oracle Database 12c introduces JIT Java compilation for Java programs. Native compilation enables ahead-of-time compilation. It changes PL/SQL and Java byte code into machine-executable programming code.

Native compilation speeds execution by eliminating JIT compilation delay, because native machine code runs immediately. Unfortunately, it takes time to compile the interpreted language programs into machine code. If you rarely change your code, the trade-off may be worth using native compilation.

There are three ways to put Java classes into the database instance. Your options are

- A two-step process: (a) compiling the Java source file, <file_name>.java, with the javac executable to generate a Java byte code program, and (b) using the Oracle loadjava utility to put the file into the database instance.

- A one-step process using the loadjava utility to compile and put the Java class file into the database instance. This stores only the class file in the data catalog.

- A one-step process using Data Definition Language (DDL) to build and compile the Java source file as a stored Java class. This stores the Java source and class files in the data catalog.

There are occasionally parser problems running DDL commands when you build Java programs. While a SQL DDL example is provided in the "Creating a Deterministic Java Library" section later in this chapter, the `loadjava` command line is recommended over SQL DDL commands. You can also call the `loadjava` procedure from the `dbms_java` package to load your Java classes. The `loadjava` command both compiles and loads class files into the database.

TIP
If you opt to use the one-step `loadjava` utility, you may encounter an ORA-29533 error for attempting to overwrite the file. The `replace` option in the `loadjava` utility does not work in some releases. Use `dropjava` with the –user option and the <file_name>.class before rerunning the `loadjava` utility.

This chapter assumes you have a basic familiarity with Java, meaning that you can compile and run Java programs. The samples include command-line instructions. There is also a Java primer in the appendix of this book. The Java primer also includes configuration instructions for JDBC interaction with an Oracle Database 12*c* database.

Java stored program units are like traditional PL/SQL program units. They are called with either definer's rights access or invoker's rights access from a single session. There are differences between how Java works externally and internally within the Oracle database instance. Some of the differences are qualified in the following subsections.

Java Execution Control

Execution control inside the database differs from native Java. While you can now have a `main()` method inside a Java resource class, it is only accessible through the `ojvmjava` utility. Internal Java resource files have two types of behaviors: stored program bodies and instantiable classes. Stored program bodies support functions and procedures whether schema or package level in scope. Instantiable classes support user-defined object types and provide the implementation for the object type. You instantiate the objects by using the `SQLData` interface, which is covered in Chapter 2.

Java Resource Storage

Java class resources are stored in clear text, Java byte code, and compressed Java ARchives (also known as JAR files). JAR files can be stored internally or externally in an Oracle Database 12*c* database instance. You can now load JAR files and concurrently define their internal object representation in the database. Oracle manages these as source, class, and resource Java objects. Schemas contain a `java$options` table, which can be accessed and configured by the `dbms_java` package, using the `set_compiler_option` and `reset_compiler_option` procedures, or `get_compiler_option` function.

Java Class Names

Internal Oracle Java class names are maintained in two forms. One is the short form that supports standard schema database objects and is limited to 30 characters. When a fully qualified package and class name exceeds the limit, Oracle automatically creates a hashed name as the class short name and stores the long name elsewhere. These hashed short names are unique within the general namespace of any schema.

Java Resolvers

The standard Java `Class.forName()` method isn't supported for internal Oracle Java classes. Oracle Database 12*c* supports multiple resolvers, and they help you locate classes. You can get unexpected results from a search when one resolver runs another. This problem involves the way classes can be distributed among different database schemas. There are several workarounds, all of which involve your qualifying the owning schema and class file. Chapter 2 in the *Oracle Database Java Developer's Guide 12*c qualifies the suggested workarounds.

Java Security and Permissions

Oracle Database 8.1.5 forward uses Java 2 security. Java 2 security wasn't created for the database world. As a result, Java 2 exhibits certain differences between its generic model and what Oracle chose to implement in the database. For example, Java 2 security defines that all applets are implicitly untrusted, and trusts all classes within the CLASSPATH environment variable because they're loaded into a secure database instance. External operating system resources are restricted by default, and inaccessible for embedded Java programs. With the noted exceptions, Java 2 security defines the privileges of database resources, operating system resources, the Oracle JVM classes, and user-loaded classes. Table 1-1 lists the installed Java 2 permissions.

After initializing the Oracle JVM, only a single role, JAVA_ADMIN, is granted the PolicyTablePermission privilege to modify the *PolicyTable*. You can only alter the Java 2 default privileges as the privileged sysdba user. There are two available default roles, JAVAUSERPRIV and JAVASYSPRIV.

The JAVAUSERPRIV role has few privileges, but generally lets you examine Java properties. The JAVASYSPRIV role enjoys major privileges, including how you update the Oracle JVM-protected packages. You can also grant fine-grained privileges in lieu of using these two default Java roles.

Type	Permissions
Java 2	java.util.PropertyPermission
	java.io.SerializablePermission
	java.io.FilePermission
	java.net.NetPermission
	java.net.SocketPermission
	java.lang.RuntimePermission
	java.lang.reflect.ReflectPermission
	java.security.SecurityPermission
Oracle specific	oracle.aurora.rdbms.security.PolicyTablePermission
	oracle.aurora.security.JServerPermission

TABLE 1-1.   *Predefined Permissions*

TIP
As a rule, JAVASYSPRIV should be granted only to administrators.

Use the dbms_java package and the grant_permission procedure to open operating resources like file IO. Managing these fine-grained privileges is the best way to control what individual users can do inside and outside the database. You can find complete coverage of the Oracle JVM security model in Chapter 10 of the *Oracle Database Java Developer's Guide 12c Release 1 (12.1)*, available at http://docs.oracle.com/.

Java Threading

Java threading works differently for Oracle internal Java classes. The Oracle JVM uses a non-preemptive threading model. This means that all threads run in a single operating system thread and the Oracle JVM merely switches contexts between threads. *Switching contexts* means that the Oracle JVM spawns one thread for a time slice and then another, in a round-robin fashion, until their execution is complete.

Oracle Database 12c also supports class loaders, which enable you to create preemptive threading solutions. This requires you to have a master class spawn instances through different class loaders. Class loaders inside the JVM run in their own thread of execution. You should note that this changes the behavior of static variables in Java, because multiple copies of static variables can discretely exist when they're not in the same class loader.

Oracle Java Connection Types

Oracle implements Java Database Connectivity (JDBC) in three ways in order to meet three different needs. These are the thin, thick, and default connections. Respectively, they map to the client-side driver, the call interface driver (or middle-tier driver), and the server-side (or internal) driver. In the following sections, you'll examine all three.

The Client-Side Driver, or JDBC Thin Driver

The Oracle thin connection is probably the most used by Java applications, Java Server Pages (JSPs), and Enterprise Java Beans (EJBs). It provides many advantages to building code without directly accessing Oracle library files.

The advantages of the Oracle JDBC thin driver are numerous for external Java applications because it requires the least setup and configuration. First, though, make sure your Java programming environment has access to the standard Java library and the Oracle JDBC library. You can set this up by configuring your CLASSPATH environment variable. You should include the Oracle ojdbc6.jar JAR file when you want the external files to match the internal JVM. You can use the ojdbc7.jar JAR file, but be careful with the newer features that aren't backward compatible with the Oracle JVM. You can find details about how to set these in the appendix of this book.

Unfortunately, you can't use the Oracle thin JDBC driver unless you've configured and started your database listener. You'll likewise need to provide the hostname, listener port number, database name, and your user ID and password each time you spawn a connection to the database instance.

TIP
The Oracle client-side or thin driver returns a rather meaningless error message if the hostname, listener port number, or database name is incorrect. In fact, it will report an ORA-17002 error. This error is found in Oracle's implementation of the JDBC API. The appendix demonstrates a clean mechanism to audit for the error.

The application of the Oracle JDBC thin driver is limited to external Java applications, JSPs, and EJBs. A multithreaded Java servlet is an example of a Java application that would implement an Oracle JDBC thin driver file. Oracle JDBC thin connections can be optimistic or pessimistic connections.

Optimistic connections are temporary connections transmitted using HTTP, which are limited to a 15-second pipelined TCP socket connection. TCP connections travel through the Oracle listener for the database instance. These solutions are ideal for JSPs but are resource-expensive because they must establish a connection for each communication.

Pessimistic connections are typically transmitted using a state-aware TCP socket that's open for the duration of the connection. Again, the Oracle listener supports these connections on the server side. Pessimistic connections are used by multithreaded Java servlets to create and maintain database connection pools. Java servlets can be implemented in two-tier or n-tier solutions.

The Oracle Call Interface Driver, or Middle-Tier Thick Driver

The Oracle Call Interface (OCI) driver is more tightly coupled with the Oracle C/C++ libraries than is the Oracle JDBC thin driver. If you use the Oracle JDBC call interface (or middle-tier thick) driver, you'll need to ensure that the PATH, CLASSPATH, and LD_LIBRARY_PATH environment variables map to Oracle libraries. The libraries need to be on the same physical platform or map through a storage area network (SAN), such as NFS in Unix.

The OCI driver can maintain persistent connection pools through Java servlets. As a rule, you'll have an easier configuration if you use the Oracle JDBC thin driver in your servlet.

The Oracle Server-Side Internal Driver, or Server-Tier Thick Driver

The Oracle server-side internal driver is likewise tightly coupled with, and dependent on, the Oracle C/C++ libraries. Unfortunately, there's no other choice available to build Java programs as stored objects in the Oracle database.

The Oracle server-side internal driver uses the getConnection() method of the DriverManager class to connect to the database. This poses a bit of a testing problem if you want to test the Java program externally, because the actual parameter for internal reference classes differs from the thin client argument. It is best if you test the Java code in your development instance with the thick connection because it moves with the database to any new platform. External JDBC code requires a separate porting activity.

Unlike the OCI driver, the server-side internal driver is faster than the Oracle JDBC thin driver. The speed increases because the libraries are all local on the server and not subject to network calls. As you read the chapter and examine the code, you'll find that embedding Java in the Oracle database requires a few tricks and techniques.

The next section examines how to build and troubleshoot class libraries and instantiable Java stored objects.

Importing Java Class Libraries

When you choose to build Java class libraries, you have two deployment choices. You can build call-interface-driven (middle-tier) libraries or server-side Java class libraries.

Call-interface libraries act like server-side includes to your Apache server. They must be replicated to all nodes of your Apache server and are managed within the structure of your web server load-balancing tool. These components act like external programs that call into the Oracle server; refer to an Enterprise Java book for further information.

NOTE
While middle-tier Java class libraries are not directly covered in this book, they do require direct reference in their path to the Oracle OCI libraries. The OCI libraries are in the Oracle Application Server but not on other web servers.

Server-side Java class libraries are stored objects within the Oracle JVM, which is a subcomponent of the Oracle database. Server-side Java class libraries are the core theme of this chapter. In the next two sections, you'll learn how to build internal server Java functions and procedures.

Java 6 (Default) or Java 7 in Oracle Database 12c

Oracle Database 12c comes preconfigured with Java 6 by default. You must run a Perl script and remake files if you want to create a database instance with Java 7. It's also possible to convert the Oracle JVM of an existing Oracle Database 12c instance. If you decide to create a database instance with Java 7 or migrate a database instance from using Java 6 to using Java 7, you must complete the following steps. There's one additional step that you must perform to convert an existing Oracle Database 12c instance.

Run the following Perl script in Linux or Unix:

```
perl $ORACLE_HOME/javavm/install/update_javavm_binaries.pl 7
```

You can then relink the Oracle executables based on the guidelines for the platform:

```
cd $ORACLE_HOME/rdbms/lib
make -f ins_rdbms.mk ioracle
```

After making the preceding changes, you can now create an instance that uses Java 7. You have a couple extra steps if you want to convert an existing database instance. You must shut down all the running databases before you run the perl script and remake the Oracle executables. After these steps, you must run the following SQL script as the SYS user:

```
$ORACLE_HOME/javavm/install/update_javavm_db.sql
```

You must run the perl script against all nodes of a RAC configuration, and you must run the SQL script as the sys user in each of the nodes.

NOTE
If you're unfamiliar with configuring and testing a Java JDBC connection, please check the appendix for instructions.

Java programming ranges from simple to complex, but these examples should be straightforward. You have two core executables to run Java programs, which you'll use in the examples. They are

- `javac`   Compiles your text file Java programs into Java byte code
- `java`   Runs your compiled Java byte code programs

The file-naming convention in Java is case sensitive, so you should ensure that you name your files consistent with the web-based code example files. If you attempt to compile a Java file when the file name and class name are different, you'll receive an error. Also, the file extension for Java programs is lowercase: `.java`.

The next subsections show you how to write and compile a sample Java program and how to load the compiled Java class file into the database.

Building a Java File

You can either build a Java program manually or build it with an IDE. You have two primary choices when using an IDE: JDeveloper or NetBeans.

It's important that you compile your Java programs with the correct version of the Java SDK. You must take several additional steps when using the default Java 6 SDK to compile Java programs, because many operating systems use Java 7 outside of the database instance.

The first step requires that you create a batch file that will alter the environment variables to point to the correct location of the Java SDK. You must also include a `CLASSPATH` environment variable that points to the current working directory (or present working directory), which is represented as a . (*dot*). The following creates an environment file for Oracle Database 12*c* on Windows:

```
C:>copy con javaenv.bat
SET PATH=%ORACLE_HOME%\jdk\bin;%PATH%
SET CLASSPATH=.
^Z
        1 file(s) copied.
```

The Linux or Unix operating system would require the following changes for a `javaenv.sh` Bash shell environment:

```
export set PATH=%ORACLE_HOME%/jdk/bin;%PATH%
export set CLASSPATH=.
```

The dot (.) on the `CLASSPATH` line puts any compiled classes in the present working directory in runtime scope. After running the environment file, you can check the default version of Java with the Oracle Database 12*c* version. This checks the runtime version:

```
C:>java -version
java version "1.6.0_37"
Java(TM) SE Runtime Environment (build 1.6.0_37-b06)
Java HotSpot(TM) 64-Bit Server VM (build 20.12-b01, mixed mode)
```

This checks the compiler version:

```
C:>javac -version
javac 1.6.0_37
```

You can navigate to Tools | Java Platforms to add a Java 6 platform to NetBeans, which allows you to compile it by using Java 6. JDeveloper lets you change the JDK by navigating to Tools | Project Properties | Libraries and Classpath.

Now, you build a simple `HelloWorld1.java` file with an IDE of your choosing. (The appendix provides a Java primer if you need help on Java basics.) By creating this small program, you verify that you can create working Java programs with JDK 6. If you're working in Microsoft Windows, open a Command Prompt window. If you're working in Unix, use a terminal window.

The following is the code for `HelloWorld1.java`:

```
// Class definition.
public class HelloWorld1 {
  public static void main(String[] args) {
    System.out.println("Hello World."); }
}
```

Java text files are compiled by the following syntax:

```
javac HelloWorld1.java
```

Successful compilation does not return anything to the console. The lack of any message is a good thing. The way to verify whether or not you have a Java byte code file is to run the Microsoft Windows directory (**dir**) command or Unix list (**ls**) command for files matching `HelloWorld1.*` in the present working directory. You should see two files displayed to the console:

```
HelloWorld1.java
HelloWorld1.class
```

After building the Java byte code compiled program, you can test its execution by entering the following:

```
java HelloWorld1
```

NOTE
Do not provide the `.class` extension when running Java programs; it is assumed. Appending `.class` to the file name will raise the following exception: `java.lang.NoClassDefFoundError: HelloWorld1/class`. This exception is also raised if you do not have your present working directory in your `$CLASSPATH` environment variables.

You'll receive the following results:

```
Hello World.
```

The next section covers how you build server-side or internal server Java programming units. You'll learn how to build Java class files to support stored functions and procedures and how to wrap them in PL/SQL packages. Make sure to read the following two sections sequentially, because the second section assumes you have worked through the first.

Creating a Deterministic Java Library

In this section you build an internal server Java function by building a Java class file that will use the server-side internal connection or JDBC thick connection. As qualified earlier in the chapter, the JDBC thick connection depends on OCI libraries. All OCI libraries are directly accessible from your Java class file when you've loaded it into the Oracle JVM.

Java internal or server-side class files are built and accessed by a three-step process. You use Java to build and compile the class file. Then, you use the Oracle loadjava utility to load the compiled class file into the server. Once the class file is built and loaded into the server, you build a PL/SQL wrapper to the Java class library. Deployment requires that you load the compiled Java class file into the database, which you do with the loadjava utility.

Building a Java Library

To build a Java library for the Oracle Database 12c server, the CLASSPATH must resolve to an ojdbc6.jar file. You can modify the earlier javaenv.bat file to include a CLASSPATH reference to the directory that contains the ojdbc6.jar file:

```
C:>copy con javaenv.bat
SET PATH=%ORACLE_HOME%\jdk\bin;%PATH%
SET CLASSPATH=%ORACLE_HOME%\jdbc\lib\ojdbc6.jar;.
^Z
        1 file(s) copied.
```

You'll get the following prompt when the javaenv.bat file already exists:

```
Overwrite javaenv.bat? (Yes/No/All): Yes
```

Naturally, you have the alternative of using any text editor of your choice. Several free or inexpensive editors are available, but we recommend Sublime as an inexpensive editor or Notepad++ as a free editor.

The Linux or Unix operating system would require the following changes for a javaenv.sh Bash shell environment:

```
export set PATH=%ORACLE_HOME%/jdk/bin:%PATH%
export set CLASSPATH=%ORACLE_HOME%\jdbc\lib\ojdbc6.jar:.
```

You need to source the javaenv.bat or javaenv.sh file before compiling the Java source file. You source the Windows batch file by simply running it from the command line, and you must use the dot (.) in the Bash or Korn shell or the keyword source in Tcsh.

Java Database Connectivity (JDBC) lets you build connections by using the DriverManager class. This is a change over the defaultConnection() method for internal Java class files and external connections. They now both use the getConnection() static method from the DriverManager class. The only difference between a thin client and a thick client is the actual parameter provided to the method. Examples in this chapter use the internal syntax, and examples in the appendix use the external thin client syntax.

The following assumes you have the correct CLASSPATH and PATH to use Java. If you are unable to compile or test the Java programs, it's possible your environment is configured incorrectly.

The `HelloWorld2.java` example builds a Java class library with two methods. These methods are overloaded, which means they have different signatures or formal parameter lists. They each return a Java string. Both of the overloaded methods will map to two overloaded PL/SQL functions that return `VARCHAR2` native Oracle data types. The first `hello()` function simply returns a static string, and the second `hello(String name)` function takes a single parameter and returns a dynamic string.

```
// Oracle class imports.
import oracle.jdbc.driver.*;

// Class definition.
public class HelloWorld2 {

  public static String hello() {
    return "Hello World."; }

  public static String hello(String name) {
    return "Hello " + name + "."; }

  public static void main(String args[]) {
    System.out.println(HelloWorld2.hello());
    System.out.println(HelloWorld2.hello("Larry")); }
}
```

The program defines two overloaded `hello` methods. One takes no formal parameters and the other takes one. You can compile `HelloWorld2.java` with the following syntax:

```
javac HelloWorld2.java
```

After you compile and run this program with this syntax:

```
java HelloWorld2
```

the method without any formal parameters always prints

```
Hello World.
```

while the one that takes one formal parameter always prints

```
Hello Larry.
```

This happens because the static `main()` method always sends either no parameter or the same actual parameter to the dynamic method. As a rule, you want to remove testing components like the `main()` method before loading them into the database and pass actual parameters to dynamic methods.

TIP
You can leave the static `main()` method in the program. It harms nothing and enables your testing of the program with the `ojvmjava` interactive utility.

Deploying a Java Library

You deploy a Java library with the `loadjava` utility, which is run from the operating system's command-line interface. This step requires the `HelloWorld2.class` file from the prior section. You should note that sometimes problems can occur with the `loadjava` utility. If you run into problems with the `loadjava` utility, check the "Building, Loading, and Dropping Java Class Library Objects" section in chapter 2.

Deploying a Java library also requires a `demo` schema, which may be a container database (CDB) or a pluggable database (PDB). If you're unfamiliar with the difference between a CDB and PDB, please refer to Appendix A in *Oracle Database 12c PL/SQL Programming*.

After creating the `demo` schema in a PDB and compiling the Java class file, you load it into the Oracle JVM with the `loadjava` utility as follows:

```
loadjava -r -f -o -user video/video@video HelloWorld2.class
```

You can verify that the `loadjava` command worked with the following query:

```
SQL> SELECT    object_name
  2  FROM       user_objects
  3  WHERE      object_name = 'HelloWorld2'
  4  AND        object_type = object_type LIKE 'JAVA%';
```

It displays:

```
OBJECT_NAME
-------------
HelloWorld2
```

NOTE
On the Microsoft platform, you may get a message that states "The procedure entry point kpuhhalo could not be located in the dynamic link library OCI.dll." If you receive this error, it means you don't have %ORACLE_HOME\bin% in your PATH environment variable.

The `loadjava` utility command loads the Java `HelloWorld2` class file into the Oracle JVM under the `demo` schema. After loading the Java class file into the database, you'll need to build a PL/SQL wrapper to use it.

Wrapping a Java Library

PL/SQL lets you wrap Java libraries. This section shows you how to wrap the previously created `HelloWorld2` Java library, which differs from wrapping a PL/SQL stored program unit.

The following `HelloWorld2.sql` script (included in the online resources file) builds the `hello_world2` package specification and a package body. The package body serves as a wrapper to the two methods implemented in the `HelloWorld2` Java class.

```
SQL> CREATE OR REPLACE PACKAGE hello_world2 AS
  2    FUNCTION hello
  3    RETURN VARCHAR2;
```

```
   4
   5    FUNCTION hello
   6    ( who  VARCHAR2 )
   7    RETURN VARCHAR2;
   8  END hello_world2;
   9  /
```

The following package body builds wrapper methods in the `HelloWorld2` Java class library:

```
SQL> CREATE OR REPLACE PACKAGE BODY hello_world2 AS
  2      FUNCTION hello
  3      RETURN VARCHAR2 IS
  4      LANGUAGE JAVA
  5      NAME 'HelloWorld2.hello() return java.lang.String';
  6
  7      FUNCTION hello
  8      ( who  VARCHAR2 )
  9      RETURN VARCHAR2 IS
 10      LANGUAGE JAVA
 11      NAME 'HelloWorld2.hello(java.lang.String) return java.lang.String';
 12  END hello_world2;
 13  /
```

Line 5 and line 11 designate a lowercase `hello` method. It is critical that the case-sensitive string description in the PL/SQL wrapper exactly match the case-sensitive method names that are used in the Java code. You raise the following exception if they don't:

```
SELECT hello_world2.hello() FROM dual
                            *
ERROR at line 1:
ORA-29531: no method hello in class HelloWorld2
```

When you ensure a case-sensitive match and run this in your schema, it creates a wrapper to the `HelloWorld2.class` file that you previously loaded. The return type of your PL/SQL wrapper is a `VARCHAR2` data type. You map it to a `java.lang.String` class, and it *must be that fully qualified path*.

You can verify that all components are present to test by querying the `user_objects` view with the following:

```
COLUMN object_name FORMAT A30
SQL> SELECT    object_name
  2  ,          object_type
  3  ,          status
  4  FROM       user_objects
  5  WHERE      object_name IN ('HelloWorld2','HELLO_WORLD2')
  6  ORDER BY CASE
  7              WHEN object_type = 'JAVA CLASS' THEN 1
  8              WHEN object_type = 'PACKAGE'    THEN 2
  9              ELSE 3
 10           END;
```

The script should output the following results:

```
OBJECT_NAME                         OBJECT_TYPE              STATUS
--------------------------------    ----------------------   -------
HelloWorld2                         JAVA CLASS               VALID
HELLO_WORLD2                        PACKAGE                  VALID
HELLO_WORLD2                        PACKAGE BODY             VALID
```

If you did not get the same output, you'll need to see what step you may have skipped. Please do that before attempting to proceed. If you did get the same output, you can now test the Java class library in SQL and PL/SQL. You can test it in SQL with a query or in PL/SQL with the dbms_ output.put_line statement. The following illustrates a SQL query of the wrapper, which uses the internal Java class file:

```
SQL> SELECT    hello_world2.hello('Paul McCartney') AS "Method Call"
  2  FROM      dual;
```

The query will return the following results:

```
Method Call
----------------------------------
Hello Paul McCartney.
```

This section has shown you how to wrap and identify Java class libraries and related PL/SQL packages. Next you'll see how to compile, deploy, and wrap a Java library.

Compiling, Deploying, and Wrapping a Java Library

As an alternative to using the loadjava utility, you can also build the entire Java source, publishing specification, and implementation in a single SQL file. Then, you can run it directly from the SQL*Plus command line. This is done by using a single Data Definition Language (DDL) command.

The prototype for the DDL command is

```
CREATE OR REPLACE AND RESOLVE JAVA SOURCE NAMED <java_class_name> AS
<java_source>
/
```

The Java class file name uniquely identifies the Java class in the Oracle JVM's CLASSPATH. You can treat a class with multiple methods like a package equivalent and define a package as a wrapper to complete the Java class. Alternatively, you can ignore the similarity to a package and implement individual Java methods as functions or procedures. Java methods that return a static value act like PL/SQL procedures, and Java methods that return a value act like PL/SQL functions.

Overloading doesn't work when you implement a schema-level function or procedure for each Java method in a Java class. You must implement PL/SQL wrappers inside a package when you want to leverage object-oriented overloading in Oracle's PL/SQL programming language.

NOTE
You must use a forward slash to execute a DDL command that builds an internal Java class. If you substitute a semicolon, you'll raise an ORA-29536 exception.

You create the Java `HelloWorldSQL` class with the following DDL command:

```
SQL> CREATE OR REPLACE AND RESOLVE JAVA SOURCE NAMED HelloWorldSQL AS
  2  // Class Definition.
  3  public class HelloWorldSQL {
  4
  5  public static String hello() {
  6    return "Hello World."; }
  7
  8  public static String hello(String name) {
  9    return "Hello " + name + "."; }
 10  }
 11  /
```

`RESOLVE JAVA SOURCE NAMED` targets the class file name and parses and compiles the Java source into the instance. You can then publish individual methods as functions or procedures, or the class as a package.

The following publishes the class as a package specification:

```
SQL> CREATE OR REPLACE PACKAGE hello_world_sql AS
  2      FUNCTION hello
  3      RETURN VARCHAR2;
  4
  5      FUNCTION hello
  6      ( who  VARCHAR2 )
  7      RETURN VARCHAR2;
  8  END hello_world_sql;
  9  /
```

And this wraps the class as a package body:

```
SQL> CREATE OR REPLACE PACKAGE BODY hello_world_sql AS
  2      FUNCTION hello
  3      RETURN VARCHAR2 IS
  4      LANGUAGE JAVA
  5      NAME 'HelloWorldSQL.hello() return String';
  6
  7      FUNCTION hello
  8      ( who  VARCHAR2 )
  9      RETURN VARCHAR2 IS
 10      LANGUAGE JAVA
 11      NAME 'HelloWorldSQL.hello(java.lang.String) return String';
 12  END hello_world_sql;
 13  /
```

The package provides an overloaded `hello` function. You can call it with or without an actual parameter. You can then publish only a single method of the class as a function, like this:

```
SQL> CREATE OR REPLACE FUNCTION hello
  2  ( who VARCHAR2) RETURN VARCHAR2 IS
  3  LANGUAGE JAVA
  4  NAME 'HelloWorldSQL.hello(java.lang.String) return String';
  5  /
```

You can query the function by using

```
SQL> SELECT hello('Nathan') AS SALUTATION
  2  FROM dual;
```

and it returns

```
SALUTATION
-------------
Hello Nathan.
```

You have now covered how to build Oracle database instance-stored Java class files that map methods to functions. The next section will examine how you build components to deliver procedure DML behaviors.

Creating a JDBC-Enabled Java Library

This section shows you how to build Java libraries that interact with data in Oracle Database 12c. Here you build Java methods to support both functions and procedures. Building a procedure follows a very similar rule to how you build functions.

While PL/SQL functions and procedures have IN, IN OUT, and OUT parameter modes, you can't use IN OUT mode in PL/SQL when wrapping a scalar parameter in a Java method. All formal parameters are defined as IN mode only. When you want output back, you should write a PL/SQL function, not a procedure.

Oracle Database 12c raises the following exception when you attempt to define a package body with a procedure using IN OUT modes:

```
PLS-00235: the external type is not appropriate for the parameter
```

In this section you create functions and procedures with IN-only mode parameters. The difference between how you implement a Java method to support a function or procedure is simple. A Java method returns any data type except a void to support a PL/SQL function wrapper, and a Java method returns only a void data type when supporting a PL/SQL procedure.

Oracle Database 12c Internal Connection Instances

The syntax for building a Java *Connection* instance had been constant from Oracle8i 8.1.5 until Oracle Database 10g. The connection was this:

```
Connection conn = new OracleDriver().defaultConnection();
```

Effective as of Oracle Database 11g, the old syntax no longer works. You will have to *migrate the connection logic* for all your stored Java libraries. The correct syntax for Oracle Database 11g and Java 1.5, and Oracle Database 12c and Java 6 or 7 is

```
Connection conn = DriverManager.getConnection("jdbc:default:connection:");
```

This syntax is used in the internal class files for this chapter.

There are two subsections. The first shows you how to work with scalar data types, such as strings. The second shows you how to work with Attribute Data Types (ADTs), which are collections of scalar data types.

JDBC Enabled Using Scalar Data Types

This section revisits how you will create a Java library externally and use the `loadjava` utility to deploy a Java class file into the database. You should note that we've tried to conserve space and show how to bind variables, which means the code passes a SQL statement and parameter to each of these Java methods.

The following Java source file supports both a function and a procedure:

```
// Oracle class imports.
import java.sql.*;
import oracle.jdbc.driver.*;

// Class definition.
public class HelloWorld3 {

  public static void doDML(String statement
                           ,String name) throws SQLException {
    // Declare an Oracle connection.
    Connection conn =
      DriverManager.getConnection("jdbc:default:connection:");

    // Declare prepared statement, run query and read results.
    PreparedStatement ps = conn.prepareStatement(statement);
    ps.setString(1,name);
    ps.execute(); }

  public static String doDQL(String statement) throws SQLException {
    // Define and initialize a local return variable.
    String result = new String();

    // Declare an Oracle connection.
    Connection conn =
      DriverManager.getConnection("jdbc:default:connection:");

    // Declare prepared statement, run query and read results.
    PreparedStatement ps = conn.prepareStatement(statement);
    ResultSet rs = ps.executeQuery();
    while (rs.next())
      result = rs.getString(1);

    return result; }
}
```

This program creates a Java *Connection* instance using the Oracle Database 12*c* process. The new process calls a static `getConnection()` method of the *DriverManager* class. Any code from your Oracle Database 10*g* instance will require that you make this change.

The program implements two methods—one to insert records and another to query records. The insert statement returns a void, and the query returns a string.

Create the example Table

The `example` table is built by using the following command:

```
SQL> CREATE TABLE example
  2  (character VARCHAR2(100));
```

TIP
While these methods don't use explicit cursors, statements and result sets persist across calls, and their finalizers do not release database cursors. You should remember to always close explicitly opened cursors.

There is no `main()` method in the `HelloWorld3.java` class file. Including a `main()` method to test the program externally to the database would require changing the connection to a client-side or OCI driver. As with the other Java libraries, `HelloWorld3.java` is a library file.

Assuming you're using a demo schema, you could load the Java class file into the Oracle JVM with the `loadjava` utility using the following:

```
loadjava -r -f -o -user video/video@video HelloWorld3.class
```

The `loadjava` utility command loads the Java `HelloWorld3` class file into the Oracle JVM under the `PLSQL` schema. After loading the Java class file into the database, you need to build a `mytable` table and PL/SQL wrapper to use it.

The following `HelloWorld3.sql` script builds the package and package body as a wrapper to the Java class library. The definition of the package specification is

```
SQL> CREATE OR REPLACE PACKAGE hello_world3 AS
  2     PROCEDURE doDML
  3     ( dml    VARCHAR2
  4     , input VARCHAR2 );
  5
  6     FUNCTION doDQL
  7     ( dql    VARCHAR2 )
  8     RETURN  VARCHAR2;
  9  END hello_world3;
 10  /
```

The definition of the package body is

```
SQL> CREATE OR REPLACE PACKAGE BODY hello_world3 AS
  2     PROCEDURE doDML
  3     ( dml    VARCHAR2
  4     , input VARCHAR2 ) IS
  5     LANGUAGE JAVA
  6     NAME 'HelloWorld3.doDML(java.lang.String,java.lang.String)';
  7
  8     FUNCTION doDQL
  9     ( dql    VARCHAR2 )
```

```
10    RETURN  VARCHAR2 IS
11    LANGUAGE JAVA
12    NAME 'HelloWorld3.doDQL(java.lang.String) return String';
13  END hello_world3;
14  /
```

This program defines two methods:

■ The doDML procedure takes two formal parameters that are VARCHAR2 data types and returns nothing as a stored procedure.

■ The doDQL function takes one formal parameter that is a VARCHAR2 and returns a VARCHAR2 data type as a stored function.

You can verify that all components are present to test by querying the user_objects view with the following:

```
SQL> COLUMN object_name FORMAT A30
SQL> SELECT    object_name
  2  ,          object_type
  3  ,          status
  4  FROM      user_objects
  5  WHERE     object_name IN ('HelloWorld3','HELLO_WORLD3')
  6  ORDER BY CASE
  7             WHEN object_type = 'JAVA CLASS' THEN 1
  8             WHEN object_type = 'PACKAGE'    THEN 2
  9             ELSE 3
 10          END;
```

The script should output the following results:

```
OBJECT_NAME                    OBJECT_TYPE             STATUS
------------------------------ ----------------------- -------
HelloWorld3                    JAVA CLASS              VALID
HELLO_WORLD3                   PACKAGE                 VALID
HELLO_WORLD3                   PACKAGE BODY            VALID
```

If you did not get the same output, you'll need to see what step you may have skipped. Please do this before attempting to proceed. If you did get the same output, you can now test the Java class library in SQL and PL/SQL.

You can test the doDML procedure inside an anonymous block program to write a string value to the mytable table:

```
SQL> BEGIN
  2    hello_world3.dodml('INSERT INTO example VALUES (?)','Bobby McGee');
  3  END;
  4  /
```

After inserting a row into the example table, you can test the doDQL function. Running a query against the pseudo dual table is the easiest way. The following illustrates a SQL query of the wrapper, which uses the internal Java class file:

```
SQL> SELECT hello_world3.doDQL('SELECT character FROM example') AS "Name"
  2  FROM    dual;
```

The query returns the following results:

```
Name
-----------------------------------
Bobby McGee
```

You've now covered how to build Oracle database instance-stored Java class files that map a Java method to a PL/SQL procedure. The next section discusses how to build real Java objects wrapped by PL/SQL object types.

JDBC Enabled Using ADT Collections

This section shows you how to create a Java library that receives and sorts an Attribute Data Type (ADT) collection of a scalar VARCHAR2 data type. It introduces how you can map an ADT collection into a Java collection, and how you can map the Java collection back into a PL/SQL collection type.

The following are four key classes available in Oracle's JDBC implementation:

- oracle.sql.ARRAY
- oracle.sql.ArrayDescriptor
- oracle.sql.Datum
- oracle.sql.STRUCT

The ARRAY class lets you implicitly cast an ADT or user-defined type (UDT) collection into a Java context without explicit conversion. You can transfer the contents of an ADT by calling the getArray() method of the ARRAY class. To transfer an Oracle collection of a scalar data type to a generic Object collection requires you to use the java.util.Map class. You map the Oracle data type to its equivalent Java data type, assuming that the Java library designates the collection's formal parameter as a list, like

```
Object[] object = (Object[])list.getArray(map);
```

Alternatively, you can avoid the expense of converting the object type by using the Oracle-specific Datum class, like

```
Datum[] arrayOracle = list.getOracleArray();
```

Chapter 2 shows you the more complex approach required to map UDT collections to Java structures. The ArrayDescriptor classes let you map a Java data type into an Oracle data type. You can find more about Oracle collections in Chapter 2, where you will work with UDT collections, or you can check Chapter 16 of the *Oracle Database JDBC Developer's Guide*.

The first step requires that you create an ADT collection. An ADT collection uses a scalar data type as its base type. Scalar data types in Oracle are like primitive data types in Java, and they're more or less numbers, dates, and strings.

The following syntax creates a table of strings:

```
SQL> CREATE OR REPLACE
  2    TYPE stringlist IS TABLE OF VARCHAR2(4000);
  3  /
```

While it would have been straightforward to create this without the use of Java generics, we wanted to make sure you knew they're available to you. Actually, you can use Java generics in both Oracle Database 11*g* and 12*c*.

The following SQL statement creates the `Sorting` Java class, which has a single `sortTitleCaseList()` method. The Java long name is the same as the short name because of its length.

```
SQL> CREATE OR REPLACE AND COMPILE JAVA SOURCE NAMED "SortList" AS
  2
  3     // Import required classes.
  4     import java.io.*;
  5     import java.security.AccessControlException;
  6     import java.sql.*;
  7     import java.util.Arrays;
  8     import java.util.Comparator;
  9     import oracle.sql.driver.*;
 10     import oracle.sql.ArrayDescriptor;
 11     import oracle.sql.ARRAY;
 12
 13     // Define class.
 14     public class Sorting {
 15       public static ARRAY sortTitleCaseList(oracle.sql.ARRAY list)
 16         throws SQLException, AccessControlException {
 17
 18       // Convert Oracle data type to Java data type.
 19       String[] unsorted = (String[])list.getArray();
 20
 21       // Sort elements.
 22       Arrays.sort(unsorted, new Comparator<String>() {
 23         public int compare(String s1, String s2) {
 24
 25         // Declare a sorting key integer for the return value.
 26         int sortKey;
 27
 28         // Check if lowercase words match and sort them.
 29         if (s1.toLowerCase().compareTo(s2.toLowerCase()) == 0)
 30            sortKey = s1.substring(0,1).compareTo(s2.substring(0,1));
 31         else
 32            sortKey = s1.toLowerCase().compareTo(s2.toLowerCase());
 33
 34         // Return the sorting index.
 35         return sortKey; }});
 36
 37       // Define a connection (this is for Oracle 11g).
 38       Connection conn =
 39         DriverManager.getConnection("jdbc:default:connection:");
 40
 41       // Declare a mapping to the schema-level SQL collection type.
 42       ArrayDescriptor arrayDescriptor =
```

```
43              new ArrayDescriptor("STRINGLIST",conn);
44
45          // Translate the Java String{} to the Oracle SQL collection type.
46          ARRAY sorted =
47            new ARRAY(arrayDescriptor,conn,((Object[])unsorted));
48
49          // Return the sorted list.
50          return sorted; }
51      }
52  /
```

Lines 10 and 11 import two key Oracle Java classes—the ARRAY and ArrayDescriptor classes. As discussed earlier in this section, the ARRAY class lets you transfer a collection of numbers, dates, strings, or any other scalar data type to a Java data type. Line 19 avoids using the java.util.Map class, shown earlier in this section, by explicitly designating the Java String data type as the natural equivalent of a VARCHAR2 data type. Line 22 implements a Java generic Comparator method that performs a natural language sort of String data type.

The ArrayDescriptor class implements a mediator pattern, and the declaration on lines 42 and 43 creates a map to the Oracle stringlist data type. Lines 46 and 47 construct an instance of the Oracle ARRAY class with a collection of the Java Object type, which is the most generalized class in the single-inheritance Java tree.

The PL/SQL wrapper for this Java library is

```
SQL> CREATE OR REPLACE
  2    FUNCTION sortTitleCaseList(list STRINGLIST) RETURN STRINGLIST IS
  3    LANGUAGE JAVA NAME
  4    'Sorting.sortTitleCaseList(oracle.sql.ARRAY) return oracle.sql.ARRAY';
  5  /
```

You can test this configuration with the following anonymous PL/SQL block:

```
SQL> DECLARE
  2    /* Declare a counter. */
  3    lv_counter  NUMBER := 1;
  4    /* Declare a unordered collection of fruit. */
  5    lv_list  STRINGLIST := stringlist('Oranges'
  6                                      ,'apples'
  7                                      ,'Apples'
  8                                      ,'Bananas'
  9                                      ,'Apricots'
 10                                      ,'apricots');
 11  BEGIN
 12      /* Read through an element list. */
 13      FOR i IN (SELECT column_value
 14                  FROM    TABLE(sortTitleCaseList(lv_list))) LOOP
 15        dbms_output.put_line('['||lv_counter||']['||i.column_value||']');
 16        lv_counter := lv_counter + 1;
 17      END LOOP;
 18  END;
 19  /
```

Line 14 has a call to the TABLE function that translates the returned collection type into a SQL result set. The anonymous PL/SQL block returns

```
[1] [Apples]
[2] [apples]
[3] [Apricots]
[4] [apricots]
[5] [Bananas]
[6] [Oranges]
```

The program also demonstrates how to accept Oracle collections into a Java program and how to return collections from a Java program to an Oracle collection.

NOTE
Check the "Troubleshooting Java Classes" section in Chapter 2 for guidelines on sorting out errors.

Supporting Scripts

The following programs are available on the McGraw-Hill Professional website to support this chapter:

- The HelloWorld1.java program is a test Java compilation program.
- The HelloWorld2.java program is a Java library file.
- The HelloWorld2.sql program is a PL/SQL wrapper to the HelloWorld2.java program file.
- The HelloWorld3.java program contains code that echoes out a string in support of PL/SQL function and procedure wrappers that perform DML statements against Oracle Database 12*c*, and supports the HelloWorld3.sql script.
- The HelloWorld3.sql program is a SQL script that writes a Java library in support of a PL/SQL wrapper and test case of DML and queries against a table in the database, uses function and procedure wrappers against Java libraries, and demonstrates how to use JDBC inside Oracle Database 12*c*.
- The list_sort.sql program contains examples that use Java to process and return ADT collections to Oracle Database 12*c*.
- The HelloWorld4.sql and HelloWorlde.sql programs contain examples of troubleshooting Java libraries and PL/SQL wrappers to Oracle Database 12*c*.

Summary

You should now have an understanding of how to implement and troubleshoot server-side or internal Java class libraries. With these skills, you can build robust solutions in Java, affording you an alternative in lieu of PL/SQL.

CHAPTER

2

Object Types

Purpose

This chapter teaches you how to configure, deploy, and troubleshoot Java libraries for Oracle object types. It shows you how to

- Create Java libraries that use the `SQLData` interface
- Create PL/SQL object types for Java libraries
- Use the `Struct` data type
- Create and use Java library instances
- Troubleshoot compilation and deployment

Some of these examples build on concepts introduced in *Oracle Database 12c PL/SQL Programming* (Oracle Press, 2014), especially Chapter 11, which covers Oracle object types. An introduction to the Java programming language is also provided as a primer in the appendix of this book.

Advantages

Oracle Database 12*c* lets you create Java objects inside the database. This means you can create instances of Java programs and use them through PL/SQL object type wrappers. These can be called from either a SQL or PL/SQL context.

As mentioned previously, a PL/SQL wrapper is a small piece of code that provides an interface between SQL and native PL/SQL program units. The PL/SQL wrapper for a Java instance is the object type. It maps the PL/SQL formal parameter and return data types to Java data types. The `SQLData` interface defines streams through which you can exchange data.

While you can't construct instances of Java classes like you do natively in Java, you can simply add default and override constructors when you implement the code outside of the database. That makes it possible to maintain a Java class structure in both the server tier and middle tier. It also means a single Java development team can write the object type logic, provided you have somebody to write the PL/SQL wrappers.

Disadvantages

The syntax differences and limitations of Java libraries inhibit some development teams from writing them. The syntax differences are imposed by implementing the `SQLData` interfaces. These interfaces prevent direct construction of the Java object types when they're deployed inside the database. They make writing internal Java classes different from writing external Java classes.

Overview

This chapter focuses on the following:

- Creating a Java class with `SQLData`
- Creating a Java superclass and object type
- Creating a Java subclass and object subtype

- Using Java classes and subclasses
- Troubleshooting how you build, load, and use Java libraries

The concepts presented in this chapter build upon each other, but if you feel you understand the basics, you should be able to jump to the section or sections of interest, though a quick browse might save you the time of looking for a missing piece later in the chapter.

Creating a Java Class with SQLData

The Java programming language is object-oriented (OO). In the previous examples of Chapter 1, Java stored objects were used as static functions. The potential to use Java to accomplish significant OO computing models lies in the Oracle object features introduced in Oracle9*i* Database Release 2. The object features haven't changed much since that release because perhaps Oracle may see very few development projects use them. Beginning with that release, you can construct instances of object types and use them as objects.

Server-side stored Java programs support full runtime object behaviors starting with Oracle9*i*. This means you can now design, develop, and implement natural Java applications beneath PL/SQL object type wrappers. These Java classes can have instance methods, which are non-static methods. You may also use static methods for libraries.

The balance of the differences covered earlier in Chapter 1 still applies. You build Java object libraries by writing the Java class file and SQL object type definition. Object type bodies are not defined when the object type implementation is written in a stored Java object.

The substantial difference between external Java objects and server internal Java objects is the way you construct an instance of the class. You do not directly instantiate the class file and cannot use overriding constructors in the Java class file. The `SQLData` interface is the key to instantiating stored Java objects. It enables instantiating the Java class by passing back and forth the parameter values. This enables a class to return a reference to a copy or instance of the class.

> **TIP**
> *There's no way to instantiate directly a default constructor when using a stored Java object class. You also cannot use overriding constructors. The `SQLData` interface allows you to pass values to an instantiated class based on known class scope instance variables. Instance variables are not static variables. These limits are imposed by the implementation of the `SQLData` interface.*

Basic Java Class with SQLData

Implementing the `SQLData` interface is done by providing a variable definition and three concrete methods in your Java class file. The following are the required components:

- A `String` data type named `sql_type`.
- A `getSQLTypeName()` method that returns a `String` data type.
- A `readSQL()` method that takes two formal parameters and returns a `void`. One formal parameter is a `SQLInput` that contains a stream. The other is a string that contains a data type name.
- A `writeSQL()` method that takes one formal parameter, which is a `SQLOutput` that contains a stream.

Oracle Database 12*c* also provides the `OracleData` and `OracleDataFactory` interfaces. Applying the *Factory* pattern is inherently more complex. Since applying the pattern requires advanced Java coding skills, they're omitted from this book.

The `SQLData` interface only maps SQL objects. The `OracleData` interface lets you map SQL objects as well as any other SQL data type. The `OracleData` interface is necessary when you want to serialize `RAW` data in Java libraries. Please check the *Oracle Database JDBC Developer's Guide* for more information on the `OracleData` and `OracleDataFactory` interfaces.

Subsequent examples in this chapter show you how to implement runtime Java classes. The `HelloWorld4.java` class file shows you a minimalist Java library to support a runtime instance of the `HelloWorld4` object.

The source code for the class is as follows (with line numbers added for your convenience while reading the discussion of the code):

```
 1 // Oracle class imports.
 2 import java.sql.*;
 3 import java.io.*;
 4 import oracle.sql.*;
 5 import oracle.jdbc.*;
 6 import oracle.oracore.*;
 7 import java.math.*; // Needed for BigDecimal maps of NUMBER data type.
 8
 9 // Class definition.
10 public class HelloWorld4 implements SQLData {
11   // Declare class instance variable.
12   private String whom;
13
14   // Declare getter for SQL data type value.
15   public String getSQLTypeName() throws SQLException {
16     return sql_type; }
17
18   // Required interface variable.
19   private String sql_type;
20
21   // Implements readSQL() method from the SQLData interface.
22   public void readSQL(SQLInput stream, String typeName)
23     throws SQLException {
24     sql_type = typeName;
25     this.whom = stream.readString(); }
26
27   // Implements writeSQL() method from the SQLData interface.
28   public void writeSQL(SQLOutput stream) throws SQLException {
29     stream.writeString(whom); }
30
31   // Declare a toString method.
32   public String toString() {
33     String datatype = null;
34
35     try {
36       datatype = getSQLTypeName(); }
37     catch (SQLException e) {}
```

```
38
39      // Return message.
40      return datatype + " says hello [" + this.whom + "]!\n"; }
41 }
```

The Java class implements the SQLData interface. You must create four elements to implement the SQLData interface. The first element requires declaring a private sql_type variable (declared on line 19). The sql_type variable holds an object type name defined in Oracle Database 12c. The second element, on lines 22 through 25, lets you read data from the database into the Java object instance through a SQLInput stream. The third element, on lines 28 and 29, lets you write any changes to the local copies of the data (held in the Java class instance) into the database. The getSQLTypeName() method lets you read the user-defined data type from the class. The sample code uses the getSQLTypeName() method to print a message from the toString() method.

If you have not built a test schema, you should do so now. The code in this chapter runs in either a container database (CDB) or a pluggable database (PDB). We're using a video PDB database with a trivial video password.

The HelloWorld4.java program contains import statements that require you to place the ojdbc6.jar file in your CLASSPATH environment variable. If you have not done so, you should do so now. The file is found in your $ORACLE_HOME/jdbc/lib directory on Linux or Unix, and %ORACLE_HOME%\jdbc\lib directory on Windows.

You can directly load *a Java source file* with the loadjava utility as follows into a CDB schema with the default listener:

```
loadjava -r -f -o -user video/video HelloWorld4.java
```

A slight change is required when you load this into a PDB. The following shows you must add the TNS alias to the credentials, which in this case is also video:

```
loadjava -r -f -o -user video/video@video HelloWorld4.java
```

The loadjava utility command behaves slightly differently when you choose this option. It parses, stores the Java source as a text entry, and compiles the stored Java source into a Java byte stream in the Oracle JVM under the video schema.

TIP
After loading the Java class file into the database this way, you won't be able to use the dropjava utility to remove the HelloWorld4.class file. Instead, use the dropjava utility to remove the HelloWorld4 .java file, which also drops the HelloWorld4.class file.

Creating the Java class file is only the first step. Next, you need to create an Oracle object type that wraps the Java class. Object types are declared as SQL data types and are implemented in PL/SQL, or callable languages such as Java.

Object Type Wrapper

You'll need to build a SQL object type to wrap the Java stored object class. That means you have to connect to the Oracle database. You can connect to a CDB or a PDB.

Assuming you have a c##student CDB schema, connect as follows:

```
sqlplus c##video/password
```

Assuming you have a video PDB schema, you connect as follows:

```
sqlplus video/password@video
```

The following HelloWorld4.sql script builds the object type as a wrapper to the Java class object:

```
SQL> CREATE OR REPLACE TYPE hello_world4 AS OBJECT
  2  ( whom   VARCHAR2(100)
  3  , MEMBER FUNCTION get_sql_type_name
  4    RETURN VARCHAR2 AS LANGUAGE JAVA
  5    NAME 'HelloWorld4.getSQLTypeName()
  6         return java.lang.String'
  7  , MEMBER FUNCTION to_string
  8    RETURN VARCHAR2 AS LANGUAGE JAVA
  9    NAME 'HelloWorld4.toString()
 10         return java.lang.String' )
 11  INSTANTIABLE FINAL;
 12  /
```

The SQL object type declares a local whom attribute. The whom attribute has a maximum length of 100 characters. Both lines 5 and 6 and lines 9 and 10 wrap the name of the Java class name, method,

Leveraging the Data Catalog

After you've defined the PL/SQL object type wrapper, you can see that both the object type and body have been registered in the Oracle instance metadata. You can see this by running the following query:

```
SQL> object_name FORMAT A30
SQL> object_type FORMAT A12
SQL> status      FORMAT A7
SQL> SELECT   object_name
  2  ,         object_type
  3  ,         status
  4  FROM     user_objects
  5  WHERE    REGEXP_LIKE(UPPER(object_name),'HELLO.*WORLD4');
```

The regular expression lets you find the HelloWorld4 Java class file and the HELLO_WORLD4 object type. The UPPER function promotes the object name to uppercase, and the regular expression makes the underscore optional in the object name.

The output, if you have run everything successfully, will be the following:

```
OBJECT_NAME                          OBJECT_TYPE   STATUS
------------------------------------ ------------- -------
HELLO_WORLD4                         TYPE          VALID
HelloWorld4                          JAVA CLASS    VALID
```

and return type across multiple lines. As signatures to your methods become longer, we recommend that you take advantage of this behavior.

You can create a table collection of the HELLO_WORLD4 type with this syntax:

```
SQL> CREATE OR REPLACE
  2    TYPE hello_tab IS TABLE OF HELLO_WORLD4;
  3  /
```

Now, you can test this in SQL with the following complex query:

```
SQL> SELECT *
  2  FROM    TABLE(
  3             SELECT CAST(COLLECT(hello_world4('Bilbo')) AS hello_tab)
  4             FROM    dual);
```

You must *collect* the object type into a table collection and *cast* it to a table collection of the hello_tab base type. Then, you use the TABLE function to return a SQL result set.

The query prints

```
WHOM
------
Bilbo
```

where whom is the column name for the single attribute in the example. Oracle discovers the attribute (column) name when the TABLE function converts the collection of one item to a SQL result set. The "Parsing Long Strings" sidebar introduces and explains the parse_rows procedure.

You can also test this small program with an anonymous block PL/SQL program. Here's a quick example:

```
SQL> DECLARE
  2    /* Declare and instantiate an instance. */
  3    lv_hello  hello_world4 := hello_world4('Bilbo');
  4  BEGIN
  5    /* Parse any string longer than 80 characters. */
  6    parse_rows(lv_hello.to_string());
  7
  8    -- Test metadata repository with DBMS_JAVA.
  9    dbms_output.put_line(
 10      '['||dbms_java.longname('HELLO_WORLD4')||']');
 11  END;
 12  /
```

You should see the following output displayed:

```
VIDEO.HELLO_WORLD4 says hello [Bilbo]!
[HELLO_WORLD4]
```

The SQLData interface allows you to pass a user-defined type (UDT), which means you can use any defined user structure. If you debug the execution of the Java instance, you'll find that each invocation of the instance method actually reinstantiates the class instance.

Parsing Long Strings

The toString() methods of Java classes often return long strings. The parse_rows procedure lets you avoid the forced line breaks imposed by the dbms_output package. Wrapping text in a call to the following parse_rows procedure lets you avoid the 80-character limit of the put_line procedures:

```
SQL> CREATE OR REPLACE PROCEDURE parse_rows
  2  ( pv_text   VARCHAR2 ) IS
  3    /* Declare parsing indexes. */
  4    lv_start       NUMBER := 1;
  5    lv_end         NUMBER := 1;
  6    lv_length      NUMBER;
  7  BEGIN
  8    /* Assign an end value by parsing line return. */
  9    IF INSTR(pv_text,CHR(10),lv_start) = 0 THEN
 10      lv_end := LENGTH(pv_text) + 1;
 11    ELSE
 12      lv_end := INSTR(pv_text,CHR(10),lv_start);
 13    END IF;
 14
 15    /* Assign a length value to parsed strings. */
 16    lv_length := lv_end - lv_start;
 17
 18    /* Print first line. */
 19    dbms_output.put_line(SUBSTR(pv_text,lv_start,lv_length));
 20
 21    /* Print the rows of a multiple line string. */
 22    WHILE (lv_end < LENGTH(pv_text)) LOOP
 23
 24      /* Assign a new start and end value. */
 25      lv_start := lv_end + 1;
 26      IF INSTR(pv_text,CHR(10),lv_start + 1) = 0 THEN
 27        lv_end := LENGTH(pv_text) + 1;
 28      ELSE
 29        lv_end := INSTR(pv_text,CHR(10),lv_start + 1);
 30      END IF;
 31      lv_length := lv_end - lv_start;
 32
 33      /* Print the individual rows. */
 34      dbms_output.put_line(SUBSTR(pv_text,lv_start,lv_length));
 35
 36    END LOOP;
 37  END;
 38  /
```

The IF block on lines 26 through 30 qualifies whether you have read a file completely or you have read a line return when parsing a text stream. The parse_rows procedure lets you take advantage of normal text formatting in Java classes.

Creating a Java Superclass and Object Types

We gave you a small sample program to show you how to implement the SQLData interface. This is a much larger example that shows you how to implement a Struct as a parameter option, and how to work with other input and output data types.

Creating the Java Superclass

The Item Java source file provides us with a lot of topics to cover. We debated about breaking the code up for display, but decided against it. In this section, we simply show you a complete Java example class. We did limit the example to one *getter*, the getRating() method, and one *setter*, the setRating() method, for single attribute values.

We also gave you a getName() method that lets you capture the Java class name, and a setItem() method that lets you set the list of class attributes with a Struct object type. The setItem() method shows you how to set the instance values through a direct method call rather than the readSQL() method implementation of the SQLData interface.

The following SQL statement creates the Item class in Oracle Database 12c, and you can find the complete source code in the Item.sql file online at the McGraw-Hill Professional website for this book:

```
SQL> CREATE OR REPLACE AND COMPILE JAVA SOURCE NAMED "Item" AS
  2
  3    // Java library imports.
  4    import java.sql.*;
  5    import java.io.*;
  6    import oracle.sql.*;
  7    import oracle.jdbc.*;
  8    import oracle.oracore.*;
  9    import oracle.jdbc2.*;
 10    import java.math.*;
 11
 12    public class Item implements SQLData
 13    {
 14      // Implement the attributes and operations for this type.
 15      private BigDecimal id;
 16      private String title;
 17      private String subtitle;
 18      private String rating;
 19      private String ratingAgency;
 20      private Date releaseDate;
 21
 22      // A getter for the rating attribute.
 23      public String getRating() {
 24        return this.rating; }
 25
 26      // A getter for the class instance name.
 27      public String getName() {
 28        return this.getClass().getName(); }
 29
```

```
30    // A getter for the rating attribute.
31    public String getUserName() {
32      // Declare local variables.
33      String userName = new String();
34      String query = "SELECT user FROM dual";
35      // Create a connection discover a user name.
36      try {
37        // Declare an Oracle connection.
38        OracleConnectionWrapper conn =
39          (oracle.jdbc.OracleConnectionWrapper)
40            DriverManager.getConnection("jdbc:default:connection:");
41
42        // Prepare and execute a statement.
43        java.sql.PreparedStatement ps = conn.prepareStatement(query);
44        ResultSet rs = ps.executeQuery();
45
46        // Read the result set.
47        while (rs.next())
48          userName = rs.getString(1); }
49      catch (SQLException e) {}
50        // Return a user name.
51          return userName; }
52
53    // A setter for this object.
54    public void setItem(Struct item) throws java.sql.SQLException {
55
56      // Get the attributes of the Item object.
57      Object[] attributes = (Object[]) item.getAttributes();
58
59      // Assign Item instance variables.
60      this.id = (BigDecimal) attributes[0];
61      this.title = (String) attributes[1];
62      this.subtitle = (String) attributes[2];
63      this.rating = (String) attributes[3];
64      this.ratingAgency = (String) attributes[4];
65      this.releaseDate =
66        new Date(((Timestamp) attributes[5]).getTime()); }
67
68    // A setter for the rating attribute.
69    public void setRating(String rating) {
70      this.rating = rating; }
71
72    // Declare an instance toString method.
73    public String toString() {
74      return "ID #    [" + this.id + "]\n" +
75             "Title   [" + this.title + ": " + this.subtitle +"]\n" +
76             "Rating  [" + this.ratingAgency +
77                     ":" + this.rating + "]\n" +
78             "Release [" + this.releaseDate + "]\n"; }
79
```

```
 80    /*   Implement SQLData interface.
 81    ||   ----------------------------------------------------------
 82    ||   Required interface components:
 83    ||   ==============================
 84    ||     1. String sql_type instance variable.
 85    ||     2. getSQLTypeName() method returns the sql_type value.
 86    ||     3. readSQL() method to read from the Oracle session.
 87    ||     4. writeSQL() method to write to the Oracle session.
 88    */
 89
 90    // Required interface variable.
 91    private String sql_type;
 92
 93    // Returns the interface required variable value.
 94    public String getSQLTypeName() throws SQLException  {
 95      return this.sql_type; }
 96
 97    // Reads the stream from the Oracle session.
 98    public void readSQL(SQLInput stream, String typeName)
 99      throws SQLException {
100      // Map instance variables.
101      this.sql_type = typeName;
102      this.id = stream.readBigDecimal();
103      this.title = stream.readString();
104      this.subtitle = stream.readString();
105      this.rating = stream.readString();
106      this.ratingAgency = stream.readString();
107      this.releaseDate = stream.readDate(); }
108
109    // Writes the stream to the Oracle session.
110    public void writeSQL(SQLOutput stream) throws SQLException {
111      // Map instance variables.
112      stream.writeBigDecimal(this.id);
113      stream.writeString(this.title);
114      stream.writeString(this.subtitle);
115      stream.writeString(this.rating);
116      stream.writeString(this.ratingAgency);
117      stream.writeDate(this.releaseDate); }
118
119    /*
120    ||   ----------------------------------------------------------
121    ||   End Implementation of SQLData interface.
122    */
123  }
124  /
```

The generic getter on lines 23 and 24 lets you get the instance value of the rating attribute, and the generic setter on lines 69 and 70 lets you override the rating instance variable. Lines 54 through 66 contain the logic for the setItem method. The setItem method takes a `Struct` parameter, which illustrates how you can use a composite data type. Line 57 converts the fields of the `Struct` parameter to an array of objects. Most of the conversions are straightforward and map through simple casting operations based on the rules in Table 2-1, shown later in this chapter in the "Mapping Oracle Types" section.

A `Date` data type in the Oracle database is a date-time data type. While you may think that an Oracle `Date` data type should convert to a Java `Date` class, it doesn't. An Oracle `Date` inside a `Struct` converts to a `Timestamp` class. You must cast the Java `Timestamp` class to a Java `Date` class through a two-step method. First, use the `getTime()` method to capture the long value of the `Timestamp`. Second, construct a new `Date` class by using the long value result from the `getTime` method.

Lines 65 and 66 from the preceding `Item` class example demonstrate the technique:

```
65      this.releaseDate =
66          new Date(((Timestamp) attributes[5]).getTime()); }
```

Line 91 declares the `sql_type` variable. Lines 94 and 95 implement the `getSQLTypeName()` method for the `SQLData` interface. Lines 98 through 107 implement the `readSQL()` method, and lines 110 through 117 implement the `writeSQL()` method for the `SQLData` interface.

After creating and compiling the `Item` class, you need to create an object type for it. The object type wraps access to the Java class file.

Creating the Object Type

The `Item` object type provides us with the syntax for mapping object methods against native Java classes. As a refresher, you create object types with a `CREATE TYPE` statement. Then, you can deploy them as persistent or transient objects. Persistent objects can be either stand-alone or embedded objects. Stand-alone objects are stored in a database table and have a unique identifier. Embedded objects are not stored in a database table but are embedded in another Oracle structure, like a stored program parameter, return type, or as an attribute of another object type. Transient objects are instances of objects that aren't stored in the database. They have a lifetime limited to the duration of their use in a PL/SQL block.

You create an instance of an object type and use an `INSERT` or `UPDATE` statement to assign it as a persistent object in a table. Alternatively, you can retrieve an object type from an `IN OUT` or `OUT`-only mode parameter, or get one as the output parameter of a function.

The following `CREATE TYPE` statement creates the object declaration in the session scope. You should note that each object type's methods point to valid Java methods from the same Java class.

```
SQL> CREATE OR REPLACE TYPE item_obj IS OBJECT
  2  ( id               NUMBER
  3  , title            VARCHAR2(60)
  4  , subtitle         VARCHAR2(60)
  5  , rating           VARCHAR2(8)
  6  , rating_agency    VARCHAR2(4)
  7  , release_date     DATE
  8  , MEMBER FUNCTION get_rating RETURN VARCHAR2
  9    AS LANGUAGE JAVA
 10    NAME 'Item.getRating() return java.lang.String'
```

```
11   , MEMBER FUNCTION get_name RETURN VARCHAR2
12     AS LANGUAGE JAVA
13     NAME 'Item.getName() return java.lang.String'
14   , MEMBER FUNCTION get_sql_type RETURN VARCHAR2
15     AS LANGUAGE JAVA
16     NAME 'Item.getSQLTypeName() return java.lang.String'
17   , MEMBER FUNCTION get_user_name RETURN VARCHAR2
18     AS LANGUAGE JAVA
19     NAME 'Item.getUserName() return java.lang.String'
20   , MEMBER PROCEDURE set_item (item   ITEM_OBJ)
21     AS LANGUAGE JAVA
22     NAME 'Item.setItem(java.sql.Struct)'
23   , MEMBER PROCEDURE set_rating (rating  VARCHAR2)
24     AS LANGUAGE JAVA
25     NAME 'Item.setRating(java.lang.String)'
26   , MEMBER FUNCTION to_string RETURN VARCHAR2
27     AS LANGUAGE JAVA
28     NAME 'Item.toString() return java.lang.String')
29   INSTANTIABLE NOT FINAL;
30   /
```

Lines 2 through 7 declare a list of attributes. The physical size assigned to the VARCHAR2 data types limits the size of the Java String attributes. Any attempt to pass a variable-length string longer than the imposed limit in the PL/SQL object type definition raises a "character string buffer too small" error.

Line 20 shows a set_item procedure that passes a SQL item_obj object type, which maps to a java.sql.Struct on line 22. All the other parameters and return types use Java String classes.

The next section shows you how to test the Java class instance by calling the PL/SQL object type in various contexts.

Testing the Java Class File

This section shows you how to insert instances of the item object type into an item_struct table, and how to query the persistent item_obj object instance from the item_struct table. Then, this section shows you how to work with transient object instances in an anonymous PL/SQL block.

The following CREATE TABLE statement creates the item_struct sample table:

```
SQL> CREATE TABLE item_struct
  2  ( item_struct_id  NUMBER
  3  , item_struct     ITEM_OBJ);
```

While Oracle Database 12c does support auto-incrementing sequences, this example uses explicitly declared and managed sequences, which are backward compatible. You create a generic sequence that starts with 1 and increments by 1 with this statement:

```
SQL> CREATE SEQUENCE item_struct_s;
```

You can construct and insert an `item_obj` object instance to the `item_struct` table with the following syntax:

```
SQL> INSERT INTO item_struct VALUES
  2  ( item_struct_s.NEXTVAL
  3  , item_obj( 1
  4           ,'The Hobbit'
  5           ,'An Unexpected Journey'
  6           ,'PG-13'
  7           ,'MPAA'
  8           ,'14-DEC-2012'));
```

Lines 3 through 8 create an instance of (*instantiate*) the `item_obj` type. The instance is assigned as a flattened object to the `VALUES` clause of the `INSERT` statement, and is inserted into the `item_struct` table.

Any attempt to access a single object type from a table in a query returns

```
ORA-22905: cannot access rows from a non-nested table item
```

To avoid this error, you create an `item_tab` or table collection of `item_obj` with the following syntax:

```
SQL> CREATE OR REPLACE
  2      TYPE item_tab IS TABLE OF item_obj;
  3  /
```

Now, you can query persistent copies of the `item_obj` data type like this:

```
SQL> COLUMN title         FORMAT A36  HEADING "Title"
SQL> COLUMN rating        FORMAT A6   HEADING "Rating"
SQL> COLUMN rating_agency FORMAT A6   HEADING "Rating|Agency"
SQL> COLUMN release_date  FORMAT A9   HEADING "Release|Date"
SQL> SELECT    title||': '||subtitle AS title
  2  ,          rating
  3  ,          rating_agency
  4  ,          release_date
  5  FROM    item_struct
  6  CROSS JOIN
  7  TABLE(
  8    SELECT CAST(COLLECT(item_struct) AS item_tab)
  9    FROM      dual);
```

The combination of the SQL `COLLECT`, `CAST`, and `TABLE` built-in functions on lines 7 and 8 let us query persistent objects. Combining these SQL functions with a `CROSS JOIN` lets us write a `SELECT` statement to query persistent object types. The preceding query prints the following when you have one or more rows in the `item_struct` table:

```
                                        Rating Release
Title                             Rating Agency Date
--------------------------------- ------ ------ ---------
The Hobbit: An Unexpected Journey PG-13  MPAA   14-DEC-12
```

An anonymous PL/SQL block provides a more robust test case solution. The following shows you how to create and assign an object type to a local variable, and shows you how to test the getter functions and setter procedures:

```
SQL> DECLARE
  2    /* Create an object type instance. */
  3    lv_item  ITEM_OBJ :=
  4      item_obj( 1
  5               ,'The Hobbit'
  6               ,'An Unexpected Journey'
  7               ,'PG-13'
  8               ,'MPAA'
  9               ,'14-DEC-2012');
 10  BEGIN
 11    /* Print the getter rating result. */
 12    dbms_output.put_line(
 13      '-------------------------------------------');
 14    dbms_output.put_line(
 15      'Rating Value: ['||lv_item.get_rating()||']');
 16
 17    /* Set the value of the rating. */
 18    lv_item.set_rating('PG');
 19
 20    /* Print the getter rating result. */
 21    dbms_output.put_line(
 22      'Rating Value: ['||lv_item.get_rating()||']');
 23    dbms_output.put_line(
 24      '-------------------------------------------');
 25
 26    /* Print user name and sql_type value. */
 27    dbms_output.put_line(
 28      'User Name:    ['||lv_item.get_user_name()||']');
 29    dbms_output.put_line(
 30      'Class Name:   ['||lv_item.get_name()||']');
 31    dbms_output.put_line(
 32      'Object Name:  ['||lv_item.get_sql_type()||']');
 33
 34    /* Print the toString value. */
 35    dbms_output.put_line(
 36      '-------------------------------------------');
 37    parse_rows(lv_item.to_string());
 38    dbms_output.put_line(
 39      '-------------------------------------------');
 40  END;
 41  /
```

Lines 3 through 9 create an instance of the item_obj object type and assign the instance to the lv_item local variable. Lines 14 and 15 print the current instance's rating value, line 18 resets the instance's rating value, and lines 21 and 22 print the modified rating value. These three activities demonstrate a call to the getter of an object type's attribute before and after the call to the setter to reset the value of an object type's attribute.

Lines 27 through 32 show how you can call several of the other getter functions, like the `get_user` function. The `get_user` function actually queries the database to determine the user's name. Line 37 calls the `to_string` procedure of the `lv_item` local variable as a parameter to the `parse_rows` procedure. As you saw in the "Parsing Long Strings" sidebar earlier in this chapter, the `parse_rows` procedure is ideal for use with Java `toString()` methods.

It prints the following:

```
-----------------------------------------------
Rating Value: [PG-13]
Rating Value: [PG]
-----------------------------------------------
User Name:    [VIDEO]
Class Name:   [Item]
Object Name:  [VIDEO.ITEM_OBJ]
-----------------------------------------------
ID #    [1]
Title   [The Hobbit: An Unexpected Journey]
Rating  [MPAA:PG]
Release [2012-12-14]
-----------------------------------------------
```

The SELECT statement and anonymous PL/SQL blocks have shown you how to work with and test Oracle object types.

Creating a Java Subclass and Object Subtype

Oracle object types support subclasses with the UNDER keyword from Oracle Database 10g forward. Naturally, you can create Java classes that subclass another Java class.

A subclass is a specialized behavior of a parent class. Parent classes are considered more generalized than their subclasses. There are certain rules and behaviors for using Java subclasses as Oracle object subtypes. That's why we wrote this section.

The two subsections show you how to implement a Java subclass and how to implement an Oracle object subtype.

Creating a Java Subclass

Like Java classes and Oracle object types, you must implement the Java class file first, and the PL/SQL wrapper second. Java subclasses rely on the existence of their parent, and object subtypes rely on the existence of their parent.

The following `ItemSt` class is a subclass or specialization of the Java `Item` class. You should take note that it doesn't redefine the attributes of the parent class. The `ItemSt` class does add one new attribute, so we can demonstrate how Java subclasses or Oracle subtypes work.

```
SQL> CREATE OR REPLACE AND COMPILE JAVA SOURCE NAMED "ItemSt" AS
  2    // Java library imports.
  3    import java.sql.*;
  4    import java.io.*;
  5    import oracle.sql.*;
  6    import oracle.jdbc.*;
```

```
 7  import oracle.oracore.*;
 8  import oracle.jdbc2.*;
 9  import java.math.*;
10
11  public class ItemSt extends Item implements SQLData
12  {
13    // Implement the attributes and operations for this type.
14    private String bluray;
15
16    // A getter for the rating attribute.
17    public String getBluray() {
18      return this.bluray; }
19
20    // A setter for the rating attribute.
21    public void setBluray(String bluray) {
22      this.bluray = new String(bluray); }
23
24    // A setter for this object.
25    public void setItem(Struct item) throws java.sql.SQLException {
26
27      // Assign Item instance variables.
28      super.setItem(item);
29
30      // Get the attributes of the Item object.
31      Object[] attributes = (Object[]) item.getAttributes();
32
33      // Assign the subtype element.
34      this.bluray = (String) attributes[6]; }
35
36    // Declare an instance toString method.
37    public String toString() {
38      return super.toString() +
39            "Blu-ray [" + this.bluray +"]\n"; }
40
41    /*  Implement SQLData interface.
42    || -------------------------------------------------------
43    ||  Required interface components:
44    ||  ==============================
45    ||    1. String sql_type instance variable.
46    ||    2. getSQLTypeName() method returns the sql_type value.
47    ||    3. readSQL() method to read from the Oracle session.
48    ||    4. writeSQL() method to write to the Oracle session.
49    */
50
51    // Required interface variable.
52    private String sql_type;
53
54    // Reads the stream from the Oracle session.
55    public void readSQL(SQLInput stream, String typeName)
56      throws SQLException {
```

```
57      // Call to parent class.
58      super.readSQL(stream, typeName);
59
60      // Map instance variables.
61      sql_type = typeName;
62      bluray = stream.readString(); }
63
64    // Writes the stream to the Oracle session.
65    public void writeSQL(SQLOutput stream) throws SQLException {
66      // Call to parent class.
67      super.writeSQL(stream);
68
69      // Map instance variables.
70      stream.writeString(bluray); }
71
72    /*
73    || ----------------------------------------------------
74    ||  End Implementation of SQLData interface.
75    */
76  }
77  /
```

Lines 25 through 34 show you how to handle a `Struct` of the `ItemSt` object type. This is where we implement a specialized `setItem()` method. You should note that in line 28 the subclass calls the parent class (or super) `setItem()` method. The balance of the `setItem()` method converts the `Struct` to an array of objects and then assigns the correct element to the `bluray` variable.

Lines 38 and 39 show you how to handle the `toString()` method of a subclass. Like the `setItem()` method, the `toString()` method must call `super` to get the behavior of the parent before adding on its own behavioral characteristics. Lines 58 and 67 also make `super` calls to the `readSQL()` and `writeSQL()` methods of the parent class.

You should discover from this example that a subclass depends on the program logic in the parent class. Also, you should see that subclass methods generally override behaviors of equivalent methods in the subclass.

Creating the Object Subtype

An Oracle object subtype is very much like an object type, except you exclude any attributes declared in the parent object type. You add any methods that augment the subtype's specialized methods, and you override any methods where the behavior changes (more or less grows):

```
SQL> CREATE OR REPLACE TYPE item_obj_st UNDER item_obj
  2  ( bluray          VARCHAR2(20)
  3  , MEMBER FUNCTION get_bluray RETURN VARCHAR2
  4    AS LANGUAGE JAVA
  5    NAME 'ItemSt.getBluray() return java.lang.String'
  6  , MEMBER PROCEDURE set_bluray (bluray  VARCHAR2)
  7    AS LANGUAGE JAVA
  8    NAME 'ItemSt.setBluray(java.lang.String)'
  9  , MEMBER PROCEDURE set_item (item  ITEM_OBJ_ST)
```

```
10     AS LANGUAGE JAVA
11     NAME 'ItemSt.setItem(java.sql.Struct)'
12   , OVERRIDING MEMBER FUNCTION to_string RETURN VARCHAR2
13     AS LANGUAGE JAVA
14     NAME 'ItemSt.toString() return java.lang.String')
15   INSTANTIABLE NOT FINAL;
16   /
```

Line 1 uses the UNDER keyword to designate that the item_obj_st object type inherits the behaviors of the item_obj object type. Line 2 adds a specialized bluray attribute to the item_obj_st and both getter and setter methods for the bluray instance variable. Lines 9 through 11 implement a set_item procedure. Looking at the item_obj_st object type, you may ask why we didn't use the OVERRIDING keyword. The answer is simple: the parameter is item_obj_st and you can't override behavior when the signature of the method differs.

You can rewrite the set_item procedure to accept a generic item_obj object type, but it would require changing the logic in the Java setItem() method. However, that's not a good idea, because you'd have to maintain that parent class for each new subclass you add.

The to_string function overrides the to_string method in the item_obj object type because the signature of both methods is the same. The overriding to_string method appends a string fragment from the parent class's string fragment.

Testing the Java Subclass

Testing subclass behavior is also known as testing polymorphic behavior. *Polymorphic behavior* occurs when a subclass performs differently from its parent and sibling classes.

We need to slip one more example in here, and that's a stand-alone function that constructs either a super class or subclass. That's done with the following get_item function. You should note two things about the get_item function. First, it takes a list of parameters necessary to create an item_obj_st instance. Second, it makes any subtype-only parameters optional parameters in the function's signature.

```
SQL> CREATE OR REPLACE FUNCTION get_item
  2  ( id             NUMBER
  3  , title          VARCHAR2
  4  , subtitle       VARCHAR2
  5  , rating         VARCHAR2
  6  , rating_agency  VARCHAR2
  7  , release_date   DATE
  8  , bluray         VARCHAR2 DEFAULT NULL )
  9  RETURN item_obj IS
 10    /* Declare a local variable. */
 11    lv_item  ITEM_OBJ;
 12  BEGIN
 13    /* Check for the subtype attribute. */
 14    IF bluray IS NULL THEN
 15      lv_item := item_obj( id
 16                         , title
 17                         , subtitle
 18                         , rating
 19                         , rating_agency
```

```
20                              , release_date);
21    ELSE
22      lv_item := item_obj_st( id
23                            , title
24                            , subtitle
25                            , rating
26                            , rating_agency
27                            , release_date
28                            , bluray);
29    END IF;
30
31    /* Return a type. */
32    RETURN lv_item;
33  END;
34  /
```

Line 8 provides the `bluray` attribute, which only belongs to the `item_obj_st` object type. The `bluray` parameter is optional because an `item_obj` instance can ignore that parameter. The `IF` statement on line 14 checks whether the subtype's `bluray` variable is null. The `get_item` function creates an `item_obj` instance when the `bluray` variable is null and an `item_obj_st` when the `bluray` variable isn't null.

The simplest way to test polymorphic behavior is an anonymous PL/SQL block. The following constructs `item_obj` and `item_obj_st` instances by leveraging our `get_item` function, and it assigns the result from the `get_item` function to a collection of the generalized `item_obj` class. Then, the anonymous block reads through the collection in a range `FOR` loop.

```
SQL> DECLARE
  2    /* Declare a generalized object type. */
  3    lv_item_tab  ITEM_TAB := item_tab();
  4  BEGIN
  5    /* Assign an object to a generalization. */
  6    lv_item_tab.EXTEND;
  7    lv_item_tab(lv_item_tab.COUNT) :=
  8      get_item(
  9         id => 2
 10       , title => 'The Hobbit'
 11       , subtitle => 'The Desolation of Smaug'
 12       , rating => 'PG-13'
 13       , rating_agency => 'MPAA'
 14       , release_date => '13-DEC-2013');
 15
 16    /* Assign an object to a specialization. */
 17    lv_item_tab.EXTEND;
 18    lv_item_tab(lv_item_tab.COUNT) :=
 19      get_item(
 20         id => 3
 21       , title => 'The Hobbit'
 22       , subtitle => 'The Battle of the Five Armies'
 23       , rating => 'PG-13'
 24       , rating_agency => 'MPAA'
```

```
25          , release_date => '17-DEC-2014'
26          , bluray => 'Sony Blu-ray');
27
28     /* Print header line. */
29     dbms_output.put_line(
30        '-------------------------------------------');
31
32     /* Print items in collection. */
33     FOR i IN 1..lv_item_tab.COUNT LOOP
34        /* Print the contents of the item_obj. */
35        parse_rows(lv_item_tab(i).to_string());
36        dbms_output.put_line(
37           '-------------------------------------------');
38     END LOOP;
39  END;
40  /
```

Lines 8 through 14 assign an `item_obj` instance to the `lv_item_tab` collection, and lines 18 through 26 assign an `item_obj_st` instance to the `lv_item_tab` collection. Line 35 uses the `parse_rows` procedure from the "Parsing Long Strings" sidebar earlier in this chapter to print the result of the `to_string` procedure.

It should print:

```
-------------------------------------------
ID #    [2]
Title   [The Hobbit: The Desolation of Smaug]
Rating  [MPAA:PG-13]
Release [2013-12-13]
-------------------------------------------
ID #    [3]
Title   [The Hobbit: The Battle of the Five Armies]
Rating  [MPAA:PG-13]
Release [2014-12-17]
Blu-ray [Sony Blu-ray]
-------------------------------------------
```

The first element prints the `item_obj` output, and the second element prints the `item_obj_st` output. Please take note that Oracle determined which to run based on their base object type, and you didn't need to write any specialized `instanceOf` logic.

The next section discusses troubleshooting the Java class library processes that build, load/drop, and use Java server stored object classes.

Troubleshooting Java Classes

This section covers how to troubleshoot Java class libraries. It becomes intuitive after performing it a few times, but initially it is very tricky.

Building, Loading, and Dropping Java Class Library Objects

When you build Java class libraries, you can encounter a number of problems. Many errors occur through simple syntax rule violations, but often the `PATH` or `CLASSPATH` environment variable excludes required Java libraries. You need to ensure that your `PATH` environment variable includes the Java SDK released with the Oracle database you're using. The best approach is to research which Java class libraries you'll require and then source them into your CLASSPATH. The following illustrates the minimum for the examples used in this chapter by operating system:

Windows

```
C:> set PATH=%PATH%;C:%ORACLE_HOME%\jdk\bin
C:> set CLASSPATH=%CLASSPATH%;C:%ORACLE_HOME%\jdbc\lib\ojdbc5.jar
```

If you want to use the JPublisher command-line tool, you need to add both of the following JAR files:

```
%ORACLE_HOME%\sqlj\lib\translator.zip
%ORACLE_HOME%\sqlj\lib\runtime12.zip
```

Unix

```
# export PATH=$PATH:/<mount>/$ORACLE_HOME/jdk/bin
# export CLASSPATH=$CLASSPATH:/<mount>/$ORACLE_HOME/jdbc/lib/ojdbc5.jar
```

If you want to use the JPublisher command-line tool, you must add both of these JAR files to your CLASSPATH environment variable:

```
$ORACLE_HOME/sqlj/lib/translator.zip
$ORACLE_HOME/sqlj/lib/runtime12.zip
```

Another potential problem in configuring Java archive access can be found in the LD_LIBRARY_PATH used in the listener.ora file. Check to make sure it's set as follows:

```
LD_LIBRARY_PATH=C:\oracle\ora92\lib;C:\oracle\ora92\jdbc\lib
```

You may also encounter an error that says you cannot drop a Java class file directly from your database instance. The error is raised by running the dropjava utility with the following syntax:

```
C:> dropjava -u username/password HelloWorld4.class
```

The following error message should then appear:

```
Error while dropping class HelloWorld4
    ORA-29537: class or resource cannot be created or dropped directly
```

The reason for the error is that you used loadjava to compile and load a Java source file, HelloWorld4.java. Thus, you should use dropjava and the source file, which will delete the class and source file.

NOTE
The behavior is generally consistent with the preceding description, but occasionally the command will work and delete both the source and class files from the Oracle JVM.

The error signaling that you have excluded something from your CLASSPATH environment variable should appear as follows:

```
C:\>loadjava -r -f -o -user video/video@video HelloWorld4.class
errors   : class HelloWorld4
    ORA-29521: referenced name oracle/jdbc2/SQLData could not be found
    ORA-29521: referenced name oracle/jdbc2/SQLInput could not be found
    ORA-29521: referenced name oracle/jdbc2/SQLOutput could not be found
The following operations failed
    class HelloWorld4: resolution
exiting  : Failures occurred during processing
```

If you get an ORA-29549 error, you're missing a Java archive reference. An ORA-29549 error is also raised when the Java class is removed and replaced the first time it's called.

TIP
If you replace your Java class files, make sure you call them once from the target schema to avoid having users manage the Java session change.

Now that you've reviewed the major issues with building, loading, and dropping Java stored object class files, let's examine some errors in the SQL and PL/SQL environment.

Using Java Class Library Objects

When you use Java stored object classes, you should ensure that you define only one constructor in the PL/SQL object type definition. The only constructor acted on by a PL/SQL object type wrapper is the default constructor.

TIP
Avoid overriding constructors unless you plan to call them from other Java libraries wrapped as procedures and functions.

The following shows you an example that attempts to implement an overriding constructor for the hello_world4 object type. Two attempts at overriding the constructor exist in the following example. One uses a null argument constructor, and the other uses a single formal parameter argument. There's no duplicate constructor in the target class file.

The following compiles successfully but fails at runtime:

```
SQL> CREATE OR REPLACE TYPE hello_world4 AS OBJECT
  2  ( whom   VARCHAR2(100)
  3  , CONSTRUCTOR FUNCTION hello_world4
  4    RETURN SELF AS RESULT
  5  , CONSTRUCTOR FUNCTION hello_world4
  6    ( whom   VARCHAR2 )
  7    RETURN SELF AS RESULT
  8  , MEMBER FUNCTION get_sql_type_name
  9    RETURN VARCHAR2 AS LANGUAGE JAVA
 10    NAME 'HelloWorld4.getSQLTypeName()
```

```
11            return java.lang.String'
12  , MEMBER FUNCTION to_string
13    RETURN VARCHAR2 AS LANGUAGE JAVA
14    NAME 'HelloWorld4.toString()
15            return java.lang.String' )
16  INSTANTIABLE FINAL;
17  /
```

The following anonymous block tests whether the object type can support an overriding constructor:

```
SQL> DECLARE
  2    /* Declare and instantiate an instance. */
  3    lv_hello  hello_world4 := hello_world4('Bilbo');
  4  BEGIN
  5    /* Parse any string longer than 80 characters. */
  6    parse_rows(lv_hello.to_string());
  7  END;
  8  /
```

The parse_rows function is presented in the "Parsing Long Strings" sidebar earlier in this chapter. This attempt to override the hello_world4 object type's constructor sends the following output to your console:

```
DECLARE
*
ERROR at line 1:
ORA-04067: not executed, type body "VIDEO.HELLO_WORLD4" does not exist
ORA-06508: PL/SQL: could not find program unit being called:
"VIDEO.HELLO_WORLD4"
ORA-06512: at line 3
```

This shows that you can't assign an overriding constructor. Any attempt to do so causes the object type declaration to fail. The real issue is that you can't override the SQLData implementation. As noted earlier, the methods used in the SQLData interface define how values are passed.

You may encounter many issues when first implementing stored Java object classes, and thus you may benefit from building a java_debug error management table like the following:

```
CREATE TABLE java_debug
( debug_number NUMBER
, debug_value VARCHAR2(4000) );
```

Adding the following method to your Java class files will enable you to write to the java_debug table:

```
// Define the debugLog() method.
public void debugLog(int debug_number
                    ,String debug_value) throws SQLException {
  String statement = "INSERT INTO java_debug VALUES (?,?)";

  // Declare an Oracle connection.
```

```
Connection conn = DriverManager.getConnection("jdbc:default:connection:");

// Declare prepared statement, run query and read results.
PreparedStatement ps = conn.prepareStatement(statement);
ps.setInt(1,debug_number);
ps.setString(2,debug_value);
ps.execute(); }
```

The two question marks in the VALUES clause of the INSERT statement let you bind positional variables from your Java program into the SQL statement. You have now covered the major issues with troubleshooting Java stored object classes. The next section summarizes the mapping of Oracle types to Java types.

Mapping Oracle Types

Oracle maps all native types and user-defined types (UDTs) to Java types. When you use SQLData, you map individual components and structures. Table 2-1 shows how Oracle SQL data types map to Java class data types.

SQL Data Types	Java Class Data Types
CHAR	oracle.sql.CHAR
LONG	java.lang.String
VARCHAR2	java.lang.Byte
	java.lang.Short
	java.lang.Integer
	java.lang.Long
	java.lang.Float
	java.lang.Double
	java.lang.BigDecimal
	java.sql.Date
	java.sql.Time
	java.sql.Timestamp
	byte
	short
	int
	long
	float
	double
DATE	oracle.sql.DATE
	java.lang.String
	java.sql.Date
	java.sql.Time
	java.sql.Timestamp

(continued)

TABLE 2-1. *Oracle Data Type Mapping to Java Object Types*

SQL Data Types	Java Class Data Types
NUMBER	oracle.sql.NUMBER
	java.lang.Byte
	java.lang.Short
	java.lang.Integer
	java.lang.Long
	java.lang.Float
	java.lang.Double
	java.lang.BigDecimal
	byte
	short
	int
	long
	float
	double
OPAQUE	oracle.sql.OPAQUE
RAW	oracle.sql.RAW
LONG RAW	byte[]
ROWID	oracle.sql.CHAR
	oracle.sql.ROWID
	java.lang.String
BFILE	oracle.sql.BFILE
BLOB	oracle.sql.BLOB
	oracle.jdbc2.Blob
CLOB	oracle.sql.CLOB
NCLOB	oracle.jdbc2.Clob
OBJECT	oracle.sql.STRUCT
Object types	java.sql.Struct
	java.sql.SqlData
	oracle.sql.ORAData
REF	oracle.sql.REF
Reference types	java.sql.Ref
	oracle.sql.ORAData
TABLE	oracle.sql.ARRAY
VARRAY | ARRAY	java.sql.Array
Associative Array	oracle.sql.ORAData
Any of the preceding SQL types	oracle.sql.CustomDatum
	oracle.sql.Datum

TABLE 2-1. *Oracle Data Type Mapping to Java Object Types*

Native types and UDTs can be used and managed by the `SQLData` conventions covered in the chapter. The Oracle JPublisher tool enables you to develop `SQLData` stubs and programs to use your UDTs.

Supporting Scripts

The following programs are available on the McGraw-Hill Professional website to support this chapter:

- The `HelloWorld4.java` and `HelloWorld4.sql` programs let you test the basic `SQLData` interface required for object instances.

- The `Item.sql` program contains all other code examples for the chapter.

- The `parsing.sql` program contains the sample that lets you parse the `toString` output from the Java libraries.

Summary

You should now have an understanding of how to implement and troubleshoot server-side or internal Java class libraries that support PL/SQL object types. With these skills, you can build internal Java libraries that mirror external Java class files.

PART

II

File I/O

CHAPTER

3

utl_file Package

Purpose

This chapter teaches you how to configure, deploy, manage, and troubleshoot the utl_file package. The utl_file package was introduced in Oracle version 7 as a PL/SQL tool to sequentially read files from and write files to the operating system. Oracle9i Database added limited ability to randomly read files by shifting the pointer forward or backward through a file. Oracle Database 10g enabled the utl_file package to use virtual directories rather than physical path locations. Oracle Database 10g also removed the physical limitation on writing external files through the dbms_output package. There are no changes to the utl_file package in Oracle Database 11g and 12c.

Advantages

The utl_file package was the first PL/SQL tool to enable Oracle 7 application developers to perform external file I/O operations. As such, it was revolutionary because no other vendor had thought about bridging internal database resources with external file system resources.

You can create, read, write, copy, move, remove, and rename external files with the utl_file package. While external tables are easier and more constructive alternatives to using the utl_file package to read comma-separated, tab-separated, and position-specific files, the utl_file package remains a key tool to

- Read unstructured data, like what may be appropriately stored in a CLOB column
- Write data into structured file extracts, large text, or binary files

Unstructured data is like an essay or customer support note. Unstructured data can also be a binary stream, such as an image file you may store in the database. Structured data is typically represented as a flat file or comma-separated value file.

The only alternatives to using the utl_file package to write external files are Java libraries, C-callable external procedures, and spooling files with SQL*Plus. Chapter 4 covers how you create Java libraries to create, read, write, copy, move, remove, and rename, and Chapter 11 demonstrates how you create C-callable external libraries. Appendix A in *Oracle Database 12c PL/SQL Programming* shows you how to spool files through SQL*Plus interactively, and it shows you how to run scripts in SQL*Plus by using its silent mode of operations. Naturally, using SQL*Plus programmatically requires mastery of a shell scripting language like Bash or Windows PowerShell (version 4 at the time of writing).

Disadvantages

The utl_file package can gain access to external files through two configuration options. One configuration option lets you set the utl_file_dir parameter in the spfile.ora file of the Oracle Database 12c server. The other configuration option uses virtual directories, which is the recommended approach.

While there's no documentation from Oracle that advises deprecation of the utl_file_dir parameter, it's probably a good idea to not use it. The value of the parameter is set when you start the database. You can set the parameter in the spfile.ora file, but then the DBA must stop and restart the database server for it to work. This limitation is actually quite severe because *during an unforeseen maintenance operation where you must move external files, you must physically shut down and restart the database server*.

A virtual directory maps an uppercase name to a physical path on the operating system. Only the sys, system, or privileged DBA user can set up virtual directories. Virtual directories abstract or hide the location of physical files from database users. The layer of abstractions should be thought of as a security layer.

A DBA can create a virtual directory without starting and stopping the database server. That's because the CREATE DIRECTORY statement is a Data Definition Language (DDL) command. After you create a virtual directory, you simply grant privileges on a virtual directory to a role or user. These changes are immediate and convenient. A user with privileges to read and write to a virtual directory enjoys the same rights as setting a physical directory in the utl_file_dir comma-delimited parameter list.

TIP
Just remember you always need to provide virtual directory names in uppercase text. A lowercase or mixed-case name fails to resolve with the virtual name in the database catalog.

The utl_file package reads line by line with minimal controls over positioning the physical locator for random access. The utl_file package doesn't have any way to read structured data without parsing the lines it reads, which is tedious and unnecessary from Oracle Database 10g forward because you can use external tables. Chapter 5 in this book covers external tables, and it shows you how to leverage Java libraries to secure external files after they're read.

Overview
This chapter shows you how to use the utl_file package to

- Access external files
- Read external files
- Copy, move, rename, and remove external files
- Create and write to external files

As mentioned in the "Advantages" section, the utl_file package lets you create, read, write, copy, move, remove, and rename external files. That makes the utl_file package an important tool. While there's no formal *create* procedure, utl_file lets you create a new file and write to an existing file by opening the file with the fopen procedure. The same fopen procedure also lets you read an existing file.

You must set the fopen procedure's *open mode* when you call the fopen procedure. You set the open mode to *read-only, read and write*, or *append* behavior with a single character, and the character options are shown in Table 3-1.

Open Mode	Description
R	Lets you open a file in read-only mode.
W	Lets you open a file in read and write mode.
A	Lets you open a file in append mode.

TABLE 3-1. *File I/O Modes of Operation*

The read-only open mode lets you read unstructured text or binary streams, or structured text. As a rule, you should use the `utl_file` package and this method only when working with unstructured data, because external tables are much more efficient, as you'll discover in Chapter 5. Essentially, external tables use SQL*Loader express mode, which is capable of reading external structured files in parallel mode.

The read and write mode lets you create a new file or edit an existing file. Naturally, you need to read a file to determine where you want to edit it. While you have sequential and limited random file access with the `utl_file` package, you can flexibly edit a document by converting the file to a `CLOB` and using the `REGEXP_REPLACE` function.

The append mode lets you add data to a file. You typically append when you keep external log files.

Some of the examples in this chapter build on PL/SQL programming concepts introduced in *Oracle Database 12c PL/SQL Programming*. For example, you should have some experience with the PL/SQL programming language, including how to use the `dbms_lob` package and how to use Oracle's regular expression functions. Chapter 3 in the referenced book provides an overview of basic PL/SQL programming functionality, Chapter 10 in the referenced book covers the `dbms_lob` package, and Appendix E covers regular expressions.

Accessing External Files

It's important to understand how you can access external files from the Oracle Database 12*c* server. As mentioned in the "Disadvantages" section earlier in this chapter, you have two configuration options. One sets the `utl_file_dir` parameter in the `spfile.ora` file and the other uses virtual directories.

Setting the utl_file_dir Database Parameter

Any directory set in the `utl_file_dir` parameter in the `spfile.ora` file enjoys read, write, and execute privileges. Any reference to a directory listed in the `utl_file_dir` parameter has full access to that directory. This approach is considered by many to be insecure and a security risk, which is why more DBAs prefer virtual directories.

By default, Oracle Database 12*c* doesn't set any values for the `utl_file_dir` parameter in the `spfile.ora` file. You can verify whether any values are set with the following `show` command as the `sys` user:

```
SQL> show parameter utl_file
```

```
NAME                  TYPE        VALUE
--------------- ----------- ------------------------------------
utl_file_dir          string
```

You can't set the parameter dynamically, but you can write the change to the `spfile.ora` file with the following command as the `sys` user:

```
SQL> ALTER SYSTEM
  2  SET utl_file_dir='C:\Data\Reader','C:\Data\Writer'
  3  SCOPE=SPFILE;
```

It's very important to note that you may create the physical directories before or after you assign them to the `utl_file_dir` parameter. While this example uses a Windows directory, it's possible to use a Linux or Unix directory. The directory and file ownership and permissions are typically the same as the Oracle database server. Any attempt to use the `utl_file_dir` targets when they don't exist on the operating system results in a failure at runtime.

If you forget to set the `scope` value on line 3 in the previous command, you raise the following exception:

```
ALTER SYSTEM SET utl_file_dir='C:\Data\Reader','C:\Data\Writer'
                 *
ERROR at line 1:
ORA-02095: specified initialization parameter cannot be modified
```

After you successfully alter the `utl_file_dir` parameter in the `spfile.ora` file, you need to stop and restart the Oracle Database 12*c* server. You can verify your changes with this `show` command as the `sys` user:

```
SQL> show parameter utl_file

NAME                    TYPE        VALUE
--------------- ----------- -----------------------------------
utl_file_dir    string       'C:\Data\Reader','C:\Data\Writer'
```

This shows that both directories are now authorized. You can read and write to the directories from the `utl_file` package.

TIP
You can't alter the system as a pluggable database (PDB). Any attempt to do so raises an `ORA-65040` exception.

The first subsection has shown you how to use the `utl_file_dir` parameter; the examples in subsequent sections will show you how to use these physical directories.

Using Virtual Directories

Virtual directories map a name stored in the database catalog to a string that (hopefully) represents a physical path on the local operating system. You can create a virtual directory that points to a pre-existing physical directory or a directory that you plan to create. The Oracle Database 12*c* server makes no attempt to validate the string you enter as a valid path until you use it in a runtime context.

Virtual directories are only accessible when you grant `read` or `write` privilege on them to a user. The `sys`, `system`, or privileged DBA user can create virtual directories and assign privileges on them to roles or users. As a rule, it's best to limit virtual directories where possible to either the `read` or `write` privilege.

At this point in the book, we must make a major assumption that you have some familiarity with the concepts of a multitenant database. If you don't but want to follow along with these examples, please check the "Multitenant Provisioning" sidebar in Chapter 5. Alternatively, you can simply configure schemas in your non-multitenant database to support these examples.

TIP
Virtual directories exist in the scope of a container database (CDB) or a PDB. You connect as the system *user to create a virtual directory for a CDB, and as the* ADMIN *user of the PDB to create a virtual directory for a PDB.*

As the sys, system, or authorized CDB administrator account, you create a reader virtual directory with the following syntax (Windows syntax). You could alternatively create a reader virtual directory as the ADMIN user of a PDB. Interestingly, the syntax to create a virtual directory is the same whether you create the directory as the CDB or the PDB.

```
SQL> CREATE DIRECTORY reader AS 'C:\data\reader';
```

You should also create a writer directory with this syntax:

```
SQL> CREATE DIRECTORY writer AS 'C:\data\writer';
```

Naturally, you can replace the Windows-specific paths with a Linux mount point and physical directory. There are simply too many possibilities of what you may opt to do in Linux for us to recommend a specific path. However, please note that, unlike in Windows, you must set both ownership and read, write, and execute privileges on the Linux directories.

You will use, or are recommended to use, an importer schema for the examples in this chapter. Assuming you follow that suggestion, you grant read permission to the importer PDB user on the reader virtual directory with this syntax:

```
SQL> GRANT READ ON DIRECTORY reader TO importer;
```

Then, you grant write permission to the importer PDB user on the writer virtual directory:

```
SQL> GRANT READ, WRITE ON DIRECTORY writer TO importer;
```

At this point you can't test these, but you will begin that process in the next section.

Reading External Files

The utl_file package contains 23 functions and procedures, but you only need to use one function and two procedures to read a file line by line. Table 3-2 lists the subroutines found inside the utl_file package. You also need to use the file_type record type declared in the utl_file package specification.

Reading a file line by line in a loop until the *end-of-file (eof)* marker raises an exception is the most common way of using the utl_file package. You may be saying "Whew!" (or something stronger) if you're new to the utl_file package. Seeing success in a program as the outcome of raising an exception can seem strange, but it's the way Oracle opted to implement the utl_file .get_line procedure.

The balance of this section is divided into a review of how to read files with the utl_file package and how to implement best practices when reading external files with the package.

Subroutine	Description
fclose procedure	Closes a file opened by fopen or fopen_nchar.
fclose_all procedure	Closes all files opened by fopen or fopen_nchar.
fcopy procedure	Copies a contiguous portion of a file to a newly created file.
fflush procedure	Physically writes all pending output to a file.
fgetattr procedure	Reads and returns the attributes of a disk file.
fgetpos function	Returns the current relative offset position within a file, in bytes.
fopen function	Opens a file for input or output.
fopen_nchar function	Opens a file in Unicode for input or output.
fremove procedure	Deletes a disk file, assuming that you have sufficient privileges.
frename procedure	Renames an existing file to a new name, similar to the Unix mv function.
fseek procedure	Adjusts the file pointer forward or backward within the file by the number of bytes specified.
get_line procedure	Reads a line of text from a file.
get_line_nchar procedure	Reads a line of Unicode text from a file.
get_raw procedure	Reads a raw string value from a file and adjusts the file pointer ahead by the number of bytes read.
is_open function	Determines if a file handle refers to an open file.
new_line procedure	Writes one or more operating system–specific line terminators to a file.
put procedure	Writes a string to a file.
put_line procedure	Writes a string and an operating system–specific line terminator to a file.
put_line_nchar procedure	Writes a string and an operating system–specific line terminator to a file.
put_nchar procedure	Writes a string to a file.
putf procedure	Writes a formatted string to a file.
putf_nchar procedure	Writes a formatted Unicode string to a file.
put_raw function	Accepts a raw input and writes the value to the output buffer.

TABLE 3-2. *The utl_file Subroutines*

Reading Files with the utl_file Package

This section provides an implementation of the `utl_file` package that opens the file, reads line by line until the *eof* marker, and then closes the file from within a `NO_DATA_FOUND` exception handler. The sample uses a four-parameter call to the `utl_file.fopen` because a three-parameter call limits the maximum size of each line to the 1,024-byte default. Writing quality reusable code requires that you avoid imposing restrictive limits. We recommend that you always override the maximum line size default value because your code becomes more robust. The maximum size is 32,767 bytes.

NOTE
While we use the maximum 32,767 bytes in these examples, you should choose a value that meets your needs.

Here's an anonymous block program that shows you how to read an external file with the `utl_file` package. For this example to work, you need to add the `'C:\Data\Direct'` directory to the `utl_file_dir` parameter and then stop and restart the Oracle Database 12*c* server.

It prints each line as it's read:

```
SQL> DECLARE
  2    /* Declare local input variables. */
  3    lv_location      VARCHAR2(60) := 'C:\Data\Direct';
  4    lv_file_name     VARCHAR2(40) := 'TextFile.txt';
  5
  6    /* Declare a file reference pointer and buffer. */
  7    lv_file    UTL_FILE.FILE_TYPE;   -- File reference
  8    lv_line    VARCHAR2(32767);      -- Reading buffer
  9  BEGIN
 10    /* Check for open file and close when open. */
 11    IF utl_file.is_open(lv_file) THEN
 12      utl_file.fclose(lv_file);
 13    END IF;
 14
 15    /* Open the file for read-only of 32,767 byte lines. */
 16    lv_file := utl_file.fopen( location    => lv_location
 17                             , filename    => lv_file_name
 18                             , open_mode   => 'R'
 19                             , max_linesize => 32767);
 20
 21    /* Read all lines of a text file. */
 22    LOOP
 23      /* Read a line of text until the eof marker. */
 24      utl_file.get_line( file   => lv_file
 25                       , buffer => lv_line );
 26
 27      /* Print the line of text. */
 28      dbms_output.put_line(NVL(lv_line,CHR(10)));
 29    END LOOP;
 30  EXCEPTION
```

```
31    /* Close file after reading the last line of a file. */
32    WHEN NO_DATA_FOUND THEN
33      utl_file.fclose(lv_file);
34    /* Close file after a thrown exception. */
35    WHEN UTL_FILE.READ_ERROR THEN
36      dbms_output.put_line(
37        'Position ['||utl_file.fgetpos(lv_file)||']');
38      utl_file.fclose(lv_file);
39      RETURN;
40  END;
41  /
```

Line 3 declares a variable with a physical directory description, which is the traditional or original way of getting a directory path. As discussed earlier in this chapter, from Oracle Database 10g forward, a virtual directory can replace a string with an absolute qualified path. Just remember one thing about the Oracle Database 12c data catalog: all literals are uppercase strings. That means you must provide an uppercase virtual directory name when calling any stored program that accepts a virtual directory as a parameter.

The following variation on line 3 uses a virtual directory:

```
3    lv_location     VARCHAR2(60) := 'READER'; -- Virtual Directory
```

CAUTION
You must pass virtual directory names in uppercase text.

Line 7 declares a local file reference by using the utl_file package's defined file_type data type. Line 8 declares a lv_line variable that is a 32,767-byte string (just to use the maximum possible value). We use the lv_line variable as our pass-by-reference variable to the utl_file package's fopen procedure. Please read the upcoming "Passing What, to Where, and Why?" sidebar if the concepts of PL/SQL pass-by-value and pass-by-reference are new to you.

Lines 11 through 13 contain an IF block that closes the file reference when it's found open in the active session. Lines 16 through 19 open an external file (using named notation) when the following three things are true:

■ The physical path points to a valid target path.
■ The physical file name points to an existing file in the target path.
■ The physical path is a valid parameter value of the utl_file_dir parameter.

A utl_file package-defined exception is raised when any of the preceding isn't true. You can check Table 3-3 for a list and description of predefined utl_file exceptions.

The max_linesize parameter call in the fopen procedure sets the maximum size of the OUT-only mode buffer parameter in the subsequent call to the get_line procedure on lines 24 and 25. Line 28 prints the contents of the buffer parameter value, which is everything except the line terminator from the last call to the get_line procedure. The get_line procedure raises a NO_DATA_FOUND error when it finds the *eof* marker, which is every time you run the program. That's why we've put the fclose procedure call inside the NO_DATA_FOUND exception handler on lines 32 and 33.

Exception Name	Description
ACCESS_DENIED	Permission to access the file location is denied.
CHARSETMISMATCH	A file is opened using fopen_nchar, but later I/O operations use non-Unicode character functions such as putf or get_line procedures.
DELETE_FAILED	The requested file delete operation failed.
FILE_OPEN	The requested operation failed because the file is open.
INTERNAL_ERROR	An unspecified PL/SQL error occurred.
INVALID_FILEHANDLE	The file handle is invalid.
INVALID_FILENAME	The file name parameter is invalid.
INVALID_MAXLINESIZE	The max_linesize value for the fopen procedure is invalid; it should be in the range of 1 to 32,767.
INVALID_MODE	The open_mode parameter in fopen is invalid.
INVALID_OFFSET	An absolute_offset value exception occurred when an absolute_offset value is less than zero or null, and when an fseek procedure goes past the end of the file.
INVALID_OPERATION	The file could not be opened or operated on as requested.
INVALID_PATH	The file location is invalid.
READ_ERROR	An operating system error occurred during the read operation.
RENAME_FAILED	The requested file-rename operation failed.
WRITE_ERROR	An operating system error occurred during the write operation.

TABLE 3-3. *utl_file Package Exceptions*

Lines 35 through 39 include a second error handler, which catches an error raised when you change the fopen procedure call on lines 16 through 19 from a four-parameter call to a three-parameter call, like this:

```
16    lv_file := utl_file.fopen( location    => lv_location
17                             , filename    => lv_file_name
18                             , open_mode   => 'R');
19
```

With this change, the get_line procedure would throw an exception when it encounters a string longer than 1,024 bytes. Each of the specialized exception handlers must include a call to the fclose procedure or there will be a lock on the file resource for the duration of the session. A generic OTHERS exception would catch all exceptions and let you include only a single call to the fclose procedure.

Passing What, to Where, and Why?

When you write PL/SQL programs, you typically care more about the business logic then how Oracle compiles and runs them. That's why the concepts of pass-by-value and pass-by-reference help explain how you work with stored functions and procedures.

At the PL/SQL level, you see two options:

■ You call a pass-by-value parameter (IN mode) with a variable or literal value. From the perspective of the calling program, you pass a copy of a value to the subprogram and never expect to see it back. Hence, you pass a value from the calling program to the called program.

■ You call a pass-by-reference parameter (IN OUT or OUT mode) with only a variable. More or less, you pass a reference to the call parameter. The reference lets the subprogram change the value of the external variable.

While we use this to describe how to work with subprograms, it is a simplification. The PL/SQL engine works differently. A pass-by-value parameter doesn't actually get a copy, because it receives an immutable (read-only) reference to an external variable or value. Likewise, a pass-by-reference parameter holds a copy of (default) or reference to an external variable. If the PL/SQL engine chooses to pass a copy, the value of the copy overwrites any value held by the original external variable at the completion of the subprogram. If the PL/SQL engine passes a reference, the subprogram can write a change to the external variable directly.

You can eliminate the need to read the *eof* marker and cease relying on closing an open file in the exception block. To accomplish this change, you need to discover the physical size of the file, track the size of each line read, and stop reading the file when the sum of the line reads exceeds the file size.

The fgetattr procedure lets you capture the file size, and a WHILE loop lets you avoid reading through to the *eof* marker where the program would raise an exception.

The following demonstrates this approach to using the utl_file package. Line 3 of this program requires that you have access to the 'C:\Data\Direct' directory. The easiest way to accomplish that is to put the physical path in the parameter list of the utl_file_dir parameter, and stop and restart the Oracle Database 12c server:

```
SQL> DECLARE
  2    /* Declare local input variables. */
  3    lv_location     VARCHAR2(60) := 'C:\Data\Direct';
  4    lv_file_name    VARCHAR2(40) := 'TextFile.txt';
  5
  6    /* Declare a file reference pointer and buffer. */
  7    lv_file    UTL_FILE.FILE_TYPE;    -- File reference
  8    lv_line    VARCHAR2(32767);       -- Reading buffer
  9
 10    /* Declare local size variables. */
 11    lv_file_size  NUMBER;
 12    lv_line_size  NUMBER;
```

```
13     lv_read_size  NUMBER :=0;
14
15     /* Declare local file attribute data. */
16     lv_file_exists  BOOLEAN := FALSE;
17     lv_block_size   BINARY_INTEGER;
18   BEGIN
19     /* Check for open file and close when open. */
20     IF utl_file.is_open(lv_file) THEN
21       utl_file.fclose(lv_file);
22     END IF;
23
24     /* Read the file attributes to get the physical size. */
25     utl_file.fgetattr( location      => lv_location
26                      , filename      => lv_file_name
27                      , fexists       => lv_file_exists
28                      , file_length  => lv_file_size
29                      , block_size    => lv_block_size );
30
31     /* Open only files that exist. */
32     IF lv_file_exists THEN
33
34       /* Open the file for read-only of 32,767 byte lines. */
35       lv_file := utl_file.fopen( location      => lv_location
36                                , filename      => lv_file_name
37                                , open_mode     => 'R'
38                                , max_linesize => 32767);
39
40       /* Read all lines of a text file. */
41       WHILE (lv_read_size < lv_file_size) LOOP
42         /* Read a line of text until the eof marker. */
43         utl_file.get_line( file   => lv_file
44                          , buffer => lv_line );
45
46         /* Print the line of text. */
47         dbms_output.put_line(NVL(lv_line,CHR(10)));
48
49         /* Add the line size to the read size. */
50         lv_read_size := lv_read_size
51                       + LENGTH(NVL(lv_line,CHR(10))) + 2;
52       END LOOP;
53
54       /* Close the file. */
55       utl_file.fclose(lv_file);
56     END IF;
57   EXCEPTION
58     /* Close file after a thrown exception. */
59     WHEN UTL_FILE.READ_ERROR  THEN
60     dbms_output.put_line(
61       'Position ['||utl_file.fgetpos(lv_file)||']');
62     RETURN;
63   END;
64   /
```

The program adds three size variables and two control variables to let you call the `fgetattr` procedure. The `fgetattr` call on lines 25 through 29 relies on three OUT-only mode pass-by-reference parameters. One, the `fexists` parameter, verifies that the file exists, which is how you avoid raising any exceptions when you try to open, read, write, copy, move, or rename the file.

While line 47 prints lines as they're read, the assignment on lines 50 and 51 adds back 2 bytes for the line terminators that it removes with the `get_line` procedure. You add 2 bytes because line terminators are that size. The WHILE loop (starting on line 41) exits when it reads the last line of text before the *eof* marker. The last instruction in the execution block closes the file reference (line 55) and leaves the exception handling section to raise errors.

Implementing Best Practices

In this section, we show you how to implement best practices for reading an external file with the `utl_file` package. Like the prior examples, the `utl_file` package returns its content as a CLOB data type.

While the following `read_file_to_clob` function illustrates best practices for reading an unstructured source from an external file into a CLOB data type, it borrows heavily from the anonymous block examples of the previous section. The logic guarantees that a missing file or incorrect directory path won't trigger a runtime error. The program accomplishes this feat by reading a Boolean value of the `fexists` parameter. The `fexists` parameter value is set after a call to the `fgetattr` procedure of the `utl_file` package.

After verifying the external file, the function's logic reads line by line the source file and writes it to the target CLOB variable. At successful completion, the CLOB variable is returned by the function.

The full implementation of the `read_file_to_clob` function is

```
SQL> CREATE OR REPLACE FUNCTION read_file_to_clob
  2  ( pv_location    VARCHAR2
  3  , pv_file_name   VARCHAR2 ) RETURN CLOB IS
  4
  5    /* Declare local input variables. */
  6    lv_location      VARCHAR2(60);
  7    lv_file_name     VARCHAR2(40);
  8
  9    /* Declare a file reference pointer and buffer. */
 10    lv_file      UTL_FILE.FILE_TYPE;   -- File reference
 11    lv_line      VARCHAR2(32767);      -- Reading buffer
 12
 13    /* Declare local sizing variables. */
 14    lv_file_size   NUMBER;
 15    lv_line_size   NUMBER;
 16    lv_read_size   NUMBER :=0;
 17
 18    /* Declare local file attribute data. */
 19    lv_file_exists   BOOLEAN := FALSE;
 20    lv_block_size    BINARY_INTEGER;
 21
 22    /* Declare a control variable and return CLOB variable. */
 23    lv_enable   BOOLEAN := FALSE;
```

```
24     lv_return  CLOB;
25  BEGIN
26     /* Declare local input variables. */
27     lv_location  := pv_location;
28     lv_file_name := pv_file_name;
29
30     /* Check for open file and close when open. */
31     IF utl_file.is_open(lv_file) THEN
32       utl_file.fclose(lv_file);
33     END IF;
34
35     /* Read the file attributes to get the physical size. */
36     utl_file.fgetattr( location    => lv_location
37                      , filename    => lv_file_name
38                      , fexists     => lv_file_exists
39                      , file_length => lv_file_size
40                      , block_size  => lv_block_size );
41
42     /* Open only files that exist. */
43     IF lv_file_exists THEN
44       /* Open the file for read-only of 32,767 byte lines. */
45       lv_file := utl_file.fopen( location    => lv_location
46                                , filename    => lv_file_name
47                                , open_mode   => 'R'
48                                , max_linesize => 32767);
49
50       /* Create a temporary CLOB in memory. */
51       dbms_lob.createtemporary(lv_return, FALSE, dbms_lob.CALL);
52
53       /* Read all lines of a text file. */
54       WHILE (lv_read_size < lv_file_size) LOOP
55         /* Read a line of text until the eof marker. */
56         utl_file.get_line( file   => lv_file
57                          , buffer => lv_line );
58
59         /* Add the line terminator or 2 bytes to its length. */
60         lv_line := NVL(lv_line,'')||CHR(10);
61         lv_read_size := lv_read_size
62                       + LENGTH(NVL(lv_line,CHR(10))) + 2;
63
64         /* Write to an empty CLOB or append to an existing CLOB. */
65         IF NOT lv_enable THEN
66           /* Write to the temporary CLOB variable. */
67           dbms_lob.write( lv_return, LENGTH(lv_line), 1, lv_line);
68
69           /* Set the control variable. */
70           lv_enable := TRUE;
71         ELSE
72           /* Append to the temporary CLOB variable. */
73           dbms_lob.writeappend( lv_return, LENGTH(lv_line),lv_line);
74         END IF;
```

```
75        END LOOP;
76
77        /* Close the file. */
78        utl_file.fclose(lv_file);
79      END IF;
80
81      /* This line is never reached. */
82      RETURN lv_return;
83    EXCEPTION
84      WHEN OTHERS THEN
85        utl_file.fclose(lv_file);
86        RETURN NULL;
87    END;
88    /
```

The IF block on lines 31 through 33 is new. It checks to see if the file handle is open and, if it is, closes the open file handle.

Line 51 uses the dbms_lob.createtemporary procedure to open a new temporary CLOB data type. You *must* create a temporary large object to secure a locator in the session's memory. While a locator value exists for all persistent large objects and those you read from a table, it doesn't exist for a transient large object. The createtemporary procedure lets you create a transient large object that acts like a persistent object.

Lines 65 through 74 write the first line of text or append it to the end of existing text. Inside, the WHILE loop continues to read lines of text until all lines of text are read. Then, the program transfers each line of text into a local CLOB variable. Line 82 returns the local CLOB variable as the result of a call to the function.

You can call the function like this:

```
SQL> SET LONG 100000
SQL> SET PAGESIZE 999
SQL> SELECT read_file_to_clob('SomeVirtualDir','TextFile.txt') AS "Output"
  2  FROM   dual;
```

The read_file_to_clob function returns a stream of input that mirrors the source file, including line returns. It returns the stream as a CLOB data type.

You can use the same approach with structured data, provided you add a parsing algorithm that translates the lv_line variable's value into a composite collection. Composite collections have a base type of a PL/SQL record structure or a SQL object type. Implementing a parsing algorithm is straightforward. You write a function that accepts a line of text as a parameter, parses the parameter into fields, and assigns the fields to a record or object type that you return from the function.

We'd recommend you implement this type of solution by using a SQL object type. A SQL object type is more flexible than a PL/SQL-only record structure.

Copying, Moving, Renaming, and Removing External Files

The utl_file package gives you the ability to copy, move, rename, and remove a file with a single procedure statement. You can move a file using the frename procedure when the source and destination directories differ, or rename a file when the source and destination directories are the same.

You can also create, write, and append to a new or an existing file with several of the utl_ file package's procedures. You can use the put, put_line, new_line, and putf procedures to write to files that you've already opened with the 'W' or 'A' open mode. The fflush procedure also works in the same open modes to force any buffered data to be written to a file.

The following subsections show you how to copy, move, rename, and remove external files. The best place to start is the utl_file package's fcopy procedure, which we'll use in subsequent examples.

Copying External Files

The utl_file package's fcopy procedure lets you copy one file to another. You need to provide the fully qualified path or a virtual directory of both files and their file names.

The following anonymous block shows you how to copy one file to another. Like the example in the "Reading Files with the utl_file Package" section, you need to put the 'C:\Data\ Direct' path in as a parameter to the utl_file_dir and stop and restart the database server.

```
SQL> DECLARE
  2    /* Declare local input variables. */
  3    lv_src_location    VARCHAR2(60) := 'C:\Data\Direct';
  4    lv_src_file_name   VARCHAR2(40) := 'TextFile.txt';
  5
  6    /* Declare local input variables. */
  7    lv_dest_location   VARCHAR2(60) := 'DIRECT';
  8    lv_dest_file_name  VARCHAR2(40) := 'TextCopy.txt';
  9  BEGIN
 10    /* Open the file for read-only of 32,767 byte lines. */
 11    utl_file.fcopy( src_location  => lv_src_location
 12                  , src_filename  => lv_src_file_name
 13                  , dest_location => lv_dest_location
 14                  , dest_filename => lv_dest_file_name);
 15  EXCEPTION
 16    /* Manage package raised exceptions. */
 17    WHEN utl_file.read_error THEN
 18      RAISE_APPLICATION_ERROR(-20001,'Read error.');
 19    WHEN utl_file.write_error THEN
 20      RAISE_APPLICATION_ERROR(-20002,'Write error.');
 21    WHEN utl_file.access_denied THEN
 22      RAISE_APPLICATION_ERROR(-20003,'Read error.');
 23  END;
 24  /
```

Line 3 declares a source location variable with a fully qualified Windows path, and line 7 declares a destination location with a virtual directory name. As mentioned earlier in this chapter, the virtual directory name must be in uppercase text.

Lines 11 through 14 show how to call the fcopy procedure. It copies the source file to the destination file, but they'll be unequal after the operation. The fcopy procedure appears to adopt the traditional reading mechanism and terminates the read after another program unit raises an *eof* error. More or less, that means it always adds 2 bytes to the last line because it adds an extra line terminator to the file. The extra line terminator is generally trivial for text files, but the additional 2 bytes may cause a binary copy to create a nonworking image.

You can wrap the utl_file package's fcopy procedure in a schema-level or user-defined package-level function. The following shows you how to wrap the procedure by implementing a copy_file function:

```
SQL> CREATE OR REPLACE FUNCTION copy_file
  2  ( pv_src_location      VARCHAR2
  3  , pv_src_file_name     VARCHAR2
  4  , pv_dest_location     VARCHAR2
  5  , pv_dest_file_name    VARCHAR2 ) RETURN NUMBER IS
  6
  7    /* Declare local input variables. */
  8    lv_src_location      VARCHAR2(60);
  9    lv_src_file_name     VARCHAR2(40);
 10    lv_dest_location     VARCHAR2(60);
 11    lv_dest_file_name    VARCHAR2(40);
 12
 13    /* Declare a local return variable. */
 14    lv_return            NUMBER := 0;
 15  BEGIN
 16    /* Assign parameters to local variables. */
 17    lv_src_location   := pv_src_location;
 18    lv_src_file_name  := pv_src_file_name;
 19    lv_dest_location  := pv_dest_location;
 20    lv_dest_file_name := pv_dest_file_name;
 21
 22    /* Open the file for read-only of 32,767 byte lines. */
 23    utl_file.fcopy( src_location  => lv_src_location
 24                  , src_filename  => lv_src_file_name
 25                  , dest_location => lv_dest_location
 26                  , dest_filename => lv_dest_file_name);
 27
 28    /* Set return variable to success. */
 29    lv_return := 1;
 30
 31    /* Return 0 for false and 1 for true. */
 32    RETURN lv_return;
 33  EXCEPTION
 ...
 41  END;
 42  /
```

Line 14 declares a return data type that can be consumed in SQL. The lv_return variable is initialized with a 0 value, which is a substitute value for FALSE in a SQL statement. Line 29 assigns 1 as a substitute for TRUE, and line 32 returns the lv_return value. Lines 34 through 40 aren't displayed but implement the same package exception handlers shown in the anonymous block example of the fcopy procedure.

The `copy_file` function doesn't write a change to the database, which means you can actually call it inside a query. Here's an example using the same concepts as the preceding anonymous block program:

```
SQL> SELECT    copy_file('C:\Data\Reader','TextFile.txt'
  2                      ,'WRITER','TextCopy.txt') AS "Copied"
  3  FROM       dual;
```

If the function works, it returns a 1. If `copy_file` raises something other than the handled exceptions, it returns 0. The `utl_file.read_error`, `utl_file.write_error`, and `utl_file.access_denied` exceptions in the exception block raise an application error.

Renaming or Moving External Files

The `frename` procedure is equivalent to a Linux or Unix `mv` command in the same directory or the `rename` command in the Windows command shell.

A simple anonymous block shows you how to call the `frename` procedure:

```
SQL> DECLARE
 ...
  9  BEGIN
 10    /* Rename the file. */
 11    utl_file.frename( src_location  => lv_src_location
 12                    , src_filename  => lv_src_file_name
 13                    , dest_location => lv_dest_location
 14                    , dest_filename => lv_dest_file_name);
 15  EXCEPTION
 ...
 23  END;
 24  /
```

As you can tell, this is very much like an `mv` command when the source and destination directories are different. The function renames a file when the source and destination locations are the same.

Removing External Files

The `utl_file` package's `fremove` procedure lets you delete a file from a `utl_file_dir` approved directory or virtual directory where you enjoy write privileges on the directory and delete privileges on the file.

A simple anonymous block shows you how to call the `fremove` procedure:

```
SQL> DECLARE
 ...
  5  BEGIN
  6    /* Remove the file. */
  7    utl_file.fremove( location => lv_src_location
  8                    , filename => lv_src_file_name);
  9  EXCEPTION
 ...
 17  END;
 18  /
```

Lines 7 and 8 contain the call to the `fremove` procedure. Like the other file management procedures in the `utl_file` package, you need to provide the fully qualified path or a virtual directory of both files and their file names.

Creating and Writing to External Files

You can create a new file or write to an existing file with unstructured data or structured data. Writing the content of a `CLOB` column or a series of large strings into a single document file is the best example of writing an unstructured data file. Likewise, writing a binary stream from a `BLOB` column is also like dealing with an unstructured data file. The binary stream is actually highly structured but not in the same sense as storing rows of a record structure, like a comma-separated value (CSV) list of columns of data from a table.

The section is divided into writing unstructured data and writing structured data. Within the following subsection on writing unstructured data, you'll see examples of writing and appending to a file. In the subsequent subsection, you'll see that one of the best uses for the `utl_file` package is writing structured data from tables into a CSV file for export into Microsoft Excel.

Writing Unstructured Data to External Files

There are two scenarios in which you write unstructured data to files. One requires that you create a new file and write a new stream of data, and the other requires that you append a new data stream to an existing set of data. The next two subsections cover both of these scenarios.

Creating a New File

Writing a new data stream to a new file sometimes requires that you eliminate a previously existing file. "Eliminate" may mean moving, renaming, or removing an existing file in the target directory that has the same file name.

The following example simply removes any existing file before writing a `CLOB` value to the new file. The `CLOB` value is actually a short string to simplify the example by eliminating parsing it into chunks to write to the file.

```
SQL> DECLARE
  2    /* Declare local input variables. */
  3    lv_location     VARCHAR2(60) := 'C:\Data\Direct';
  4    lv_file_name    VARCHAR2(40) := 'TextNew.txt';
  5
  6    /* Declare a file reference pointer and buffer. */
  7    lv_file    UTL_FILE.FILE_TYPE;   -- File reference
  8    lv_line    VARCHAR2(32767);      -- Reading buffer
  9
 10    /* Declare local file source. */
 11    lv_source  CLOB := 'Not really a long CLOB.';
 12
 13    /* Declare local file attribute data. */
 14    lv_file_size   NUMBER;
 15    lv_file_exists  BOOLEAN := FALSE;
 16    lv_block_size   BINARY_INTEGER;
 17  BEGIN
```

```
18      /* Check for open file and close when open. */
19      IF utl_file.is_open(lv_file) THEN
20        utl_file.fclose(lv_file);
21      END IF;
22
23      /* Read the file attributes to get the physical size. */
24      utl_file.fgetattr( location     => lv_location
25                       , filename     => lv_file_name
26                       , fexists      => lv_file_exists
27                       , file_length  => lv_file_size
28                       , block_size   => lv_block_size );
29
30      /* Remove file that exist. */
31      IF lv_file_exists THEN
32        utl_file.fremove( location  => lv_location
33                        , filename  => lv_file_name );
34      END IF;
35
36      /* Open the file for read-only of 32,767 byte lines. */
37      lv_file := utl_file.fopen( location     => lv_location
38                               , filename     => lv_file_name
39                               , open_mode    => 'W'
40                               , max_linesize => 32767);
41
42      /* Write a line of text. */
43      utl_file.put_line( file   => lv_file
44                       , buffer => lv_source );
45
46      /* Flush any buffer to file. */
47      utl_file.fflush( file   => lv_file );
48
49      /* Close the file. */
50      utl_file.fclose(lv_file);
51    EXCEPTION
...
59    END;
60    /
```

Lines 19 through 21 check for an open file handle and close it. The `fgetattr` call on lines 24 through 28 determines whether the file exists, and lines 31 through 34 delete the file from the file system with a call to the `fremove` procedure. Lines 37 through 40 hold a call to the `fopen` procedure, and the call opening the file uses a `'W'` (*write*) mode.

The data is written by the `put_line` procedure on lines 43 and 44. The `fflush` procedure on line 47 guarantees any data in a buffer is flushed to the file, and line 50 closes the open file handle.

If you looked at the content of the `TextNew.txt` file, you should see

```
Not really a long CLOB.
```

This example has shown you how to guarantee you're creating a new file and how you can write unstructured data into an external file.

Appending to an Existing File

The file must exist for you to append to it. The following sample code opens the file in append mode and writes a second line to the same target file used in the previous section. This example uses ellipses to replace most of the declaration and exception blocks because they're the same as in the prior example. Only the CLOB value assigned in the declaration block differs. An ellipsis also replaces the check for an open file handle and the call to the fgetattr procedure.

```
SQL> DECLARE
  ...
 17  BEGIN
  ...
 30    /* Check for existing file. */
 31    IF lv_file_exists THEN
 32
 33      /* Open the file for read-only of 32,767 byte lines. */
 34      lv_file := utl_file.fopen( location    => lv_location
 35                               , filename    => lv_file_name
 36                               , open_mode   => 'A'
 37                               , max_linesize => 32767);
 38
 39      /* Write a line of text. */
 40      utl_file.put_line( file   => lv_file
 41                       , buffer => lv_source );
 42
 43      /* Flush any buffer to file. */
 44      utl_file.fflush( file   => lv_file );
 45    END IF;
 46
 47    /* Close the file. */
 48    utl_file.fclose(lv_file);
 49  EXCEPTION
  ...
 57  END;
 58  /
```

Line 31 checks for the existence of the file, which is the result of one of the pass-by-reference parameters of the fgetattr call. The key difference in this example is that you don't open the file unless it already exists, and you open the file in 'A' (*append*) mode on line 36.

If you look at the modified content of the TextNew.txt file, you should see

```
Not really a long CLOB.
A second not really a long CLOB.
```

This example has shown you how to guarantee you're appending data to an existing file and how you can write unstructured data into that file.

Writing Structured Data to External Files

Like the previous section, the example in this section reuses much of the base example from the "Creating a New File" section. Ellipses are present where the code mirrors the prior example.

This example adds a cursor that queries the `item` table, and a `FOR` loop that governs the writes with the `utl_file` package's `put_line` procedure.

```
SQL> DECLARE
  . . .
  18    /* Declare a cursor. */
  19    CURSOR get_items IS
  20      SELECT   i.item_title
  21      ,        i.item_subtitle
  22      FROM     item i;
  23  BEGIN
  . . .
  49    FOR i IN get_items LOOP
  50      /* Concatenate the results into a CSV format. */
  51      lv_source := i.item_title||','||i.item_subtitle;
  52
  53      /* Write a line of text. */
  54      utl_file.put_line( file   => lv_file
  55                       , buffer => lv_source );
  56    END LOOP;
  . . .
  63  EXCEPTION
  . . .
  71  END;
  72  /
```

The cursor on lines 19 through 22 returns two columns, and that makes creating a CSV file easy. The `FOR` loop from line 49 through line 56 governs the writes of new data to the file. Line 51 concatenates (or glues) the records together with an intervening comma. Line 54 writes the concatenated line of text.

The content of the target file would look as follows (only the first three lines are shown):

```
Around the World in 80 Days,Two-Disc Special Edition
Around the World in 80 Days,
Casino Royale,
```

This section has shown you how to write structured data to an external file.

Supporting Scripts

The following programs are available on the McGraw-Hill Professional website to support this chapter:

- The `utl_file_append.sql` program shows how to append data to an existing file with the `utl_file` package's `put_line` procedure.
- The `utl_file_copy.sql` program shows how to copy one file to another with the `utl_file` package's `fcopy` procedure.
- The `utl_file_move.sql` program shows how to copy one file to another with the `utl_file` package's `frename` procedure.

- The `utl_file_read1.sql` program creates an anonymous block program that reads through a file line by line until it reads an *eof* marker and raises an exception.

- The `utl_file_read2.sql` program creates an anonymous block program that determines the file size before it reads through a file line by line until adding 2 bytes makes the string size greater than the file size.

- The `utl_file_read3.sql` program creates a schema-level function that reads an external file and returns a CLOB by using the same logic as the `utl_file_read2.sql` script.

- The `utl_file_write.sql` program shows how to write unstructured data to a new data file with the `utl_file` package's `put_line` procedure.

- The `utl_file_write.sql` program shows how to write structured data to a new data file with the `utl_file` package's `put_line` procedure.

Summary

You should now have an understanding of how to use the `utl_file` package to manage unstructured and structured data. These skills lay a foundation for the next two chapters.

CHAPTER
4

Java I/O Libraries

Purpose

This chapter teaches you how to replace the `utl_file` and `dbms_lob` packages with Java libraries. It shows you how to develop and deploy Java I/O libraries inside the database, and how to wrap these libraries with PL/SQL. To accomplish this, we'll show you how to gain access to the physical directories that map to Oracle Database 12*c*'s virtual directories.

Advantages

As of Oracle Database 10*g* forward, you can write and deploy Java libraries that extend the reach of the Oracle database. Java I/O libraries enable you to develop tools that can interact directly with external files. The external files can be on the same physical machine or on another physical machine. In fact, the external files can be web pages from any site on the company intranet or the Internet.

Java I/O libraries provide alternatives to using the `utl_file` and `dbms_lob` packages. That means you can avoid the shortfalls of those packages. For example, you can avoid adding an extra line return when you copy a file with the `utl_file` package. You can also avoid the complexity of using the pass-by-reference procedures in both the `utl_file` and `dbms_lob` packages. In this chapter you'll see how to write Java I/O libraries that hide that complexity by putting all the steps inside PL/SQL functions. These functions abstract the complexity from any SQL or PL/SQL calls.

Oracle Database 12*c* now lets you compile a white list of callers of functions, procedures, packages, and object types. White listing any functions that call Java I/O libraries ensures the DBA can manage the risk of exposing access to a hardened OS, or outbound network calls.

Disadvantages

When you let the database interact with the OS or the network, you create potential security risks. These security risks should be your focus when you choose to use Java I/O in Oracle Database 12*c*.

The risks of implementing Java I/O are similar to the risks of using external tables, the `utl_file` package, or the `dbms_lob` package. The differences between Java I/O and the PL/SQL packages are the programming language and the ability to assess and manage risk. These differences mean the DBA and application development teams need one or more members who are fluent in reading and assessing the risk in the Java programs.

Overview

This chapter shows you how to write and deploy Java I/O libraries. It presents the information as follows:

- Mapping virtual directories to physical directories
- Learning how to set Java privileges
- Developing and deploying Java I/O libraries

Some of these examples build on concepts introduced earlier in Chapters 1 and 2 of this book, and the general concepts found in *Oracle Database 12c PL/SQL Programming*.

Mapping Virtual Directories to Physical Directories

Oracle lets you define virtual directories that map a name in the database catalog to a physical file directory path. Virtual directories typically support the source files for external tables or BFILE column values. They can also simply hold ordinary files that you want to manage through Java I/O libraries.

The next three subsections describe

- How you create a virtual directory
- How you translate a virtual directory to a physical directory path
- How you discover a fully qualified file name of a BFILE column

Ordinary files are accessible through a combination of creating a virtual directory, translating a virtual directory to a physical directory path, and discovering file names in that directory. BFILE locator values can sometimes point to what would appear as ordinary files in a virtual directory. Unfortunately, there's no way to disambiguate between these two types of ordinary files because you can't map them to a BFILE locator.

You can extract the full path name and file name from any BFILE column value. The "Extracting a File Path and Name" subsection shows you how to find the fully qualified file name of any BFILE column.

Creating a Virtual Directory

Virtual directories let you map a name in the database to an external directory. They're stored in the data catalog, and the physical directories are intentionally hidden. In this section, you learn how to configure a loader virtual directory and grant privileges on that directory to the importer schema.

As the sys, system, or authorized CDB administrator account, you create a virtual loader directory with the following syntax:

```
SQL> CREATE DIRECTORY loader AS 'C:\data\loader';
```

In Oracle Database 12c's multitenant architecture, you can also create a virtual directory in the ADMIN user account of a pluggable database (PDB). Chapter 5 contains a "Multitenant Provisioning" sidebar that shows how to create and manage a PDB.

Next, you need to grant read and write privileges on the virtual loader directory. You need to have these permissions to work with the Java I/O library examples in this chapter. You grant read and write permission to the importer schema like this:

```
SQL> GRANT READ, WRITE ON DIRECTORY loader TO importer;
```

After creating a virtual directory and granting privileges to the virtual directory, you need to create a function that takes the virtual directory and returns the physical path. That's what you learn in the next section.

Translating Virtual Names to Paths

Oracle Database 12*c* provides a robust architecture for developing internal Java libraries. The Oracle database also creates several layers of security to limit what you can do with Java libraries.

One of the Oracle Database 12*c* security precautions hides the physical directory tied to a virtual directory. As discussed in Chapter 3, the utl_file package isn't limited the same way, and you can use it to translate a virtual directory to a physical directory. The logic to translate a virtual directory to a physical directory was added to the utl_file package in Oracle Database 10*g*. Unfortunately, Java I/O libraries and generic PL/SQL programs can't natively translate a virtual directory to a physical directory.

PL/SQL programs are blocked by the abstraction barrier that hides physical directories, and Java libraries require a physical directory to find a file. That leaves you with the problem of how to overcome the imposed limit of the data catalog. When you do choose to remove a security shield, it's important that you replace it with your own. What you implement as a new security barrier should be better than what you removed or disabled.

The best solution that's available in Oracle Database 12*c* is twofold. First, you use schemas and grants to limit access to the module that lets you translate virtual directories to physical directories. Second, you co-locate any modules that perform Java I/O inside a single schema and white list their PL/SQL wrappers. White listing provides fine-grained security to your Java I/O libraries.

You begin the process of translating virtual directories to physical paths by leveraging an administrative view owned by the sys schema. The cdb_, all_, and dba_directories administrative views all contain the mapping between virtual and physical directories. You can query these administrative views from sys, system, and any authorized user. You can also query these views as the ADMIN account of a PDB.

Administrative Views

You can find the list of administrative views by querying the DICTIONARY view. More or less, you have four types of administrative views in a multitenant Oracle Database 12c. The CDB_ views don't exist in non-multitenant databases. They are

- A CDB_ view displays all relevant information in the multitenant database, including pluggable databases. CDB_ views are intended only for administrators. They can be accessed only by the super users, like sys and system.

- A DBA_ view displays all relevant information in the database, either a non-multitenant database or a pluggable database in a multitenant database. DBA_ views are intended only for administrators. They can be accessed only by users that enjoy the SELECT ANY TABLE privilege. The SELECT ANY TABLE privilege is assigned to the DBA role when you install a database.

- An ALL_ view displays all the information accessible to the current user, including information from the current user's schema as well as information from objects in other schemas. The key determinant of what can be seen are the grants of privilege through a direct grant of a privilege or role.

- A USER_ view displays all the information from the schema of the current user. The user has these by default and they require no special privileges.

The following query shows you how a physical directory links to a virtual directory:

```
SQL> SELECT    directory_path
  2  FROM      sys.dba_directories
  3  WHERE     directory_name = UPPER('virtual_dir_name');
```

It returns a result like the following for a Windows operating system when the `virtual_dir_name` value is the uppercase LOADER:

```
DIRECTORY_PATH
--------------------
C:\Data\Loader
```

TIP
It's important to recall that Oracle maintains all data catalog key values in uppercase text.

As discussed in Chapter 3, the `utl_file` package can translate a virtual directory to a physical directory from Oracle Database 10g forward. PL/SQL programs can't natively translate a virtual directory to a physical directory. Fortunately, you can use PL/SQL to unblock the abstraction barrier that hides physical directories.

The next three sections contain the steps to unblock your ability to translate virtual directories into physical directories.

Relaxing Data Catalog Security

It's possible to query the `cdb_`, `all_`, and `dba_directories` administrative views as a privileged user, but you can't embed them in a PL/SQL block without a special privilege. You need to relax the security over one of these views before you can create a PL/SQL function that translates the virtual directory to a physical directory.

Connect as the `sys` user, and grant the SELECT privilege on the `dba_directories` view to the `system` user, like this:

```
GRANT SELECT ON dba_directories TO system;
```

Having granted the SELECT privilege to the `system` user, you can now create a PL/SQL function that translates the virtual directory to a physical one.

Creating an Unmapping Directory

The `system` user now enjoys the privilege to create a PL/SQL function that includes a query against the `dba_directories` view. You can create the `get_directory_path` function as the `system` user. The `get_directory_path` function lets you translate any virtual directory name into a physical directory path:

```
SQL> CREATE OR REPLACE FUNCTION get_directory_path
  2  ( virtual_directory IN VARCHAR2 )
  3  RETURN VARCHAR2 IS
  4
  5    /* Define return variable. */
  6    directory_path VARCHAR2(256) := '';
  7
```

```
 8    /* Define dynamic cursor. */
 9    CURSOR get_directory
10    (virtual_directory VARCHAR2) IS
11      SELECT   directory_path
12      FROM     sys.dba_directories
13      WHERE    directory_name = UPPER(virtual_directory);
14
15    /* Define an exception for a name violation. */
16    directory_name EXCEPTION;
17    PRAGMA EXCEPTION_INIT(directory_name,-22284);
18  BEGIN
19    OPEN  get_directory (virtual_directory);
20    FETCH get_directory
21    INTO  directory_path;
22    CLOSE get_directory;
23
24    /* RETURN file name. */
25    RETURN directory_path;
26  EXCEPTION
27    WHEN directory_name THEN
28      RETURN null;
29  END get_directory_path;
30  /
```

Line 2 takes a formal parameter of a virtual directory name. Lines 9 through 13 declare a cursor that reads the dba_directories administrative view for a specific virtual directory and returns a physical directory path. Line 13 goes one step beyond what the utl_file package supports because it ensures a case-insensitive virtual directory maps to a physical directory path. Line 25 returns the directory path when it's found, and line 28 returns a null value when one isn't found.

Granting Privilege on the Mapping Function

After creating the get_directory_path function, you grant the EXECUTE privilege to any schema. As mentioned earlier, you should only grant privileges to specific schemas and white list any functions implemented in those schemas.

For the purpose of our example, we use the importer schema. The following grants the EXECUTE privilege on the get_directory_path to the importer schema:

```
GRANT EXECUTE ON system.get_directory_path TO importer;
```

With this grant to the importer schema, you can now write a query to translate a virtual directory to a physical directory name. Unfortunately, you can't call it natively without disclosing the owning schema and creating a synonym.

You can create the following synonym as the importer user:

```
SQL> CREATE SYNONYM get_directory_path FOR system.get_directory_path;
```

With the synonym in place, you can translate the LOADER virtual directory into a physical path by calling the get_directory_path function:

```
SQL> COLUMN path_directory FORMAT A40 HEADING "Path Directory"
SQL> SELECT  get_directory_path('LOADER') AS path_directory
  2  FROM     dual;
```

It should return the following:

```
Path Directory
----------------------------------------
C:\Data\Loader
```

Now, you have the ability to translate a virtual directory to a physical directory name. The next section shows you how to unmask the locator value of any BFILE column.

Extracting a File Path and Name

You use the filegetname procedure from the dbms_lob package to extract a file path and name from a BFILE column. The BFILE process differs from the earlier examples in this chapter, and here we introduce another function that should be used only with BFILE columns.

The get_canonical_bfilename function uses a Native Dynamic SQL (NDS) approach to solve for all potential BFILE columns in Oracle Database 12c. The NDS in this function enables you to return a string value that matches a fully qualified file name for a BFILE column's external file. The NDS statement requires a table name, BFILE column name, primary key column name, and primary key value. The primary key column name and value ensure that the NDS statement inside the function always returns a unique row.

The definition of the get_bfile_name is

```
SQL>  CREATE OR REPLACE FUNCTION get_canonical_bfilename
  2  ( pv_table_name      IN  VARCHAR2
  3  , pv_bfile_column    IN  VARCHAR2
  4  , pv_primary_key     IN  VARCHAR2
  5  , pv_primary_value   IN  VARCHAR2
  6  , pv_operating_sys   IN  VARCHAR2 := 'WINDOWS')
  7  RETURN VARCHAR2 IS
  8
  9    /* Declare default delimiter. */
 10    delimiter          VARCHAR2(1) := '\'; -- '''
 11
 12    /* Define statement variable. */
 13    stmt               VARCHAR2(200);
 14
 15    /* Declare a locator. */
 16    locator            BFILE;
 17
 18    /* Define alias and file name. */
 19    dir_alias          VARCHAR2(255);
 20    directory          VARCHAR2(255);
 21    file_name          VARCHAR2(255);
 22
 23    /* Define a local exception for size violation. */
 24    directory_num EXCEPTION;
 25    PRAGMA EXCEPTION_INIT(directory_num,-22285);
 26  BEGIN
 27    /* Assign dynamic string to statement. */
```

```
28     stmt := 'BEGIN'||CHR(10)
29          || '   SELECT '||pv_bfile_column||CHR(10)
30          || '   INTO    :column_name'||CHR(10)
31          || '   FROM   '||pv_table_name||CHR(10)
32          || '   WHERE  '||pv_primary_key||'='||CHR(10)
33          || ''''||pv_primary_value||''''||';'
34          || 'END;';
35
36     /* Run dynamic statement. */
37     EXECUTE IMMEDIATE stmt USING OUT locator;
38
39     /* Check available locator. */
40     IF locator IS NOT NULL THEN
41       dbms_lob.filegetname(locator,dir_alias,file_name);
42     END IF;
43
44     /* Check for Linux or Unix OS. */
45     IF pv_operating_sys <> 'WINDOWS' THEN
46       delimiter := '/';
47     END IF;
48
49     /* Create a fully qualified file name. */
50     file_name := get_directory_path(dir_alias)||delimiter||file_name;
51
52     /* Return file name. */
53     RETURN file_name;
54   EXCEPTION
55     WHEN directory_num THEN
56       RETURN NULL;
57 END get_canonical_bfilename;
58 /
```

Line 6 lets you designate the operating systems for the function. The default operating system is set to Windows. A call to the `get_canonical_bfilename` function with any value other than `'WINDOWS'` as the `pv_operating_sys` parameter changes the default `delimiter` value. While line 10 sets the default `delimiter` to a backslash, the `IF` block on lines 45 through 47 resets the `delimiter` to a forward slash when the `pv_operating_sys` parameter holds a value different than `'WINDOWS'`.

Lines 28 through 34 create a dynamic anonymous PL/SQL block that returns a `BFILE` column into a local `BFILE` variable. The `IF` block on lines 40 through 42 checks for a valid `BFILE` value and then uses the `dbms_lob` package to extract a valid physical path and file name. Line 53 returns the valid fully qualified file name, or line 56 returns a null value, when any part of the function fails.

The next section shows you how to set Java privileges to perform Java I/O.

Setting Java Privileges

Chapter 1 discussed basic concepts about how Oracle implements Java inside the database. This section explores the Oracle JVM security model and shows you how to set specific privileges for the `JAVASYSPRIV` role.

Oracle JVM security differs from Java 2 security. You still assign permissions to Java libraries on a *class-by-class basis*, but you do so through Oracle Database 12c management tools. Oracle JVM permissions are stored in a `permission` table that's made up of target and action attributes, which are more or less a name and value pair.

You can read about Java 2 security at the following website:

http://docs.oracle.com/javase/7/docs/api/java/security/BasicPermission.html

Java 2 security labels applets as implicitly unsecure and trusts all classes with the `CLASSPATH` environment variable. The Oracle JVM doesn't trust any classes, notwithstanding their installation in a secure database. The Oracle JVM also has its own `SecurityManager`. Oracle Database 12c allows you to replace the default `SecurityManager`, but you shouldn't!

You also have the ability to grant administrative and action permissions to specified users, which goes beyond our scope of modifying the `JAVASYSPRIV` role's privileges. When you change the administrative and action privileges, you change the rules under which basic Oracle JVM security works. If you're interested in enabling fine-grained control, please check Chapter 10 of the *Oracle Database 12c Java Developer's Guide*.

Table 4-1 contains the default permissions for the `JAVASYSPRIV` role. In this chapter, we focus on showing you how to modify the `java.io.FilePermission` permissions. We'd also recommend you not enable `java.net.SocketPermission` permissions.

Table 4-1 contains the default permissions for the `JAVASYSPRIV` role. In the three subsections we focus on showing you how to modify the `java.io.FilePermission` permissions with the `grant_permission` procedure of the `dbms_java` package. You must connect as the Oracle `sys` user with superuser privileges conferred by using the `as dba` qualifier in a non-multitenant

Permission Type	Permission Name	Action
`java.io.SerializablePermission`	`*`	N/A
`java.io.FilePermission`	`<<ALL FILES>>`	read, write, execute, delete
`java.net.SocketPermission`	`*`	accept, connect, listen, resolve
`java.sql.SQLPermission`	`setLog`	

`java.lang.RuntimePermission`	`createClassLoader`
	`getClassLoader`
	`setContextClassLoader`
	`setFactory`
	`setFileDesciptor`
	`readFileDescriptor`
	`writeFileDescriptor`	

TABLE 4-1. *JAVASYSPRIV Permissions*

database or for a user-defined container database (CDB). Alternatively, you can connect as the ADMIN user for a PDB.

TIP
You must perform this command as the user who installed Oracle Database 12c.

The syntax for this command is

```
sqlplus sys / as sysdba
```

The grant_permission procedure lets you enable reading from, writing to, deleting of, and execution of external files. The grant_permission procedure has four required IN parameters and one optional OUT parameter, as qualified in Table 4-2. The optional KEY parameter enables or disables specific permissions.

The grantee parameter can be any schema name or PUBLIC. We strongly advise against making any of these grants to PUBLIC.

The optional KEY parameter isn't required to grant read, write, or delete permissions for our examples. So, the subsections call the grant_permission procedure with only the four mandatory parameters—grantee, permission_type, permission_name, and permission_action.

You can find the current settings for any schema with a query against the CDB_, DBA_, and USER_JAVA_POLICY views. While it's an exception to the general rule on administrative views, there isn't an ALL_JAVA_POLICY view. The USER_JAVA_POLICY view also changes the GRANTEE column name to GRANTEE_NAME.

While you wouldn't see answers to these queries until after you complete the next three subsections, it's helpful to show diagnostic commands. A diagnostic query against the CDB_, DBA_, and USER_JAVA_POLICY views would look like the following:

```
SQL> SELECT  *
  2  FROM    cdb_java_policy
  3  WHERE   type_name = 'java.io.FilePermission'
  4  AND     grantee = 'IMPORTER'
  5  AND     name LIKE '%Loader%';
```

Position	Field Name	Required	Mode	Data Type
1	GRANTEE	Mandatory	IN	VARCHAR2
2	PERMISSION_TYPE	Mandatory	IN	VARCHAR2
3	PERMISSION_NAME	Mandatory	IN	VARCHAR2
4	PERMISSION_ACTION	Mandatory	IN	VARCHAR2
5	KEY	Optional	OUT	NUMBER

TABLE 4-2. *GRANT_PERMISSION Signature*

As previously noted, line 4 refers to the GRANTEE column for superuser views, but would refer to the GRANTEE_NAME column. You also can rewrite line 5 to use a regular expression function, like

```
5   AND    REGEXP_LIKE(name,'^.*Loader.*$');
```

The problem with the foregoing is that the text wraps. You can get row-by-row output formatted by borrowing the vertical_query function from the "Dynamic Statements with Variable Inputs and Outputs" section of Chapter 13 in *Oracle Database 12c PL/SQL Programming*. For convenience, the code is online at the McGraw-Hill Professional website for both of these books.

You need to create the vertical_query function as the sys user, and then you grant the SELECT privilege to the system user with the following syntax:

```
SQL> GRANT SELECT ON  vertical_query TO system;
```

Reconnect as the system user and create a synonym for the vertical_query function. The syntax to create the vertical_query synonym is

```
SQL> CREATE SYNONYM vertical_query FOR sys.vertical_query;
```

After you have created the vertical_query synonym, you can write a query that displays the column names on the left and values on the right. The following is a query that leverages the vertical_query function:

```
SQL> SELECT column_value
  2  FROM    TABLE(
  3              vertical_query(
  4                  'CDB_JAVA_POLICY'
  5                , 'WHERE type_name = ''java.io.FilePermission'''
  6                ||'AND    grantee = ''IMPORTER'''
  7                ||'AND    REGEXP_LIKE(name,''^.*Loader.*$'',''i'')'));
```

You need to change the GRANTEE column to GRANTEE_NAME when you query against the USER_JAVA_POLICY view. After you complete the next three subsections, you can use the vertical_query function to return formatted output like

```
*************************** 1. row ***************************
KIND         : GRANT
GRANTEE      : IMPORTER
TYPE_SCHEMA  : SYS
TYPE_NAME    : java.io.FilePermission
NAME         : C:\Data\Loader
ACTION       : read
ENABLED      : ENABLED
SEQ          : 245
CON_ID       : 4
*************************** 2. row ***************************
KIND         : GRANT
GRANTEE      : IMPORTER
TYPE_SCHEMA  : SYS
TYPE_NAME    : java.io.FilePermission
NAME         : C:\Data\Loader\Hobbit1.txt
ACTION       : read
ENABLED      : ENABLED
```

```
SEQ          : 244
CON_ID       : 4
**************************** 3. row *****************************
KIND         : GRANT
GRANTEE      : IMPORTER
TYPE_SCHEMA  : SYS
TYPE_NAME    : java.io.FilePermission
NAME         : C:\Data\Loader\Hobbit1_copy.txt
ACTION       : read,write,delete
ENABLED      : ENABLED
SEQ          : 248
CON_ID       : 4
*********************************************************************
```

Row 1 returns a read and write permission on the physical directory pointed to by the loader virtual directory. Row 2 returns a `read` permission on the `Hobbit1.txt` file, and row 3 returns a read, write, and delete permission on the `Hobbit1_copy.txt` file. While you should never directly edit the underlying data shown in this view, the `dbms_java` package lets you interact with the data found in this and other views.

The following subsections qualify how to set appropriate permissions for the Java I/O programs for this chapter.

Reading from an External Directory

Reading files with Java from an external directory only requires read permission on the directory where the file is located. You can call it like this for the physical directory where your `loader` virtual directory points on a Windows OS:

```
SQL> BEGIN
  2    DBMS_JAVA.GRANT_PERMISSION(
  3        grantee => 'IMPORTER'
  4      , permission_type =>'SYS:java.io.FilePermission'
  5      , permission_name => 'C:\Data\Loader'
  6      , permission_action => 'read');
  7    END;
  8    /
```

The `grantee` is the `importer` schema, the `permission_type` value is the `java.io.FilePermission`, and the `permission_name` value is a Windows OS fully qualified path. You would change the `permission_name` value for a Linux or Unix server to a fully qualified path that starts with a *mount point* rather than the logical drive (`C:\`) of a Windows OS. The `permission_action` value is set to read-only on a directory.

Reading from an External File

Reading files with Java from an external directory requires read permission on individual physical files. You must provide the fully qualified path for each physical file. The following is an example for the Windows OS:

```
SQL> BEGIN
  2    DBMS_JAVA.GRANT_PERMISSION(
  3        grantee => 'IMPORTER'
```

```
4        , permission_type =>'SYS:java.io.FilePermission'
5        , permission_name => 'C:\Data\Loader\some_file.file_ext'
6        , permission_action => 'read');
7  END;
8  /
```

Like the prior example for an external directory, the grantee is the importer schema, the permission_type value is the java.io.FilePermission, and the permission_name value is a Windows OS fully qualified path. You would change the permission_name value for a Linux or Unix server to a fully qualified path that starts with a mount point rather than the logical drive (C:\) of a Windows OS. The permission_action value is set to read-only on a directory.

Writing to an External File

Writing new files with Java to an external directory requires read, write, and delete permissions to individual files. That's because you must check for the existence of the file and then delete a previously existing file. Alternatively, you can append to a file with only the read and write permissions.

You can call the grant_permission procedure like this for the physical file where your loader virtual directory points on a Windows OS:

```
SQL> BEGIN
2      DBMS_JAVA.GRANT_PERMISSION(
3          grantee => 'IMPORTER'
4        , permission_type =>'SYS:java.io.FilePermission'
5        , permission_name => 'C:\Data\Loader\some_file.file_ext'
6        , permission_action => 'read,write,delete');
7  END;
8  /
```

Like the previous example of reading from an external file, the grantee is the importer schema, the permission_type value is the java.io.FilePermission, the permission_name value is a Windows OS fully qualified path, and the permission_action value holds read and write privileges on individual physical files.

Deleting from an External File

Deleting files from an external directory requires that you grant both read and delete permissions to that file. If you grant only the delete permission, you'd raise the following exception (manually edited for display):

```
ORA-29532: Java call terminated by uncaught Java exception:
java.security.AccessControlException: the Permission
(java.io.FilePermission C:\Data\Loader\Hobbit1_delete.txt read)
has not been granted to IMPORTER. The PL/SQL to grant this is
dbms_java.grant_permission('IMPORTER','SYS:java.io.FilePermission', 'C:\Data\
Loader\Hobbit1_delete.txt','read')
ORA-06512: at "IMPORTER.DELETE_FILE", line 1
ORA-06512: at line 2
```

Essentially, deleting a file requires the ability to check for the file's existence before you delete it. You call the `grant_permission` procedure with the following values to enable deleting a physical file:

```
SQL> BEGIN
  2     DBMS_JAVA.GRANT_PERMISSION(
  3         grantee => 'IMPORTER'
  4       , permission_type =>'SYS:java.io.FilePermission'
  5       , permission_name => 'C:\Data\Loader\some_file.file_ext'
  6       , permission_action => 'read,write,delete');
  7   END;
  8   /
```

Like the previous examples, the `grantee` is the `importer` schema, the `permission_type` value is the `java.io.FilePermission`, the `permission_name` value is a Windows OS fully qualified path, and the `permission_action` value holds read, write, and delete privileges on individual physical files.

Developing and Deploying Java I/O Libraries

This section shows you how to create Java libraries to read a text file, how to copy one text file to another and one binary file to another, and how to delete a file. You should ensure that the operating system permissions allow the `oracle` user to access the files.

NOTE
You should deploy the Java I/O libraries in the importer *schema.*

Reading a Directory

Beyond granting read permissions on the target directory, you must create a collection data type in the target schema for the following Java library. The collection data type is a collection of strings.
The syntax to create a collection data type is

```
SQL> CREATE OR REPLACE TYPE file_list
  2     AS TABLE OF VARCHAR2(255);
  3   /
```

After you create the collection data type, you can create a `ListVirtualDirectory` Java library. The following Java library uses an `ARRAY` JDBC class as a return type and Oracle's `ArrayDescriptor` JDBC class. The `ArrayDescriptor` class maps a native Java collection to the `ARRAY` Java library.
You can create the file by running the following:

```
SQL> CREATE OR REPLACE AND COMPILE JAVA SOURCE
  2     NAMED "ListVirtualDirectory" AS
  3
  4     // Import required classes.
  5     import java.io.*;
  6     import java.security.AccessControlException;
  7     import java.sql.*;
  8     import java.util.Arrays;
```

```
 9   import oracle.sql.driver.*;
10   import oracle.sql.ArrayDescriptor;
11   import oracle.sql.ARRAY;
12
13   // Define the class.
14   public class ListVirtualDirectory {
15
16     // Define the method.
17     public static ARRAY getList(String path) throws SQLException {
18
19     // Declare variable as a null.
20     ARRAY listed = null;
21
22     // Define a connection (this is for Oracle 11g forward).
23     Connection conn =
24       DriverManager.getConnection("jdbc:default:connection:");
25
26     // Use a try-catch block to trap a Java permission
27     // error on the directory.
28     try {
29       // Declare a class with the file list.
30       File directory = new File(path);
31
32       // Declare a mapping schema SQL collection type.
33       ArrayDescriptor arrayDescriptor =
34         new ArrayDescriptor("FILE_LIST",conn);
35
36       // Translate the Java String[] collection type.
37       listed = new ARRAY(arrayDescriptor
38                          ,conn
39                          ,((Object[]) directory.list())); }
40     catch (AccessControlException e) {
41       throw new AccessControlException(
42                 "Directory permissions restricted."); }
43   return listed; }}
44 /
```

Line 17 declares the getList method that returns a collection of the Oracle ARRAY class. The statement on lines 33 through 34 creates an ArrayDescriptor instance with the file_list collection type. Lines 37 through 39 construct a new ARRAY instance with the ArrayDescriptor instance, a connection to the database, and a generic Java collection of the base Java Object class.

You wrap the Java ListVirtualDirectory class with the following PL/SQL statement:

```
SQL> CREATE OR REPLACE FUNCTION list_files(path VARCHAR2)
  2    RETURN FILE_LIST IS LANGUAGE JAVA NAME
  3    'ListVirtualDirectory.getList(java.lang.String) return oracle.sql.ARRAY';
  4  /
```

After creating all the necessary elements, you can query the contents of a directory with this SQL statement and a fully qualified path:

```
SQL> SELECT column_value
  2    FROM   TABLE(list_files('C:\JavaDev\Loader'));
```

The `get_directory_path` and `get_canonical_bfilename` functions give you an alternative over a literal path value. They were introduced earlier in this chapter.

Reading a File

You can read an external text file with a Java library when you need to read a file into a SQL context with a query or as the return value from a PL/SQL function. In most cases, you can use the `dbms_lob` package to read an external file as a `BFILE` data type. The downside to using the `dbms_lob` package is that both the `loadclobfromfile` and `loadblobfromfile` procedures return a `CLOB` or `BLOB` data type, respectively, as an `OUT`-mode parameter. You can find examples of these approaches in Chapter 10 of *Oracle Database 12c PL/SQL Programming*.

Alternatively, you can use external tables to read comma-separated value (CSV) files. We'd recommend you do that as a rule, because you can read those files through parallel streams by simply appending the `PARALLEL` keyword. Appendix B of *Oracle Database 12c PL/SQL Programming* has a discussion of how to use external tables. Chapter 5 shows you a complete external table framework, which combines some Java I/O skills from this chapter.

You will need to grant permissions to external files to enable the Java I/O libraries from this section. Connect as the superuser (either `sys` or a pluggable database's `ADMIN` user) to grant these permissions on the specific target files before you test any of these Java I/O libraries.

The next three subsections show you how to read a text file with Java, how to read a text file with a Java I/O library, and how to read a binary file with a Java I/O library and PL/SQL wrapper.

Reading a Text File with Java

This section shows you how to read a file with Java. The `ReadFile.java` file is designed to work outside the database. The `ReadFile` Java class reads the file from the operating system and loads it into a Java `String` variable. Then, the `readText()` method of the `ReadFile` Java class returns the file contents as a `String` value. The test case for the stand-alone Java class is in the `main()` method of the class.

While Java I/O has numerous stream possibilities, the following example file uses the `FileReader` and `BufferedReader` classes. Java requires a combination of stream readers to read different types of files. The combination of the `FileReader` and `BufferedReader` classes is well suited to reading text files.

The `ReadFile.java` file is shown here with line numbers:

```
1   // Java library imports.
2   import java.io.File;
3   import java.io.BufferedReader;
4   import java.io.FileNotFoundException;
5   import java.io.IOException;
6   import java.io.FileReader;
7   import java.security.AccessControlException;
8
9   // Class definition.
10  public class ReadFile {
11  // Declare class variables.
12  private static File file;
13  private static FileReader inTextFile;
14  private static BufferedReader inTextReader;
15  private static StringBuffer output = new StringBuffer();
```

```
16  private static String outLine, outText;
17
18  // Define readText() method.
19  public static String readText(String fromFile)
20     throws AccessControlException, IOException {
21     // Read file.
22     try {
23       // Initialize File.
24       file = new File(fromFile);
25
26       if (file.exists()) {
27
28         // Assign file to a stream.
29         inTextFile = new FileReader(file);
30         inTextReader = new BufferedReader(inTextFile);
31
32         // Read character-by-character.
33         while ((outLine = inTextReader.readLine()) != null) {
34           output.append(outLine + "\n"); }
35         // Passing the StringBuffer to a String.
36         outText = output.toString();
37
38         // Close File.
39         inTextFile.close(); }}
40     catch (IOException e) {
41       outText = new String("Empty");
42       return outText; }
43     return outText; }
44
45  // A main method to test the class.
46  public static void main(String args[]) {
47
48     // Create an instance of a class for testing.
49     ReadFile rf = new ReadFile();
50     try {
51       System.out.println(rf.readText(args[0])); }
52     catch (IOException e) {
53       System.out.println("Static main ..."); }
54  }}
```

Lines 29 and 30 create a stream that reads an external file. Lines 33 and 34 read a file row by row and write it into a StringBuffer variable. Line 36 transfers the contents of the file from the output (a StringBuffer data type) variable to an outText variable, and line 43 returns the file content as a String variable. As covered in the appendix, the main method contains the test case for the Java class. This test case instantiates an instance of the ReadFile class on line 49 and calls the readText method on line 51 as the sole argument to a standard out (STDOUT) call, which prints the file to the console.

You compile the preceding ReadFile.java program with the following command, provided you've sourced the PATH and CLASSPATH environment variables. Sourcing these environment variables is typically done automatically for you by a Java IDE, like JDeveloper, NetBeans, or

Eclipse. Although, you may have to do it yourself when compiling and running the Java file from the operating system's command-line interface.

```
javac ReadFile.java
```

You would then run the program with this command:

```
java ReadFile
```

The program displays the complete content of the physical file. That's possible because a Java `String` can be a very large string. The next section shows you how to factor the `ReadFile` class file into a Java I/O library, explains the limit on mapping a Java `String` class, and then shows you how to replace the `String` return type with an Oracle `CLOB` data type.

Reading a Text File with a Java I/O Library

This section shows you how to implement a Java I/O library that reads text files from the operating system. Like the prior example, it uses the `FileReader` and `BufferedReader` classes to manage the read operation of the external file.

The following Java I/O library is more or less the same as the stand-alone `ReadFile.java` class file. Just make sure you've granted the appropriate JVM permissions to the target file. The `readText()` method of the following `ReadFile` class reads an external text file and writes the file's contents to a `VARCHAR2` string variable:

```
SQL> CREATE OR REPLACE AND COMPILE JAVA SOURCE NAMED "ReadFile" AS
  2    // Java library imports.
  3    import java.io.File;
  4    import java.io.BufferedReader;
  5    import java.io.FileNotFoundException;
  6    import java.io.IOException;
  7    import java.io.FileReader;
  8    import java.security.AccessControlException;
  9
 10    // Class definition.
 11    public class ReadFile {
 12      // Define class variables.
 13      private static File file;
 14      private static FileReader inTextFile;
 15      private static BufferedReader inTextReader;
 16      private static StringBuffer output = new StringBuffer();
 17      private static String outLine, outText;
 18
 19      // Define readText() method.
 20      public static String readText(String fromFile)
 21        throws AccessControlException, IOException {
 22        // Read file.
 23        try {
 24          // Initialize File.
 25          file = new File(fromFile);
 26
 27          // Check for valid file.
 28          if (file.exists()) {
 29
```

```
30              // Assign file to a stream.
31              inTextFile = new FileReader(file);
32              inTextReader = new BufferedReader(inTextFile);
33
34              // Read character-by-character.
35              while ((outLine = inTextReader.readLine()) != null) {
36                output.append(outLine + "\n"); }
37
38              // Passing the StringBuffer to a String.
39              outText = output.toString();
40
41              // Close File.
42              inTextFile.close(); }
43            else {
44              outText = new String("Empty"); }}
45          catch (IOException e) {
46            outText = new String("");
47            return outText; }
48        return outText; }}
49 /
```

The ReadFile class creates a single readText() method. The readText() method reads an external file and writes it to a String return type, as qualified on line 20. Line 25 creates a new File instance, and line 28 validates whether a file was found. Lines 35 through 36 read *line by line* the file's data before appending it to the StringBuffer instance. Line 39 assigns the StringBuffer instance to a String instance.

After successfully compiling the library, you can wrap its functionality with the following PL/SQL statement:

```
SQL> CREATE OR REPLACE FUNCTION read_text_file
  2  (from_file VARCHAR2) RETURN VARCHAR2 IS
  3  LANGUAGE JAVA
  4  NAME 'ReadClobFile.readFile(java.lang.String)
  5        return java.lang.String';
  6  /
```

This works to read a small file, which must be 4,000 characters or less. This may surprise you, because Oracle Database 12c supports VARCHAR2 data types up to 32,767 bytes. Unfortunately, 4,000 characters is the limitation for mapping java.lang.String to a VARCHAR2 data type. You can rewrite the Java library to return an oracle.sql.CLOB class instance when you want to work with text files larger than 4,000 bytes.

A simple query like the following demonstrates how to call the read_text_file PL/SQL function, which calls the readFile() method in the Java I/O library:

```
SQL> SET PAGESIZE 9999
SQL> COLUMN astring FORMAT A60
SQL> SELECT read_text_file('C:\Data\loader\SmallHobbit1.txt') AS "AString"
  2  FROM   dual;
```

The first two commands are SQL*Plus commands. They set the number of rows where line breaks occur and how to format output from the AString column.

Unfortunately, trying to use the `readFile()` method for a text file larger than 4,000 bytes raises the `ORA-24345` and `ORA-01002` exceptions:

```
FROM dual
       *
ERROR at line 2:
ORA-24345: A Truncation or null fetch error occurred
ERROR:
ORA-01002: fetch out of sequence
```

You can fix this problem by rewriting the program to return a `CLOB` data type instead of a `VARCHAR2` data type. The only downside to this approach is that the lifetime of the `CLOB` is the session, which means you must run it only once in the scope of any session. If you run it twice in the same session, it'll append to the existing temporary `CLOB` variable.

The following `ReadClobFile` class makes those changes and lets you read files larger than 4,000 bytes. You should notice that it requires a connection to the local database server to allocate space for the temporary `CLOB`.

You need to reset the `DEFINE` SQL*Plus environment variable to `OFF` before running a file when it includes an ampersand in the Java code. The SQL*Plus command to disable the default value of the `DEFINE` environment variable is

```
SQL> SET DEFINE OFF
```

After running the preceding SQL*Plus command, you can create the `ReadClobFile` class with this SQL statement that creates and compiles a Java I/O library:

```
SQL> CREATE OR REPLACE AND COMPILE JAVA SOURCE NAMED "ReadClobFile" AS
  2      // Java library imports.
  3      import java.io.File;
  4      import java.io.BufferedReader;
  5      import java.io.FileNotFoundException;
  6      import java.io.IOException;
  7      import java.io.FileReader;
  8      import java.security.AccessControlException;
  9      import java.sql.*;
 10      import oracle.sql.driver.*;
 11      import oracle.sql.*;
 12
 13      // Class definition.
 14      public class ReadClobFile {
 15        // Define class variables.
 16        private static int i;
 17        private static File file;
 18        private static FileReader inTextFile;
 19        private static BufferedReader inTextReader;
 20        private static StringBuffer output = new StringBuffer();
 21        private static String outLine, outText;
 22        private static CLOB outCLOB;
 23
 24        // Define readFile() method.
 25        public static oracle.sql.CLOB readFile(String fromFile)
 26          throws AccessControlException, IOException, SQLException  {
```

```
27          // Read file.
28          try {
29            // Initialize File.
30            file = new File(fromFile);
31
32            // Check for valid file.
33            if (file.exists()) {
34
35              // Assign file to a stream.
36              inTextFile = new FileReader(file);
37              inTextReader = new BufferedReader(inTextFile);
38
39              // Read character-by-character.
40              while ((outLine = inTextReader.readLine()) != null) {
41                output.append(outLine + "\n"); }
42
43              // Passing the StringBuffer to a String.
44              outText = output.toString();
45
46              // Declare an Oracle connection.
47              Connection conn =
48                DriverManager.getConnection("jdbc:default:connection:");
49
50              // Transfer the String to CLOB.
51              outCLOB =
52                CLOB.createTemporary(
53                  (oracle.jdbc.OracleConnectionWrapper) conn
54                  , true, CLOB.DURATION_CALL);
55              i = outCLOB.setString(1,outText);
56
57              // Close File.
58              inTextFile.close(); }
59            else {
60              i = outCLOB.setString(1,"Empty"); }}
61          catch (IOException e) {
62            i = outCLOB.setString(1,"");
63            return outCLOB; }
64      return outCLOB; }}
65  /
```

Lines 10 and 11 add two additional Oracle-specific Java class library imports that weren't in the earlier ReadFile class. Line 22 adds a new outCLOB variable.

The statement on lines 51 through 54 creates a temporary CLOB in the scope of the current database connection and assigns it to the outCLOB variable. Line 54 designates the duration of the temporary CLOB as the duration of the call. It doesn't appear to work as it does when used in the dbms_lob package. It appears to endure for the entire session because its JVM garbage collector doesn't flush it from memory after the call to the temporary CLOB. Unfortunately, there isn't any documentation explaining the observed behavior.

Line 55 uses the setString() method to assign the outText variable to the outCLOB variable. The value of i is the physical length of the string.

You should re-enable the `DEFINE` environment command after creating the Java I/O `ReadClobFile` Java I/O library. You do that like this:

```
SQL> SET DEFINE ON
```

Having made the return type change, you need a new PL/SQL wrapper that maps the new `CLOB` return type correctly. The following is the modified PL/SQL wrapper:

```
SQL> CREATE OR REPLACE FUNCTION read_text_file
  2  (from_file VARCHAR2) RETURN VARCHAR2 IS
  3  LANGUAGE JAVA
  4  NAME 'ReadFile.readText(java.lang.String)
  5       return java.lang.String';
  6  /
```

Assuming you've granted Java permissions to read the `Hobbit1.txt` file and included the following SQL*Plus commands, the following query displays the large file with its physical size:

```
SQL> SET LONG 100000
SQL> SET PAGESIZE 9999
SQL> COLUMN atext FORMAT A60 HEADING "Text"
SQL> COLUMN asize FORMAT 99,999 HEADING "Size"
SQL> SELECT   read_clob_file('C:\Data\loader\Hobbit1.txt') AS AText
  2  ,         LENGTH(read_clob_file('C:\Data\loader\Hobbit1.txt')) AS ASize
  3  FROM dual;
```

It should print this:

```
Text                                                          Size
------------------------------------------------------------ -------
Approaching his 111th birthday, the hobbit Bilbo Baggins beg  8,496
ins writing down the full story of his adventure 60 years ea
rlier for the benefit of his nephew Frodo. Long before Bilbo
's involvement, the Dwarf king Thror brings an era of prospe
rity for his kin under the Lonely Mountain until the arrival
 of the dragon Smaug. Destroying the nearby town of Dale, Sm
aug drives the Dwarves out of their mountain and takes their
 hoard of gold. Thror's grandson Thorin sees King Thranduil
and his Wood-elves on a nearby hillside, and is dismayed whe
n they take their leave rather than aid his people, resultin
g in Thorin's everlasting hatred of Elves.
```

Querying the data is easy and is not typically a reason for writing this Java I/O library file as a function. However, we'd like to call your attention to the 8,496 file size returned. It's incorrect because the actual size of the file is 4,246 bytes. The two calls to the Java I/O library double the size of the temporary `CLOB` because the query that calls the `read_clob_file` function runs twice in the scope or same session. Each subsequent call to the same Java I/O library in the same session adds another 8,496 bytes to the temporary `CLOB`.

There is no way to avoid the behavior of a temporary `CLOB` inside a Java method call like the `readText()` method. While you can use a single call to `read_clob_file` PL/SQL to read an external text file into a `CLOB` variable, the call scope is *session-level* and can't be set to *call-level*.

Then, you can insert the value into a table. For example, let's create a `temp` table with a `CLOB` column and then insert the `CLOB` value into the table.

The following `CREATE TABLE` statement creates a `temp` table for testing purposes:

```
SQL> CREATE TABLE temp
  2  ( temp_id    NUMBER GENERATED ALWAYS AS IDENTITY
  3  , temp_clob  CLOB
  4  , CONSTRAINT temp_pk PRIMARY KEY (temp_id));
```

Line 2 uses an identity column, which is a new feature in Oracle Database 12c. If you're running against an earlier version of the Oracle database server, remove the `identity` clause from the `CREATE TABLE` statement.

You can now insert the external file directly into a table like this:

```
SQL> INSERT INTO temp
  2  (temp_clob)
  3  VALUES
  4  (read_clob_file('C:\Data\loader\Hobbit1.txt'));
```

Line 2 provides an override signature for the `INSERT` statement, which lets the `VALUES` clause provide only the `temp_clob` column value. A query against this table should yield the following result:

```
Text                                                    Size
------------------------------------------------------- ------
Approaching his 111th birthday, the hobbit Bilbo Baggins beg   4,246
ins writing down the full story of his adventure 60 years ea
rlier for the benefit of his nephew Frodo. Long before Bilbo
's involvement, the Dwarf king Thror brings an era of prospe
rity for his kin under the Lonely Mountain until the arrival
 of the dragon Smaug. Destroying the nearby town of Dale, Sm
aug drives the Dwarves out of their mountain and takes their
 hoard of gold. Thror's grandson Thorin sees King Thranduil
and his Wood-elves on a nearby hillside, and is dismayed whe
n they take their leave rather than aid his people, resultin
g in Thorin's everlasting hatred of Elves.
```

Travel the Road to No Locator

Developers are different from programmers because we question whether limits exist. The session limitation of temporary `CLOB`, `NCLOB`, and `BLOB` values is one of those things that many developers will question. Assuming you're curious, you can try it for yourself by running the variation of the `ReadClobFile` class (`no_bananas_today.sql`) provided on the McGraw-Hill Professional website for this book.

Rather than reprint the whole code set, here are the components you'd need to add to try working around the limitation. You'll need to change imports, change variable declarations, add some code to the `readFile()` method, and write a `toByteArrayUsingJava()` method that translates an `InputStream` to a byte array.

(continued)

The additional import statements are

```
import java.io.ByteArrayOutputStream;
import java.io.InputStream;
```

The changes to variable declarations are

```
private static byte[] b;
private static CLOB outCLOB, tempCLOB;
```

Add the following code after you create the temporary CLOB column:

```
// Transfer the String to CLOB.
tempCLOB =
  CLOB.createTemporary(
         (oracle.jdbc.OracleConnectionWrapper) conn
       , true, CLOB.DURATION_SESSION);
i = tempCLOB.setString(1,outText);

// Assign the contents of the CLOB to a byte array.
byteArray = toByteArrayUsingJava(tempCLOB.getAsciiStream());

// Create a new CLOB instance.
outCLOB = new CLOB(
              (oracle.jdbc.OracleConnectionWrapper) conn
            , byteArray);

// Free resources from the temporary CLOB.
CLOB.freeTemporary(tempCLOB);
```

You need to write the toByteArrayUsingJava method code because you can't use the Apache Software Foundation's generic org.apache.commons.io.IOUtils class file inside Oracle Database 12c. Here's how you write the method:

```
private static byte[] toByteArrayUsingJava(InputStream is)
  throws IOException {
  // Declare a new ByteArrayOutputStream.
  ByteArrayOutputStream baos = new ByteArrayOutputStream();

  // Transfer InputStream to byte array.
  int i = is.read();
  while(i != -1) {
    baos.write(i);
    i = is.read(); }
  return baos.toByteArray(); }
```

Hopefully, this sidebar resolves any lingering question about working around the problem. It's always possible that Oracle may yet provide an alternative in a future release.

You should note that the physical size is half of the previous value because we closed the session after we ran the INSERT statement. Clearly, session management is a concern and limitation when using Java to open a temporary CLOB variable. The problem is that when you return a temporary CLOB, you can't remove it from the current session of the JVM.

There's a natural tendency among programmers to not believe something like the preceding limitation exists, but it does exist because Oracle Database 12c only allocates LOB locator values to CLOB, NCLOB, and BLOB columns or to a temporary CLOB, NCLOB, or BLOB variable. Oracle SQL disallows creating a CLOB outside of the stated context.

You raise an ORA-24345, or *a truncation or null fetch error occurred*, message when you implement the code changes from the "Travel the Road to No Locator" sidebar. The error is really misdirection because you didn't really construct a new CLOB locator. An ORA-22275 error, or *an invalid LOB locator specified* error message, is the real problem. You can find that out by assigning the file's outText string to the outCLOB variable.

In short, use this approach with care. While it's extremely powerful, it has gotchas that can hurt production code. We recommend it provided that you take the appropriate precautions.

Reading a Binary File with a Java I/O Library

This section shows you how to implement a Java I/O library that reads binary files from the operating system. Like the ReadClobFile class example, implementing this Java I/O library has the same limitation: you can call the Java I/O library only once in any session.

The following ReadImageFile class shows you how to read a binary file and return its contents as a BLOB variable:

```
SQL> CREATE OR REPLACE AND COMPILE JAVA SOURCE NAMED "ReadImageFile" AS
  2    // Java library imports.
  3    import java.io.File;
  4    import java.io.FileInputStream;
  5    import java.io.ByteArrayOutputStream;
  6    import java.io.FileNotFoundException;
  7    import java.io.IOException;
  8    import java.security.AccessControlException;
  9    import java.sql.*;
 10    import oracle.sql.driver.*;
 11    import oracle.sql.*;
 12
 13    // Class definition.
 14    public class ReadImageFile {
 15      // Define class variables.
 16      private static int i;
 17      private static byte [] byteArray, emptyArray;
 18      private static File file;
 19      private static FileInputStream inImageFile;
 20      private static ByteArrayOutputStream outImageFile;
 21      private static BLOB outBLOB;
 22
 23      // Define readText() method.
 24      public static oracle.sql.BLOB readBinary(String fromFile)
 25        throws AccessControlException, IOException, SQLException  {
 26        // Read file.
 27        try {
```

```
28            // Initialize File.
29            file = new File(fromFile);
30
31            // Check for valid file.
32            if (file.exists()) {
33
34               // Assign file to a stream.
35               inImageFile  = new FileInputStream(file);
36
37               // Declare an output stream.
38               outImageFile = new ByteArrayOutputStream();
39
40               // Transfer InputStream to byte array.
41               int i = inImageFile.read();
42               while(i != -1) {
43                 outImageFile.write(i);
44                 i = inImageFile.read(); }
45
46               // Assigning output stream to a byte array.
47               byteArray = outImageFile.toByteArray();
48
49               // Declare an Oracle connection.
50               Connection conn =
51                 DriverManager.getConnection("jdbc:default:connection:");
52
53               // Transfer the String to CLOB.
54               outBLOB =
55                 BLOB.createTemporary(
56                     (oracle.jdbc.OracleConnectionWrapper) conn
57                   , true, BLOB.DURATION_CALL);
58
59               // Assign the byte stream to a BLOB.
60               outBLOB.setBytes(1,byteArray);
61
62               // Close Stream(s).
63               inImageFile.close(); }
64            else {
65              i = outBLOB.setBytes(1,emptyArray); }}
66          catch (IOException e) {
67            i = outBLOB.setBytes(1,emptyArray);
68            return outBLOB; }
69      return outBLOB; }}
70  /
```

As opposed to a variable-length string, you need to return the file contents as a byte array. Line 17 declares the byte array, and lines 19 and 20 declare the input and output streams required for reading a binary file. While there are other alternatives, those implemented seemed the simplest to illustrate how to handle reading the file content into a byte array.

Lines 41 through 44 read the bytes of the file into an output stream. Line 47 uses a toByteArray() method to convert the output stream into a byte array. You create a temporary BLOB on lines 54 through 57 much as you created the temporary CLOB in the earlier "Reading a

Text File with a Java I/O Library" section. Line 60 calls the Oracle BLOB class's setBytes() method to write the file content from an image file into a BLOB variable. Ultimately, the ReadFile() method returns a BLOB variable as the output value on line 69.

The following read_blob_file function wraps the ReadImageFile class's readBinary() method:

```
SQL> CREATE OR REPLACE FUNCTION read_blob_file
  2   (from_file VARCHAR2) RETURN BLOB IS
  3   LANGUAGE JAVA
  4   NAME 'ReadImageFile.readBinary(java.lang.String)
  5        return oracle.sql.BLOB';
```

While it might be fun to demonstrate reading a BLOB variable in a query, it doesn't display at the command-line interface or in the generic IDE tools. The space required to show you how to call the function in a web-based application would take too much space. Please check Chapter 10 of *Oracle Database 12c PL/SQL Programming* for ideas on handling BLOB columns in web-based and GUI applications.

Like the earlier "Reading a Text File with a Java I/O Library" section, creating a table and inserting the BLOB from the function seems like a great test case. While it's not too original, we're using a temp table in this example. The difference from the prior CLOB example is that the second column uses a BLOB data type.

You would create the new temp table with the following statement:

```
SQL> CREATE TABLE temp
  2   ( temp_id     NUMBER GENERATED ALWAYS AS IDENTITY
  3   , temp_blob   BLOB
  4   , CONSTRAINT temp_pk PRIMARY KEY (temp_id));
```

Line 2 uses an identity column, like the earlier example. Identity columns are a new feature in Oracle Database 12c. You'll need to change the preceding statement if you're running against an earlier version of the Oracle database server.

You can insert the BLOB column with the following:

```
SQL> INSERT INTO temp
  2   (temp_blob)
  3   VALUES
  4   (read_blob_file('C:\Data\loader\Hobbit1.png'));
```

As shown in the previous section, line 2 provides an override signature for the INSERT statement. An override signature lets the VALUES clause limit itself to a single temp_blob column value.

A query against this table should yield the following result:

```
SQL> COLUMN assize FORMAT 99,999,999
SQL> SELECT    LENGTH(temp_blob) AS ASize
  2   FROM      temp;
```

The query returns the following output:

```
      ASIZE
-----------
    107,671
```

This section has shown you how to read a binary file into a BLOB data type, and how to consume the result of the function in an INSERT statement. This approach would also work with an UPDATE statement.

Copying a File

The process of copying a file is a bit more complex with Java I/O libraries because you have one set of I/O streams for text and another for binary. So, we took the liberty of writing a single Copy class file that contains one method for copying text files and another method for copying binary files. The copyText() method copies text, and the copyImage() method copies image files.

This library also requires us to again touch on the DEFINE option in SQL*Plus. By default, DEFINE is on because it lets you use substitution variables. Substitution variables are preceded by an ampersand (&). The ampersand lets you provide runtime variables to anonymous block programs. Unfortunately, Java uses the ampersand as part of a comparison operator.

You must disable the DEFINE environment variable before trying to create, replace, and compile the following Java library. This syntax disables the DEFINE environment variable:

```
SQL> SET DEFINE OFF
```

Now, you can build the Copy Java I/O library with the following SQL statement:

```
SQL> CREATE OR REPLACE AND COMPILE JAVA SOURCE NAMED "Copy" AS
  2    // Java library imports.
  3    import java.io.File;
  4    import java.io.IOException;
  5    import java.io.FileReader;
  6    import java.io.FileWriter;
  7    import javax.imageio.stream.FileImageInputStream;
  8    import javax.imageio.stream.FileImageOutputStream;
  9    import java.security.AccessControlException;
 10
 11    // Class definition.
 12    public class Copy
 13    {
 14      // Define variables.
 15      private static int c;
 16      private static File file1,file2;
 17      private static FileReader inTextFile;
 18      private static FileWriter outTextFile;
 19      private static FileImageInputStream inImageFile;
 20      private static FileImageOutputStream outImageFile;
 21
 22      // Define copyText() method.
 23      public static int copyText(String fromFile,String toFile)
 24        throws AccessControlException
 25      {
 26        // Create files from canonical file names.
 27        file1 = new File(fromFile);
 28        file2 = new File(toFile);
 29
```

```
30       // Copy file.
31       try
32       {
33         // Define and initialize FileReader and FileWriter.
34         inTextFile  = new FileReader(file1);
35         outTextFile = new FileWriter(file2);
36
37         // Delete older file when present.
38         if (file2.isFile() && file2.delete()) {}
39
40         // Read character-by-character.
41         while ((c = inTextFile.read()) != -1) {
42           outTextFile.write(c); }
43
44         // Close Streams.
45         inTextFile.close();
46         outTextFile.close(); }
47       catch (IOException e) {
48         return 0; }
49     return 1; }
50
51     // Define copyImage() method.
52     public static int copyImage(String fromFile,String toFile)
53       throws AccessControlException
54     {
55       // Create files from canonical file names.
56       file1 = new File(fromFile);
57       file2 = new File(toFile);
58
59       // Copy file(s).
60       try
61       {
62
63       // Define and initialize FileReader(s).
64       inImageFile  = new FileImageInputStream(file1);
65       outImageFile = new FileImageOutputStream(file2);
66
67       // Delete older file when present.
68       if (file2.isFile() && file2.delete()) {}
69
70       // Read character-by-character.
71       while ((c = inImageFile.read()) != -1) {
72         outImageFile.write(c); }
73
74       // Close Stream(s).
75       inImageFile.close();
76       outImageFile.close(); }
77     catch (IOException e) {
78       return 0; }
79     return 1; }}
80 /
```

Line 23 declares the `copyText` method, which takes two file paths and returns 1 when it is successful and 0 when it fails. Lines 34 and 35 declare the `FileReader` and `FileWriter` as text processing streams. Line 38 checks for the existence of a file and, if found, deletes it. Lines 41 and 42 read the text from one file to another, line 48 returns a 0 when an error occurs, and line 49 returns a 1 when the files are successfully copied.

Line 52 declares the `copyImage` method, which works like the `copyText` method. The only external differences between the methods are that the string inputs point to binary files. The internals of the method are different. Rather than using text processing streams, it uses the binary `FileImageInputStream` and `FileImageOutputStream` to manage moving the data from one file to another. Lines 64 and 65 declare the two binary streams. Lines 71 and 72 move the data from one file to the other.

After you create the Java `Copy` class file, you should re-enable the `DEFINE` environment variable. You do it with the following SQL*Plus statement:

```
SQL> SET DEFINE OFF
```

The next two sections show the PL/SQL wrapper functions that hide the complexity of the Java I/O libraries.

Copying a Text File

The PL/SQL `copy_text_file` function wraps the Java `copyText()` method of the `Copy` class. It returns a 1 for success and returns a 0 for failure. The integer return type lets you call the `copy_text_file` function from a SQL or PL/SQL statement.

```
SQL> CREATE OR REPLACE FUNCTION copy_text_file
  2  (from_file VARCHAR2, to_file VARCHAR2)
  3  RETURN NUMBER IS LANGUAGE JAVA NAME
  4  'Copy.copyText(java.lang.String,java.lang.String) return java.lang.int';
  5  /
```

Before you can test the `copy_text_file` function, you need to create the `external_file` table, which you can do with the following `CREATE TABLE` statement:

```
CREATE TABLE external_file
( file_id     NUMBER
, text_file   BFILE
, image_file  BFILE);
```

After you create the `external_file` table, you need to insert two rows. The following `INSERT` statements add the needed rows for subsequent testing of the next anonymous block:

```
SQL> INSERT INTO external_file
  2  VALUES
  3  ( external_file_s.NEXTVAL
  4  , BFILENAME('LOADER','Hobbit1.txt')
  5  , BFILENAME('LOADER','Hobbit1.png'));
SQL> INSERT INTO external_file
  2  VALUES
  3  ( external_file_s.NEXTVAL
  4  , BFILENAME('LOADER','Hobbit1_copy.txt')
  5  , BFILENAME('LOADER','Hobbit1_copy.png'));
```

The following anonymous block PL/SQL program shows you how to call the `copy_text_file` function. The two parameters are the result of separate calls to the `get_canonical_bfilename` function. Each call to the `get_canonical_bfilename` function requires the ability to look up individual rows in the `external_file` table. So, please insert the two rows before testing the next anonymous block, because if you haven't done so, the following block will fail.

```
SQL> DECLARE
  2    file1 BFILE := BFILENAME('LOADER','Hobbit1.png');
  3    file2 BFILE := BFILENAME('LOADER','Hobbit1_Copy.png');
  4  BEGIN
  5    IF copy_text_file(
  6            get_canonical_bfilename(
  7              pv_table_name    => 'EXTERNAL_FILE'
  8            , pv_bfile_column  => 'TEXT_FILE'
  9            , pv_primary_key   => 'FILE_ID'
 10            , pv_primary_value => '1')
 11          , get_canonical_bfilename(
 12              pv_table_name    => 'EXTERNAL_FILE'
 13            , pv_bfile_column  => 'TEXT_FILE'
 14            , pv_primary_key   => 'FILE_ID'
 15            , pv_primary_value => '2')) = 1 THEN
 16      DBMS_OUTPUT.put_line('It copied an image file.');
 17    END IF;
 18  END;
 19  /
```

While the example uses the `get_canonical_bfilename` function, it isn't necessary to call the `copy_text_file` function. It's an ideal solution when you want to move BFILE source files from one location to another on the physical OS. A SELECT statement can also call the `copy_text_file` function.

Copying a Binary File
The PL/SQL `copy_image_file` function wraps the Java `copyImage()` method of the Copy class. Like its text counterpart, it returns a 1 for success and returns a 0 for failure, and it lets you call the `copy_image_file` function from a SQL or PL/SQL statement.

```
SQL> CREATE OR REPLACE FUNCTION copy_image_file
  2  (from_file VARCHAR2, to_file VARCHAR2)
  3  RETURN NUMBER IS LANGUAGE JAVA NAME
  4  'Copy.copyImage(java.lang.String,java.lang.String) return java.lang.int';
  5  /
```

Like the `copy_text_file` function, the `copy_image_file` function is an effective solution when you want to copy or move external files from one location to another.

Deleting a File
Deleting an external file requires managing the SQL*Plus DEFINE parameter by disabling it before and re-enabling it after you create the Java I/O library. The DeleteFile class has only the `deleteFile()` method. It takes a file name and returns a 1 when it deletes the file and 0 when it fails to delete the file.

Remember to disable the SQL*Plus DEFINE environment variable before running the next block of code, which is the DeleteFile class:

```
SQL> CREATE OR REPLACE AND COMPILE JAVA SOURCE NAMED "DeleteFile" AS
  2    // Java import statements
  3    import java.io.File;
  4    import java.security.AccessControlException;
  5
  6    // Class definition.
  7    public class DeleteFile
  8    {
  9      // Define variable(s).
 10      private static File file;
 11
 12      // Define copyTextFile() method.
 13      public static void deleteFile(String fileName)
 14        throws AccessControlException {
 15
 16        // Create files from canonical file names.
 17        file = new File(fileName);
 18
 19        // Delete file(s).
 20        if (file.isFile() && file.delete()) {}}}
 21  /
```

The key statement in the deleteFile() method is on line 20. It deletes the file when it exists. The wrapper for this method isn't a function like those previously shown. This example shows you how to wrap it with a procedure:

```
SQL> CREATE OR REPLACE PROCEDURE delete_file (dfile VARCHAR2) IS
  2    LANGUAGE JAVA
  3    NAME 'DeleteFile.deleteFile(java.lang.String)';
  4  /
```

You can call the delete_file procedure from an anonymous block, like

```
SQL> BEGIN
  2      delete_file('C:\Data\Loader\Hobbit1_copy.txt');
  3  END;
  4  /
```

While we wanted to show you at least one example with a procedure, we recommend you always write the PL/SQL wrappers as stored functions. Naturally, it makes sense to package these into a single class and wrap them with a stored package.

Writing a File

Writing files from the database typically happens when you export data. More often than not, you export text data. We'll assume you want a Java I/O library that works with code that you or your team members write in PL/SQL, because most backend development in an Oracle database is written using PL/SQL.

There is a use case for exporting binary data. It happens when you want to move a value from a BLOB column to a BFILE column. We see this type of use case (a binary storage conversion) as very viable, and it provides us with an opportunity to show you how to write a package with overloading that wraps multiple Java libraries.

As a result of our assumption and the BLOB to BFILE conversion use case, the Java I/O library accepts two parameters. The first parameter is the target file name, and the second parameter is a CLOB or BLOB. The PL/SQL wrapper is an overloaded write function, which we deploy in a package because overloading is an object-oriented language feature. Packages were the first object introduced along with PL/SQL 2.0 in Oracle 7.

Writing LOBs Through Procedures

It's not possible to insert a string longer than 32,767 bytes into an uninitialized CLOB, NCLOB, or BLOB column with SQL. An attempt with an INSERT or UPDATE statement would fail. You can insert or update a very large string by using a PL/SQL function or procedure.

A pass-by-reference procedure lets you use the RETURNING INTO clause with an UPDATE statement. The RETURNING INTO clause lets you use a *call locator* to identify a LOB column, and calling it lets you return a *return locator*. The return locator acts as a duplex (two-way) pipe to write very large text or binary strings.

The following illustration of an UPDATE statement comes from Chapter 10 of *Oracle Database 12c PL/SQL Programming*. The UPDATE statement shows how the RETURNING INTO clause lets us manage a return locator.

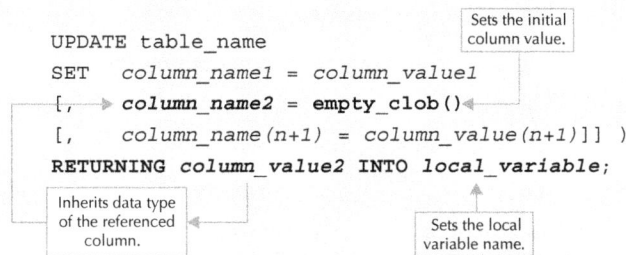

```
                                            ┌──────────────────┐
                                            │ Sets the initial │
                                            │ column value.    │
                                            └──────────────────┘
        UPDATE table_name

        SET    column_name1 = column_value1

        [,  ➤  column_name2 = empty_clob()◄──────────────┘

        [,     column_name(n+1) = column_value(n+1)]] )

        RETURNING column_value2 INTO local_variable;
   ┌──────────────────┐                    ┌──────────────────┐
   │ Inherits data type│                   │ Sets the local   │
   │ of the referenced │                   │ variable name.   │
   │ column.           │                   └──────────────────┘
   └──────────────────┘
```

You can then enclose this type of UPDATE statement in a stored procedure. The stored procedure should treat the return locator as a pass-by-reference or IN OUT mode formal parameter.

The following demonstrates that approach with the item table and a CLOB column:

```
SQL> CREATE OR REPLACE PROCEDURE load_clob_from_file
  2  ( pv_item_id  IN      NUMBER
  3  , descriptor  IN OUT CLOB ) IS
  4  BEGIN
  5    /* This a DML transaction. */
  6    UPDATE     item
  7    SET        item_desc = empty_clob()
  8    WHERE      item_id = pv_item_id
  9    RETURNING item_desc INTO descriptor;
 10  END load_clob_from_file;
 11  /
```

(continued)

This `load_clob_from_file` procedure lets you open a CLOB locator and access it from an external program. There are three key features in this procedure. First, the formal parameter on line 3 is a CLOB locator with an IN OUT mode access. Second, the RETURNING INTO clause on line 9 provides a local variable gateway into the SET clause's column variable on line 7. Third, the lack of a COMMIT in the stored procedure leaves the CLOB locked and the DML transaction scope open for a calling external program.

The next three sections show you how to write the Java library, how to test the individual methods, and how to overload the methods in a package. As with earlier sections, you need to grant Java permissions to act on external files for each file.

Writing Files in Java I/O Libraries

The Java I/O library for writing files should support two methods. One method should write a text file, and the other should write an image file. You have the option of writing one class for each method or two classes, but we'd recommend that you create only one class file when deploying both methods inside a package.

The `Write` class has two methods. The `writeText()` method writes a text file, and the `writeImage()` method writes a binary image file. Naturally, they rely on the `sys` user or a PDB ADMIN user granting read, write, and delete permissions on the file names.

The following `Write` class requires that you disable the DEFINE parameter before you run it because it uses the Java logical `&&` (*and*) operator:

```
SQL> CREATE OR REPLACE AND COMPILE JAVA SOURCE NAMED "Write" AS
  2    // Java library imports.
  3    import java.io.File;
  4    import java.io.IOException;
  5    import java.io.FileReader;
  6    import java.io.FileWriter;
  7    import javax.imageio.stream.FileImageInputStream;
  8    import javax.imageio.stream.FileImageOutputStream;
  9    import java.security.AccessControlException;
 10    import oracle.sql.driver.*;
 11    import oracle.sql.*;
 12
 13    // Class definition.
 14    public class Write {
 15      // Define variable(s).
 16      private static File file;
 17      private static FileReader inTextFile;
 18      private static FileWriter outTextFile;
 19      private static FileImageInputStream inImageFile;
 20      private static FileImageOutputStream outImageFile;
 21
 22      // Define writeText() method.
 23      public static int writeText(String toFile, CLOB clob)
 24        throws AccessControlException, java.sql.SQLException {
 25
```

```
26          // Create files from canonical file names.
27          file = new File(toFile);
28
29          // Write file.
30          try {
31
32            // Define and initialize FileReader.
33            outTextFile = new FileWriter(file);
34
35            // Delete older file when present.
36            if (file.isFile() && file.delete()) {}
37
38            // Write character stream.
39            outTextFile.write(
40              clob.getSubString(1L,(int) clob.length()));
41
42            // Close Stream(s).
43            outTextFile.close(); }
44          catch (IOException e) {
45            return 0; }
46        return 1; }
47
48        // Define writeImage() method.
49        public static int writeImage(String toFile, BLOB blob)
50          throws AccessControlException, java.sql.SQLException {
51
52          // Create files from canonical file names.
53          file = new File(toFile);
54
55          // Write file.
56          try {
57
58            // Define and initialize binary file streams.
59            outImageFile = new FileImageOutputStream(file);
60
61            // Delete older file when present.
62            if (file.isFile() && file.delete()) {}
63
64            // Write binary stream.
65            outImageFile.write(
66              blob.getBytes(1L,(int) blob.length()));
67
68            // Close Stream(s).
69            outImageFile.close(); }
70        catch (IOException e) {
71          return 0; }
72        return 1; }}
73  /
```

Line 14 declares the Write class. Line 23 declares the writeText() method, which continues through line 46. The writeText() method declares a text stream writer on line 33, and uses the `FileWriter` stream to write the `CLOB` parameter's value to a file. Line 49 declares the second method, the `writeImage()` method. The `FileImageOutputStream` writes the `BLOB` parameter's value to an image file.

Testing Java I/O Libraries that Write Files

It's important to test the `writeText()` and `writeImage()` methods of the `Write` class individually before you test them in an overloaded context. Testing the individual methods requires that you write two schema-level functions that wrap the `Write` class's methods. The two subsections show you how to write text and image files.

Test Writing a Text File   The following declares the `write_text_file` function that wraps the `writeText()` method of the `Write` class:

```
SQL> CREATE OR REPLACE FUNCTION write_text_file
  2  (to_file VARCHAR2, text CLOB)
  3  RETURN NUMBER IS LANGUAGE JAVA NAME
  4  'Write.writeText(java.lang.String,oracle.sql.CLOB)
  5   return java.lang.int';
  6  /
```

After creating the schema-level `write_text_file` function, you can test it with the following PL/SQL anonymous block:

```
SQL> SET SERVEROUTPUT ON SIZE UNLIMITED
SQL> BEGIN
  2    IF write_text_file(
  3           'C:\Data\loader\Hobbit21.txt'
  4         , read_clob_file('C:\Data\loader\Hobbit1.txt')) = 1 THEN
  5      dbms_output.put_line('Success');
  6    END IF;
  7  END;
  8  /
```

The `IF` statement on lines 2 through 4 calls the `write_text_file` function, which maps to the `writeText()` method of the `Write` class. The call to the `write_text_file` function takes a qualified file name and `CLOB` data type.

The qualified file name must resolve to a physical file to which you've previously granted read, write, and delete permissions with the `dbms_java` package. The return value of the call to the `read_clob_file` must retrieve a `CLOB` variable. The preceding anonymous block prints the following when the two criteria are met:

```
Success.
```

This section has shown you how to test the `Write` class by writing a text file with its `writeText()` method.

Test Writing an Image File   The following declares the `write_image_file` function that wraps the `writeImage()` method of the `Write` class:

```
SQL> CREATE OR REPLACE FUNCTION write_image_file
  2  (to_file VARCHAR2, blob BLOB)
  3  RETURN NUMBER IS LANGUAGE JAVA NAME
```

```
4  'Write.writeImage(java.lang.String,oracle.sql.BLOB)
5   return java.lang.int';
6  /
```

After creating the schema-level `write_image_file` function, you can test it with the following PL/SQL anonymous block:

```
SQL> SET SERVEROUTPUT ON SIZE UNLIMITED
SQL> BEGIN
  2    IF write_image_file(
  3          'C:\Data\loader\Hobbit21.png'
  4          , read_blob_file('C:\Data\loader\Hobbit1.png')) = 1 THEN
  5      dbms_output.put_line('Success');
  6    END IF;
  7  END;
  8  /
```

Like the test case that wrote a text file, the `IF` statement on lines 2 through 4 calls the `write_image_file` function. The `write_image_file` function maps to the `writeImage()` method of the `Write` class, and the second parameter of the `write_image_file` function takes a `BLOB` data type instead of a `CLOB` data type.

Like the anonymous block that tested the `write_text_file` function, the preceding anonymous block tests the `write_image_file` function and prints the following when similar criteria are met:

```
Success.
```

This section has shown you how to test the `Write` class by writing a binary file with its `writeImage()` method.

Overloading Java I/O Libraries
The process to overload Java I/O libraries doesn't differ much from the process to overload PL/SQL functionality. You must declare a package specification that is *language neutral* before you can create a package body that implements functionality in the Java language.

Writing the Package Wrapper   The following `write_file` package specification declares two write functions. We choose write functions over procedures to guarantee the files are written. While functions and procedures that run in the same transaction scope as the caller are wait programs, only functions can later be rewritten as autonomous programs that cause a calling program to wait on their completion. When writing large files, it's possible that you may want to rewrite these libraries to run as autonomous transactions.

The `write_file` package specification is

```
SQL> CREATE OR REPLACE PACKAGE write_file IS
  2    /* Write a text file. */
  3    FUNCTION write
  4    ( to_file  VARCHAR2
  5    , text        CLOB)
  6    RETURN NUMBER;
  7
```

```
 8     /* Write a binary file. */
 9     FUNCTION write
10     ( to_file   VARCHAR2
11     , blob      BLOB)
12     RETURN NUMBER;
13   END write_file;
14   /
```

Overloading requires that the signatures (or list of parameter data types) differ between the two `write` functions. The first parameter of both `write` functions uses the same `VARCHAR2` data type, while the second parameter differs by using a `CLOB` on line 5 and a `BLOB` on line 11. The difference between the two signatures lets a call to the `write_file.write` function choose the one that's correct.

The `write_file` package body implements the Java language:

```
SQL> CREATE OR REPLACE PACKAGE BODY write_file AS
  2     /* Write a text file. */
  3     FUNCTION write
  4     ( to_file   VARCHAR2
  5     , text      CLOB)
  6     RETURN NUMBER IS LANGUAGE JAVA NAME
  7       'Write.writeText(java.lang.String,oracle.sql.CLOB)
  8        return java.lang.int';
  9
 10     /* Write a binary file. */
 11     FUNCTION write
 12     ( to_file   VARCHAR2
 13     , blob      BLOB)
 14     RETURN NUMBER IS LANGUAGE JAVA NAME
 15       'Write.writeImage(java.lang.String,oracle.sql.BLOB)
 16        return java.lang.int';
 17   END write_file;
 18   /
```

Lines 3 and 11 declare two overloaded write functions. They both take a fully qualified file name and either a `CLOB` or `BLOB` data type. The first `write` function maps to the `writeText()` method of the `Write` class, and the second `write` function maps to the `writeImage()` method of the same `Write` class. While the method names are unique, the PL/SQL function names inside the package are the same. The same function name inside the `write_file` package with different parameter lists supports overloading.

Test Writing a CLOB Variable to a File   To test overloading, we'll create another `temp` table. This `temp` table differs from the earlier versions because it has three columns. One column is a surrogate key that uses a `NUMBER` data type, and the other two columns have a `CLOB` and `BLOB` data type, respectively.

The following creates the three-column `temp` table:

```
SQL> CREATE TABLE temp
  2   ( temp_id    NUMBER GENERATED ALWAYS AS IDENTITY
  3   , textclob   CLOB
  4   , imageblob  BLOB);
```

You insert a CLOB value by using an INSERT statement with the read_clob_file PL/SQL wrapper function from the earlier "Reading a Text File with a Java I/O Library" section of this chapter. The following INSERT statement adds a CLOB value into the textclob column:

```
SQL> INSERT INTO temp
  2  (textclob)
  3  VALUES
  4  (read_clob_file('C:\Data\loader\Hobbit1.txt'));
```

Now, you use an UPDATE statement to add a BLOB value to the same row of the temp table. The PL/SQL read_blob_file wrapper function lets you read the file from the operating system as qualified in the earlier "Reading a Binary File with a Java I/O Library" section.

The following UPDATE statement adds a BLOB value into the imageblob column:

```
SQL> UPDATE temp
  2  SET    imageblob = read_blob_file('C:\Data\loader\Hobbit1.png')
  3  WHERE  temp_id = 1;
```

It's possible to use the two libraries in the same session because one creates a temporary CLOB and the other a temporary BLOB variable. The data type difference ensures that they're unique in the scope of the session.

You can query to determine the success of the INSERT and UPDATE statements with the following:

```
SQL> COLUMN clobsize FORMAT 9,999,999
SQL> COLUMN blobsize FORMAT 9,999,999
SQL> SELECT    LENGTH(textclob) AS clobsize
  2  ,          LENGTH(imageblob) AS blobsize
  3  FROM       temp;
```

If you're using the sample files provided with this book's source code, you should see the following result:

```
  CLOBSIZE   BLOBSIZE
---------- ----------
     4,246    107,671
```

After populating the two columns with valid CLOB and BLOB values, you can now query the results as follows:

```
SQL> COLUMN writetext  FORMAT 9 HEADING "WriteText"
SQL> COLUMN writeimage FORMAT 9 HEADING "WriteImage"
SQL> SELECT write_file.write(
  2              'C:\Data\loader\Hobbit21.txt'
  3             ,textclob) AS writetext
  4  ,        write_file.write(
  5              'C:\Data\loader\Hobbit21.png'
  6             ,imageblob) AS writeimage
  7  FROM       temp;
```

The two write_file.write calls in the SELECT statement return 1, which means the query successfully writes the two target files. It reads the column data types as the second parameter.

The calls to the overloaded `write` function choose the appropriate version from the `write_file` package based on the data type of the second parameter.

Writing Structured Data Through Java I/O Libraries

In the previous section, we qualified how to use Java I/O libraries and PL/SQL wrapper functions to write data to external files, though we limited the discussion to writing CLOB and BLOB data streams because the principal use case was to move internal BLOB images to external files.

There is another use case, which is often managed by the `utl_file` package. It is the use case for writing structured data to external files, like CSV files. This section demonstrates how you load a CLOB variable with structured records, and how you write a CLOB variable with structured data as a CSV file.

Creating a CLOB Variable Holding Structured Data

This example is simple and not very extendable, but our purpose is to simply show how to put structured data into a transient CLOB variable. It uses the `dbms_lob` package, which is covered in Chapter 10 of *Oracle Database 12c PL/SQL Programming*.

The following `write_item_records` function takes no formal parameters and writes a simplistic two-column row of comma-delimited data to a transient CLOB variable:

```
SQL> CREATE OR REPLACE FUNCTION write_item_records
  2  RETURN CLOB IS
  3    /* Declare a file reference pointer and buffer. */
  4    lv_clob     CLOB;              -- File reference
  5    lv_line     VARCHAR2(32767); -- Reading buffer
  6    first_line  BOOLEAN := TRUE; -- First line flag.
  7
  8    /* Declare a cursor. */
  9    CURSOR get_items IS
 10      SELECT   i.item_title
 11      ,        i.item_subtitle
 12      FROM     item i
 13      WHERE    REGEXP_LIKE(i.item_title,'Star.*$');
 14  BEGIN
 15    /* Create a temporary CLOB for the scope of the call. */
 16    dbms_lob.createtemporary(lv_clob, FALSE, dbms_lob.call);
 17
 18    /* Read the cursor for values. */
 19    FOR i IN get_items LOOP
 20      /* Concatenate the results into a CSV format. */
 21      lv_line := i.item_title||','||i.item_subtitle||CHR(10);
 22
 23      /* Write or append a line of text. */
 24      IF first_line THEN
 25        dbms_lob.write(
 26            lob_loc => lv_clob
 27          , amount  => LENGTH(lv_line)
 28          , offset  => 1
 29          , buffer  => lv_line);
 30
 31        /* Reset logical first line control flag. */
 32        first_line := FALSE;
```

```
33      ELSE
34        dbms_lob.writeappend(
35           lob_loc => lv_clob
36         , amount  => LENGTH(lv_line)
37         , buffer  => lv_line);
38      END IF;
39    END LOOP;
40    /* Return a CLOB variable. */
41    RETURN lv_clob;
42  EXCEPTION
43    /* Manage raised exceptions. */
44    WHEN OTHERS THEN
45      dbms_output.put_line(SQLERRM);
46  END;
47  /
```

Line 16 creates a temporary CLOB in memory, which provides a locator value to a transient and internally stored LOB. The locator value lets you manage references to the CLOB when passing it between PL/SQL program units. Line 21 builds a record of data by concatenating together the data and delimiting commas.

An IF statement lets you write the first record or append subsequent records to the CLOB variable. The write procedure of the dbms_lob package occurs on lines 25 through 29, and the writeappend procedure occurs on lines 35 through 37. Line 41 returns the CLOB variable from the write_item_records function.

You can test the write_item_records function with this query:

```
SQL> SET LONG 1000000
SQL> SET PAGESIZE 0
SQL> SELECT   write_item_records
  2  FROM      dual;
```

It prints a list of *Star Wars* videos in inventory, like this:

```
Star Wars - Episode I,The Phantom Menace
Star Wars - Episode II,Attack of the Clones
 ...
Star Wars - Episode VI,Return of the Jedi
```

This section has shown you how to gather structured data and assign it to a CLOB variable. The next section shows you how to write the CLOB to a physical file.

Writing a CSV File with a CLOB Variable   The last step in writing structured data to a CSV file requires that you call the write_item_records or some other function that returns structured data to a CLOB variable. The following anonymous block writes the results from the write_item_records to a physical CSV file.

You can view the contents of the physical file by using a text editor, or by using the cat command in Linux or Unix or the type command in Windows, like this:

```
SQL> BEGIN
  2    IF write_file.write(
  3         'C:\Data\loader\ItemText.csv'
```

```
4          , write_item_records()) = 1 THEN
5        dbms_output.put_line('Success');
6     END IF;
7   END;
8   /
```

It displays the following when it works:

Success.

The only question that remains is whether you should use Java to write CSV files or use the utl_file package to do so. We'd recommend the utl_file package as the preferred option. Although, the Java I/O library approach is ideal when you want to call a function to write the data to a CSV file because the utl_file doesn't support that approach. The utl_file package requires pass-by-reference procedures to write CSV files.

Supporting Scripts

The following programs are available on the McGraw-Hill Professional website to support this chapter:

- The copy_external_files.sql program shows how to copy text and image files.
- The create_get_directory_path.sql program shows how to translate a virtual directory name to a physical path.
- The delete_file.sql program shows how to delete external files.
- The get_canonical_bfilename.sql program shows how to translate a BFILE reference into a fully qualified file name.
- The get_directory_list.sql program demonstrates how to read an external directory.
- The ReadNullClobFile.sql program demonstrates the limits of trying to drop-transfer a temporary CLOB variable to a transient data type (one without a locator, or pointer in memory).
- The ReadBlobFile.sql program creates the internal Java library to read an external file into a BLOB variable.
- The ReadClobFile.sql program creates the internal Java library to read an external file into a CLOB variable.
- The ReadFile.java program shows how to read and print a file's content in a purely exclusive Java mode of operation.
- The write_file.sql program shows how to write CLOB and BLOB files.
- The write_csv_data.sql program shows how to write structured data into a CLOB and then through the CLOB into an external CSV file.

Summary

You should now have an understanding of how to implement Java I/O libraries and the PL/SQL wrappers that make them effective tools inside Oracle Database 12*c*.

CHAPTER
5

External Tables

Purpose

This chapter teaches you how to configure, deploy, manage, and troubleshoot external tables. It builds a manageable framework for how you can handle imports of data sets through a push (upload to server) paradigm. It shows you how to

- Create and use external tables
- Use PL/SQL to unmask physical directories from virtual directories
- Use Java to read external files
- Verify the presence of external files
- Shield reads of external files from cartridge errors
- Clean up and store source files

Some of these examples build on concepts introduced in *Oracle Database 12c PL/SQL Programming*. Other new Oracle Database 12c features, like using a wildcard character in the LOCATION clause, specifying a date-time format and NULLIF criteria, and using field name identification, are covered in this chapter.

Additional Oracle Database 12c new features include three new parameters (dnfs_disable, dnfs_enable, and dnfs_readbuffers) that let you enable or disable *Direct NFS Client* on input data files while reading external files. The Direct NFS Client API provides DBAs with a tool to improve performance. The dnfs_readbuffers parameter is set to 4 by default. Increasing the value of the dnfs_readbuffers parameter may compensate for inconsistent I/O from the Direct NFS Client, but it will increase server memory usage. These parameters are covered in Chapter 15 of the *Oracle Database Utilities* manual.

Advantages

Since Oracle9i Database, you've been able to read data stored in external files, and from Oracle Database 10g forward, you've been able to read and write data from external files. Oracle9i lets you read files by using the Oracle SQL*Loader utility to read comma-separated value (CSV), tab-separated value (TSV), and position-specific files. Since the release of Oracle Database 10g, you can now read and write files by using the Oracle Data Pump utility.

External tables provide a natural way to perform large file and bulk upload processing. They also provide logging mechanisms to capture problems with loading data from external files when they don't agree with their defined specification. Oracle Database 12c and its predecessors read the external files using Oracle's SQL*Loader express mode, and with large files, you should enable parallel processing.

Disadvantages

External tables point to files that are outside the database, and as such they may expose data to operating system users. The risk of exposing data to prying eyes in external tables must be minimized by limiting the time of exposure after import, which is the time between staging the data and deleting the data.

Overview

This chapter focuses on an external file management framework, which covers the following:

■ How to use external tables

■ How to leverage the data catalog

■ How to wrap access to external tables

■ How to clean up the external table files

The chapter builds on your understanding of SQL, PL/SQL, and general extract, transform, and load (ETL) concepts. While the materials are organized to read from start to finish, you should be able to jump to any section of interest if you understand the previous concepts, though a quick browse might save you the time of looking for a missing piece later in the chapter.

Using External Tables

Oracle lets you define externally organized tables. Externally organized tables appear like ordinary tables in the database, but are structures that are read-only files or read and write files from the operating system. Read-only files can be comma-separated value (CSV), tab-separated (TSV), or position-specific files. Read and write files are stored in an Oracle Data Pump proprietary format. However, both of these file types are known as *flat files*.

Oracle SQL*Loader lets you read these flat files with a SELECT statement from what appear as standard tables. Oracle Data Pump also lets you read with a SELECT statement, but, unlike Oracle SQL*Loader, Oracle Data Pump lets you write with an INSERT statement. The write creates a proprietary formatted file, and the read extracts the data from the file.

Two key preparation steps are required whether you're working with externally organized read-only or read-write files. These steps help you create virtual directories and grant database privileges to read from and write to them. You should have a working knowledge of Oracle Database 12c's multitenant architecture before tackling the configuration of users, and should probably read the nearby "Multitenant Provisioning" sidebar if you're not familiar with the procedure. However, you should also know that this type of approach doesn't require a multitenant architecture, and you can skip it when you're not working in a multitenant database server.

Multitenant Provisioning

If you're new to Oracle Database 12c, then it's important to understand that the pluggable database (PDB) is a private data context. Most of its data catalog is private and separate from the overall database. Only a small portion of the database catalog is stored in the container database (CDB) catalog, and new CDB_ administrative views are added to the database. A PDB is a great solution when you're leveraging the *Editioning* feature introduced in Oracle Database 11g.

You should note the following guarantee reproduced from page 9 of Oracle's *Oracle Multitenant* white paper (June 2013).

(continued)

From the point of view of the client connecting via Oracle Net, the PDB *is* the database. A PDB is fully compatible with a non-CDB. We shall refer to this from now on as the *PDB/non-CDB compatibility guarantee*. In other words, the installation scheme for an application backend that ran without error against a non-CDB will run, with no change, and without error, in a PDB and will produce the same result.

The full document can be found at the time of writing at this URL:

www.oracle.com/technetwork/database/multitenant-wp-12c-1949736.pdf
Here are the steps that work on Linux or Windows.

Create a Pluggable Database
You can create a `videodb` PDB with a `videoadm` administrative user assigned to it:

```
CREATE PLUGGABLE DATABASE videodb
  ADMIN USER videoadm IDENTIFIED BY Video1
  ROLES = (dba)
  DEFAULT TABLESPACE videots
    DATAFILE 'C:\APP\ORACLE\ORADATA\ORCL\VIDEO01.DBF' SIZE 500M ONLINE
  FILE_NAME_CONVERT = ('C:\APP\ORACLE\ORADATA\ORCL\PDBSEED\',
                       'C:\APP\ORACLE\ORADATA\ORCL\VIDEOPDB\');
```

NOTE
Don't try to create the DEFAULT TABLESPACE before you provision the database. If you do, you'll get an ORA-01537 error, which tells you that you can't create the tablespace before you create the database.

Configure the Oracle listener.ora File
You need to stop the Oracle listener and modify the `listener.ora` file, as follows (line numbers don't exist in the `listener.ora` file; they're provided to help illustrate the changes to the file):

```
 1 SID_LIST_LISTENER =
 2  (SID_LIST =
 3    (SID_DESC =
 4      (SID_NAME = CLRExtProc)
 5      (ORACLE_HOME = C:\app\oracle\product\12.1.0\dbhome_1)
 6      (PROGRAM = extproc)
 7      (ENVS = "EXTPROC_DLLS=ONLY:C:\...\dbhome_1\bin\oraclr12.dll")
 8    )
 9    (SID_DESC =
10      (SID_NAME = VIDEODB)
11      (ORACLE_HOME = C:\app\oracle\product\12.1.0\dbhome_1)
12    )
13  )
14  LISTENER =
15    (DESCRIPTION_LIST =
16      (DESCRIPTION =
17        (ADDRESS = (PROTOCOL = IPC)(KEY = EXTPROC1521))
```

```
18          (ADDRESS = (PROTOCOL = TCP)(HOST = localhost)(PORT = 1521))
19    )
20    )
```

Lines 9 through 12 configure a `videodb` Oracle SID. After you make the changes, start the Oracle listener. This configuration doesn't take effect until you stop and restart the Oracle listener, which is covered in the "Manage the Oracle Listener" section later in this series of steps.

After you make a change to the `listener.ora` file, you must stop and restart the Oracle listener. You stop the listener with the following commands:

```
lsnrctl stop
```

and you start it with this command:

```
lsnrctl start
```

If you're running on the Windows operating system, the alternative is to use the `services.msc` utility. With the Windows Services console, you can start, stop, and restart the Oracle listener service.

Configure the Oracle tnsnames.ora File

You also need to add a `video` TNS alias to the bottom of the `tnsnames.ora` file for the `videodb` PDB. It should look like this:

```
VIDEO =
  (DESCRIPTION =
    (ADDRESS = (PROTOCOL = TCP)(HOST = localhost)(PORT = 1521))
    (CONNECT_DATA =
      (SERVER = DEDICATED)
      (SERVICE_NAME = videodb)
    )
  )
```

This `tnsnames.ora` file is configured like you'd find it on a workstation, with the `host` value set to `localhost`. This type of configuration lets you use a DNS-supplied dynamic IP address and work with a local copy of the Oracle Database 12c database on a laptop. A real server deployment would use the `hostname` value of the server, which is also listed in the corporate DNS server. As a rule, the `hostname` value creates a layer of abstraction that lets you change the IP address of the server. The map between the hostname and IP address is generally maintained in the corporate DNS server. For testing purposes, you can also map this type of relationship in

- **Unix or Linux**   `/etc/hosts` file
- **Windows**   `C:\Windows\System32\drivers\etc\hosts` file

It's called *file resolution* when you map the IP address to the hostname. File resolution should only be used in very small shops or test environments isolated from the company's DNS server. Isolated test environments typically run on subnets set up inside the company intranet.

(continued)

Manage the Oracle Listener

The Oracle listener must be running for you to make a connection across the network through a TCP connection. If you're running this code on your laptop and the Windows operating system, the Oracle listener is running as a Windows service. To avoid covering the different release variants, you can start and stop the listener by typing the following in a terminal session:

```
C:\> services.msc
```

Alternatively, you can status, start, and stop the Oracle listener by using the command line, like this:

```
C:\> lsnrctl status
```

The keywords `status`, `start`, and `stop` are interchangeable at the command line. If you're the `oracle` user on a Linux or Unix system, you can use the same command-line syntax.

Start the videodb PDB

You connect to the CDB `sys` user or PDB `sys` user using the `sysdba` role to start the `videodb` PDB. You can connect to the `videodb` PDB database directly with the following syntax:

```
sqlplus sys@video AS sysdba
```

After authenticating as the `sys` user with the `sysdba` role, you can start it like this:

```
SQL> startup
Pluggable DATABASE opened.
```

You can connect as the CDB `sys` user with the `sysdba` role:

```
SQL> ALTER SESSION SET container=videodb;
SQL> ALTER PLUGGABLE DATABASE videodb OPEN;
```

Create a PDB User with Privileges

You create a PDB `importer` user by using the following syntax:

```
SQL> CREATE USER importer IDENTIFIED BY importer;
SQL> GRANT create cluster, create indextype, create operator
  2  ,      create procedure, create sequence, create session
  3  ,      create synonym, create table, create trigger
  4  ,      create type, create view, unlimited tablespace
  5  TO importer;
```

This sidebar has shown you how to create a `videodb` PDB and a PDB `importer` user. While you don't need to provision a PDB for the example in this chapter, the examples are provided for scenarios where you may do so. Moreover, this sidebar should help you work through examples in this chapter when in a PDB.

The first subsection walks you through the two preparation steps, and the next two subsections show you how to work with read-only and read-write files.

Creating Virtual Directories and Granting Database Privileges

Virtual directories are structures in the Oracle database, and they're stored in the data catalog. They map virtual directory names to physical operating system directories. Virtual directories make a few assumptions, which can become critical fail points. For the database grants to work successfully, the physical directories must be accessible to the operating system user who installed the Oracle server. That means the operating system user should have read and write privileges to the related physical directories.

As the `sys`, `system`, or authorized CDB administrator account, you can create a virtual directory with the following syntax:

```
SQL> CREATE DIRECTORY upload AS 'C:\data\upload';
```

NOTE
It's not necessary to create the physical file before you create the virtual directory, but the virtual directory can't resolve a physical location until the physical directories are available.

While the `upload` directory is where you put the data file, there should be a separate virtual directory for the log files. The reason for separating them is that you may want to grant only read privileges on the `upload` directory. However, the framework cleans up files and requires that you grant read and write privileges to the directory.

The following creates a virtual directory for the log files:

```
SQL> CREATE DIRECTORY logs AS 'C:\data\logs';
```

After you create the virtual directories, you must grant permission to read from the `upload` directory and grant permission to write to the `log` directory. The division of the two virtual directories is necessary unless you grant read-write permissions to a single virtual directory. It's necessary to grant read and write permissions because you need read permission to read the file and write permissions to write log files. Any read of an external file may write errors, discards, and log files.

You grant read permission to the `importer` PDB user on the upload directory like this:

```
SQL> GRANT READ ON DIRECTORY upload TO importer;
```

Then, you grant write permission to the `importer` PDB user on the `log` directory:

```
SQL> GRANT WRITE ON DIRECTORY log TO importer;
```

NOTE
If you're unfamiliar with the difference between a container database (CDB) user and a pluggable database (PDB) user, please refer to Appendix in Oracle Database 12c PL/SQL Programming.

You grant read and write permissions to the `importer` PDB user on the `upload` directory when the data and log files are stored in the same virtual directory. You can also grant read and write permissions to an `importer` PDB user like this:

```
SQL> GRANT READ, WRITE ON DIRECTORY upload TO importer;
```

NOTE
The framework in this chapter requires that you grant read and write privileges to all directories because you clean up files after reading them.

After creating a virtual directory, you can find the mapping of virtual directories to operating system directories in the `DBA_DIRECTORIES` data dictionary view. Only a `sys` or `system` superuser can gain access to this conceptual view. Unlike many other administrative views, there is no `USER_DIRECTORIES` view.

For reference, virtual directories are also used for `BFILE` data types. Web developers need to know the list of virtual directories and their physical directories. They need that information to ensure their programs place the uploaded files where they belong.

Oracle SQL*Loader Files

After the preparation steps, you can define an externally organized table that uses a read-only file.

```
SQL> CREATE TABLE CHARACTER
  2  ( character_id NUMBER
  3  , first_name VARCHAR2(20)
  4  , last_name VARCHAR2(20))
  5    ORGANIZATION EXTERNAL
  6    ( TYPE oracle_loader
  7      DEFAULT DIRECTORY upload
  8      ACCESS PARAMETERS
  9      ( RECORDS DELIMITED BY NEWLINE CHARACTERSET US7ASCII
 10        BADFILE     'LOG':'character.bad'
 11        DISCARDFILE 'LOG':'character.dis'
 12        LOGFILE     'LOG':'character.log'
 13        FIELDS TERMINATED BY ','
 14        OPTIONALLY ENCLOSED BY "'"
 15        MISSING FIELD VALUES ARE NULL )
 16      LOCATION ('character.csv'))
 17  REJECT LIMIT UNLIMITED;
```

Line 6 sets the `TYPE` value as Oracle SQL*Loader (designated as `oracle_loader` in the creation statement) as the communication layer, and line 7 sets the `DEFAULT DIRECTORY` as the virtual directory name you created previously. Lines 10 through 12 set the virtual log directories and files for any read from the externally organized table. Logs are written with each `SELECT` statement against the `character` table when data succeeds or fails to conform to the definition.

The `character.csv` is a small file and it is set up as a non-parallelized read. You would change the create statement by appending a `PARALLEL` clause when the external source file is large. The PARALLEL clause lets Oracle read your external file through concurrent SQL*Loader threads:

```
16   PARALLEL
17   REJECT LIMIT UNLIMITED;
```

After the log file setup, the delimiters define how to read the data in the external file. Line 13 sets the delimiter, FIELD TERMINATED BY, as a comma. Line 14 sets the optional delimiter, OPTIONALLY ENCLOSED BY, as a single quote mark or apostrophe—this is important when you have a comma in a string.

The character file reads a file that follows this format:

```
1,'Indiana','Jones'
2,'Ravenwood','Marion'
3,'Marcus','Brody'
4,'Rene','Belloq'
```

A query like this:

```
SELECT * FROM character;
```

returns the following, which mimics the content of the character.csv external file:

```
CHARACTER_ID FIRST_NAME           LAST_NAME
------------ -------------------- --------------------
           1 Indiana              Jones
           2 Ravenwood            Marion
           3 Marcus               Brody
           4 Rene                 Belloq
```

Sometimes, you won't want to use CSV files because you've received position-specific files. That's the case frequently when the information comes from mainframe exports. You can create a position-specific table with the following syntax:

```
SQL> CREATE TABLE grocery
  2  ( grocery_id   NUMBER
  3  , item_name    VARCHAR2(20)
  4  , item_amount NUMBER(4,2))
  5    ORGANIZATION EXTERNAL
  6    ( TYPE oracle_loader
  7      DEFAULT DIRECTORY upload
  8      ACCESS PARAMETERS
  9      ( RECORDS DELIMITED BY NEWLINE CHARACTERSET US7ASCII
 10        BADFILE     'LOG':'grocery.bad'
 11        DISCARDFILE 'LOG':'grocery.dis'
 12        LOGFILE     'LOG':'grocery.log'
 13        FIELDS
 14        MISSING FIELD VALUES ARE NULL
 15        ( grocery_id   CHAR(3)
 16        , item_name    CHAR(20)
 17        , item_amount CHAR(4)))
 18      LOCATION ('grocery.csv'))
 19  REJECT LIMIT UNLIMITED;
```

When the physical directory, physical file, and virtual directory are configured, a query like the following:

```
SELECT * FROM grocery;
```

returns the following values:

```
GROCERY_ID ITEM_NAME            ITEM_AMOUNT
---------- -------------------- -----------
         1 Apple                       1.49
         2 Orange                         2
```

The major difference between the CSV-enabled table and a positionally organized external table is the source signature on lines 15 through 17. The CHAR data type specifies fixed-length strings, which can be implicitly cast to number data types. When a SELECT statement reads the external source, it casts the values from fixed-length strings to their designated numeric and variable-length string data types.

An alternative position-specific syntax replaces lines 14 through 16 with exact positional references, like this:

```
14          ( grocery_id  POSITION(1:3)
15          , item_name    POSITION(4:23)
16          , item_amount POSITION(24:27)))
```

The casting issue works the same way because POSITION(1:3) expects to find a fixed-length string. The value in the flat file can be cast successfully only when it is a number.

The grocery table reads values from a positionally specific flat file, like this:

```
GROCERY_ID ITEM_NAME            ITEM_AMOUNT
---------- -------------------- -----------
         1 Apple                       1.49
         2 Orange                         2
```

These are the preferred solutions when importing large amounts of data. Many data imports include values that belong in multiple tables. Import sources that include data for multiple tables are called *composite import files*. Most import source files generally ignore or exclude surrogate key values because they'll change in the new database. Importing the data is important, but taking data from an externally managed table into the normalized business model can be tricky. The MERGE statement lets you import data, and, based on some logic, you can determine whether it's new or existing information. The MERGE statement in the Oracle database then lets you insert new information or update rows of existing data. You can find a full example of this implementation in the "MERGE Statement" section of Appendix B in *Oracle Database 12*c *PL/SQL Programming*.

Oracle Data Pump Files

Oracle Data Pump lets you read and write data in an Oracle-proprietary format. Oracle Data Pump is most often used for backup and recovery. You have import files for reading Oracle-proprietary formatted files and export files for saving data in a proprietary format.

The next example requires you to create a new download virtual directory and grant the directory read and write permissions. You would need to connect to the superuser sys account in a non-multitenant database. Alternatively, you would connect as the CDB's superuser `sys` account or the PDB's superuser `sys` account in a multitenant architecture.

You connect to a non-multitenant database with this syntax:

```
sqlplus / as sysdba
```

Or, like this in a PDB:

```
sqlplus sys/password@tns_alias AS sysdba
```

Once connected as the appropriate superuser, you create the `download` virtual directory with this statement:

```
GRANT READ, WRITE ON DIRECTORY download TO importer;
```

After you've created the `download` directory and granted the appropriate privileges, you can reconnect with this syntax:

```
SQL> CONNECT importer/password@tns_alias;
```

The following creates a table that exports data to an Oracle Data Pump–formatted file:

```
SQL> CREATE TABLE item_export
  2  ORGANIZATION EXTERNAL
  3  ( TYPE oracle_datapump
  4    DEFAULT DIRECTORY download
  5    LOCATION ('item_export.dmp')
  6  ) AS
  7  SELECT    item_id
  8  ,         item_barcode
  9  ,         item_type
 10  ,         item_title
 11  ,         item_subtitle
 12  ,         item_rating
 13  ,         item_rating_agency
 14  ,         item_release_date
 15  ,         created_by
 16  ,         creation_date
 17  ,         last_updated_by
 18  ,         last_update_date
 19  FROM    item;
```

The exporting process with externally organized tables has only one very noticeable problem—it throws a nasty error when the file already exists, like so:

```
CREATE TABLE item_export
*
ERROR at line 1:
ORA-29913: error IN executing ODCIEXTTABLEOPEN callout
ORA-29400: data cartridge error
KUP-11012: file item_export.dmp IN C:\data\download already EXISTS
```

Our advice on this type of process is that you create an operating system script, a Java application, or a web solution that checks for the existence of the file before inserting data into the `item_export` table. Alternatively, you can create a set of utilities in Java libraries. You deploy the libraries inside the database and wrap them with PL/SQL function definitions.

These Java libraries can clean up the file system for you, and you have the ability to call them before you query the table. You can check Chapter 4 for details on writing and deploying Java I/O libraries on the Oracle database.

Cleanup on Oracle Data Pump files should be performed after you remove the external table. Ideally, cleanup of Oracle Data Pump files should be performed after you remove the external table, although you do have flexibility to choose when to delete the file.

NOTE
Java libraries work only in the Standard or Enterprise Editions of Oracle Database 12c.

Reversing the process and importing from the external file source isn't complex. There are a few modifications to the CREATE TABLE statement. Here's a sample:

```
SQL> CREATE TABLE item_import
  2  ( item_id             NUMBER
  3  , item_barcode        VARCHAR2(20)
  4  , item_type           NUMBER
  5  , item_title          VARCHAR2(60)
  6  , item_subtitle       VARCHAR2(60)
  7  , item_rating         VARCHAR2(8)
  8  , item_rating_agency  VARCHAR2(4)
  9  , item_release_date   DATE
 10  , created_by          NUMBER
 11  , creation_date       DATE
 12  , last_updated_by     NUMBER
 13  , last_update_date    DATE)
 14  ORGANIZATION EXTERNAL
 15  ( TYPE oracle_datapump
 16    DEFAULT DIRECTORY download
 17    LOCATION ('item_export.dmp'));
```

Notice that the table definition mirrors the source file. This means you must know the source before you can define the external table CREATE TABLE statement.

Importing a Framework's External Table

This section creates a framework for working with external files, which is similar to the table we used to demonstrate Oracle Data Pump. The framework shows you how to use PL/SQL and Java to manage delivery and upload of the raw data, store the raw source and log files, and delete the raw source and log files from the physical directory.

This section revisits some of the content previously discussed, but does so to present the complete syntax for the framework. It works with a sample `item_import` table and the contents of the small sample file.

This section relies on your completing the following steps from Chapter 4:

- The `sys` user granting the `SELECT` privilege on `DBA_DIRECTORIES` to the `system` user
- The `system` user creating the `get_directory_path` function in the `system` schema
- The `system` user granting the `EXECUTE` privilege to the `import` user
- The `import` user creating a `get_directory_path` synonym to the `system` `.get_directory_path` function

Sometimes, you may have created tables, functions, procedures, or packages from prior testing. It's important to note that you should check before trying to create objects and delete old copies. For example, the following drops a table without raising an error when the table isn't already there:

```
SQL> BEGIN
  2    FOR i IN (SELECT    object_name
  3              FROM      user_objects
  4              WHERE     object_name = 'ITEM_IMPORT') LOOP
  5      EXECUTE IMMEDIATE 'DROP TABLE '||i.object_name||' '
  6                                      ||'CASCADE CONSTRAINTS';
  7    END LOOP;
  8  END;
  9  /
```

You have many more ways of writing a conditional `DROP TABLE` statement, but this is the simplest with the fewest moving parts. Just remember that the name of the table on line 4 is generally always uppercase letters unless you replace it by using double quotes when you created a case sensitive name for the table, function, procedure, or package.

Having ensured that the configuration of the directory and privileges were complete and that the `item_import` table doesn't exist, the following creates the `item_import` table:

```
SQL> CREATE TABLE item_import
  2  ( asin_number         VARCHAR2(10)
  3  , item_type           VARCHAR2(15)
  4  , item_title          VARCHAR2(60)
  5  , item_subtitle       VARCHAR2(60)
  6  , item_rating         VARCHAR2(8)
  7  , item_rating_agency  VARCHAR2(4)
  8  , item_release_date   DATE)
  9    ORGANIZATION EXTERNAL
 10    ( TYPE oracle_loader
 11      DEFAULT DIRECTORY UPLOAD
 12      ACCESS PARAMETERS
 13    ( RECORDS DELIMITED BY NEWLINE CHARACTERSET US7ASCII
 14      BADFILE    'LOG':'item_import.bad'
 15      DISCARDFILE 'LOG':'item_import.dis'
```

```
16      LOGFILE     'LOG':'item_import.log'
17      FIELDS TERMINATED BY ','
18      OPTIONALLY ENCLOSED BY "'"
19      MISSING FIELD VALUES ARE NULL )
20    LOCATION ('item_import.csv'))
21  PARALLEL
22  REJECT LIMIT UNLIMITED;
```

Line 10 sets the external type as read-only because it's using Oracle SQL*Loader. Line 11 sets the data file's virtual directory, which you created earlier in this chapter. Lines 14 through 16 set the logging virtual directory. Line 21 designates that the file is read through concurrent SQL*Loader threads by providing the PARALLEL clause. If you didn't provide the PARALLEL clause, Oracle SQL*Loader returns the following error message:

```
KUP-05004:   Warning: Intra source concurrency disabled because
             parallel select was not requested.
```

The data set uses ellipsis for text to prevent wrapping on the page. You can find the data file on this book's web page on the McGraw-Hill Professional website. The item_import.csv file is

```
'B000W74EQC','DVD','Harry ... Stone',,'PG','MPAA','11-DEC-2007'
'B000W746GK','DVD','Harry ... Secrets',,'PG','MPAA','11-DEC-2007'
'B000W796OM','DVD','Harry ... Azkaban',,'PG','MPAA','11-DEC-2007'
'B000E6EK2Y','DVD','Harry ... Fire',,'PG-13','MPAA','07-MAR-2006'
'B000W7F5SS','DVD','Harry ... Phoenix',,'PG-13','MPAA','11-DEC-2007'
'B002PMV9FG','DVD','Harry ... Prince',,'PG','MPAA','08-DEC-2009'
'B001UV4XHY','DVD','Harry ... Part 1',,'PG-13','MPAA','15-APR-2011'
'B001UV4XIS','DVD','Harry ... Part 2',,'PG-13','MPAA','11-NOV-2011'
```

Whether you're reading or testing this along the way is impossible for us to know as authors, but we're guessing that you may test it. So, at this point you should see if you can read the data from the external file. The following query requires the SQL*Plus formatting commands when you run it from within the SQL*Plus command-line interface (CLI). Simply ignore the SQL*Plus formatting when running from Oracle SQL Developer.

```
SQL> SET PAGESIZE 99
SQL> COLUMN asin_number        FORMAT A11 HEADING "ASIN #"
SQL> COLUMN item_title         FORMAT A46 HEADING "ITEM TITLE"
SQL> COLUMN item_rating        FORMAT A6  HEADING "RATING"
SQL> COLUMN item_release_date  FORMAT A11 HEADING "RELEASE|DATE"
SQL> SELECT    asin_number
  2 ,          item_title
  3 ,          item_rating
  4 ,          TO_CHAR(item_release_date
  5                 ,'DD-MON-YYYY') AS item_release_date
  6 FROM       item_import;
```

The query should return the sample eight rows of data. The next section describes how you can leverage the Oracle Database 12c data catalog to empower your Java NIO libraries to discover the physical directory.

Leveraging the Data Catalog

Oracle Database 12c provides you with a robust architecture for developing server-side or internal Java programming components. The Oracle database also takes many security precautions. One of these security precautions prevents a stored program unit from querying the cdb_, all_, and dba_directories administrative views.

This means that while the privileged system user can query the cdb_, all_, and dba_directories administrative views, it can't query the same view inside a function or procedure. Any attempt to deploy such a function in the system schema would raise an ORA-00942 error. While that error signals that the table or view does not exist, it can also mean the database user querying the view doesn't have SELECT privileges on the view. The latter is the reason the system can't deploy a function or procedure querying the cdb_, all_, and dba_directories administrative view.

As a workaround, you need to create a get_directory_path function in the system schema that reads data from the cdb_, all_, and dba_directories administrative view. That means you need the sys user (who owns the administrative view) to grant the SELECT privilege to the system user. Then, you use the Java ListVirtualDirectory library and PL/SQL list_files ADT (Attribute Data Type) table function from Chapter 4 to read the external file system.

The syntax to grant the SELECT privilege to the system user is

```
GRANT SELECT ON sys.dba_directories TO system;
```

This grant makes the cdb_, all_, and dba_directories administrative views available to the system schema. After making this grant, you can create the following get_directory_path function in the system user's schema:

```
SQL> CREATE OR REPLACE FUNCTION get_directory_path
  2  ( virtual_directory IN VARCHAR2 )
  3  RETURN VARCHAR2 IS
  4
  5    /* Define RETURN variable. */
  6    directory_path VARCHAR2(256) := '';
  7
  8    /* Define dynamic cursor. */
  9    CURSOR get_directory (virtual_directory VARCHAR2) IS
 10      SELECT   directory_path
 11      FROM     sys.dba_directories
 12      WHERE    directory_name = UPPER(virtual_directory);
 13
 14    /* Define a LOCAL exception FOR name violation. */
 15    directory_name EXCEPTION;
 16    PRAGMA EXCEPTION_INIT(directory_name,-22284);
 17  BEGIN
 18    /* Open the cursor and fetch a row. */
 19    OPEN  get_directory (virtual_directory);
 20    FETCH get_directory INTO directory_path;
 21    CLOSE get_directory;
 22
 23    /* RETURN file name. */
 24    RETURN directory_path;
```

```
25  EXCEPTION
26    WHEN directory_name THEN
27      RETURN NULL;
28  END get_directory_path;
29  /
```

Line 2 takes a virtual directory name, line 12 makes sure the virtual directory input is case insensitive, and line 24 returns the physical file path from the dba_directories administrative view. Unlike the fopen procedure in the utl_file package, most programs simply have no way of discovering which physical directory maps to a virtual directory. While the utl_file package is wrapped, you (and we) may wonder if it doesn't perform this logic in a private function.

After creating the get_directory_path function, you grant the EXECUTE privilege to the importer schema. That means you should connect as the system user. Then, you grant the EXECUTE privilege on the get_directory function to the importer user:

```
SQL> GRANT EXECUTE ON get_directory_path TO importer;
```

The next command requires that you connect as the importer user. You create a synonym to simplify all calls to the get_directory_path function in the system schema.

```
SQL> CREATE SYNONYM get_directory_path FOR system.get_directory_path;
```

Now the importer user can submit the upload virtual directory name and return the physical file. The following query tests whether it works:

```
SQL> COLUMN upload  FORMAT A30  HEADING "Upload Directory"
SQL> COLUMN log     FORMAT A30  HEADING "Log Directory"
SQL> SELECT get_directory_path('upload') AS upload
  2  ,      get_directory_path('log') AS log
  3  FROM   dual;
```

It returns the following result:

```
Upload Directory                Log Directory
------------------------------  ------------------------------
C:\data\upload                  C:\data\log
```

Having leveraged the data catalog, you can now make a call to the list_files ADT table function from Chapter 4, like this:

```
SELECT  column_value AS "File Names"
FROM    TABLE(list_files(get_directory_path('UPLOAD')));
```

You need to set up directory permissions correctly, or you may encounter an ORA-29913 or ORA-29532 error. If you run into one of these errors, it means you should revisit how you granted permissions on the virtual directory or how you granted Java privileges. Chapter 4 covers how you should grant Java privileges.

At this point, you have the portion of the framework to secure the list of potential files found in the physical directory pointed to by an Oracle virtual directory. What you don't have is the ability to associate which file in the directory belongs to a specific external table. That's what you learn how to do in the next section.

Wrapping Access to External Tables

This section shows you how to use the function you built in the last section, which relies on the Java `ListVirtualDirectory` library and PL/SQL `list_files` ADT table function you built in Chapter 4. As a group they let you read the contents of a directory pointed to by an Oracle virtual directory.

Every schema has access to the `user_external_tables` and `user_external_locations` administrative views. These two views together with the `list_files` and `get_directory_path` functions let you use an external table name to find the related physical file. The physical file is the location value in the `CREATE TABLE` statement.

The following query uses the two administrative views coupled with the results from the `list_files` and `get_directory_path` functions to return a list of external table and physical file names. The two SQL*Plus commands let you format the query results, and they're not required unless you're running inside the SQL*Plus CLI.

```
SQL> COLUMN table_name FORMAT A30
SQL> COLUMN file_name  FORMAT A30
SQL> SELECT   xt.table_name
  2  ,        xt.file_name
  3  FROM          (SELECT   uxt.table_name
  4                 ,         ixt.column_value AS file_name
  5                 FROM      user_external_tables uxt CROSS JOIN
  6                 TABLE(
  7                   list_files(
  8                     get_directory_path(
  9                       uxt.default_directory_name))) ixt) xt
 10  JOIN          user_external_locations xl
 11  ON   xt.table_name = xl.table_name
 12  AND          xt.file_name = xl.location;
```

Lines 6 through 9 contain a trick that creates a runtime (or common table expression) view of all the physical files found in the directory pointed to by the virtual directory. That's why you leveraged the data catalog earlier.

Unfortunately, a blanket result set doesn't let you have what you need. You need to submit a specific external table name and return an indicator of whether the external file exists. This requires a local function, like the following `external_file_found` function:

```
SQL> CREATE OR REPLACE FUNCTION external_file_found
  2  ( table_in VARCHAR2 ) RETURN NUMBER IS
  3    -- Define a default return value.
  4    retval NUMBER := 0;
  5
  6    -- Declare a cursor to find external tables.
  7    CURSOR c (cv_table VARCHAR2) IS
  8      SELECT   xt.table_name
  9      ,        xt.file_name
 10      FROM     (SELECT   uxt.table_name
 11               ,          ixt.column_value AS file_name
 12               FROM      user_external_tables uxt CROSS JOIN
 13               TABLE(
```

```
14                      list_files(
15                        get_directory_path(
16                          uxt.default_directory_name))) ixt) xt
17       JOIN      user_external_locations xl
18       ON        xt.table_name = xl.table_name
19       AND       xt.file_name = xl.location
20       AND       xt.table_name = UPPER(cv_table);
21   BEGIN
22     FOR i IN c(table_in) LOOP
23       retval := 1;
24     END LOOP;
25     RETURN retval;
26   END;
27   /
```

The FOR loop on lines 22 through 24 opens and fetches results only when one or more physical files are found. The loop implicitly exits after opening when no physical records are found, which means the retval variable can only be set to 1 when files are found. So, the external_file_found function takes an external table name and returns a 1 when it finds the external file exists and returns a 0 when it doesn't. This means that if you wrap an external table in a view with a WHERE clause like this:

```
WHERE     external_file_found('ITEM_IMPORT_EXT_TABLE') = 1;
```

the view only returns a value when the external file exists, and you avoid raising the following error when the file is missing or the virtual directory fails to resolve for any reason:

```
SELECT * FROM item_import
*
ERROR at line 1:
ORA-29913: error IN executing ODCIEXTTABLEOPEN callout
ORA-29400: DATA cartridge error
KUP-04040: file item_import.csv IN UPLOAD_FILES NOT found
```

The best way to wrap an external table is to use an object table function, which you can find fully explained in Chapter 8 of *Oracle Database 12c PL/SQL Programming*. You need two elements before you can write an object table function. One is an object type, which acts like a record data structure, and the other is a collection of the object type.

You would create the following item_import_object object type that mirrors the table structure of the external table:

```
SQL> CREATE OR REPLACE TYPE item_import_object IS OBJECT
  2  ( asin_number           VARCHAR2(10)
  3  , item_type             VARCHAR2(15)
  4  , item_title            VARCHAR2(60)
  5  , item_subtitle         VARCHAR2(60)
  6  , item_rating           VARCHAR2(8)
  7  , item_rating_agency    VARCHAR2(4)
  8  , item_release_date     DATE);
  /
```

After creating the `item_import_object` object type, you create a collection of the object type with the following:

```
SQL> CREATE OR REPLACE
  2    TYPE item_import_object_table IS TABLE OF item_import_object;
  3  /
```

Before you create the object table function, you need to determine if a query should trigger an action. While you can't write a trigger on a `SELECT` statement, you can write an object table function that mimics a trigger by calling autonomous program units from within the object table function.

In this case, you want an object table function that returns a result set or a *no rows found* message. Although, you can have more data returned by writing the object table function as an autonomous function. An autonomous object table function can take action based on whether or not an external file is found, which we'll examine in the last section of this chapter. Oracle PL/SQL doesn't support a natural object-oriented programming language (OOPL) adapter pattern. That means you need to write an object table function for each external table.

Here's an example of an object table function that meets your needs with the `item_import` table:

```
SQL> CREATE OR REPLACE FUNCTION external_file_contents
  2    RETURN item_import_object_table IS
  3    -- Define a local counter.
  4    lv_counter NUMBER := 1;
  5    -- Construct an empty collection.
  6    lv_item_import_table ITEM_IMPORT_OBJECT_TABLE :=
  7      item_import_object_table();
  8    -- Declare a cursor to find external tables.
  9    CURSOR c IS
 10      SELECT  *
 11      FROM    item_import
 12      WHERE   external_file_found('ITEM_IMPORT') = 1;
 13  BEGIN
 14    FOR i IN c LOOP
 15      lv_item_import_table.EXTEND;
 16      lv_item_import_table(lv_counter) :=
 17        item_import_object(i.asin_number
 18                          ,i.item_type
 19                          ,i.item_title
 20                          ,i.item_subtitle
 21                          ,i.item_rating
 22                          ,i.item_rating_agency
 23                          ,i.item_release_date);
 24      lv_counter := lv_counter + 1;
 25    END LOOP;
 26
 27    -- This is where you can place autonomous function calls:
 28    RETURN lv_item_import_table;
 29  END;
 30  /
```

Between the assignment to the collection and the return statement of the function, you have the ability to call any number of autonomous functions on line 27. Any schema-level function can call autonomous functions that read and write tables with DML statements, such as the INSERT, UPDATE, and DELETE statements. You can also call schema-level functions that wrap Java libraries that delete external files.

You can confirm that the steps work by running the following query, with or without the SQL*Plus formatting:

```
SQL> SET PAGESIZE 99
SQL> COLUMN asin_number        FORMAT A11 HEADING "ASIN #"
SQL> COLUMN item_title         FORMAT A46 HEADING "ITEM TITLE"
SQL> COLUMN item_rating        FORMAT A6  HEADING "RATING"
SQL> COLUMN item_release_date  FORMAT A11 HEADING "RELEASE|DATE"
SQL> SELECT    asin_number
  2  ,         item_title
  3  ,         item_rating
  4  ,         TO_CHAR(item_release_date,'DD-MON-YYYY') AS release_date
  5  FROM      TABLE(external_file_contents('ITEM_IMPORT'));
```

This query returns the original eight rows from the source file. The source file is introduced in the beginning of the earlier "Importing a Framework's External Tables" section.

Cleaning Up the External Table Files

This section examines how you can capture the data source and log files from an external table. The first step requires that you set up tables in which you can store the contents of the data and log files. While you need one table for the data, you need three others for the log, discard, and bad files.

You create import_master, import_data, import_log, import_discard, and import_bad tables for this model. Only the import_master table and the import_data table are shown in the book, but you can download the script that creates the import_log, import_discard, and import_bad log tables from the website.

```
SQL> CREATE TABLE import_master
  2  ( import_master_id  NUMBER CONSTRAINT pk_import_master PRIMARY KEY
  3  , import_table      VARCHAR2(30));
SQL> CREATE SEQUENCE import_master_s;
SQL> CREATE TABLE import_data
  2  ( import_data_id    NUMBER CONSTRAINT pk_import_data PRIMARY KEY
  3  , import_master_id  NUMBER
  4  , import_data       CLOB
  5  , CONSTRAINT fk_import_data FOREIGN KEY (import_data_id)
  6    REFERENCES import_master (import_master_id))
  7  LOB (import_data) STORE AS BASICFILE item_import_clob
  8  (TABLESPACE users ENABLE STORAGE IN ROW CHUNK 32768
  9  PCTVERSION 10 NOCACHE LOGGING
 10  STORAGE (INITIAL 1048576
 11          NEXT      1048576
 12          MINEXTENTS 1
 13          MAXEXTENTS 2147483645));
SQL> CREATE SEQUENCE import_data_s;
```

All of these tables store the data source or log contents in a single CLOB column. The named sequences follow a pattern of table name plus an _s for a sequence. As you'll see later in this chapter, the cleanup_external_files function that you adopted uses this pattern to support how you clean up physical log files.

These logging tables set the targets for uploading the source and log files. You should note that the table name is also the column name for the CLOB column. This approach becomes convenient when supporting a Native Dynamic SQL (NDS) statement in a single autonomous function. The load_clob_from_file function supports reading the external source and log files and writing them into their respective tables.

There is a *deadlock possibility* with this type of architecture. Because of that possibility, the program commits the base row in the import_master table before it attempts to insert data into any of the dependent tables.

You already set the access privileges for the dbms_lob package when you granted the user privileges to read and write to the upload and log virtual directories. While you only need to grant read privileges to the virtual directories for the load_clob_from_file function, the subsequent cleanup_external_files function will require both read and write permissions. It uses techniques similar to those discussed in Chapter 10 of *Oracle Database 12c PL/SQL Programming*.

```
SQL> CREATE OR REPLACE FUNCTION load_clob_from_file
  2  ( pv_src_file_name   IN VARCHAR2
  3  , pv_virtual_dir     IN VARCHAR2
  4  , pv_table_name      IN VARCHAR2
  5  , pv_column_name     IN VARCHAR2
  6  , pv_foreign_key     IN NUMBER ) RETURN NUMBER IS
  7
  8    -- Declare placeholder for sequence generated primary key.
  9    lv_primary_key  NUMBER;
 10
 11    -- Declare default return value.
 12    lv_retval  NUMBER := 0;
 13
 14    -- Declare local DBMS_LOB.LOADCLOBFROMFILE variables.
 15    des_clob    CLOB;
 16    src_clob    BFILE := BFILENAME(pv_virtual_dir,pv_src_file_name);
 17    des_offset  NUMBER := 1;
 18    src_offset  NUMBER := 1;
 19    ctx_lang    NUMBER := dbms_lob.default_lang_ctx;
 20    warning     NUMBER;
 21
 22    -- Declare pre-reading size.
 23    src_clob_size  NUMBER;
 24
 25    -- Declare variables for handling NDS sequence value.
 26    lv_sequence          VARCHAR2(30);
 27    lv_sequence_output   NUMBER;
 28    lv_sequence_tagline  VARCHAR2(10) := '_s.nextval';
 29
 30    -- Define local NDS statement variable.
```

```
31   stmt       VARCHAR2(2000);
32
33   -- Declare the function as an autonomous transaction.
34   PRAGMA AUTONOMOUS_TRANSACTION;
35
36 BEGIN
37
38   -- Open file only when found.
39   IF          dbms_lob.fileexists(src_clob) = 1
40   AND NOT dbms_lob.isopen(src_clob) = 1 THEN
41     src_clob_size := dbms_lob.getlength(src_clob);
42     dbms_lob.OPEN(src_clob,dbms_lob.lob_readonly);
43   END IF;
44
45   -- Concatenate the sequence name with the tagline.
46   lv_sequence := pv_table_name || lv_sequence_tagline;
47
48   -- Assign the sequence through an anonymous block.
49   stmt := 'BEGIN '
50       || ' :output := '||lv_sequence||';'
51       || 'END;';
52
53   -- Run the statement to extract a sequence value through NDS.
54   EXECUTE IMMEDIATE stmt USING IN OUT lv_sequence_output;
55
56   --  Create a dynamic statement for all source and log files.
57   -- ----------------------------------------------------------------
58   --  NOTE: This statement requires that the row holding the primary
59   --        key has been committed because otherwise it raises the
60   --        following error because it can't verify the integrity of
61   --        the foreign key constraint.
62   -- ----------------------------------------------------------------
63   --        DECLARE
64   --        *
65   --        ERROR at line 1:
66   --        ORA-00060: deadlock detected while waiting for resource
67   --        ORA-06512: at "IMPORT.LOAD_CLOB_FROM_FILE", line 50
68   --        ORA-06512: at line 20
69   -- ----------------------------------------------------------------
70   stmt := 'INSERT INTO '||pv_table_name||' '||CHR(10)||
71           'VALUES '||CHR(10)||
72           '('||lv_sequence_output||CHR(10)||
73           ','||pv_foreign_key||CHR(10)||
74           ', empty_clob())'||CHR(10)||
75           'RETURNING '||pv_column_name||' INTO :locator';
76
77   -- Run dynamic statement.
78   EXECUTE IMMEDIATE stmt USING OUT des_clob;
79
80   -- Read and write file to CLOB, close source file and commit.
81   dbms_lob.loadclobfromfile( dest_lob       => des_clob
```

```
82                                  , src_bfile     => src_clob
83                                  , amount        => dbms_lob.getlength(src_clob)
84                                  , dest_offset   => des_offset
85                                  , src_offset    => src_offset
86                                  , bfile_csid    => dbms_lob.default_csid
87                                  , lang_context  => ctx_lang
88                                  , warning       => warning );
89
90      -- Close open source file.
91      dbms_lob.close(src_clob);
92
93      -- Commit write and conditionally acknowledge it.
94      IF src_clob_size = dbms_lob.getlength(des_clob) THEN
95        COMMIT;
96        lv_retval := 1;
97      ELSE
98        RAISE dbms_lob.operation_failed;
99      END IF;
100
101     RETURN lv_retval;
102   END load_clob_from_file;
103   /
```

The `load_clob_from_file` function uses NDS, which is covered in Chapter 13 of *Oracle Database 12c PL/SQL Programming*. The NDS statements enable the `load_clob_from_file` function to load a CLOB data type to any type of table that conforms to the design of the logging tables.

The next step is to write a master function that writes the master row and calls the `load_clob_from_file` function for the source file and each of the log files. That's what the following `cleanup_external_files` function provides:

```
SQL> CREATE OR REPLACE FUNCTION cleanup_external_files
  2  ( table_in           VARCHAR2
  3  , data_directory_in  VARCHAR2
  4  , log_directory_in   VARCHAR2 ) RETURN NUMBER IS
  5
  6    -- Declare a local Attribute Data Type (ADT).
  7    TYPE list IS TABLE OF VARCHAR2(3);
  8
  9    -- Declare a collection.
 10    lv_extension LIST := list('csv','log','bad','dis');
 11
 12    -- Define a default return value.
 13    retval NUMBER := 0;
 14
 15    -- Declare base target table name.
 16    lv_target_table  VARCHAR2(30)  := 'IMPORT';
 17    lv_foreign_key   NUMBER;
 18
 19    -- Declare a cursor to find external tables.
 20    CURSOR check_source (cv_table_name VARCHAR2) IS
```

```
21        SELECT    xt.file_name
22        ,         xt.path_name
23        FROM      (SELECT   uxt.table_name
24                  ,                get_directory_path(
25                                     uxt.default_directory_name) AS path_name
26                  ,                ixt.column_value AS file_name
27                  FROM       user_external_tables uxt CROSS JOIN
28                  TABLE(
29                    list_files(
30                      get_directory_path(
31                        uxt.default_directory_name))) ixt) xt
32        JOIN      user_external_locations xl
33        ON        xt.table_name = xl.table_name
34        AND       xt.file_name = xl.location
35        AND xt.table_name = UPPER(cv_table_name);
36
37     -- Declare a cursor to find files and compare them.
38     CURSOR check_logs ( cv_file_name VARCHAR2
39                       , cv_dir_name  VARCHAR2 ) IS
40        SELECT    get_directory_path(cv_dir_name) AS path_name
41        ,         list.column_value AS file_name
42        FROM      TABLE(
43                    list_files(
44                      get_directory_path(cv_dir_name))) list
45        JOIN      (SELECT cv_file_name AS file_name FROM dual) filter
46        ON        list.column_value = filter.file_name;
47
48     -- Declare the function as autonomous.
49     PRAGMA AUTONOMOUS_TRANSACTION;
50
51  BEGIN
52
53     -- Master loop to check for source and log files.
54     FOR i IN check_source (table_in) LOOP
55
56       -- Assign next sequence value to local variable.
57       lv_foreign_key := import_master_s.NEXTVAL;
58
59       -- Write the master record and commit it for autonomous threads.
60       INSERT INTO import_master
61       VALUES (lv_foreign_key,'ITEM_IMPORT');
62       COMMIT;
63
64       -- Process all file extensions.
65       FOR j IN 1..lv_extension.COUNT LOOP
66
67         -- The source data file based on the file extension.
68         IF lv_extension(j) = 'csv' THEN
69
70           --  Load the source data file.
71           -- -------------------------------------------------------
```

```
72        --  The RETVAL holds success or failure, this approach
73        --  suppresses an error when the file can't be loaded.
74        --  It should only occur when there's no space available
75        --  in the target table.
76        retval := load_clob_from_file(i.file_name
77                                      ,data_directory_in
78                                      ,lv_target_table||'_DATA'
79                                      ,lv_target_table||'_DATA'
80                                      ,lv_foreign_key);
81
82        -- Increment the foreign key value.
83        lv_foreign_key := lv_foreign_key + 1;
84
85        -- Delete the file; the backslash needs to replaced by
86        -- a forward slash when working in Linux or Unix.
87        delete_file(i.path_name||'\'||i.file_name);
88      ELSE
89
90        -- Verify the log file exists before trying to load it.
91        FOR k IN check_logs ( LOWER(table_in)||'.'||lv_extension(j)
92                              , log_directory_in) LOOP
93
94          --  Load the log, bad, or dis(card) file.
95          -- ----------------------------------------------------
96          --  The RETVAL holds success or failure value.
97          retval :=
98            load_clob_from_file(LOWER(table_in)||'.'||lv_extension(j)
99                                ,log_directory_in
100                               ,lv_target_table||'_'||lv_extension(j)
101                               ,lv_target_table||'_'||lv_extension(j)
102                               ,lv_foreign_key);
103
104         -- Delete the file; the backslash needs to be replaced by
105         -- a forward slash when working in Linux or Unix.
106         delete_file(k.path_name||'\'||k.file_name);
107        END LOOP;
108      END IF;
109    END LOOP;
110    retval := 1;
111  END LOOP;
112  RETURN retval;
113 END;
114 /
```

Lines 87 and 106 call the `delete_file` procedure, which is a PL/SQL wrapper that uses the `DeleteFile` Java library. The lines glue a backslash between the file path and name, which must be changed to a forward slash in a Linux or Unix environment.

After you put this last script in place, you have a framework to manage the import of files through external tables.

Supporting Scripts

The following programs are available on the McGraw-Hill Professional website to support this chapter:

- The `CreateExportFramework.sql` program is a SQL script with both SQL and PL/SQL statements.

- The `CreateVirtualDirectories.sql` script creates the upload and log virtual directories.

- The `GrantPrivileges.sql` program lets you grant Java privileges that are necessary for reading, writing, and deleting external files. You run this script as the `sys` user by using the `sysdba` role.

- The `MapDirectories.sql` program lets you leverage the data catalog and needs to be run as the `sys` user by using the `sysdba` role.

Summary

You should now have an understanding of how to implement a framework for external files. With these skills, you can build robust import solutions.

CHAPTER

6

High-Speed Data Transfer

Purpose

The purpose of this chapter is to introduce you to various methods of high-speed data transfer. It is not intended to sway your decision between products. There are many successful vendors with products that can help you move data at or near real-time speeds. Most of these tools are used in data warehousing. Their claim to fame is that they offload processing burdens so that your database servers are freed up to give attention to their applications and users. Two such products that have been popular in the past are Oracle Streams and Oracle Change Data Capture (CDC); however, Oracle announced that it is deprecating both products in favor of its GoldenGate offerings.

Now, it is up to companies to license other commercial products, write their own scripts, or purchase GoldenGate. No matter what the outcome of your decision-making processes, you will be making changes. We hope that this chapter will provide you with a deeper knowledge of the variety of products and their abilities.

Advantages

High-speed data transfer has many advantages. Some are critical to the business. For example, successful data warehouses provide executives with information that helps them to make key decisions. If the information is stale or of low quality, the executives may make costly mistakes that have the potential of ruining the company's ability to make money and stay solvent. On the other hand, if the information is timely, relevant, and of good quality, executives are able to make good decisions that potentially yield strong earnings and win sales over their competitors.

The problem is that data synchronization either takes a long time or chews up massive amounts of CPU, I/O, and network resources (see Figure 6-1). If data warehouses cannot deliver accurate data in a timely manner, they will undoubtedly fail. We have spent many years working on successful data warehouses. Because of our success, we have often been asked to use our data-moving skills to synchronize data between disparate online transaction processing (OLTP) systems as well as data warehouses.

Most of our work has utilized some kind of extract, transform, and load (ETL) tool. There are many such tools available, and they all have a similar look and feel. A very short list of popular products includes

- Data Integrator (Oracle)
- Data Services (SAP)
- SQL Service Integration Services (SSIS; Microsoft)
- InfoSphere (IBM)
- Data Integration Studio (SAS)
- PowerCenter (Informatica)
- Pentaho (open source)

With such tools, we've been able to extract data from source databases, transform it so that it is of higher quality and easier to query, and load it into target systems that serve as warehouses or additional transactional systems. The order of the load and transform functions are interchangeable and varied depending on business requirements. In cases where we've had enough disk space in

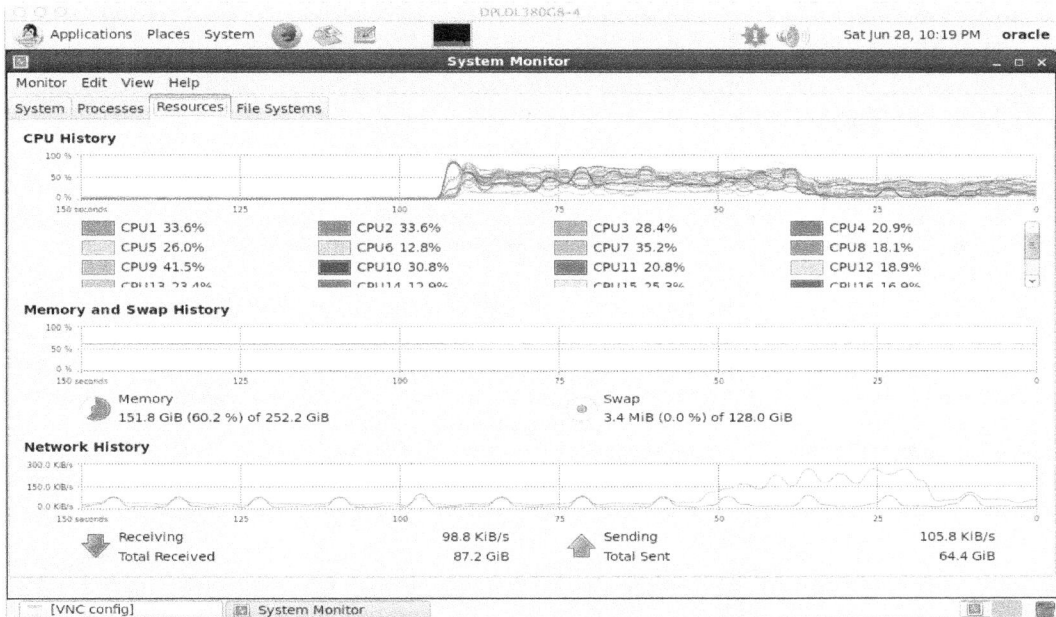

FIGURE 6-1. *Massive CPU load*

the target, oftentimes, it has been cheaper on resources to simply make a copy of source systems in target databases and then transform the data as needed, versus in-flight transformations.

Sometimes, we've employed technologies like SQL*Loader, expdp, and impdp to perform data copies between systems. Other times, those methods were too slow or did not allow us to order the data for improved query speed during our transformations. What's more, in systems that employed staging schemas, we've faced lengthy downtime of live production tables when we've had to move staged tables to production.

To solve this quandary, we've created custom programs that move staged data into production tables as fast as the system can process the data without negatively affecting user queries. Three tables are necessary in these programs: a live table, which has to be online 99.999 percent of the time, a new table that can be loaded offline, and a backup table in case we need to roll back our changes. Once all of the data is loaded, our custom programs check the data for consistency and assign all the necessary rights needed to ensure that users retain their access. The last thing that our programs do is rename the online and offline tables so that new queries point to the newly synchronized table. The process is ingenious. We have used it over and over again. What's more, this method allows us to compress, compact, and reorganize data without noticeable downtime. In some cases, our actions have reduced hour-long queries into seconds because the data is contiguous, compressed, and organized well.

Oracle's GoldenGate product also has the ability to move data at extreme rates. This product has an advantage over custom scripts in that it is able to mine online database log files and move the data before it is committed to disk on OLTP systems. However, target systems receive only a copy of production because transformations are not as flexible as custom scripts. Custom scripts are not for the faint of heart. They require a deep understanding of Oracle internals. In the end, it may be easier to purchase a commercial product like GoldenGate, because vendors have already figured out the complexities associated with extremely fast data movers.

Disadvantages

Given enough money to spend on resources, it is possible to move data so quickly that end users do not realize that they are querying separate systems. But there's the rub: real-time synchronization costs a *lot of money*! It would be better for you to communicate clearly to management about the resources required for such a feat and to determine if and why business users need real-time synchronization.

A few years ago, we were involved in the development of a product that synchronized bank transactions with our own databases. Our business analyst *insisted* that all tables had to be queried in real time and that no materialization was possible. Upon further investigation, it was discovered that bank transaction logs only came once per week, except for a few banks that sent their data once per day. The analyst had heard about real-time data synchronization and automatically added it to the project before asking the business what it needed. When the business heard that it could have real-time synchronization, it hopped on board and wanted it done; however, this ability neither benefited the client nor could be delivered adequately because external banks could/did not deliver data at the same rate of speed.

As a result of our investigation, we presented a plan to synchronize data once per day, after the more active banks sent their records. We also created views that materialized long-running queries, greatly reducing the overhead produced by many concurrent queries. The end result gave users a better experience and synchronized data at the right time. Many of our business managers and engineers switched their vernacular from "real time" to "right time." The business received just the right amount of acceleration and spent much less money.

One disadvantage to running non-commercial scripts is that they can quickly become overwhelming, eclipsing the hard cost you might spend on licenses. Your company would do well to follow a process that first reuses technology that you have, then buys prebuilt programs, and finally builds custom programs where needed. If that paradigm is inverted, you will find that your company must dedicate entire teams of people to the development and maintenance of such programs.

Overview

This chapter covers the following topics:

- Importing and exporting with `impdp` and `expdp`
- Importing and exporting with `dbms_datapump`
- SQL*Loader
- Custom data-moving scripts

Database professionals should already be familiar with importing, exporting, and using SQL*Loader. We covered external tables in the previous chapter, so we will not be discussing that topic here. Our data-moving scripts are a greatly simplified version of what we use in our work, but we hope you will glean enough know-how from them to help you in your endeavors.

Before we get started, we need to step you through the creation of some very large tables. We do so out of a desire to simulate real-life data-moving scenarios. We were lucky enough to have Fusion-io set up a nice lab for us. Their ION storage appliances were so fast that we were forced to increase the size of our sample data set, populating some tables with billions of rows in order to get a test to run long enough for adequate stats collection.

Our intention is not to exclusively showcase Fusion-io. We have a great deal of respect for all storage vendors; however, we are very impressed with Fusion-io products, and they were immediately willing to give us lab space to prove our theories. In fact, other storage vendors have expressed their interest in our advanced techniques. Over the next year, we will be creating several flash-books that will showcase each vendor, including detailed setup, testing, and teardown, so you can test the results for yourself.

We are using a simple star-schema approach to the data. You can download our `video_store` schema creation scripts to create the base schema; however, you will need to apply the `video_store_star.sql` file to obtain the following tables (see Figure 6-2). By far, the largest table in our `video_store` star is the `rental_item_fact`. It holds mocked-up sales data for a

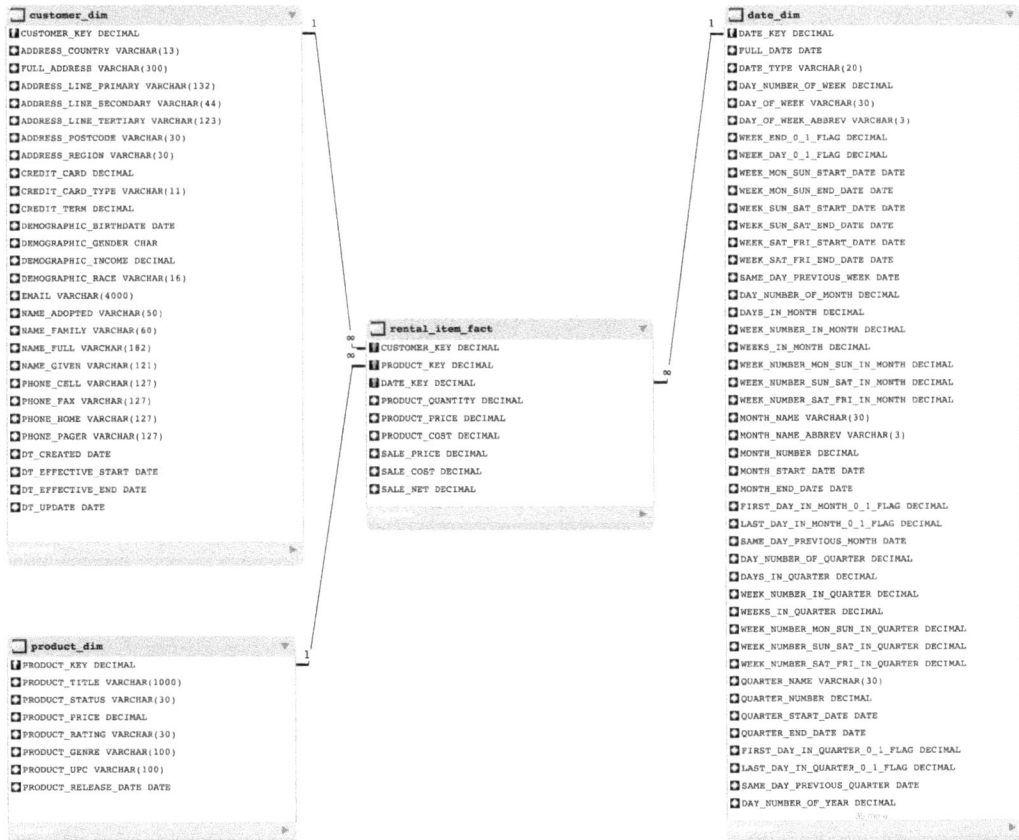

customer_dim
- CUSTOMER_KEY DECIMAL
- ADDRESS_COUNTRY VARCHAR(13)
- FULL_ADDRESS VARCHAR(300)
- ADDRESS_LINE_PRIMARY VARCHAR(132)
- ADDRESS_LINE_SECONDARY VARCHAR(44)
- ADDRESS_LINE_TERTIARY VARCHAR(123)
- ADDRESS_POSTCODE VARCHAR(30)
- ADDRESS_REGION VARCHAR(30)
- CREDIT_CARD DECIMAL
- CREDIT_CARD_TYPE VARCHAR(11)
- CREDIT_TERM DECIMAL
- DEMOGRAPHIC_BIRTHDATE DATE
- DEMOGRAPHIC_GENDER CHAR
- DEMOGRAPHIC_INCOME DECIMAL
- DEMOGRAPHIC_RACE VARCHAR(16)
- EMAIL VARCHAR(4000)
- NAME_ADOPTED VARCHAR(50)
- NAME_FAMILY VARCHAR(60)
- NAME_FULL VARCHAR(182)
- NAME_GIVEN VARCHAR(121)
- PHONE_CELL VARCHAR(127)
- PHONE_FAX VARCHAR(127)
- PHONE_HOME VARCHAR(127)
- PHONE_PAGER VARCHAR(127)
- DT_CREATED DATE
- DT_EFFECTIVE_START DATE
- DT_EFFECTIVE_END DATE
- DT_UPDATE DATE

rental_item_fact
- CUSTOMER_KEY DECIMAL
- PRODUCT_KEY DECIMAL
- DATE_KEY DECIMAL
- PRODUCT_QUANTITY DECIMAL
- PRODUCT_PRICE DECIMAL
- PRODUCT_COST DECIMAL
- SALE_PRICE DECIMAL
- SALE_COST DECIMAL
- SALE_NET DECIMAL

product_dim
- PRODUCT_KEY DECIMAL
- PRODUCT_TITLE VARCHAR(1000)
- PRODUCT_STATUS VARCHAR(30)
- PRODUCT_PRICE DECIMAL
- PRODUCT_RATING VARCHAR(30)
- PRODUCT_GENRE VARCHAR(100)
- PRODUCT_UPC VARCHAR(100)
- PRODUCT_RELEASE_DATE DATE

date_dim
- DATE_KEY DECIMAL
- FULL_DATE DATE
- DATE_TYPE VARCHAR(20)
- DAY_NUMBER_OF_WEEK DECIMAL
- DAY_OF_WEEK VARCHAR(30)
- DAY_OF_WEEK_ABBREV VARCHAR(3)
- WEEK_END_0_1_FLAG DECIMAL
- WEEK_DAY_0_1_FLAG DECIMAL
- WEEK_MON_SUN_START_DATE DATE
- WEEK_MON_SUN_END_DATE DATE
- WEEK_SUN_SAT_START_DATE DATE
- WEEK_SUN_SAT_END_DATE DATE
- WEEK_SAT_FRI_START_DATE DATE
- WEEK_SAT_FRI_END_DATE DATE
- SAME_DAY_PREVIOUS_WEEK DATE
- DAY_NUMBER_OF_MONTH DECIMAL
- DAYS_IN_MONTH DECIMAL
- WEEK_NUMBER_IN_MONTH DECIMAL
- WEEKS_IN_MONTH DECIMAL
- WEEK_NUMBER_MON_SUN_IN_MONTH DECIMAL
- WEEK_NUMBER_SUN_SAT_IN_MONTH DECIMAL
- WEEK_NUMBER_SAT_FRI_IN_MONTH DECIMAL
- MONTH_NAME VARCHAR(30)
- MONTH_NAME_ABBREV VARCHAR(3)
- MONTH_NUMBER DECIMAL
- MONTH_START_DATE DATE
- MONTH_END_DATE DATE
- FIRST_DAY_IN_MONTH_0_1_FLAG DECIMAL
- LAST_DAY_IN_MONTH_0_1_FLAG DECIMAL
- SAME_DAY_PREVIOUS_MONTH DATE
- DAY_NUMBER_OF_QUARTER DECIMAL
- DAYS_IN_QUARTER DECIMAL
- WEEK_NUMBER_IN_QUARTER DECIMAL
- WEEKS_IN_QUARTER DECIMAL
- WEEK_NUMBER_MON_SUN_IN_QUARTER DECIMAL
- WEEK_NUMBER_SUN_SAT_IS_QUARTER DECIMAL
- WEEK_NUMBER_SAT_FRI_IN_QUARTER DECIMAL
- QUARTER_NAME VARCHAR(30)
- QUARTER_NUMBER DECIMAL
- QUARTER_START_DATE DATE
- QUARTER_END_DATE DATE
- FIRST_DAY_IN_QUARTER_0_1_FLAG DECIMAL
- LAST_DAY_IN_QUARTER_0_1_FLAG DECIMAL
- SAME_DAY_PREVIOUS_QUARTER DATE
- DAY_NUMBER_OF_YEAR DECIMAL

FIGURE 6-2. *Rental Item data mart*

five-year period. It is also 10 billion rows deep. Its creation script is quite simple but will take some time depending on your hardware setup. Please modify our scripts so that they create much less data, unless you have a lot of hardware you can throw at it.

Note that this simple star schema has many of the components you generally see in data warehouse tables. If you query the data, it looks realistic. In fact, you would have a hard time determining if it was made up or real if you did not know otherwise. We start by making a table that will help us iterate through our random data creation:

```
SQL> DROP TABLE iterator CASCADE CONSTRAINTS PURGE;
SQL> CREATE TABLE iterator_100m
  2    AS SELECT LEVEL i FROM dual CONNECT BY LEVEL <= 100000000;
```

We create a 100-million-row iterator table with the previous commands. Next, we use the table to produce randomly generated product, customer, and date keys for our `rental_item_fact` table. We also churn out product quantities and their price:

```
SQL> CREATE TABLE rental_item_fact
  2    PARALLEL 32
  3    TABLESPACE fio_001 AS
  4    WITH base_values AS
  5    (SELECT   ROUND(dbms_random.value(1, 258248)) AS product_key
  6    ,         ROUND(dbms_random.value(1, 5000000)) AS customer_key
  7    ,         SYSDATE -
  8              ROUND(dbms_random.value(1, 1825)) AS date_key
  9    ,         ROUND(dbms_random.value(1, 15)) AS product_quantity
 10    ,         ROUND(dbms_random.value(5, 15)) AS product_price
 11    FROM      iterator_100m CROSS JOIN
 12              (SELECT LEVEL FROM dual CONNECT BY LEVEL <= 100))
, ... Continued ...
```

Observe that we perform a cross-join between the iterator table and `dual` table. This multiplies the data by a factor of 100. Our resultant data set is 10 billion records; however, we are not done yet. We must still determine a realistic product cost, total sale price, total sale cost, and total net sales values. We do so with the following statements:

```
 13    , product_cost AS
 14    (SELECT   pv.*
 15    ,         product_price *
 16              ROUND(dbms_random.value(.1, .9),4) product_cost
 17    FROM      base_values pv)
 18    , sale_total AS
 19    (SELECT   pc.*
 20    ,         pc.product_quantity * pc.product_price sale_price
 21    ,         pc.product_quantity * pc.product_cost  sale_cost
 22    FROM      product_cost pc)
 23    SELECT    st.*
 24    ,         st.sale_price - st.sale_cost sale_net
 25    FROM      sale_total st;
```

You can do this kind of thing with one SELECT statement on `dual`; however, it is likely that you will run out of memory long before the 10-billion-row table is finished. Our test servers are

A Cautionary Tale when Generating Data

If your server is too small, you can always decrease the size of your sample database by reducing or eliminating the CROSS JOIN operation that we used in our scripts. In addition, our random data generation might create a data set that is slightly bigger or smaller than yours. Please do not be alarmed if the end result is not the same.

using a 42GB/Instance SGA limits, and we hit that limitation just before finishing. Your resulting table will be around 400GB. We used this same methodology to create a customer dimension and item dimension. Altogether, the sample data that we will be using is 402GB.

Importing and Exporting with impdp and expdp

Some of you may not remember the older import and export (expdp and impdp) utilities that were used in Oracle9i Database and earlier. In those days, DBAs used the expdp/impdp utilities almost exclusively even though other alternatives like RMAN were available.

The exp/imp utilities were easy to use but had a few problems. For one, they were single threaded and very slow compared to modern methods. In addition, importing and exporting often broke when data architects got creative with data types. Another problem was that the imp utility had difficulty remapping schemas. If you wanted to change the schema in a target database, you had to make all of the tables first. Then, you could import the data.

Oh! There was one other nuance...all of the export files were unencrypted. Anyone who had the know-how and access to your export file could replicate your data anywhere they wanted. DBAs were forced to use tools like the GNU Privacy Guard (GPG) utility to encrypt important exports. We still like GPG to this day because it is a pretty slick way to encrypt and decrypt files, but it's really nice to have a single call that both creates the export file and encrypts it in flight.

Nowadays, the Oracle Data Pump versions of the import and export utilities (expdp/impdp) are vastly improved. You can easily remap schemas, import directly through database links, limit the logging performed during importing, compress or decompress the data in the target, and even encrypt the export files to keep them safe from prying eyes.

In the following subsections, we go over the more commonly used and beneficial options to the expdp and impdp executables.

To start, you need to make sure your user account has the correct setup. You will need the following:

- A common directory where export and log files can be stored
- Read and write permissions to the directory
- OS logon with rights to the expdp and impdp executables
- Environmental variables to ease the use of exp/imp commands
- The export full database right
- The import full database right

- The ability to create, attach to, and modify jobs
- The ability to remap tables to other schemas

The Oracle database comes with several directories by default, and our sample server has most of the possible set because we installed our instance with default options. You can find out what directories your server has by issuing the following query as the `sys` or `system` user:

```
SQL> COLUMN owner FORMAT A10
SQL> COLUMN directory_name FORMAT A30
SQL> COLUMN directory_path FORMAT A70
SQL> SET PAGESIZE 50
SQL> SET LINESIZE 200
SQL> SELECT   directory_name
  2  ,         directory_path
  3  FROM     dba_directories;
```

The results from our query are all owned by the `sys` user, and the query returns ten directories; however, we've left out the `$ORACLE_BASE` and `$ORACLE_HOME` directories because they only return a "/." Pay particular attention to the `DATA_PUMP_DIR` directory:

```
DIRECTORY_NAME              DIRECTORY_PATH
--------------------------  --------------------------------------------------
OPATCH_LOG_DIR              /u01/app/.../dbhome_1/QOpatch
OPATCH_SCRIPT_DIR           /u01/app/.../dbhome_1/QOpatch
DATA_PUMP_DIR               /u01/app/oracle/admin/T001/dpdump/
ORACLE_OCM_CONFIG_DIR       /u01/app/.../dbhome_1/ccr/hosts/DPLHP380G8-4/state
ORACLE_OCM_CONFIG_DIR2      /u01/app/.../dbhome_1/ccr/state
PDB1_DPD                    /u01/app/oracle/admin/PDB1/dpdump
XSDDIR                      /ade/b/3593327372/oracle/rdbms/xml/schema
ORACLE_OCM_CONFIG_DIR2      /u01/app/.../dbhome_1/ccr/state
SCHEDULER$_LOG_DIR          /u01/app/.../dbhome_1/scheduler/log
```

The default Data Pump directory shown in the code can be used by anyone who has OS user rights to do so. That means that their user is part of the group that owns the Oracle install. If you are running Windows, these directory paths will be slightly different.

We strongly suggest that you do not allow common users access to your server's OS. It's not a good practice. Furthermore, access to your `$ORACLE_HOME` or `$ORACLE_BASE` directory should be completely outlawed...that is, unless you want a database that is more suited for the Wild West than a corporate IT shop. Heck! You could set up a saloon complete with spittoons. Then, you could name your databases WWST001, WWST002, and so on. When the hackers come, you could act surprised just like the Hollywood shop owners did when an outlaw holed up in their shop because they had the whiskey and ammo. Contrariwise, you should do everything in your power to harden your OS and DB. Only allow the `sys` and `system` accounts access to your `$ORACLE_BASE`.

Instead of regressing to the Wild West, let's create a common directory elsewhere with the following commands:

```
SQL> CREATE DIRECTORY wwest_001 AS
  2    '/u02/pdb1/analyst/dpump_dir';
SQL> GRANT READ, WRITE ON DIRECTORY wwest_001 TO video_store;
```

Observe that we created a directory just below the /u02 folder, specific to the database we want to work with. You want to follow this practice to keep things tidy and secure. You will also need to make sure you create the directories in the OS, as these commands do not do that automatically for you. A listing of your more public-facing directories should look like so:

```
[oracle@DPLHP380G8-4 u02]$ cd /u02
[oracle@DPLHP380G8-4 u02]$ ll
total 56
drwx------   2 oracle oinstall 16384 Apr 18 19:02 lost+found
drwxr-xr-x   3 oracle oinstall  4096 Apr 18 19:25 oradata
drwxr-x---   3 oracle oinstall  4096 Apr 18 19:25 fast_recovery_area
dr-xr-xr-x. 28 root   root      4096 Apr 18 23:37 ..
drwxr-xr-x   3 oracle oinstall  4096 May  3 12:09 pdb5
drwxr-xr-x   3 oracle oinstall  4096 May  3 12:09 pdb4
drwxr-xr-x   3 oracle oinstall  4096 May  3 12:09 pdb3
drwxr-xr-x   3 oracle oinstall  4096 May  3 12:09 pdb2
drwxr-xr-x   3 oracle oinstall  4096 May  3 12:09 pdb1
drwxr-xr-x   3 oracle oinstall  4096 May  3 12:09 pdb6
drwxr-xr-x  11 oracle oinstall  4096 May  5 02:06 .
```

Exporting Files with expdp

The expdp utility is an excellent way to create a temporary backup of a schema or to move it from one database to another. In the following examples, we use the oracle OS account and the /u02/pdb1/analyst/dpump_dir directory to make a backup of one of our schemas. We will use the export files created there to import the data later on.

One simple way for you to freshen your memory of the expdp options is to issue the expdp command with the -help switch. We will issue it and show you what the output looks like:

```
[oracle@DPLHP380G8-4 dpump_dir]$ expdp -help | more
... omitted for brevity ...
The Data Pump export utility provides a mechanism for transferring data objects
between Oracle databases. The utility is invoked with the following command:
   Example: expdp scott/tiger DIRECTORY=dmpdir DUMPFILE=scott.dmp
... omitted for brevity ...
-------------------------------------------------------------------------
The available keywords and their descriptions follow. Default values are listed within
square brackets.
ATTACH
Attach to an existing job.
For example, ATTACH=job_name.
... omitted for brevity ...
```

Notice the great examples that Oracle gives in just the first few lines of output. You can use these examples to generate complex expdp/impdp commands. We won't describe every option here because other resources already exist for that. Instead, we simply want to show how we have used these tools to speed up our data-moving efforts. Refer to author Darl Kuhn's *Pro Oracle Database 12c Administration* for a complete listing of switches available in the expdp/impdp executables. Other excellent sources for these and many other commands are Michael McLaughlin's blog at http://blog.mclaughlinsoftware.com/ and Tim Hall's blog at www.oracle-base.com.

We used the help generated in the output of the expdp -help statement to create the following export examples.

Example 6-1 *Exporting Schemas with Multiplexed Dump Files and Parallelism*

```
expdp admjmh/abc123@pdb1 \
  cluster=Y \
  directory=WWEST_001 \
  dumpfile=video_store1.dmp,video_store2.dmp,video_store3.dmp,video_store4.dmp \
    video_store5.dmp,video_store6.dmp,video_store7.dmp,video_store8.dmp \
  encryption=all \
  encryption_password=abc123 \
  parallel=8 \
  schemas=admjmh
```

Example 6-2 *Exporting a Table*

```
expdp admjmh/abc123@pdb1 \
directory=WWEST_001 \
dumpfile=vse_product1.dmp \
tables=video_store.product_dim
```

Example 6-3 *Exporting over a Network Link*

```
expdp admjmh/abc123@pdb1 \
directory=WWEST_001 \
dumpfile=vse_product1.dmp \
tables=video_store.product_dim
```

We purposefully used some of the more interesting switches in the expdp command. The cluster switch tells the expdp utility to push its job across its entire RAC cluster. This will allow you to move the data using a very high degree of parallelism. The directory switch simply tells expdp to use the directory we created earlier. Next, we wanted to maximize the export, so we created the same number of dump files as our degree of parallelism. Lastly, we encrypted all of the export and told the expdp utility to move all of the data in the admjmh schema.

The export will start immediately after issuing the command. Its output will look something like this:

```
Export: Release 12.1.0.1.0 - Production on Mon May 5 02:10:36 2014
Copyright (c) 1982, 2013, Oracle and/or its affiliates.  All rights reserved.Connected
to: Oracle Database 12c Enterprise-Edition Release 12.1.0.1.0
With the Partitioning, OLAP, Advanced Analytics and Real Application Testing
Starting "ADMJMH"."SYS_EXPORT_SCHEMA_01":  admjmh/********@pdb1 cluster=Y
directory=WWEST_001 dumpfile=video_store1.dmp,video_store2.dmp,video_store3.dmp,video_
store4.dmp video_store5.dmp,video_store6.dmp,video_store7.dmp,video_store8.dmp
```

```
encryption=all encryption_password=******** parallel=8 schemas=admjmh
Estimate in progress using BLOCKS method...
Processing object type SCHEMA_EXPORT/TABLE/TABLE_DATA
Total estimation using BLOCKS method: 400.7 GB
Processing object type SCHEMA_EXPORT/USER
Processing object type SCHEMA_EXPORT/SYSTEM_GRANT
Processing object type SCHEMA_EXPORT/ROLE_GRANT
Processing object type SCHEMA_EXPORT/DEFAULT_ROLE
Processing object type SCHEMA_EXPORT/PRE_SCHEMA/PROCACT_SCHEMA
Processing object type SCHEMA_EXPORT/DB_LINK
Processing object type SCHEMA_EXPORT/TABLE/TABLE
Processing object type SCHEMA_EXPORT/TABLE/COMMENT
Processing object type SCHEMA_EXPORT/PROCEDURE/PROCEDURE
Processing object type SCHEMA_EXPORT/PROCEDURE/ALTER_PROCEDURE
Processing object type SCHEMA_EXPORT/TABLE/INDEX/INDEX
Processing object type SCHEMA_EXPORT/TABLE/CONSTRAINT/CONSTRAINT
Processing object type SCHEMA_EXPORT/TABLE/INDEX/STATISTICS/INDEX_STATISTICS
Processing object type SCHEMA_EXPORT/VIEW/VIEW
Processing object type SCHEMA_EXPORT/TABLE/STATISTICS/TABLE_STATISTICS
Processing object type SCHEMA_EXPORT/STATISTICS/MARKER
. . exported "ADMJMH"."CUSTOMER_DIM"                   1.575 GB 5000000 rows
. . exported "ADMJMH"."DATE_DIM"                       69.21 MB  735358 rows
. . exported "ADMJMH"."PRODUCT_DIM"                    21.52 MB  231205 rows
... omitted for brevity ...
Job "ADMJMH"."SYS_EXPORT_SCHEMA_01" successfully completed at Mon May 5 02:27:16 2014
elapsed 0 00:16:39
```

It was exciting to see the CPU counter jump as the job churned. You can see that the total time was quite short for the volume of data. Notice that the estimated file size was *400.7GB* and the time to complete was *only 16 minutes and 39 seconds*. Incidentally, we bumped the parallel degree to 24 and finished the same 400.7GB export in 9 minutes and 37 seconds, as shown in Figure 6-3. A three- or four-node cluster with 24 physical cores per node could easily complete the job in around 2 minutes. Now that is really cooking!

Importing Files with impdp

The impdp utility is very much like its sibling expdp, except it has a few extra tricks up its sleeves. For one, you can disable archive logging on import. This option will save you loads of time. Other really great options are the ability to export views as tables, change the compression level, prompt the importing user for a password, and import data via a database link. We'll issue the impdp command with the -help switch, just as we did with the expdp command, and see the results:

```
[oracle@DPLHP380G8-4 dpump_dir]$ impdp -help
... omitted for brevity ...
    Example: impdp scott/tiger DIRECTORY=dmpdir DUMPFILE=scott.dmp
... omitted for brevity ...
ATTACH
Attach to an existing job.
For example, ATTACH=job_name.
... Omitted for brevity ...
```

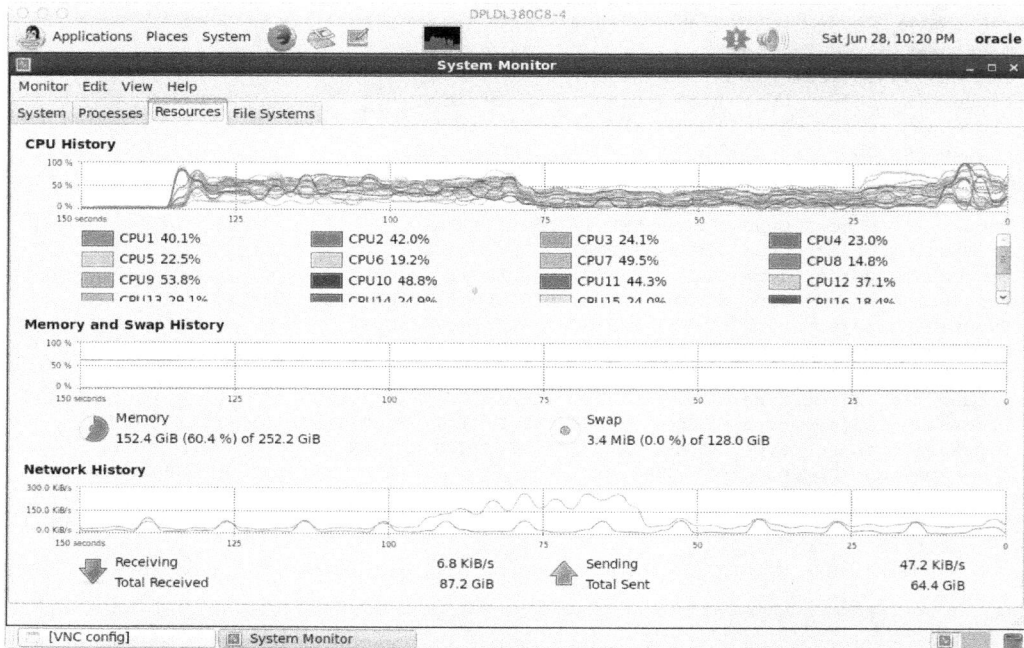

FIGURE 6-3. *CPU counter with 24 parallel jobs* `expdp`

The output is very similar to `expdp`. We used this help output to build the following command:

```
impdp admjmh/abc123@pdb1 \
  directory=WWEST_001 \
  dumpfile=video_storeu%.dmp \
  encryption_password=abc123 \
  parallel=24 \
  remap_tablespace=fio_001:fio_002 \
  remap_schema=admjmh:video_store
```

In this case, the `impdp` command is shorter than its sibling `expdp` and the majority of its switches are identical. For example, the number of dump files, degree of parallelism, and encryption password have not changed; however, there are two additional switches, `remap_tablespace` and `remap_schema`. These two switches are crucial if you regularly move data between production, test, and development servers. In our case, the test data generated is extremely large, and we wanted to see how much time it takes to use `impdp` to move data from one schema to the other. The total job time took 25 minutes and 2 seconds, which is a bit longer than we expected, but it is still impressive when you consider the total file size. Most DBAs would be ecstatic to move 400GB of data in less than 30 minutes, especially when the data has also been remapped to a new schema and tablespace.

Importing Across the Network

We really like the `network_link` switch. It allows you to move data directly into a schema, with all of the options listed previously. Your transfer speeds will not be as fast as the prior example because your network is considerably limited. A completely saturated 10-Gigabit Ethernet connection has a theoretical maximum of 1.2 Gbps. We would be surprised if you actually got that.

We suggest you use a set of bonded network interfaces on a private network to pull large sets of data. That way, your users will still be able to access your database during data extraction and importing activities. We modified the previous `impdp` command to show you how to import data via a database link:

```
impdp admjmh/abc123@pdb1 \
    directory=WWEST_001 \
    dumpfile=video_store%u.dmp \
    encryption_password=abc123 \
    parallel=24 \
    remap_tablespace=fio_001:fio_002 \
    remap_schema=admjmh:video_store \
    network_link=pdb1
```

In this example, we increased our degree of parallelism from 8 to 24 to see how quickly the import would complete.

Importing and Exporting with dbms_datapump

If you are using the scripts we supplied at the McGraw-Hill Professional website and you ran the last two examples, you have already been using Data Pump. You must have the same rights to use Data Pump inside the database as you had outside with the `expdp` and `impdp` utilities. In our next few examples, we will use the same directory as before, but we need to grant the `video_store` user rights to it. We also need to give that user execute rights on `dbms_datapump`. Finally, if the `video_store` user plans to export schemas outside its own, we need to give the user the `datapump_exp_fulldatabase` and `datapump_imp_fulldatabase` roles as the `sys` user like so:

```
SQL> GRANT EXECUTE ON dbms_datapump TO video_store;
SQL> GRANT datapump_exp_full_database TO video_store;
SQL> GRANT datapump_imp_full_database to video_store;
SQL> GRANT READ, WRITE ON DIRECTORY wwest_001 TO video_store;
```

The `dbms_datapump` package has some worker and job status types that can be handy in troubleshooting, tracking progress, or instrumenting your use of the package. For example, one such type is `ku$_dumpfile_info`. It's an associative array that can hold information about a dump file (check Chapter 6 of *Oracle Database 12c PL/SQL Programming* for details on collections). It is always a good idea to check your dump files before processing them, especially if your expcrt is spread across many files.

You do so like this:

```
SQL> DECLARE
  2    lv_info_table    ku$_dumpfile_info;
  3    lv_filetype      NUMBER;
  4    lv_item_decoded  dbms_sql.varchar2_table;
  5  BEGIN
  6    dbms_datapump.get_dumpfile_info( filename    => 'video_store24.dmp'
  8                                   , directory   => 'WWEST_001'
  9                                   , info_table  => lv_info_table
 10                                   , filetype    => lv_filetype );
```

NOTE
The item codes are found in the Oracle PL/SQL package and type documentation.

Calling get_dumpfile_info is pretty straightforward. It takes input values of the filename and directory. Its output is the file type and the associative array. Because the output is an associative array, you can simply loop through it after it is populated, like so:

```
 12    FOR a IN 1 .. lv_info_table.COUNT LOOP
 13      CASE
 14        WHEN lv_info_table(a).item_code = 1 THEN
 15          lv_item_decoded(a) := 'FILE VERSION';
 16        WHEN lv_info_table(a).item_code = 2 THEN
... omitted for brevity ...
 57          lv_item_decoded(a) := 'ENCRYPTION MODE';
 58        WHEN lv_info_table(a).item_code = 23 THEN
 59          lv_item_decoded(a) := 'COMPRESSION ALGORITHM';
 60        ELSE lv_item_decoded(a) := lv_info_table(a).item_code;
 61      END CASE;
 62      dbms_output.put_line(  RPAD( lv_item_decoded(a),'25','.' )
 63                          || ': '
 64                          || lv_info_table(a).value );
 65    END LOOP;
 66  END;
```

We took the time to add a decoded version of the item_code to make it easier for you to read. We like it this way much better than the original number:value list. Here is the output of the previous PL/SQL block:

```
FILE VERSION.............:  4.1
DB VERSION...............:  12.01.00.00.00
MASTER TABLE PRESENT.....:  0
INTERNAL FLAG............:  514
EXPORT GUID..............:  F8A40C5DF99EB300E04365F1320A8D7C
```

```
CHARACTER SET...........: 873
FILE NUMBER.............: 24
JOB NAME................: "ADMJMH"."SYS_EXPORT_SCHEMA_01"
PLATFORM................: x86_64/Linux 2.4.xx
INSTANCE................: T001
LANGUAGE................: AL32UTF8
CREATE DATE.............: Mon May 05 02:37:58 2014
BLOCK SIZE..............: 4096
METADATA COMPRESSED.....: 1
DATA COMPRESSED.........: 0
COMPRESSION ALGORITHM...: 3
METADATA ENCRYPTED......: 0
DATA ENCRYPTED..........: 0
COLUMNS ENCRYPTED.......: 0
ENCRYPTION MODE.........: 2
```

You should never, ever store database exports in their unencrypted form on a network or removable drive. That is why security nuts like us think that the encryption output is of great interest. It is also a good idea to run a small block like this before you spin all of the importing processes. Oracle has created similar objects for worker status, log entry, log errors, job status, job information, and general status. Most of these types are prefixed with ku$_. It will be helpful for you to at least skim through Oracle's documentation on them.

Our next example will use ku$_logentry, ku$_jobstatus, ku$_jobdesc, and ku$_status objects. We really had to dig, but we were lucky enough to find this wonderful example in the older Oracle Database 10g documentation. It fulfilled nearly everything we wanted to discuss about exporting jobs, so we modified it slightly and used it to export our video_store schema:

```
SQL> DECLARE
  2      lv_jobname      VARCHAR2(30) := 'VS_' ||
  3                          dbms_scheduler.generate_job_name;
  4      ind             NUMBER;
  5      spos            NUMBER;
  6      slen            NUMBER;
  7      h1              NUMBER;
  8      percent_done    NUMBER;
  9      job_state       VARCHAR2(30);
 10      le              ku$_LogEntry;
 11      js              ku$_JobStatus;
 12      jd              ku$_JobDesc;
 13      sts             ku$_Status;
```

Notice the ku$_ objects. We are fortunate because this example shows how to use them effectively. We don't have to fully qualify the ku$_ objects because Oracle creates public synonyms for them. We added the lv_jobname variable and caused it to iterate sequentially so

Data Warehouse Scenario

We simulated a possible data warehouse scenario for you in our performance tests. In our scenario, we created a user named `fred`. Then, we created two versions of the `rental_item_fact` table, named `rental_item_fact_1` and `rental_item_fact_2`. One of the tables in our scenario is live and can be queried by `fred`, but the other can be dropped and re-created, or truncated and loaded even while `fred` queries the live table. To do this, we made a public synonym called `rental_item_fact_live` and pointed it to the table we were not building. We had to grant `fred` user `SELECT` on both the `rental_item_fact_1` and `rental_item_fact_2` tables. We loved the results, hitting around 6.7 Gbps and completing the 10-billion-row load in 5 minutes and 55 seconds. `fred`'s query came back just fine, all while our simulated ETL was happening. The following illustration shows the Flash results of ETL during user query:

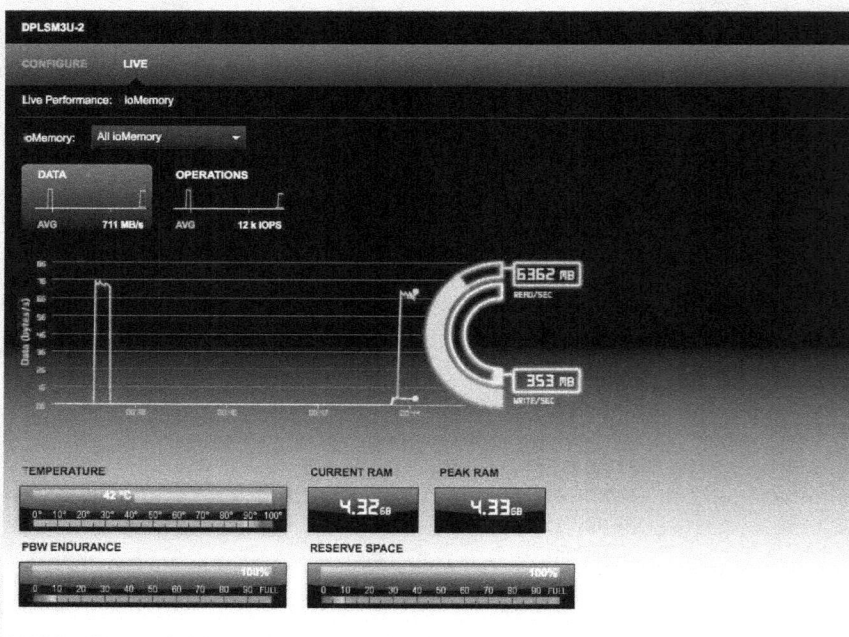

You can query the results with the following when you run it as the `admin` user:

```
SQL> CREATE TABLE video_store.rental_item_fact_2
  2    PARALLEL 32
  3    TABLESPACE fio_001
  4    NOLOGGING
  5    AS
  6    SELECT * FROM video_store.rental_item_fact;
```

You can then count the rows as the `fred` user:

```
SQL> SELECT COUNT(*) FROM rental_item_fact_live;
  COUNT(*)
----------
1.0000E+10
```

After the prior block, we reran `fred`'s query while re-creating the public synonym. Of course, `fred`'s query returned without interruption; however, this time `fred` was able to use all 6.7 Gbps in his query.

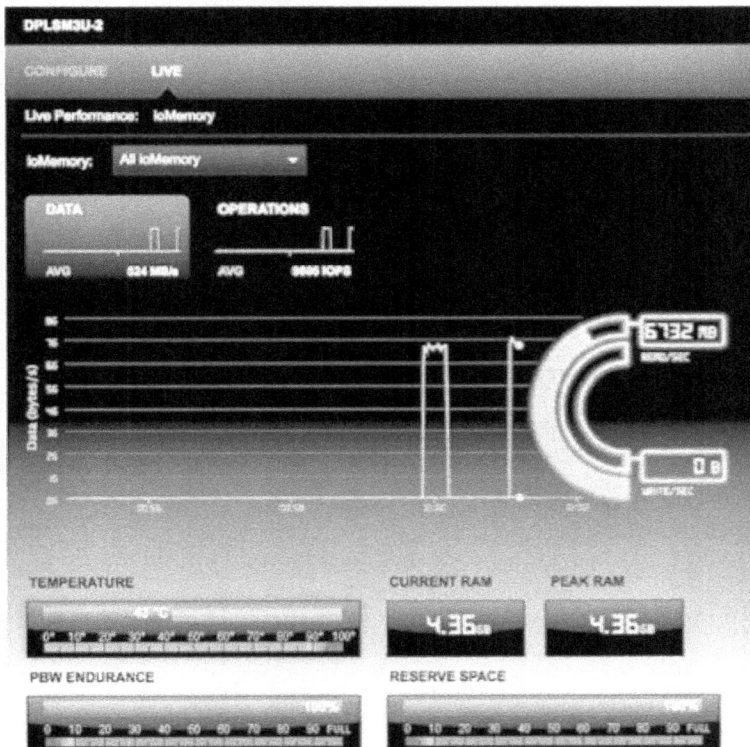

Finally, we reissued `fred`'s query one last time to ensure that his ability to query the table was not broken. Viola! `fred` experienced no downtime even though the loading of our 10-billion-row `rental_item_fact_table` took a little over 5 minutes to complete. You can use this method to load very large tables that must remain up; however, this method would be overkill for smaller tables that already load in subseconds.

In all, this test was extremely impressive. We could not dream of obtaining those kinds of numbers against spindled disks.

that you won't get caught with the dreaded *job name already exists* error. Next, we instantiate the job handle by calling dbms_datapump.open:

```
14    BEGIN
15      h1 := dbms_datapump.open(
16              'EXPORT','SCHEMA',NULL,lv_jobname,'LATEST');
17      dbms_datapump.add_file( h1
18                           ,'video_store%U.dmp'
19                           ,'WWEST_01');
20      dbms_datapump.metadata_filter( h1
21                                   ,'SCHEMA_EXPR'
22                                   ,'IN (''VIDEO_STORE'')');
23      dbms_datapump.set_parallel(h1,16);
24    BEGIN
25      dbms_datapump.start_job(H1);
26      dbms_output.put_line('Data Pump job started successfully');
27      EXCEPTION
28        WHEN OTHERS THEN
29          IF SQLCODE = dbms_datapump.success_with_info_num THEN
30            dbms_output.put_line(
31              'Data Pump job started with info available:');
32            dbms_datapump.get_status(
33              h1
34            , dbms_datapump.ku$_status_job_error
35            , 0
36            , job_state
37            , sts);
38            IF BITAND(
39                sts.mask,dbms_datapump.ku$_status_job_error) != 0 THEN
40              le := sts.error;
41              IF le IS NOT NULL THEN
42                ind := le.FIRST;
43                WHILE ind IS NOT NULL LOOP
44                  dbms_output.put_line(le(ind).logtext);
45                  ind := le.NEXT(ind);
46                END LOOP;
47              END IF;
48            END IF;
49          ELSE
50            RAISE;
51          END IF;
52    END;
```

If the job does not start correctly, we perform a nesting of commands. The first evaluates the dbms_datapump.add_file procedure for the success_with_info exception. If that exception exists, we have further information available via the dbms_datapump.get_status procedure. Once we establish that information is available, we populate the le (log exists) associative array with the output from get_status. Then, we loop through the results and use dbms_output to output the results to the screen. If the job starts correctly, we automatically move on to the next section:

```
54    percent_done := 0;
55    job_state := 'UNDEFINED';
56    WHILE (job_state != 'COMPLETED') AND (job_state != 'STOPPED') LOOP
57      dbms_datapump.get_status
58      ( h1
59      , dbms_datapump.ku$_status_job_error +
60          dbms_datapump.ku$_status_job_status +
61          dbms_datapump.ku$_status_wip
62      , -1
63      , job_state, STS );
64      js := sts.job_status;
65      IF js.percent_done != percent_done THEN
66        dbms_output.put_line( '*** Job percent done = ' ||
67          TO_CHAR(js.percent_done));
68        percent_done := js.percent_done;
69      END IF;
70      IF BITAND(sts.mask,dbms_datapump.ku$_status_wip) != 0 THEN
71        le := sts.wip;
72      ELSE
73        IF BITAND(sts.mask,dbms_datapump.ku$_status_job_error) != 0 THEN
74          le := sts.error;
75        ELSE
76          le := NULL;
77        END IF;
78      END IF;
79      IF le IS NOT NULL THEN
80        ind := le.FIRST;
81        WHILE ind IS NOT NULL LOOP
82          dbms_output.put_line(le(ind).LogText);
83          ind := le.NEXT ( ind );
84        END LOOP;
85      END IF;
86    END LOOP;
```

The previous section simply populates the js (job status) associative array and pipes the output to the screen with dbms_output. Once this loop is complete, we print the 'Job has completed' and 'Final job state' messages to the screen and detach from the job handle:

```
88    dbms_output.put_line('Job has completed' );
89    dbms_output.put_line('Final job state = ' || job_state );
90    dbms_datapump.detach(h1);
```

If there are any unhandled exceptions, we get the status similarly to the way we did on lines 27-51, as shown next.

NOTE
The item codes are found in the Oracle PL/SQL package and type documentation.

```
 92     EXCEPTION
 93       WHEN OTHERS THEN
 94         dbms_output.put_line('Exception in Data Pump job');
 95         dbms_datapump.get_status(
 96             h1
 97           , dbms_datapump.ku$_status_job_error
 98           , 0
 99         , job_state
100         , sts);
101         IF BITAND(sts.mask,dbms_datapump.ku$_status_job_error) != 0 THEN
102           le := sts.error;
103           IF le IS NOT NULL THEN
104             ind := le.FIRST;
105             WHILE ind IS NOT NULL LOOP
106               spos := 1;
107               slen := LENGTH(le(ind).LogText);
108               IF slen > 255 THEN
109                 slen := 255;
110               END IF;
111               WHILE slen > 0 LOOP
112                 dbms_output.put_line(SUBSTR(le(ind).LogText,spos,slen));
113                 spos := spos + 255;
114                 slen := LENGTH ( le(ind).LogText ) + 1 - spos;
115               END LOOP;
116               ind := le.NEXT(ind);
117             END LOOP;
118           END IF;
119         END IF;
120   END;
121   /
```

If everything goes as planned, we get similar output to the following block:

```
Data Pump job started successfully
Starting 'ADMJMH'."VS_JOB$_690":
Estimate in progress using BLOCKS method...
Processing object type SCHEMA_EXPORT/TABLE/TABLE_DATA
Total estimation using BLOCKS method: 5.918 GB
Processing object type SCHEMA_EXPORT/USER
Processing object type SCHEMA_EXPORT/SYSTEM_GRANT
Processing object type SCHEMA_EXPORT/ROLE_GRANT
Processing object type SCHEMA_EXPORT/DEFAULT_ROLE
. . exported "VIDEO_STORE"."RENTAL_ITEM_FACT":"SYS_P763"  12.66 MB  282579
rows
. . exported "VIDEO_STORE"."RENTAL_ITEM_FACT":"SYS_P762"  12.64 MB  282374
rows
... omitted for brevity ...
Master table "ADMJMH"."VS_JOB$_690" successfully loaded/unloaded
******************************************************************************
Dump file set for ADMJMH.VS_JOB$_690 is:
/u02/pdb1/analyst/dpump_dir/video_store01.dmp
```

```
/u02/pdb1/analyst/dpump_dir/video_store02.dmp
/u02/pdb1/analyst/dpump_dir/video_store03.dmp
/u02/pdb1/analyst/dpump_dir/video_store04.dmp
/u02/pdb1/analyst/dpump_dir/video_store05.dmp
*** Job percent done = 100
/u02/pdb1/analyst/dpump_dir/video_store06.dmp
/u02/pdb1/analyst/dpump_dir/video_store07.dmp
/u02/pdb1/analyst/dpump_dir/video_store08.dmp
/u02/pdb1/analyst/dpump_dir/video_store09.dmp
/u02/pdb1/analyst/dpump_dir/video_store10.dmp
/u02/pdb1/analyst/dpump_dir/video_store11.dmp
/u02/pdb1/analyst/dpump_dir/video_store12.dmp
/u02/pdb1/analyst/dpump_dir/video_store13.dmp
/u02/pdb1/analyst/dpump_dir/video_store14.dmp
/u02/pdb1/analyst/dpump_dir/video_store15.dmp
/u02/pdb1/analyst/dpump_dir/video_store16.dmp
Job "ADMJMH"."VS_JOB$_690" successfully completed at Wed May 7 22:29:29 2014
elapsed 0 00:00:13
Job has completed
Final job state = COMPLETED
```

The import process is quite a bit shorter than the export process. We added the `lv_jobname`
and parallelism in the same way that we did for the export example. However, in this case, we
simply called the `dbms_datapump.get_status` job as long as its status was not set to
"completed." Then, we piped the output to the screen using `dbms_output` as before:

NOTE
*The item codes are found in the Oracle PL/SQL package and type
documentation.*

```
SQL> DECLARE
  2    lv_jobname VARCHAR2(30) := 'VS_'||DBMS_SCHEDULER.GENERATE_JOB_NAME;
  3    ind NUMBER;                -- Loop index
  4    h1 NUMBER;                 -- Data Pump job handle
  5    percent_done NUMBER;       -- Percentage of job complete
  6    job_state VARCHAR2(30);    -- To keep track of job state
  7    le ku$_LogEntry;           -- For WIP and error messages
  8    js ku$_JobStatus;          -- The job status from get_status
  9    jd ku$_JobDesc;            -- The job description from get_status
 10    sts ku$_Status;            -- The status object returned by get_status
 11  BEGIN
 12    h1 := dbms_datapump.open('IMPORT','FULL',NULL,lv_jobname);
 13    dbms_datapump.add_file(h1,'video_store%U.dmp','WWEST_01');
 14    dbms_datapump.metadata_remap(h1,'REMAP_SCHEMA','VIDEO_STORE','FRED');
 15    dbms_datapump.set_parameter(h1,'TABLE_EXISTS_ACTION','SKIP');
 16    dbms_datapump.set_parallel(h1,16);
 17    dbms_datapump.start_job(h1);
 18    percent_done := 0;
 19    job_state := 'UNDEFINED';
 20    WHILE (job_state != 'COMPLETED') AND (job_state != 'STOPPED') LOOP
```

```
21        dbms_datapump.get_status(
22          h1
23        , dbms_datapump.ku$_status_job_error +
24            dbms_datapump.ku$_status_job_status +
25            dbms_datapump.ku$_status_wip,-1,job_state,sts);
26      js := sts.job_status;
27      IF js.percent_done != percent_done THEN
28        dbms_output.put_line('*** Job percent done = ' ||
29                             to_char(js.percent_done));
30        percent_done := js.percent_done;
31      END IF;
32      IF bitand(sts.mask,dbms_datapump.ku$_status_wip) != 0 THEN
33        le := sts.wip;
34      ELSE
35        IF bitand(sts.mask,dbms_datapump.ku$_status_job_error) != 0 THEN
36          le := sts.error;
37        ELSE
38          le := null;
39        END IF;
40      END IF;
41      IF le IS NOT NULL THEN
42        ind := le.FIRST;
43        WHILE ind IS NOT NULL LOOP
44          dbms_output.put_line(le(ind).LogText);
45          ind := le.NEXT(ind);
46        END LOOP;
47      END IF;
48    END LOOP;
49    dbms_output.put_line('Job has completed');
50    dbms_output.put_line('Final job state = '||job_state);
51    dbms_datapump.detach(h1);
52  END;
53  /
```

If the job had any errors, we print that information to the screen using lines 32–51. Otherwise, we print to the screen that the job has completed and its ending state, as shown in this output:

```
Master table "ADMJMH"."VS_JOB$_698" successfully loaded/unloaded
Starting "ADMJMH"."VS_JOB$_698":
Processing object type SCHEMA_EXPORT/USER
ORA-31684: Object type USER:"FRED" already exists
Processing object type SCHEMA_EXPORT/SYSTEM_GRANT
Processing object type SCHEMA_EXPORT/ROLE_GRANT
Processing object type SCHEMA_EXPORT/DEFAULT_ROLE
Processing object type SCHEMA_EXPORT/PRE_SCHEMA/PROCACT_SCHEMA
Processing object type SCHEMA_EXPORT/TABLE/TABLE
Processing object type SCHEMA_EXPORT/TABLE/TABLE_DATA
. . imported "FRED"."RENTAL_ITEM_FACT":"SYS_P763"      12.66 MB   282579 rows
. . imported "FRED"."RENTAL_ITEM_FACT":"SYS_P762"      12.64 MB   282374 rows
Processing object type SCHEMA_EXPORT/TABLE/STATISTICS/TABLE_STATISTICS
Processing object type SCHEMA_EXPORT/STATISTICS/MARKER
```

```
Job "ADMJMH"."VS_JOB$_698" completed with 1 error(s) at Wed May 7 23:28:12
2014
elapsed 0 00:00:53
Job has completed
Final job state = COMPLETED
```

We aren't quite sure why the Oracle Database 12*c* documentation omitted this little golden nugget. Whatever the reason, we hope you will enjoy the fruits of our documentation mining beyond the Oracle Database 12*c* documentation libraries.

SQL*Loader

This chapter wouldn't be complete without mention of SQL*Loader. The fact is that most DBAs are very familiar with this technology. In some shops, the utility may seem mundane and routine, while in others, external tables have replaced older SQL*Loader methods. Nevertheless, we created a very good example, presented in Chapter 9, that shows a modern way to use SQL*Loader to quickly import XML files into your database. We refer you to that example. We have also added multiple pages to our blog site (security.mclaughlinsoftware.com) if you require a basic understanding of SQL*Loader.

Supporting Scripts

The following programs are available on the McGraw-Hill Professional website to support this chapter:

- ■ The ch_06_examples.sql program contains the code used to create our EXPDP/IMPDP and Data Pump jobs.

- ■ The ch_06_performance_tests.sql program contains the code used to create our CTAS performance tests.

Summary

By now, you should be very familiar with terms like ETL and right-time data. In addition, your prowess with expdp/impdp and dbms_datapump should be heightened. You should also benefit from the example we found in the old Oracle Database 10*g* documentation.

Our performance tests and supporting scripts have shown you how the CREATE TABLE as techniques coupled with table renaming can move data very quickly and provide you with data warehouse tables that stay live 99.999 percent of the time. They also give you a good idea of how flash storage performs versus alternatives like an SaS RAID array. We would be surprised if you can't maximize your CPU and IO resources now that you are armed with the techniques found in this chapter.

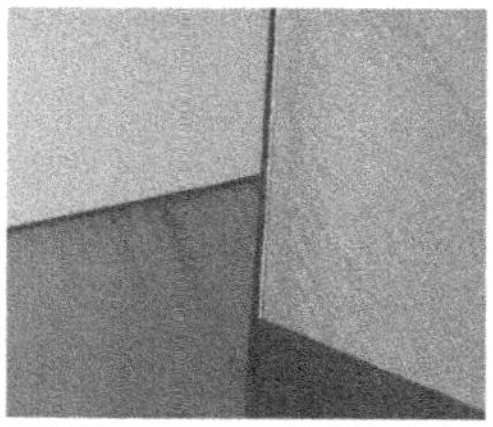

PART
III

Application Security

CHAPTER
7

Database Security

Purpose

This chapter introduces you to the threat of database attacks. It uses real-world examples to point out reasons why attackers were successful. We're not presenting the examples to highlight security flaws of the victimized organizations. Instead, we use these examples to illustrate the common weak points of many organizations. These examples should provide you with facts that let you identify security weaknesses and fix them.

This chapter explains why you need effective database security measures. It also helps you gain senior management support for improved measures. This chapter also lays a foundation for technical solutions we discuss in Chapter 8, which covers how you should implement database security.

We've seen a shift in the field of database security recently. While professionals believed firewalls were adequate protection for their servers (back-end systems), that's no longer true. Firewalls proved no more difficult to breach than any other hacker intrusion measures. System architects are now placing a much higher priority on security activities.

Advantages

There are many advantages to securing your databases. These advantages are the hard-to-quantify avoidance of the cost from security breaches.

When current security measures work, it can be hard to get funds for new measures. New measures are important because hackers constantly evolve attack methods. Some security changes can be incredibly expensive, like the setup and implementation of multiple firewalls. There's even more expense creating and maintaining honeypots (rogue databases that have tripwires) to trap hackers.

It's easy to quantify dollar amounts *after* your database has been breached. Sharp drops in sales and large legal fees/fines can be easily tied to loss of data. Your overall success hinges on your ability to make your executives aware of the potential consequences of a breach before one happens and keep them focused on real issues. Your executives are like eaglets ensconced in a nest underneath a severely eroding cliff overhang. The hatchlings are completely unaware of the looming threat that hangs above them. In fact, they may even feel that the large slab of rock protects them. Figuratively, it's your job to make them aware that the small fissures forming in the ledge above them *will* lead to catastrophe.

At a minimum, the following advantages should be reason enough to fund and begin your security work:

- Savings in legal fees
- Defense of customer confidence
- Continued ability to do business
- Job security

Take into account that the cost of a breach associated with this list typically falls between $125 and $200 per record. In some cases, costs can be much higher, as shown in our Utah Department of Technology Services example, later in this chapter. That said, if your company had a breach of 5 million records, and it was lucky enough to pay only $150 per record, it would have to dish out $750 million dollars in fees and lost revenue.

Disadvantages

Some engineers may resist security changes because they are complex or costly. For example, some engineers might think they are saving money by implementing one firewall between the Internet and local area network (LAN). This firewall is known as a DMZ (demilitarized zone). While this action may save their company thousands of dollars up front, it may cost the company far more from a future hack.

Firewalls merely provide speed bumps to hacks. You *must* work under the assumption that your firewalls have already been compromised, and create detection and alerting mechanisms. Detection and alerting programs are known as *tripwires*, and they let you detect probes before a full-blown hack. You also need an attractive hacking target that acts as a distraction, drawing the hacker's attention away from the real database and into a mockup database. A mockup database doesn't contain any real customer data but data made to look real. The combination of a fake database and tripwires that identify attempted entry is known as a honeypot. Honeypots are expensive to create, and they require maintenance programming to keep them attractive targets to would-be hackers.

Using a DMZ, a honeypot, activity monitoring, and listener hardening is a strong beginning because it creates multiple zones. To move between zones, users and hackers need proper credentials, much like an international traveler needs a passport and/or visas to move through the borders of different countries. Zoning your intranet is an effective, albeit expensive, solution (qualified in Figure 7-1).

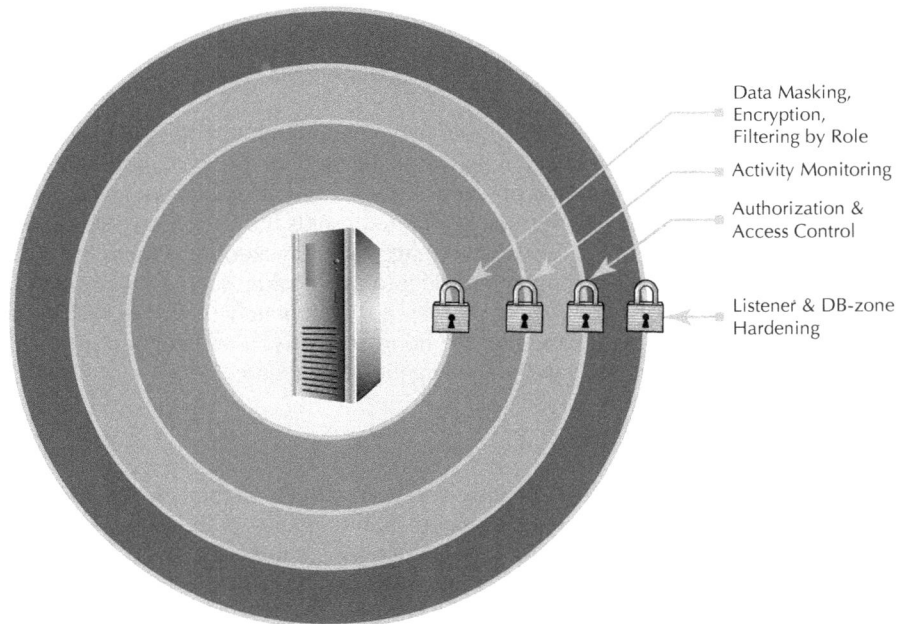

FIGURE 7-1. *Multilayered DB hardening*

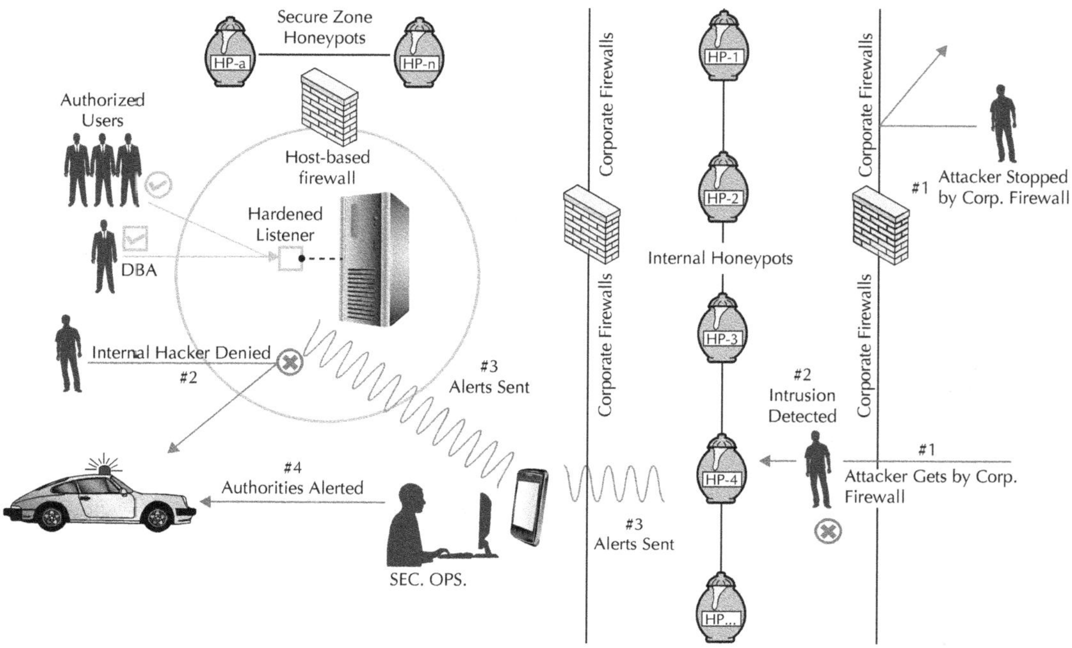

FIGURE 7-2. *Honeypots*

Once you have adequately applied a multilayered approach to your database environment, you must monitor it for intrusions. An analogy to this would be for you to think of your zones as a sonar net around your vessel in a time of war and your server as your vessel. You need to monitor for an intruder, such as submarine. The submarine represents the hacker's assault or hack. If you did your job well, the honeypot (a false sonar image to the hacker) lures them in to take a look.

When you catch the hacker trying to intrude into the mockup server, you should also discover what they know about your system. Then, you should immediately secure or shut down anything they were able to use to penetrate and find the honeypot. As you're doing that, you should gather all forensics available so that you can pursue litigation (see Figure 7-2).

Overview

Most of this chapter will follow an example-solution pattern. In those sections, we'll present well-known data breaches. We also suggest remediation strategies for the well-known data breaches. After the example-solution sections, we'll introduce you to methods and resources used by the NIST (National Institute of Standards and Technology) and SANS Institute. Then, we describe what you should do to be successful in planning and implementing database security.

Our example-solution cases are probably familiar to you because they were highly publicized hacks. Our *LinkedIn Corporation* and *Utah Department of Technology Services* examples show problems with database security. On the other hand, our *Target Corporation* and *National Security Agency* examples show hacks that involve a combination of database and infrastructure issues. The latter cases are included because they were accomplished by less direct hacking methods. We cover these to highlight direct and indirect vulnerabilities; you must be aware of the multifaceted techniques of hackers to protect your corporate data.

The breaches we cover will be presented as follows:

- LinkedIn Corporation
- Target Corporation
- National Security Agency (NSA)
- Utah Department of Technology Services

LinkedIn Breach

In June 2012, the business/social-networking site LinkedIn was hacked. Russian attackers found flaws in the way LinkedIn implemented cookies and exploited LinkedIn's non-HTTPS services via SQL injection. Assailants used stolen credentials to download around 6.5 million usernames with their encrypted passwords. The attackers quickly discovered that LinkedIn passwords used an out-of-date SHA1 hash that did not include *salting*—a practice of appending extra bits to the password before one-way hashing functions mangle the phrase. Hackers were able to decode the easier passwords, posting them to a public website the very next day.

In a defensive move, LinkedIn invalidated all of the leaked accounts and sent e-mails to registered users asking them to reset their passwords. In addition, LinkedIn implemented HTTPS and refactored its iOS application. Apparently, LinkedIn's iOS application siphoned contact information from smartphone databases. The news of this "borrowing of contacts" and the initial leak sparked controversy that eventually led to a $5 million class-action lawsuit. Fortunately for LinkedIn, the lawsuit was overturned. Even so, the debacle forced LinkedIn to spend more than $1 million in defending against the lawsuit.

Vendors such as Apple revisited the code that had been published on their application storefront and discovered that other programmers were borrowing contact lists, locations, and Internet activity from smartphones. They also found that some programmers nefariously used this data to harvest millions of contacts and private usage information via their applications. Then, the programmers stored this information in central databases and sold it for gain. At least LinkedIn had the moral fortitude to ask mobile phone users for access to their on-phone databases. What's more, they did not cave to the temptation of harvesting said data. Apple either removed data harvesting programs from their store or forced programmers to remediate risky programs.

LinkedIn posted several articles via its website asking users to help prevent future database leaks. These articles encouraged users to use only trusted networks, not widely used public networks; to change their password often and use passwords that contained significant entropy; to install, use, and keep up-to-date antivirus/malware software; and finally, to not use the same password across accounts.

Key Points of the LinkedIn Breach

LinkedIn had five key areas that would have prevented their data breach. Granted, when they began their social networking company, hacking efforts were not so numerous or acute. In review, those areas are

- LinkedIn did not restrict cookie information.
- LinkedIn did not use the HTTPS protocol.
- LinkedIn web programs were weak to SQL injection attacks.
- Passwords were not salted in the LinkedIn database.
- LinkedIn's iOS application borrowed from on-phone contact databases.

Solutions to Avoid a Similar Breach

As the previous list indicates, LinkedIn could have done several things to prevent the attack. Only one of the items was truly database related; however, you may be one of only a few engineers in your company to advocate security measures. As such, you may not write the front-end code, but you can have influence on it. For now, we will simply show how to hash and salt passwords.

If you followed along in Chapter 6 and ran our `video_store` schema creation scripts, you will already have the following tables in your database. If you did not, then run the schema creation scripts as the `sys` user with `sysdba` privilege. Then, grant the `EXECUTE` privilege on the `dbms_crypto` package to the `video_store` user:

```
SQL> GRANT EXECUTE ON DBMS_CRYPTO TO video_store;
```

Connect to the `video_store` user, conditionally drop the `contact` and `system_user` tables, and create the `contact` table with this syntax:

```
SQL> DROP TABLE contact CASCADE CONSTRAINTS PURGE;
SQL> DROP TABLE system_user CASCADE CONSTRAINTS PURGE;
SQL> CREATE TABLE contact
  2  ( contact_id        NUMBER        CONSTRAINT pk_contact    PRIMARY KEY
  3  , member_id         NUMBER        CONSTRAINT nn_contact_1 NOT NULL
  4  , contact_type      NUMBER        CONSTRAINT nn_contact_2 NOT NULL
  5  , last_name         VARCHAR2(20)  CONSTRAINT nn_contact_3 NOT NULL
  6  , first_name        VARCHAR2(20)  CONSTRAINT nn_contact_4 NOT NULL
  7  , middle_name       VARCHAR2(20)
  8  , favorite_color    VARCHAR2(20)  CONSTRAINT nn_contact_9 NOT NULL
  9  , favorite_food     VARCHAR2(20)  CONSTRAINT nn_contact_10 NOT NULL
 10  , created_by        NUMBER        CONSTRAINT nn_contact_5 NOT NULL
 11  , creation_date     DATE          CONSTRAINT nn_contact_6 NOT NULL
 12  , last_updated_by   NUMBER        CONSTRAINT nn_contact_7 NOT NULL
 13  , last_update_date  DATE          CONSTRAINT nn_contact_8 NOT NULL
 );
```

Notice that we put the `favorite_food` and `favorite_color` columns in the `contact` table. We use those values as part of our salt, and we don't want hackers to inadvertently discover that fact. That's why they are in a different table and are related to contact information instead of authorization.

Create the `system_user` table as the `video_store` user with this code:

```
SQL> CREATE TABLE system_user
  2  ( system_user_id             NUMBER
  3    CONSTRAINT pk_system_user  PRIMARY KEY
  4  , system_contact_id          NUMBER
  5  , system_user_name           VARCHAR2(20)
       CONSTRAINT nn_system_user_1 NOT NULL
  6  , system_user_group_id       NUMBER
       CONSTRAINT nn_system_user_2 NOT NULL
  7  , system_user_type           NUMBER
       CONSTRAINT nn_system_user_3 NOT NULL
  8  , system_password            VARCHAR2(250)
       CONSTRAINT nn_system_user_8 NOT NULL
  9  , created_by                 NUMBER
       CONSTRAINT nn_system_user_4 NOT NULL
 10  , creation_date              DATE
       CONSTRAINT nn_system_user_5 NOT NULL
 11  , last_updated_by            NUMBER
       CONSTRAINT nn_system_user_6 NOT NULL
 12  , last_update_date           DATE
       CONSTRAINT nn_system_user_7 NOT NULL);
```

In this block, we created a column large enough to hold our new SHA2 512-bit hash. In the following function, we make a very simple one-way hashing program. While you may want the ability to decrypt values such as credit card numbers or salaries, you do not want that ability with passwords. That would be like locking your front door but leaving the key in the lock. Burglars could simply turn the key and walk in. You will want to wrap the following function if you decide to use it in production.

You can create the `hashed` function as the `video_store` user:

```
SQL> CREATE OR REPLACE FUNCTION hashed
  2  ( pv_username   IN VARCHAR2
  3  , pv_password   IN VARCHAR2
  4  , pv_phrase1    IN VARCHAR2    -- secret answer 1
  5  , pv_phrase2    IN VARCHAR2    -- secret answer 2
  6  RETURN VARCHAR2 AS
  7    -- Declare return variable.
  8    lv_salted VARCHAR2(250);
  9  BEGIN
 10    lv_salted := UPPER (
 11                 pv_username
 12            || pv_phrase1
 13            || pv_password
 14            || pv_phrase2);
 15    RETURN dbms_crypto.hash( utl_raw.cast_to_raw(lv_salted)
 16                           , dbms_crypto.hash_sh512);
 17  END;
 18  /
```

Only key people should know about special security functions like this. The point is that you reduce the overall attack-surface area by restricting knowledge about the algorithm used to create the hash, thus preventing *external and internal* hackers from reverse engineering it.

In the following block, we insert a couple of people in our `contact` and `system_user` tables. We use the same password for both users to show how the salted hash looks different.

The following `INSERT` statements should be run as the video_store user:

```
SQL> INSERT
  2  INTO    contact
  3  VALUES
  4  ( 10, 1, 1, 'Thornton', 'Billy', 'Bob', 'Red', 'Pizza'
  5  , 1, SYSDATE, 1, SYSDATE );
SQL> INSERT
  2  INTO    system_user
  3  VALUES
  4  ( 1, 10, 'thorntonbb', 2, 1
  5  , hashed('thorntonbb', 'abc123', 'pizza', 'red')
  6  , 1, SYSDATE, 1, SYSDATE );
SQL> INSERT
  2  INTO    contact
  3  VALUES
  4  ( 11, 1, 1, 'Voight', 'Angelina', 'Jolie', 'Red', 'Pizza'
  5  , 1, SYSDATE, 1, SYSDATE );
SQL> INSERT
  2  INTO    system_user
  3  VALUES
  4  ( 2, 11, 'voightaj', 2, 1
  5  , hashed('voightaj', 'abc123', 'cheerios', 'black')
  6  , 1, SYSDATE, 1, SYSDATE );
```

We issue the following query as the `video_store` user against our newly created rows to see what the hashed passwords look like:

```
SQL> COLUMN system_password FORMAT A60
SQL> COLUMN system_user_name FORMAT A20
SQL> SELECT   system_user_name
  2  ,        system_password
  3  FROM system_user;
```

The query should return the following:

```
SYSTEM_USER_NAME    SYSTEM_PASSWORD
--------------------------------------------------------------------------------
thorntonbb          306999E31B3BEEAB84B120C4C131151C5BF12E9C30374C919919CAD1F719
                    75D62930ECF99035E42640BCEDD10059F200F031AC2B6EFFB2CB2C6EF04D
                    8E87AF4E

voightaj            0F00D2C3DA3E0B67E87D8FB167F72F85FA908BD8A747AA71B0AA760B1D12
                    5635494B871C1B69D9C3AA056B84DDA34E0C8D9EF8A75FA0C45EF5284B53
                    D1DDB574
```

The hackers would have to perform both their easy-guess and known-password attacks first. Then, they would be hard-pressed to get anywhere if all they had was the hash. The next step for you is to create a password verification function that will prevent easy passwords like *abc123* from getting into your databases in the first place.

The following statement creates a `security` virtual directory as the `system` user:

```
SQL> CREATE DIRECTORY security
  2  AS '/u01/app/oracle/admin/T12101/pdb1/sec';
```

This block creates a `password_dictionary` table. We need to drop it and re-create it in the `video_store` schema:

```
SQL> DROP TABLE password_dictionary CASCADE CONSTRAINTS PURGE;
SQL> CREATE TABLE password_dictionary
  2  ( password_id     INTEGER GENERATED ALWAYS AS IDENTITY
  3  , password_fwd    VARCHAR2(30)
  4  , password_rev    VARCHAR2(30)
  5  , password_rnk    INTEGER
  6  , password_cnt    INTEGER
  7  , created_by      INTEGER
  8  , created_dt      DATE
  9  , updated_by      INTEGER
 10  , updated_dt      DATE);
```

Next, we create a temporary `password_dictionary` external table that pulls in the dictionary text file:

```
SQL> DROP TABLE PASSWORD_DICTIONARY_STAGE;
SQL> CREATE TABLE PASSWORD_DICTIONARY_STAGE
  2  ( password  VARCHAR2(50)
  3  , frequency VARCHAR2(50))
  4  ORGANIZATION EXTERNAL
  5  ( TYPE ORACLE_LOADER
  6    DEFAULT DIRECTORY security
  7    LOCATION
  8    ('tenThousandPasswords.dat'))
  9  REJECT LIMIT UNLIMITED;
```

Now, we insert the passwords into the `password_dictionary` table and drop the temporary table. The commit is implied when we perform the `DROP TABLE` statement in the next block.

```
SQL> INSERT  /*+ append */
  2  INTO  password_dictionary
  3  ( password_fwd
  4  , password_rev
  5  , password_cnt
  6  , password_rnk
  7  , created_by
  8  , created_dt
  9  , updated_by
```

```
10    , updated_dt)
11    WITH passwords AS
12    (SELECT password_fwd
13    , password_rev
14    , TO_NUMBER(TRIM(REPLACE(password_cnt, CHR(13), ' '))) password_cnt
15    , created_by
16    , created_dt
17    , updated_by
18    , updated_dt
19      FROM pwd_stg)
20    SELECT  p.password_fwd
21    ,  p.password_rev
22    ,  p.password_cnt
23    ,  RANK () OVER(ORDER BY password_cnt DESC) password_rnk
24    ,  p.created_by
25    ,  p.created_dt
26    ,  p.updated_by
27    ,  p.updated_dt
28    FROM  passwords p;
SQL> DROP TABLE password_dictionary_stage;
```

In the previous INSERT statement, we use the RANK() function to tally the password_cnt column and return the rank of the password by its use. This is a typical analytic SQL function. More information about SQL analytics can be found in *Oracle Database SQL Language Reference 12c Release 1 (12.1)*.

Our password list comes from Mark Burnett's security blog. In 2005, he wrote a book called *Perfect Passwords* (Syngress). At the same time, he published a list of the top 500 worst passwords. His list became widely distributed across the Internet. Since then, he has collected another 6 million unique username and password combinations. Some very interesting stats about his new list include

- The phrases *password*, *123...8*, and *qwerty* were used nearly 78,000 times.
- Ninety-one percent of users employ one of the top 1,000 passwords.
- The top 20 password list rarely changes.

We are aware that many of the passphrases have some vulgar reference; however, their use is frequent enough that it would be irresponsible for you to remove those phrases from your password dictionary. We kept the list and added the reversed password phrase.

Now that we have a significant list, let's make a decent password verification function. You need to understand that the function Oracle supplies is only a starter and should not be merely implemented in your environment. Our new function makes use of regular expressions, greatly simplifies the logic, and nixes the loops that Oracle used:

```
SQL> CREATE OR REPLACE FUNCTION ora12c_verify_function
  2    ( username        VARCHAR2
  3    , password        VARCHAR2
  4    , old_password    VARCHAR2)
  5    RETURN BOOLEAN IS
  6      lv_un_fwd VARCHAR2(30);
```

```
 7    lv_un_rev VARCHAR2(30);
 8    lv_hn_fwd VARCHAR2(64);
 9    lv_hn_rev VARCHAR2(64);
10    lv_in_fwd VARCHAR2(30);
11    lv_in_rev VARCHAR2(30);
12    lv_dcount NUMBER;
13  BEGIN
...
```

You must return a Boolean true/false value, and your input parameters must exclusively hold the username, new password, and old password. We use the variables to hold the forward and reverse values of the username, instance name, and server name. In the next block, we use the REVERSE SQL function to automatically flip the input strings. This is much more efficient than looping.

```
14    ---------------------------------------------------------------
15    -- The REVERSE function is much more efficient than looping.
16    ---------------------------------------------------------------
17    SELECT  username
18    ,       REVERSE(username)
19    ,       host_name
20    ,       REVERSE(host_name)
21    ,       instance_name
22    ,       REVERSE(instance_name)
23    INTO    lv_un_fwd
24    ,       lv_un_rev
25    ,       lv_hn_fwd
26    ,       lv_hn_rev
27    ,       lv_in_fwd
28    ,       lv_in_rev
29    FROM    v$instance vi;
```

Now that we have put in memory all of the values that we want to check, we will go through our string comparisons first. We do so because these comparisons are much faster than table lookups. The errors raised explain what each regular expression is looking for in the next section.

```
30    ---------------------------------------------------------------
31    -- Get all of the string comparisons out of the way first
32    ---------------------------------------------------------------
33    IF    LENGTH(password) < 8 THEN
34      RAISE_APPLICATION_ERROR(-20001
35      ,'password must be more than 8 characters');
36    ELSIF LENGTH(password) > 30 THEN
37      RAISE_APPLICATION_ERROR(-20002
38      ,'password must be no more than 30 characters');
39    ELSIF REGEXP_INSTR(password, '"') > 0 THEN
40      RAISE_APPLICATION_ERROR(-20003
41      ,'password must not contain the " symbol');
42    ELSIF REGEXP_INSTR(password, '^[a-zA-Z]') < 1 THEN
43      RAISE_APPLICATION_ERROR(-20004
44      ,'password must start with a letter');
```

```
45    ELSIF REGEXP_INSTR(password, '\d{1,}') < 1 THEN
46      RAISE_APPLICATION_ERROR(-20005
47      ,'password must contain at least one digit');
48    ELSIF REGEXP_INSTR(password, '[A-Z]{1,}') < 1 THEN
49      RAISE_APPLICATION_ERROR(-20006
50      ,'password must contain at least one upper');
51    ELSIF REGEXP_INSTR(password, '[a-z]{1,}') < 1 THEN
52      RAISE_APPLICATION_ERROR(-20007
53      ,'password must contain at least one lower');
54    ELSIF REGEXP_INSTR(password
55      ,'(%|~|#|_|!|\^|\-|\[|\]|\+|\,|\.){1,}') < 1 THEN
56      RAISE_APPLICATION_ERROR(-20008
57      ,'password must contain one of the following '
58                             ||'symbols %~#!^-[]+,.');
59    ELSIF UTL_MATCH.JARO_WINKLER(password, old_password) > .5 THEN
60      RAISE_APPLICATION_ERROR(-20009
61      ,'password is too close to the old one');
62    ELSIF INSTR(LOWER(password), lv_un_fwd) > 0 THEN
63      RAISE_APPLICATION_ERROR(-20010
64      ,'password cannot contain the username');
65    ELSIF INSTR(LOWER(password), lv_un_rev) > 0 THEN
66      RAISE_APPLICATION_ERROR (-20011
67      ,'password cannot contain the reversed username');
68    ELSIF INSTR(LOWER(password), lv_hn_fwd) > 0 THEN
69      RAISE_APPLICATION_ERROR(-20012
70      ,'password cannot contain the server name');
71    ELSIF INSTR(LOWER(password), lv_hn_rev) > 0 THEN
72      RAISE_APPLICATION_ERROR(-20013
73      ,'password cannot contain the reversed server name');
74    ELSIF INSTR(LOWER(password), lv_in_fwd) > 0 THEN
75      RAISE_APPLICATION_ERROR(-20014
76      ,'password cannot contain the instance name');
77    ELSIF INSTR(LOWER(password), lv_in_rev) > 0 THEN
78      RAISE_APPLICATION_ERROR(-20015
79      ,'password cannot contain the reversed instance_name');
80    ELSIF REGEXP_INSTR(password,'(.+{3,}).*\1' ) > 0 THEN
81      RAISE_APPLICATION_ERROR(-20016
82      ,'password cannot contain 3+ repeated characters');
83    END IF;
```

Note that our regular expressions allowed us to perform seven very complex matches. We shrunk Oracle's code from 500 lines to 100. What's more, we added several checks that Oracle did not consider in its password verification function. We especially like the (.+{3,}).*\1 and (%|~|#|_|!|\^|\-|\[|\]|\+|\,|\.){1,} expressions, which tell the function not to accept repeating characters over 3 and to require at least one of the following special characters: %~#_!^-[]+,.. Our final check looks at the password_dictionary table we created. This block will throw an error if the new password matches the forward or reverse word in the dictionary:

```
 84    -----------------------------------------------------------------
 85    -- Check the password dictionary.
 86    -----------------------------------------------------------------
 87    SELECT    COUNT(*)
 88    INTO      lv_dcount
 89    FROM      password_dictionary
 90    WHERE     password_fwd = password
 91    OR        password_rev = password;
 92
 93    IF lv_dcount > 0 THEN
 94      RAISE_APPLICATION_ERROR(-20017
 95      , 'password is a dictionary word' );
 96    END IF;
 97
 98    RETURN TRUE;
 99  END;
100  /
```

The very last thing we need to do is create or modify a profile so that the password verification function is executed. We do so in the next block as the system user:

```
SQL> GRANT EXECUTE ON ora12c_verify_function TO PUBLIC;
SQL> ALTER PROFILE DEFAULT LIMIT
  2  PASSWORD_LIFE_TIME 180 -- 6 months
  3  PASSWORD_GRACE_TIME 7  -- 7 days
  4  PASSWORD_REUSE_TIME 1095 -- 3 years before reuse
  5  PASSWORD_REUSE_MAX  3 -- only 3 uses max
  6  FAILED_LOGIN_ATTEMPTS 10
  7  PASSWORD_LOCK_TIME 4 -- 4 hour of lock per profile violation
  8  PASSWORD_VERIFY_FUNCTION ora12c_verify_function
  9  /
```

Notice that we limited the password lifetime to 180 days. In our opinion, this should really be 90 days or less, but you may not have that luxury. We also added a one-week grace time for users to change their password, beyond the 180 days. Next, we limited the reuse of the same password for 3 years and stipulated that users could use the same password only three times before it is retired permanently. Then, we limited the maximum failed logon attempts to 10 and set the lockout time to 4 hours if that limit is reached. Finally, we attach the ora12c_verify_function to the policy.

Your new function is capable of preventing nearly any weak password from entering your database. What's more, you can add passwords to your password dictionary table to strengthen the function even more. Be careful in applying checks, because you may make it impossible for users to create a password that passes. You have to apply just enough scrutiny to ensure that your database is protected without impeding business processes.

LinkedIn could have avoided its data breach entirely if it had implemented HTTPS, salted password hashing, and strong password validation software. Hackers may have been turned away from their attempts or would have lost interest in the data if it was too difficult to crack. That doesn't mean that they will not continue to hack away at your data files, because the amount of work they put into harvesting and cracking your data files is directly proportional to how much they believe they can gain monetarily or politically.

Target Breach

Late in the fourth quarter of 2013, Target Corporation announced that account data from 40 million credit and debit cards, along with other identifying information, had been stolen from its point-of-sale terminals. Before the incident, Target installed FireEye security software, which is designed to stop malware and web-based attacks. The software worked as designed, isolating and alerting security staff of initial breaches; however, the security team disregarded those alerts because of the vastness of data collected across Target's networks. Granted, Target's security teams evaluated the alerts as best as they could, but because of the size of data and noise in the data, they determined that further activity was not warranted.

Attackers accomplished this breach by installing malware on Target's point-of-sale terminals. The malware acted much like key-logging software, but it intercepted and copied database transactions instead of keystrokes. Unimpeded, attackers went on to conduct one of the largest data breaches to date.

After Target's announcement, security experts reevaluated their claims and discovered that not 40 million but as many as 70 million customers had been affected. Moreover, recent financial reports from Target showed a sharp drop in sales, as much as 40 percent. Target has yet to recover fully. According to Target reports on the incident, they were forced to spend more than $61 million in efforts to remediate vulnerabilities and to address the PR nightmare that followed.

As a result, Target's CEO and CIO have resigned their posts. Since this attack, many other retailers have admitted that they were victims of the same tactics that the Eastern European group used to blitz Target.

Key Points of the Target Breach

The Target breach did not attack databases directly. Instead, hackers performed man-in-the-middle attacks against their point-of-sale terminals. The DBA and database programmer *must* be aware of all attacks that can compromise the data set. Furthermore, DBAs and database programmers *must* make their voice heard on any vector that jeopardizes their systems. The key points behind the Target breach are

- Massive data logs masked the criticality of the attacks.
- Malware attacks were ignored.
- The CEO and CIO resigned because of associated fallout.
- Target's sales dropped as much as 40 percent following the announcement.
- Target has spent more than $61 million to date in remediation efforts.

Suggested Remediation for the Breach

The Target breach did not attack database systems directly; instead, hackers replicated and then stole data transactions just before they reached the database. DBAs and database programmers should be aware of this attack vector and insist that steps be taken to prevent similar data breaches. You must think of databases in a broader term than ORDBMS because your data exists in a myriad of places en route to and from your database system.

NSA Breach

Edward Snowden's story sounds more like a Jason Bourne novel than reality. Like Bourne, Snowden found his loyalty to the United States steadily deteriorating. Snowden eventually decided to breach his trust with his employer, and stole tens of thousands of classified documents. This is an internally mounted hack. Internal hacks are the hardest type of breach to defend against because organizations often trust their employees.

According to news accounts and interviews with Snowden, he felt obligated to divulge the data collection and mining efforts conducted by the U.S. National Security Agency (NSA) and its multinational confederates. He felt that the Fourth and Fifth Amendments of the U.S. Constitution were being violated. Then, he concluded that it was his personal duty to expose what he deemed illegal activity by the U.S. government.

Snowden stated that the turning point for him was when he witnessed key, high-level NSA managers lie to the U.S. Congress about their activities. Contrariwise, the NSA managers felt strongly that their surveillance measures were designed to protect the American people from terrorist threats.

According to Snowden, over a nine-year period, his loyalties shifted from vehemently defending the U.S. government to outright hatred of its intelligence agencies and the intelligence agencies' indifference toward its governing bodies. He began thinking about divulging data as early as 2008. Between 2008 and 2013, he used internally fabricated SSH keys to mask his activities. Then, on May 20, 2013, he exposed tens of thousands of Top Secret documents to *The Guardian*, *Der Spiegel*, *The Washington Post*, *The New York Times*, and many more news agencies.

Some say that his treachery stemmed from management's mistreatment of his skillset and his desire to play a larger role in intelligence efforts. Others call him a hero and thank him for whistle blowing. Regardless of the overall moral implications, U.S. officials state that Snowden's actions endangered thousands of lives and exposed what should be classified government programs according to the NSA.

We use this example not to debate who was right or wrong. Rather, we hope to create a poignant illustration of the havoc that can be wreaked by once-loyal employees who become, for whatever reason, bent on breaching their employer's trust.

Key Points of the NSA Breach

Snowden's approach used SSH keys to mask his stealing of restricted documents. He may have pulled them from a document database, but our guess is that he must have touched a few database systems in his efforts. Snowden's theft might have been slowed down if employee use of SSH keys was managed and monitored by the government. Clearly, he held those keys to do his assigned job. The key points behind the NSA breach are

- Snowden was loyal when he was originally vetted for Top Secret clearance.
- Snowden used encryption keys to mimic normal activity and hide his true actions.
- Snowden exposed many documents that were harmful to the United States and its affiliates.
- The cost of Snowden's breach goes way beyond financial consequences.

Suggested Remediation for the Breach

This breach has very little to do with relational database systems; however, it represents the kind of damage that can be done when system administrators have complete access to your database operating system and the ability to create encrypted, auto-logon access to external servers to or from your servers. It is a best practice to demand that persons in these roles be vetted on a regular basis to ensure that they remain loyal to your organization. This means an organization requires a well-trained internal Electronic Data Processing (EDP) auditing team with clear policies and procedures. It also means you must develop a black box (hidden from those with keys) auditing system that randomly checks how employees use their authorized credentials (including encrypted keys).

Utah Department of Technology Services Breach

In March 2012, the Utah Department of Technology Services (DTS) became yet another victim in the recent onslaught of cybercrime. Hackers from an Eastern European organization compromised a multilayered security system and discovered a test database server with a very weak password. They exploited this weak password and made a direct connection to the production database server. The cloning of the database from production to test wasn't shielded from outside access because the production database was concurrently being used by the organization.

The medical records in the database were associated with internal Medicaid payments. By April, hackers had downloaded 780,000 records, including 250,000 Social Security numbers; 500,000 records contained address, birth date, and name information. This breach came as no surprise to us because hackers deem medical records and Medicaid payments to be high-value targets.

It is possible that the state of Utah could face fines of up to $1,000 per record; however, victims of the breach have very little recourse. The victims must prove that the state was negligent in its efforts to secure personal information.

It turns out that this breach could have been easily prevented, but state employees did not consider the attackers to be as sophisticated and organized as they actually were. Luckily, operation engineers discovered the attack and stopped the transmission after looking into the unusually large amount of data that was being off loaded to a European site.

The employee who put the database in place was disciplined. What's more, the governor promptly fired the CIO/director of the DTS. State employees also put in place better intrusion detection and alerting routines. The costs of remediation were staggering and approached $406 million. The state of Utah has paid more than $9 million, leaving the bulk of the $406 million to victims, who must shoulder nearly $1,000 per breach if it results in identity theft.

Key Points of the Utah DTS Breach

It is our opinion that Governor Herbert acted as quickly and decisively as he could. His methods protected as many Utah citizens as was feasibly possible, but it would have been much better if the DBA had followed already established policies. The key points behind the DTS breach are

- Attackers were not stopped by complex layering of firewalls.
- Test database servers had live production data on them.
- Intrusion detection methods were substandard.
- Brute-force attacks were successful against weak passwords.
- The governor promptly fired the CIO.

- The overall cost of remediation is staggering, at $406 million.
- Victims often shoulder the largest burden.

Solutions to Avoid a Similar Breach

The database engineer in this example failed to follow some very basic principles. For one, the engineer built a test database that had unlocked default accounts with well-known passwords. This is plain bad…never do this! We suggest you employ similar tactics to our password verification function (presented earlier in the chapter) to seek out default accounts with weak passwords.

First, you need a special password dictionary called a rainbow table. This kind of table is easy to create. You simply write a routine that takes a user's password and alters it many times over. Then, you store the resultant hash in your rainbow table.

The following program loops through your dba_users and the password_dictionary table. Then, it modifies the users' passwords and places the resultant MD5 and SHA1 hash patterns in the rainbow table.

This block creates the password_dictionary table:

```
SQL> DROP TABLE sys.password_rainbow CASCADE CONSTRAINTS PURGE;
SQL> CREATE TABLE sys.password_rainbow
  2  ( password_id    INTEGER GENERATED ALWAYS AS IDENTITY
  3  , password_fwd   VARCHAR2(30)
  4  , password_sh1   VARCHAR2(50)
  5  , password_md5   VARCHAR2(50)
  6  , db_username    VARCHAR2(30)
  7  , created_by     INTEGER
  8  , created_dt     DATE
  9  , updated_by     INTEGER
 10  , updated_dt     DATE);
```

Now create the procedure as the system user:

```
SQL> CREATE OR REPLACE PROCEDURE sys.collect_rainbow
  2  ( pv_username    VARCHAR2
  3  , pv_password    VARCHAR2) AS
  4    lv_hash_sh1    VARCHAR2(250);
  5    lv_hash_md5    VARCHAR2(100);
  6  BEGIN
  7    EXECUTE IMMEDIATE 'ALTER USER ' || pv_username
  8                   || ' IDENTIFIED BY "' || pv_password ||'"';
  9    SELECT    password
 10    ,         spare4
 11    INTO      lv_hash_md5
 12    ,         lv_hash_sh1
 13    FROM      sys.user$
 14    WHERE     name = pv_username;
 15
 16    INSERT
 17    INTO      sys.password_rainbow
```

```
18    ( password_fwd
19    , password_sh1
20    , password_md5
21    , db_username
22    , created_by
23    , created_dt
24    , updated_by
25    , updated_dt)
26    VALUES
27    ( pv_password
28    , lv_hash_sh1
29    , lv_hash_md5
30    , pv_username
31    , 1, SYSDATE, 1, SYSDATE );
32  END;
33  /
```

This program is really quite simple and somewhat scary at the same time. Even a junior-level PL/SQL programmer is capable of doing something like this. The spookiest thing of all is that hackers don't have to do this on your database. Instead, they can create their own database and run this procedure for hours, days, and weeks. The result is a Cartesian product between the password_dictionary table and specific users that the hacker wants to exploit.

The next block loops through all of the passwords in the password_dictionary table for the user Fred:

```
SQL> DECLARE
  2    CURSOR c IS
  3      SELECT   *
  4      FROM     dba_users du CROSS JOIN sys.password_dictionary pd
  5      WHERE    du.username in ( 'FRED' );
  6  BEGIN
  7    FOR r IN c LOOP
  8      sys.collect_rainbow(r.username, r.password_fwd);
  9    END LOOP;
 10    COMMIT;
 11  END;
 12  /
PL/SQL procedure successfully completed.

Elapsed: 00:00:36.17
```

Hold the phone! This program completed the entire process of changing Fred's password and storing the hashes in a little over 36 seconds, for 10,000 known passwords. At that rate, a hacker could create a worthy rainbow table in very little time at all.

Ask yourself, "How should I use the ability to create rainbow tables to help me harden my databases?" The answer is to combat hackers by thinking like they do. Thereby, you get ahead of them by performing the same kinds of penetration tests that they might perform. But wait! Before you begin hacking away at your own database, obtain executive approval for performing hacking tests. Make sure you obtain a printed "get-out-of-jail-free card" from the corporate counsel just in

Status of Impossible Passwords

Oracle may choose to deprecate the use of impossible passwords. If they do, you may want to choose an approach that evaluates the user based on its SYS_CONTEXT. Issue a kill session if the user does not match your in-database rules.

case someone decides to challenge you about the process after the fact. That type of authorization generally comes from the corporate legal department. Never miss that step, or you may find yourself fired, the defendant in a civil lawsuit, or even criminally charged.

After you have adequately ensured that you have permission to proceed and face no culpability, expand your password_dictionary table and run this program for all of your accounts. Did we say "all"? Yup! Lastly, you scan all of your databases, looking for hashes that match your very large rainbow table. We promise that the results will surprise you. Your final step is to set up a good password verification function, assign it to your profiles, and invalidate any password that is known.

We will finish our discussion on passwords with this one last note. Back in Oracle version 7, database administrators had to mangle user passwords in order to lock accounts. When they did so, a user could not log on to the database until a valid password was given. The reason was that the authentication subroutines expected the hash value, and they could not do anything with clear text. This is how they did it:

```
SQL> ALTER USER fred IDENTIFIED BY VALUES 'impossible';
```

That was it. It's probably one of the simplest commands you could issue against the database, but it's very powerful. We're lucky, because Oracle kept this ability in all of its following releases. If it were up to us, we would set all default account passwords to an impossible value. We say that with some trepidation because we know there will always be exceptions. What you don't want is for your entire database to be compromised because it serviced an application that relied on a default account with a well-known password.

NIST

The National Institute of Standards and Technology (NIST) is a thought leader in computer security, specializing in encryption, security architecture, and risk management. They have two departments that you should be very familiar with: the National Cybersecurity Center of Excellence (NCCoE) and the Computer Security Division (CDS).

According to http://csrc.nist.gov/nccoe/The-Center/About/About.html, "The NCCoE is part of the NIST Information Technology Laboratory (ITL) and operates in close collaboration with the Computer Security Division." Both groups are anxious and ready to help you if you reach out to them. They offer their standards and help freely because NIST's official mandate is to protect the information technology that is relied upon by the U.S. economy, citizens, and government.

SANS

The Systems Administration, Networking, and Security (SANS) Institute was founded in 1989. Originally, SANS focused on providing cybersecurity conferences; however, in the mid-1990s it matured into the commercialized company that it is today. SANS is the premier source of security training, and we advise you to pay heed to its publications.

One of SANS' best-known publications is its *Top 20 Critical Security Controls* (www.sans.org/ critical-security-controls/). Version 5 of this publication lists the following as its Top 20 Critical Security Controls:

- Inventory of Authorized and Unauthorized Devices
- Inventory of Authorized and Unauthorized Software
- Secure Configurations for Hardware/Software on Mobile Devices, Laptops, Workstations, and Servers
- Continuous Vulnerability Assessment and Remediation
- Malware Defenses
- Application Software Security
- Wireless Access Control
- Data Recovery Capability
- Security Skills Assessment and Appropriate Training to Fill Gaps
- Secure Configurations for Network Devices such as Firewalls, Routers, and Switches
- Limitation and Control of Network Ports, Protocols, and Services
- Controlled Use of Administrative Privileges
- Boundary Defense
- Maintenance, Monitoring, and Analysis of Audit Logs
- Controlled Access of Information Based on the Need to Know
- Account Monitoring and Control
- Data Protection
- Incident Response and Management
- Secure Network Engineering
- Penetration Testing and Red Team Exercises

Your security efforts will be greatly enhanced if you do nothing more than implement these security controls. Believe us when we say that doing so is a monumental task. Without guidance, you may never completely cover each item. Possibly the most important task you have is to obtain executive support for the creation of policies and programs that support this list. Your entire success hinges on whether or not your executive staff actually believes that cybersecurity is important.

Planning and Implementing Cybersecurity

In a large organization, your first task in the creation of a security program is to carefully create *nontechnical* presentations that explain in simple terms why cybersecurity is important. Stress the costs and effort associated with remediating data breaches. When given the opportunity to present these ideas to executives or other key decision-makers, do so patiently and positively. Nothing will kill your efforts to gain buy-in faster than a lack of patience with your audience's level of knowledge, or by responding to their questions with techno-babble. Remember that executives are not stupid; they simply have a different focus. Your technical jargon may seem to them just as illogical as their business jargon may sound to you. Finally, stress the costs associated with security breaches, because dollars always speak louder to executives than security principles or technical terms.

Once you obtain executive support and funding (that last bit is very important), seek the aid of your chief engineers (or team leads in a small organization) and legal department to create policies that provide more than lip service. Nothing is more frustrating than trying to exact accountability when the offending engineers know you can't hold them responsible. Make sure that each of your policy items is defined clearly and has measurable steps. We suggest making a grid of the SAN Top 20 Critical Security Controls. Cater each item to your database-centric needs and schedule the rollout of remediation items in a steady fashion. We also suggest that you create a delivery schedule, an example of which is provided in Table 7-1. Please note that the following table uses both a SANS and Maturity Level (ML) identifier.

As soon as you complete your planning, policy creation, and procedure setup, you must educate employees. Our suggestion is that you get your internal graphics department to make up

SANS	ML	Remediation	Delivery Schedule			
			Q1-2015	Q2-2015	Q3-2015	Q4-2015
1-1	1	Deploy an automated asset discovery tool to find all database instances	*			
1-2	1	Create DHCP logging to help detect rogue database instances	*			
1-3	1	Create/update inventory systems that track all database instances		*		
8-1	1	Ensure that all databases are backed up			*	
8-2	1	Test backups on a regular basis			*	
8-3	1	Encrypt all backups			*	
17-1	2	Deploy hard drive encryption software throughout the enterprise				*
17-2	2	Deploy encryption key management				*
2-2	2	Perform data discovery and assessment activities to vet data sensitivity				*

TABLE 7-1. *Sample Remediation Schedule*

some nifty posters that advertise the benefits of your new program. Don't be afraid to ham it up a bit. You can offer prizes to the first groups of people who go to your company intranet and learn about a particular security measure.

Once you get everyone on board, host a mandatory training session (or sessions) and show recognition for employee groups who have already begun their quest for database security nirvana. Remember to reinforce this training by distributing continual reminders…educate, educate, educate! Finally, use your executive support to push down accountability for the policies you create. This accountability will most certainly drive employees to do more remediation tasks than any other activity, and if you remember to make it fun, you won't be labeled the bad guy.

Separation of Duties

In our experience, you will need to set up a separate team of database administrators who specialize in database security. Their entire purpose will be to police what the other DBAs, software engineers, and users do. They won't have average day-to-day tasks like database backups and recoveries. Instead, they will use discovery tools like Oracle Audit Vault and Database Firewall to monitor activity and ensure that your database security program remains vibrant. You will find this bit of advice very helpful because priorities from database managers inherently clash with security efforts. For example, it becomes easy for a manager who is in charge of both security and operations to overload the operations side, making unnecessary security allowances to ensure overall uptime. After all, uptime is more visible than the dark workings of hackers.

It may prove difficult to set up a separate team. Some of the organizations we have worked with installed a single engineer on a database security team. Other organizations have allocated a portion of a database administrator's time. Whatever the case, you will have to continue garnering support until the principles of database security gain credence.

Supporting Scripts

The following programs are available on the McGraw-Hill Professional website to support this chapter:

- The `ch_07_linkedin.sql` program contains the code used in the "LinkedIn" section.
- The `ch_07_udots.sql` program contains the code used in the "Utah Department of Technology Services" section.
- The `ch_07_passwords.sql` program contains the code used to create the `password_dictionary` table.
- The `ch_07_rainbow.sql` program contains the code used to create the `password_rainbow` table.

Summary

Ultimately, database security is everyone's responsibility, and it surprises us when we hear database engineers balk at the suggestion of implementing security measures. You must be vigorous in your efforts to communicate the benefits of secure database administration and design to fellow engineers and management and to get them to buy into the planning and implementation. We hope this chapter helped make you aware of the overall costs associated with a data breach. In addition, you should be armed with information on how to create and move forward with your database security program.

CHAPTER
8

Developing Secure
Applications

Purpose

The purpose of this chapter is to illustrate some of the technical options and best practices to provide a secure and stable database environment for users. Recall that all of the security breach case studies in Chapter 7 had associated costs that easily reached into the millions. It would behoove you to pay particular attention to Chapter 7 and this chapter so that you can begin to harden your database systems against attackers.

Typically, engineers who fare better are constant readers. There isn't a day or week that goes by without them learning something new. Many computer hackers are like the engineers just mentioned. They are curious and they do their homework—lots of it. They are masters of multiple computer-related disciplines, and in some areas they can be considered expert or industry leading. If you approach your hardening skills with the same gusto, you might be able to thwart their attacks, but you constantly have to be on your guard.

Advantages

The greatest advantage of adopting the methods presented in this chapter is business continuity. Think of your company assets, and data might not come to mind immediately, but it's a valuable asset. Unfortunately, data alone isn't good enough anymore. Companies simply cannot function unless their data is of high quality and is delivered in a timely fashion. You must collect, constrain, and cleanse your data regularly so that it clearly represents the common and accurate truth about the condition of your business. Data does not help business owners and corporate executives make good decisions unless it is on time, truthful, and safe.

The second greatest advantage to running a well-maintained database is job security. Business owners will recognize your efforts when you show that you care about their data. You build trust with them when you responsibly protect it. Database engineers who consistently show their worth to the company are seldom let go.

In order to obtain the respect of business owners, you must let your success speak for you. Make sure that you quantify everything that you do. Then, find a way to channel the importance of your work to management. Don't get carried away. Blabbing all the time about how great you are will not impress the top brass. If possible, keep track of your project's cost-to-implement and overall savings ratio. Remember that your achievements are often the result of many small successes.

You must remain focused. As we stated earlier, hackers are masters at multiple disciplines, and it would be easier for you to boil the ocean than to present a perfect defense against firewall and OS penetration. That is why we suggested in Chapter 7 that you implement the *Top 20 Critical Security Controls*, published by SANS (www.sans.org/critical-security-controls/).

Disadvantages

The biggest potential disadvantage of securing your database systems arises only if you lose track of why the database was created in the first place. For example, you may focus so much on creating the perfect password complexity function that you impede business efforts. True, your users will be forced to create incredibly strong passwords, thereby providing a very good defense against data breach. However, the function may be so difficult to pass that developers, engineers, and business users will begin to hate it. Instead of generating trust and loyalty, your effort will spawn resentment and disloyalty. Think about it…the purpose of the database is to do business and keep track of business. If your all-too-perfect password function interferes with the business, then you have looked beyond the mark and stymied the basic reason databases exist.

Another potential disadvantage of securing your database systems is that the database architects may over-engineer their systems, as they tend to do, and spend more money than is budgeted for the project. Sometimes the rigidity of their systems comes from their desire to control every aspect of a process or group of people. Other times, their negative past experiences heavily influence their designs and decision-making processes. For whatever reason, their added requirements go well beyond what the business actually needs, and the costs of their projects soar.

Overview

This chapter introduces the following topics related to developing secure applications. We realize that nearly every one of these topics is sufficiently substantive to warrant its own chapter, but such deep coverage would exceed the scope of this book.

- Programming patterns
- Auditing and Oracle Audit Vault
- Secure application roles
- Oracle's new multitenant architecture
- Sanitizing SQL and PL/SQL

You can improve program reuse by applying programming patterns. Programming patterns let you innovate from a common framework and produce better generalized coding solutions. Auditing and Oracle Audit Vault let you secure the use of your code. Just make sure you also implement secure application roles, which gives you more visibility into who does what within the database. You also can more effectively leverage your Oracle licensing cost by using Oracle's new multitenant architecture. A multitenant architecture typically reduces the number of physical database installations in your organization. Lastly, you should sanitize SQL and PL/SQL because sanitized code becomes easier to troubleshoot and maintain.

Programming Patterns

All too often, we see database programmers create programs that either try to do too much or reinvent an already built-in package. One programmer we knew attempted to create a fuzzy match between search terms and products. Instead of using Oracle's text-based indexes or its `utl_match` built-in package, the engineer created a function that spanned more than 500 lines of code. By chance, we were asked to look at the code, and we immediately asked why so much effort had been put into the function. No one knew the answer.

Programming patterns are designs that solve types of coding problems. A solid knowledge of programming patterns can help you solve problems more quickly with less code. Programming patterns also give you a framework for solving unstructured problems with tried and true methods.

We offered a better method. Instead of gyrating and contorting through superficial checks, we created a very simple search function based on the `utl_match.jarow_winkler` function. For those of you who haven't heard of this function, it has two variants. The first calculates the number of changes required to make the first string match the second string. The second variant predicts similarity between the two strings.

To test our theory, we created a table containing 80,000 English words (the instructions for creating the English word table are in the online code). Then, we created a simple 11-line function that wrapped the `utl_match.jarow_winkler_similarity` function as follows:

```
SQL> CREATE OR REPLACE FUNCTION compare_me
  2  ( thing_1 IN VARCHAR2
  3  , thing_2 IN VARCHAR2 ) RETURN NUMBER
  4  PARALLEL_ENABLE
  5  DETERMINISTIC AS
  6  BEGIN
  7    RETURN utl_match.jaro_winkler_similarity(
  8           NVL(thing_1,' '),NVL(thing_2,' '));
  9  END;
 10  /
```

In this code, we wrapped the `utl_match` function because it was not enabled for parallel execution. We also wanted to take advantage of the `deterministic` keyword that allows Oracle to cache responses and return answers precalculated if they have been called before.

If you want a more precise score, you can use the `jarow_winkler` function instead. Make sure you multiply by 100 and round your results to the desired precision. Simply replace lines 8 and 9 with this one:

```
  7    RETURN utl_match.jaro_winkler(
  8           NVL(thing_1,' '),NVL(thing_2,' '));
```

Next, we created a SQL statement that cross-joined all of the values in our English words table with itself. This step rendered a comprehensive coverage of all 80,000 words. In this case, we wanted to compare all of the words that started with the letter *a* as follows:

```
SQL> WITH litmus AS
  2  (SELECT   ew1.column1 stuff1
  3  ,         ew2.column1 stuff2
  4  ,         compare_me(ew1.column1,ew2.column1) cm
  5  FROM      ew ew1 CROSS JOIN ew ew2
  6  WHERE     SUBSTR(ew1.column1,1,1) IN ('a','A')
  7  AND       SUBSTR(ew2.column1,1,1) IN ('a','A'))
  8  SELECT  *
  9  FROM    litmus
 10  WHERE   cm > 95;
```

In this query, the `compare_me` function is used to provide a closeness score between the source column and its list of words. The score for `jarow_winkler_similarity` is 0–100, meaning that a 100 score is a 100 percent match. The value is rounded to the nearest percent. This query returns the following results:

STUFF1	STUFF2	CM
affectation	affectation	100
affectation	affectations	98
affectation	affectation's	96
affectation	affection	96
affectations	affectation	98

```
affectations              affectations              100
affectations              affection's                98
affection's               affection                 96
affection's               affectations               98
affection's               affection's               100
affected                  affected                  100
affected                  affectedly                 96
affectedly                affected                   96
...
10176 rows selected.
Elapsed: 00:00:19.69
```

Wow! Our little server did 10,176 comparisons in 19.69 seconds. Bear in mind that this function will make your processors spike. If you use it, you will certainly have to set up resource management groups. If you have enough money in your budget and the search term is sufficiently complex, you will want to create a server farm where subordinate databases compare chunks of the search and return their results to a query coordinator. In the end, our little 11-line function, paired with an ingenious cross-join, created a much better approach than the developer's 500 lines of code.

When we speak of best programming patterns, we mean the ability of an engineer to create sustainable code, using the least amount of code, by reuse of existing methods. In order to create this kind of thing, database engineers must really know their craft. This requires that they know their technology. The database engineer who designed the 500-line fuzzy match function was not aware of built-in programs and thus created a function that was difficult to read, let alone maintain.

We have seen similar efforts made with encryption tasks. Our password-hashing example from Chapter 7 is a prime example of coding simply. Recall that our business objective was to create a one-way, salted hash. Instead of re-creating the wheel, we used Oracle's dbms_crypto .hash function, combined with concatenation. Voilà! Our application passwords instantly became much more secure, as follows:

```
SQL> CREATE OR REPLACE FUNCTION hashed
  2 ( pi_username   IN VARCHAR2
  3 , pi_password   IN VARCHAR2
  4 , pi_phrase1    IN VARCHAR2    -- secret answer 1
  5 , pi_phrase2    IN VARCHAR2    -- secret answer 2)
  6 RETURN VARCHAR2 AS
  7   lv_salted VARCHAR2(250);
  8 BEGIN
  9   lv_salted := UPPER( pi_username
 10              ||          pi_phrase1
 11              ||          pi_password
 12              ||          pi_phrase2);
 13   RETURN dbms_crypto.hash(
 14              utl_raw.cast_to_raw(lv_salted)
 15            , dbms_crypto.hash_sh512);
 16 END;
 17 /
```

You should strive for simplicity instead of coding all-or-nothing functions and procedures. Break large tasks down into their smallest functional chunks and then code each of those. Package the smaller chunks into reusable program groups that are independent of the larger task as a whole. It may be tempting for you to write larger chunks of code. Don't do it. Your code will not be reusable and will become rigid the very instant you complete it.

Now…drink your own Kool-Aid. Use your packages as code libraries. If possible, reuse these libraries instead of writing new code. At first, your library will be meager and will not seem very helpful. As it grows, you will discover that this approach saves you an incredible amount of time and provides system continuity.

Auditing with Oracle Audit Vault

A few years ago, Oracle set out on a quest to centralize audit data. To achieve that goal, Oracle built a simple data warehouse, created an intelligent agent that could be installed on multiple operating systems, and built a reporting and alerting application on top of the warehouse. Oracle Audit Vault is our reporting and alerting application.

For the most part, the warehouse works well, until it is loaded with hundreds of millions or billions of rows. If it were up to us, we would redesign the warehouse to use a star schema instead of placing all of the audit events in a single table (`event_table`). With that redesign, the warehouse would function well even if its fact tables contained several billion records.

We have also encountered a few instances in which the agent stopped responding. That is to be expected. We have never seen an agent-driven application run perfectly every time. Our solution to this problem was to write a heartbeat program that checks for agent vitality. If the agent goes down, we simply restart it. Using this method made the entire product solid, and we were able to collect audit data even on our busiest systems.

It was interesting to see the results. On one occasion, we caught unauthorized users poking around HR data. Catching unauthorized activity was possible before we implemented Audit Vault, but the data was disparate, making it difficult for us to get an overall view of such activity. Audit Vault's conglomeration of data empowered us to *see* what was going on.

Within the Audit Vault application, you can audit database objects, build alerts on simple events, maintain audit policy and user entitlement, and control the audit data lifecycle. Audit Vault's agents are able to connect to the following databases:

- SQL Anywhere Database
- MySQL
- Oracle Database
- Microsoft SQL Server
- Sybase
- DB2
- Windows Active Directory
- LDAP

Oracle plans to increase this list, but for now it is rather impressive. In some cases, third-party databases don't have the level of auditing and reporting that Oracle does. Installing the agent on those servers gives you the ability to pull back system logs and any audit data that the third-party database has to offer. That way, you have a single homogenous warehouse of all your database activity (see Figure 8-1).

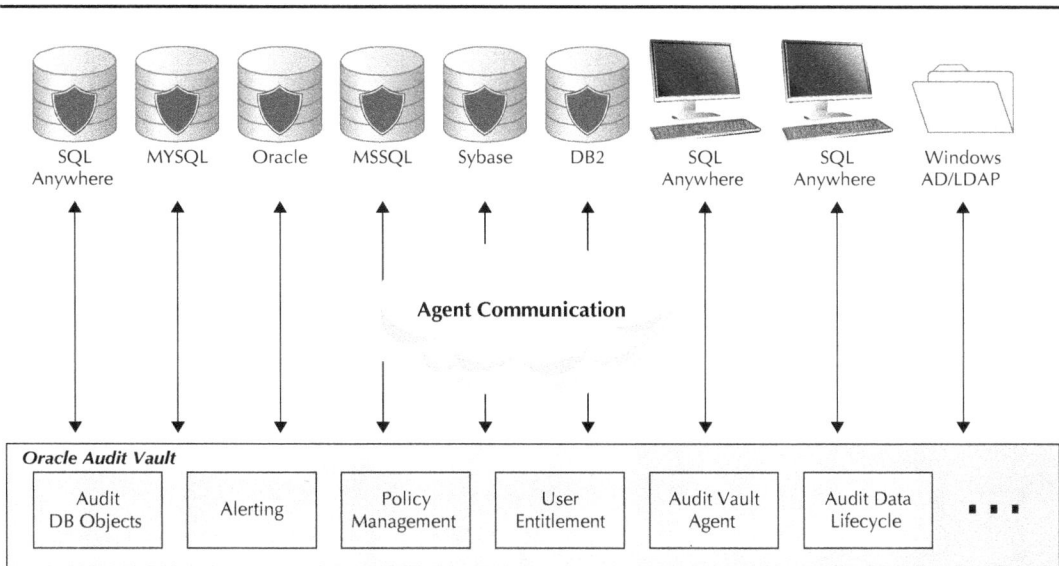

FIGURE 8-1. *Oracle Audit Vault connectivity*

We have to say that we were impressed with the level of hardening that Oracle put into its Audit Vault Server. Currently, it uses the same kernel as Oracle Exadata and the 11.2.0.3 database instance. The installation and updates were a breeze, but they knocked out any customization done to system files like /etc/fstab. We discovered this after using an NFS mount to back up our files. Granted, Oracle has a backup utility built into its web application, but we wanted the ease of simply pushing information to a network-mounted device.

Oracle developed the front-end application in Apex. It's a web-based tool that supplies an end-user interface and e-mail alerting (see Figure 8-2). This is where you will spend most of your time, unless you plan to directly attach to the internal database to do complex analytics. Your end users should never do this. Oracle suggests that you only attach to it for support reasons.

You need to develop an incident management process before you push Audit Vault into production. If you don't, one of three things will happen:

- Your company won't be able to litigate when hackers are successful in their attacks, because you will have no way of proving that your evidence has not been tampered with.

- Your company will fire internal hackers and then get sued by them for damages for wrongful dismissal.

- Your processes will break down and you won't be able to do anything about the hack when it does happen.

It would be much better for your company to iron out your incident management process before Audit Vault goes into production. What's more, a small incident management team should be trained on external laws and internal policy. They and HR should be the team to coordinate disciplinary action, not you (see Figure 8-3).

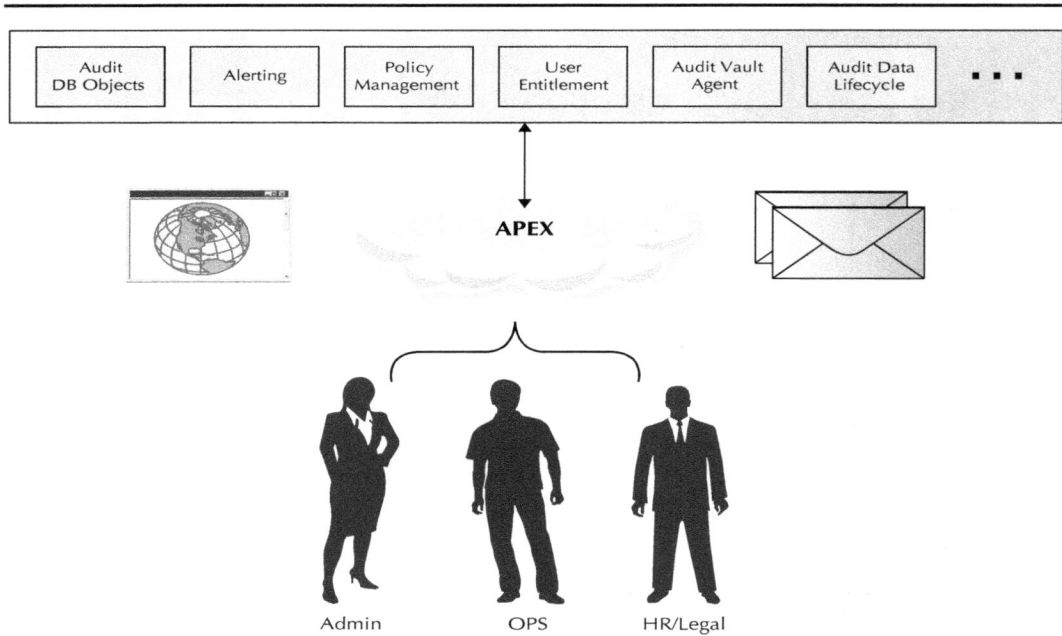

FIGURE 8-2. *Audit Vault user interaction*

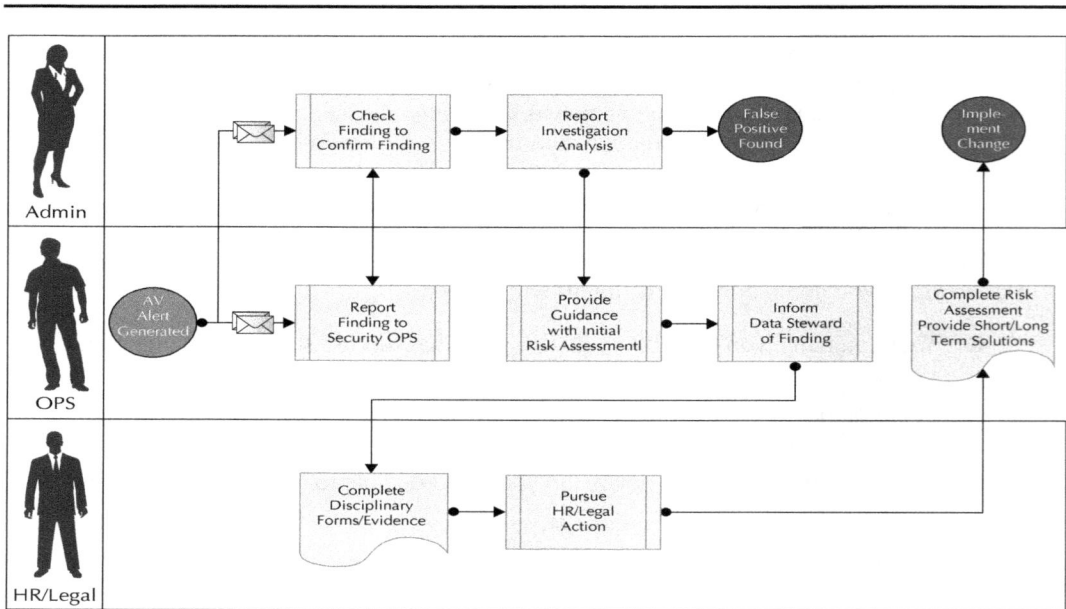

FIGURE 8-3. *Possible incident management process*

Secure Application Roles

Secure application roles (SARs), like any other roles in the database, can receive grants and be assigned to users. The benefit that you get from these kinds of roles over others is that a governing program is run to validate that the role can be active. The disadvantage to SARs is that the validation procedure must be run after logon and you cannot simply create a logon trigger to handle it for you.

Secure application roles are easy enough to set up. You can program them statically or make them table-driven. We suggest the table-driven approach because you won't have to change the program each time you want to add or subtract a set of rules. For now, we will explain how to make a secure application role with static checks.

We create two users, Fred and Wilma. Fred has the ability to select from the video_store .product_dim table and Wilma does not; however, we will attempt to run the SAR while logged in as both users. This creates users Fred and Wilma:

```
SQL> CONN / AS SYSDBA
SQL> CREATE USER fred IDENTIFIED BY fioora12;
SQL> GRANT CREATE SESSION TO fred;
SQL> CREATE USER wilma IDENTIFIED BY fioora12;
SQL> GRANT CREATE SESSION TO wilma;
```

Next, we create the secure application role procedure. It white lists the users and grants access only if the user meets its criteria. This method is static, but we will show you how to make dynamic table-driven white lists in the "Proxy Users" section following this one.

NOTE
We create the dbsec schema and the examples in this chapter in the supporting scripts.

```
SQL> CREATE OR REPLACE PROCEDURE dbsec.grant_vsp_select
  2    AUTHID CURRENT_USER AS
  3      lv_counter        NUMBER;
  4      lv_db_user        VARCHAR2(50) :=
  5                          LOWER(SYS_CONTEXT('userenv','current_user'));
  6      lv_time           varchar2(50) := TO_CHAR(sysdate,'HH24:MI:SS');
  7    BEGIN
  8      IF lv_db_user = 'fred' AND
  9         lv_time between '01:00:00' and '24:00:00' THEN
 10         lv_counter := 1;
 11      ELSE
 12         NULL;
 13      END IF;
 14      IF lv_counter > 0 THEN
 15        dbms_output.put_line('VSP_SELECT Granted');
 16        dbms_session.set_role('VSP_SELECT');
 17      ELSE
 18        dbms_output.put_line(
 19          'What are you doing ''||lv_db_user||''?'' );
 20        dbms_output.put_line ( lv_db_user );
 21        dbms_output.put_line ( lv_time    );
 22        null;
```

```
23    END IF;
24   END;
25   /
```

Notice our output on lines 18 and 19. You don't want to do this kind of thing in a production environment because it will give a hacker hints about what must be done to compromise the validation procedure. Next, we create the role and grant it to both Fred and Wilma:

```
SQL> create role vsp_select identified using dbsec.grant_vsp_select;
SQL> grant select on video_store.product_dim to vsp_select;
SQL> grant vsp_select to fred;
SQL> grant execute on dbsec.grant_vsp_select to fred;
```

Now, as Fred, we log on and attempt to select from the video_store.product_dim table. It fails because we haven't run the procedure yet.

```
***AS FRED***
SQL> conn fred/fioora12
SQL> SELECT COUNT(*) FROM video_store.product_dim;

SELECT COUNT(*) FROM video_store.product_dim
                              *
ERROR at line 1:
ORA-00942: table or view does not exist
```

We grant the secure application role to Fred and reattempt the previous query in the following block:

```
SQL> SET SERVEROUTPUT ON
SQL> SET TIMING ON
SQL> SET TAB OFF
SQL> EXECUTE sec.grant_vsp_select;
VSP_SELECT Granted
SQL> SELECT COUNT(*) FROM video_store.product_dim;
```

It should print:

```
  COUNT(*) ----------    1234567
```

Observe that Fred is finally able to select from the video_store.product_dim table, but only after he executes the procedure. Our attempt with Wilma won't be so lucky. She has rights to execute the procedure, but according to our rules, only Fred can actually set the role:

```
***AS WILMA***
SQL> SET SERVEROUTPUT ON
SQL> SET TIMING ON
SQL> SET TAB OFF
SQL> EXECUTE sec.grant_vsp_select;
What are you doing Wilma?
wilma
14:46:07
```

As you can see, applying secure application roles is a handy way to provide yet another layer of security between the data and your users. There are only two drawbacks to this method. The first is that the user must execute the procedure in order to gain rights, and if the user is an application account, it may not be able to do so. The second problem is that Fred cannot make any objects in his schema until he has direct rights granted to him on tables, and that thwarts the whole mechanism. Fred's attempt to do so fails in the next block:

```
SQL> conn fred/fioora12
SQL> EXECUTE sec.grant_vsp_select;

SQL> CREATE VIEW test AS SELECT * FROM video_store.product_dim;
CREATE VIEW test AS SELECT * FROM video_store.product_dim;

                                        *

ERROR at line 1:
ORA-01031: insufficient privileges
```

Proxy Users

We suggest an entirely different approach…

Think about your current method. Most likely, you have three types of users. The first type represents people who can only log on. Most of their rights are granted through roles because they don't need to create named objects or even own a schema. The second type represents your power users, who need to create objects and thereby need to have rights granted through roles and directly to them. The third type represents your applications, which log directly in and manipulate database objects that they own.

It might take you a week or more to create a report showing all of the rights that your users have. A diagram of the rights might look more like a bowl of spaghetti than anything else (see Figure 8-4). What's more, your developers know the application password and you constantly have to convince them that they don't need to know the production passwords. Unfortunately, you must give them application passwords occasionally so that they can troubleshoot. That means you have to change the passwords and coordinate with other system administrators to have them change their passwords as well. There may even be legacy application accounts that you would like to permanently lock out but can't because the application would break. So…what do you do?

The secure application role won't help you to clean up your spaghetti bowl of user rights. You can see from our previous code that Fred is not able to create named objects based on his role-granted rights. Our approach starts with a new way of thinking about users, roles, and rights. It uses already built-in methods and requires only a change of perspective. It can be implemented such that authenticating users never have any more rights than create session. Finally, it enables logon triggers to revoke their proxy access to your data layer if they don't meet all of your rules.

The key mechanism in this new method is the proxy user. Proxy users are easy to create, but most DBAs and users do not know about them. Proxy rights allow connecting users to assume another identity. They literally become the user they have proxied into. We show you how to do this in the following block:

```
SQL> ALTER USER wilma GRANT CONNECT THROUGH fred;
SQL> CONNECT fred[wilma]@a002
SQL> SHOW USER
```

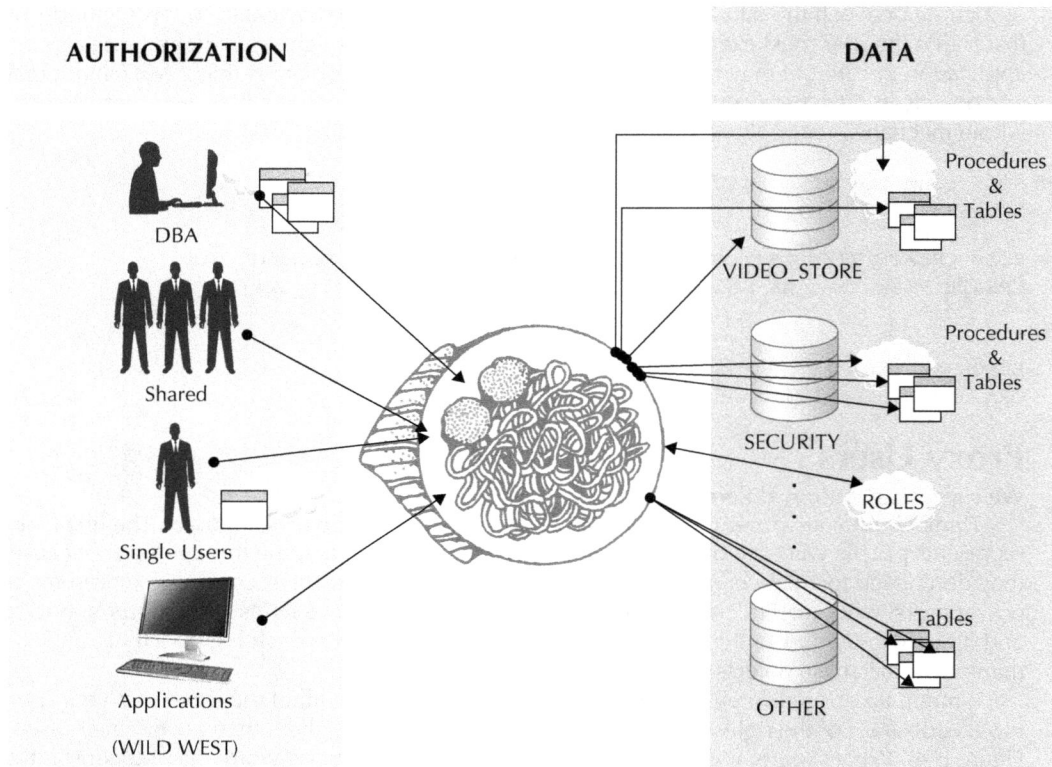

FIGURE 8-4. *User rights before proxy*

It should print

```
USER is "WILMA"
```

By itself, this may not seem very special to you. In fact, you may think, "Sure, Fred can become Wilma...big deal." To this thought we smile and say, "Quite the contrary! This ability means everything."

Imagine a three-layered database system (see Figure 8-5). The innermost layer (Data) holds data and programs. The users who own these accounts are permanently locked and have their passwords set to impossible values. This is where your data lives and can be protected. At no point can anyone log on at this level, and you have triggers set up to alert you if anyone attempts to do so.

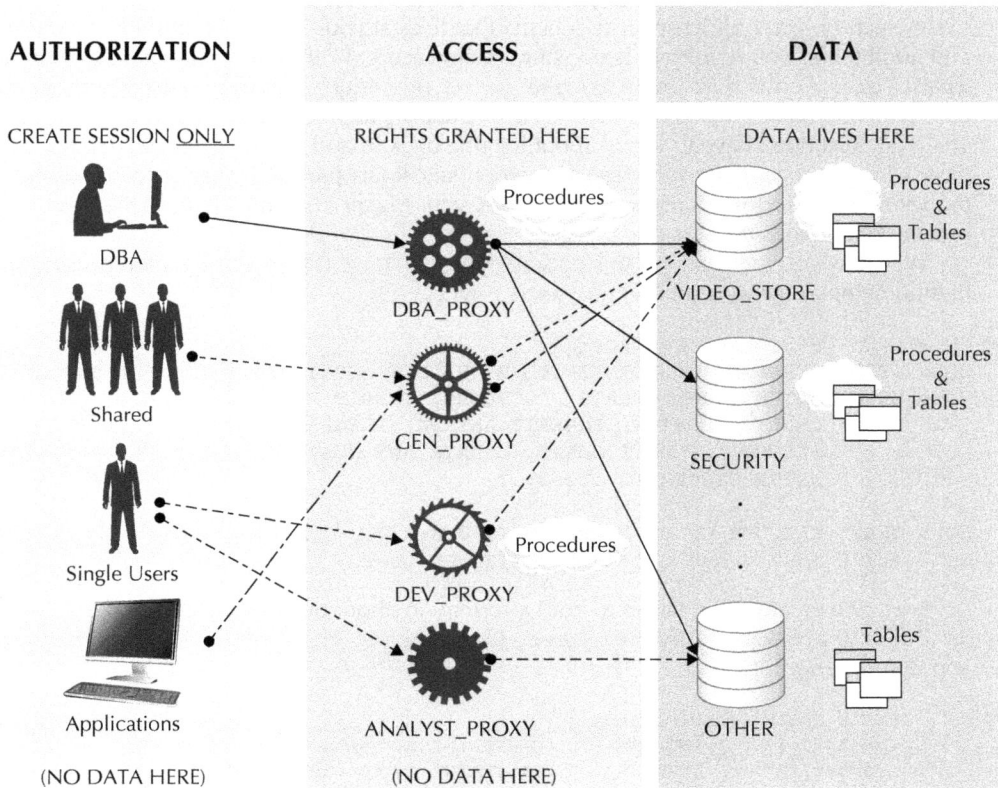

FIGURE 8-5.   *Proxy-based access*

The next layer (Access) represents a finite set of users by their role. They are not human users and have 30-character passwords that change on a regular basis (every week or month). You only have 5, 10, or even 15 of these accounts. They represent all of the functional roles that your database maintains. For example, you may have DBA_SENIOR, DBA_JUNIOR, DEVELOPER, and QA accounts. At no time does anyone know the password to these accounts, as they are randomly generated strings. This layer never holds any data, but can have programs and views. You assign your rights and set up auditing on this layer.

The outermost layer (Authorization) represents all of the application and human user accounts. At no point do any accounts created here own or create objects. In fact, the only right that they have is create session. That's it! No more! You grant proxy access to this layer as needed and on a timed basis. For example, Fred could be a senior-level developer and may help you with your junior-level DBA work. His proxy access to the DEVELOPER account has a 365-day timeout, but his DBA_JUNIOR access is granted on an as-needed basis. In fact, you seldom grant Fred more than a day or week of proxy access on the DBA_JUNIOR account.

The Database Security Schema

In this section, you build a security schema that lives at your data layer. It holds the packages and audit tables you require to keep your system secure. Within the main package, you have a `grant_proxy` procedure and a `revoke_proxy` procedure. The `grant_proxy` procedure automatically grants access but also sets a secondary job at a desired period to revoke that access. That way, you don't have to worry about logging back in and revoking access. What's more, you have a logon trigger that evaluates user credentials. If any part of the user account does not match the values in your `dbsec.proxy_rule` table, your trigger immediately calls the `revoke_proxy` procedure and kills the session.

We show you the basics of this package next. First, we create a user called `dbsec`, and run the following as the `sys` user with `sysdba` privileges:

```
SQL> DROP USER dbsec cascade;
SQL> CREATE USER dbsec IDENTIFIED BY VALUES 'S0m3 R341ly B1g P4$$w0rd';
SQL> GRANT ALTER USER, CREATE PROCEDURE, CREATE ROLE
  2  ,       CREATE SESSION, INHERIT ANY PRIVILEGES
  3  ,       SELECT ANY DICTIONARY, CREATE ANY JOB
  4  ,       ALTER SYSTEM TO dbsec;

SQL> GRANT EXECUTE ON DBMS_CRYPTO TO dbsec;
SQL> ALTER USER dbsec QUOTA UNLIMITED ON users;
```

Next, we create a few tables to hold information about our users. They are the `dbsec_contact`, `dbsec_system_user`, `dbsec_proxy_rule_type`, `dbsec_proxy_rule`, and `dbsec_logon` tables:

```
SQL> CREATE TABLE dbsec.contact
  2  ( contact_id      INTEGER     CONSTRAINT pk_contact    PRIMARY KEY
  3  , member_id       INTEGER     CONSTRAINT nn_contact_1 NOT NULL
  4  , contact_type    INTEGER     CONSTRAINT nn_contact_2 NOT NULL
  5  , last_name       VARCHAR(20) CONSTRAINT nn_contact_3 NOT NULL
  6  , first_name      VARCHAR(20) CONSTRAINT nn_contact_4 NOT NULL
  7  , middle_name     VARCHAR(20)
  8  , favorite_color  VARCHAR(20) CONSTRAINT nn_contact_9 NOT NULL
  9  , favorite_food   VARCHAR(20) CONSTRAINT nn_contact_10 NOT NULL
 10  , created_by      INTEGER     CONSTRAINT nn_contact_5 NOT NULL
 11  , created_dt      DATE        CONSTRAINT nn_contact_6 NOT NULL
 12  , updated_by      INTEGER     CONSTRAINT nn_contact_7 NOT NULL
 13  , updated_dt      DATE        CONSTRAINT nn_contact_8 NOT NULL);


SQL> CREATE TABLE dbsec.system_user
  2  ( system_user_id       INTEGER      CONSTRAINT pk_system_user   PRIMARY KEY
  3  , contact_id           INTEGER
  4  , system_user_name     VARCHAR(20)  CONSTRAINT nn_system_user_1 NOT NULL
  5  , system_user_group_id INTEGER      CONSTRAINT nn_system_user_2 NOT NULL
  6  , system_user_type     INTEGER      CONSTRAINT nn_system_user_3 NOT NULL
  7  , system_password      VARCHAR(250) CONSTRAINT nn_system_user_4 NOT NULL
  8  , created_by           INTEGER      CONSTRAINT nn_system_user_5 NOT NULL
  9  , created_dt           DATE         CONSTRAINT nn_system_user_6 NOT NULL
```

```
 10  , updated_by            INTEGER      CONSTRAINT nn_system_user_7 NOT NULL
 11  , updated_dt            DATE         CONSTRAINT nn_system_user_8 NOT NULL);


SQL> CREATE TABLE dbsec.proxy_rule_type
  2  ( proxy_rule_type_id    INTEGER CONSTRAINT pk_proxy_rule_type PRIMARY KEY
  3  , proxy_rule_description VARCHAR(50) CONSTRAINT nn_proxy_rule_type_1 NOT NULL
  4  , created_by            INTEGER CONSTRAINT nn_proxy_rule_type_2 NOT NULL
  5  , created_dt            DATE        CONSTRAINT nn_proxy_rule_type_3 NOT NULL
  6  , updated_by            INTEGER CONSTRAINT nn_proxy_rule_type_4 NOT NULL
  7  , updated_dt            DATE        CONSTRAINT nn_proxy_rule_type_5 NOT NULL);
SQL> CREATE TABLE dbsec.proxy_rule
  2  ( proxy_rule_id        INTEGER       CONSTRAINT pk_proxy_rule      PRIMARY KEY
  3  , proxy_rule_type_id INTEGER       CONSTRAINT nn_proxy_rule_1  NOT NULL
  4  , system_user_id       INTEGER       CONSTRAINT nn_proxy_rule_2  NOT NULL
  5  , value                VARCHAR2(50) CONSTRAINT nn_proxy_rule_3  NOT NULL
  6  , created_by           INTEGER       CONSTRAINT nn_proxy_rule_4  NOT NULL
  7  , created_dt           DATE          CONSTRAINT nn_proxy_rule_5  NOT NULL
  8  , updated_by           INTEGER       CONSTRAINT nn_proxy_rule_6  NOT NULL
  9  , updated_dt           DATE          CONSTRAINT nn_proxy_rule_7  NOT NULL);

SQL> CREATE TABLE dbsec.logon
  2  ( sid          NUMBER
  3  , serial#      NUMBER
  4  , db_user      VARCHAR2(50)
  5  , proxy_user   VARCHAR2(50)
  6  , os_user      VARCHAR2(50)
  7  , ip_address   VARCHAR2(50)
  8  , message      VARCHAR2(50)
  9  , update_dt    DATE);
```

The next two scripts add foreign key constraints to the dbsec_proxy_rule and dbsec_system_user tables:

```
SQL> ALTER TABLE dbsec.proxy_rule
  2     ADD CONSTRAINT fk_proxy_rule_1
  3     FOREIGN KEY (proxy_rule_type_id)
  4     REFERENCES dbsec.proxy_rule_type(proxy_rule_type_id)
  5     ADD CONSTRAINT fk_proxy_rule_2
  6     FOREIGN KEY (system_user_id)
  7     REFERENCES dbsec.system_user(system_user_id);

SQL> ALTER TABLE dbsec.system_user
  2     ADD CONSTRAINT fk_system_user_1
  3     FOREIGN KEY (contact_id)
  4     REFERENCES dbsec.contact(contact_id);
```

The utl_sec Package

The utl_sec package has three procedures and one function in it. The function is our password-hashing program that we used in Chapter 7. The grant_proxy procedure automatically gives users proxy access and it schedules the revocation of that access. That way, the DBA doesn't have to remember to revoke proxy access when the authorization period is up. The `revoke_proxy` procedure is simple and merely wraps the following command:

```
ALTER USER <target username>
REVOKE CONNECT THROUGH <proxy username> command
```

Lastly, the `kill_session` procedure enables us to disconnect users that do not meet our proxy rules. Finally, we create the package body and specification. This package has our password-hashing program that we used in Chapter 7. It also has simple grant and revoke proxy procedures. We wanted to keep the example simple, but our production packages contain more logic than these.

We create the specification in the following block:

```
SQL> CREATE OR REPLACE PACKAGE dbsec.utl_sec AS
  2    FUNCTION hashed
  3    ( pi_username   IN VARCHAR2
  4    , pi_password   IN VARCHAR2
  5    , pi_phrase1    IN VARCHAR2    -- secret answer 1
  6    , pi_phrase2    IN VARCHAR2    -- secret answer 2)
  7    RETURN VARCHAR2;
  8    PROCEDURE grant_proxy
  9    ( pi_user       IN VARCHAR2
 10    , pi_target     IN VARCHAR2
 11    , pi_expiry_dt  IN DATE);
 12    PROCEDURE revoke_proxy
 13    ( pi_user       IN VARCHAR2
 14    , pi_target     IN VARCHAR2);
 15    PROCEDURE kill_session
 16    ( pi_sid        IN NUMBER
 17    , pi_serial#    IN NUMBER);
 18  END utl_sec;
 19  /
```

We created the package body as follows:

```
SQL> CREATE OR REPLACE PACKAGE BODY dbsec.utl_sec AS
  2    FUNCTION hashed
  3    ( pi_username   IN VARCHAR2
  4    , pi_password   IN VARCHAR2
  5    , pi_phrase1    IN VARCHAR2    -- secret answer 1
  6    , pi_phrase2    IN VARCHAR2    -- secret answer 2)
  7    RETURN VARCHAR2 IS
  8      lv_salted VARCHAR2(250);
  9    BEGIN
 10      lv_salted := UPPER (
 11                          pi_username
 12                      ||  pi_phrase1
 13                      ||  pi_password
 14                      ||  pi_phrase2);
 15      RETURN dbms_crypto.hash(
```

```
16                      utl_raw.cast_to_raw(lv_salted)
17                    , dbms_crypto.hash_sh512);
18      END hashed;
```

You've seen the previous function before. It's a nifty little program that can be used just about anywhere you need to hash something with a salting ability. The next section of our package is the grant_proxy procedure. It is created like so:

```
20      PROCEDURE grant_proxy
21      ( pi_user        IN VARCHAR2
22      , pi_target      IN VARCHAR2
23      , pi_expiry_dt   IN DATE) IS
24        lv_security_check VARCHAR2(30);
25        lv_job                 VARCHAR2(30);
26        lv_sql                 VARCHAR2(100);
27      BEGIN
28        lv_security_check := DBMS_ASSERT.SIMPLE_SQL_NAME(pi_user);
29        lv_security_check := DBMS_ASSERT.SIMPLE_SQL_NAME(pi_target);
30        lv_job := DBMS_SCHEDULER.GENERATE_JOB_NAME('proxy');
31        lv_sql := 'BEGIN '
32               || '  EXECUTE IMMEDIATE '
33               || '    ''ALTER USER $1'
34               || '      GRANT CONNECT THROUGH $2'';'
35               || ' END;';
36        lv_sql := REGEXP_REPLACE (lv_sql,'\$1',pi_target);
37        lv_sql := REGEXP_REPLACE (lv_sql,'\$2',pi_user);
38        dbms_output.put_line(lv_sql);
39        dbms_scheduler.create_job
40        ( job_name     => lv_job
41        , job_type     => 'PLSQL_BLOCK'
42        , job_action   => lv_sql
43        , enabled      => TRUE
44        , auto_drop    => TRUE);
45        lv_job := dbms_scheduler.generate_job_name('proxy');
46        lv_sql := 'BEGIN '
47               || '  EXECUTE IMMEDIATE '
48               || '    ''ALTER user $1'
49               || '      REVOKE CONNECT THROUGH $2'';'
50               || '  END;';
51        lv_sql := REGEXP_REPLACE(lv_sql,'\$1',pi_target);
52        lv_sql := REGEXP_REPLACE(lv_sql,'\$2',pi_user   );
53        dbms_scheduler.create_job(
54            job_name => lv_job
55          , job_type => 'PLSQL_BLOCK'
56          , job_action => lv_sql
57          , start_date => pi_expiry_dt
58          , enabled => TRUE
59          , auto_drop => TRUE);
60      END grant_proxy;
```

We use the `dbms_assert` program to validate that user input is never anything more than schema names. This keeps the procedure safe from fuzzing efforts. Then, we create two jobs. The first job runs immediately and grants the specified user connect-through rights to the targeted user. The second job is automatically scheduled on the date specified by the parameter `pi_expiry_date`. Your users must know that they only have that period before their proxy access will be revoked. This step eliminates one of the biggest threats that databases face... derelict accounts with stale passwords.

In the next section, we create the `revoke_proxy` procedure:

```
61    PROCEDURE revoke_proxy
62    ( pi_user       IN VARCHAR2
63    , pi_target     IN VARCHAR2) IS
64      lv_security_check VARCHAR2(30);
65      lv_job            VARCHAR2(30);
66      lv_sql            VARCHAR2(100);
67    BEGIN
68      lv_security_check := dbms_assert.simple_sql_name(pi_user);
69      lv_security_check := dbms_assert.simple_sql_name(pi_target);
70      lv_job := dbms_scheduler.generate_job_name('proxy');
71      lv_sql := 'BEGIN '
72              || '  EXECUTE IMMEDIATE '
73              || '    ''ALTER USER $1'
74              || '      REVOKE CONNECT THROUGH $2'';'
75              || 'END;';
76      lv_sql := REGEXP_REPLACE(lv_sql,'\$1',pi_target);
77      lv_sql := REGEXP_REPLACE(lv_sql,'\$2',pi_user);
78      dbms_output.put_line(lv_sql);
79      dbms_scheduler.create_job(
80          job_name => lv_job
81        , job_type => 'PLSQL_BLOCK'
82        , job_action => lv_sql
83        , enabled => TRUE
84        , auto_drop => TRUE);
85    END revoke_proxy;
```

This program is a little less complicated than `grant_proxy`. It doesn't need a scheduled date, as its purpose is to immediately revoke proxy access when triggered. You will want to protect this package. Do not grant access to it inadvertently. Our last section is the `kill_session` procedure. It is created as follows:

```
86    PROCEDURE kill_session
87    ( pi_sid        IN NUMBER
88    , pi_serial#    IN NUMBER) AS
89      lv_sql            VARCHAR2(4000);
90      lv_job            VARCHAR2(30);
91    BEGIN
92      lv_job := dbms_scheduler.generate_job_name('kill');
93      lv_sql := 'BEGIN '
94              || '  EXECUTE IMMEDIATE '
95              || '    ''ALTER SYSTEM KILL SESSION ''''$1, $2'''' IMMEDIATE '';'
```

```
 96              || 'END;';
 97       lv_sql := REGEXP_REPLACE(lv_sql,'\$1',pi_sid);
 98       lv_sql := REGEXP_REPLACE(lv_sql,'\$2',pi_serial#);
 99       dbms_scheduler.create_job(
100           job_name      => lv_job
101         , job_type      => 'PLSQL_BLOCK'
102         , job_action    => lv_sql
103         , enabled       => TRUE
104         , auto_drop     => TRUE);
105     END kill_session;
106   END utl_sec;
107   /
```

Now that we have created our `dbsec.utl_sec` package, we are armed enough to make a trigger that evaluates user credentials at logon and revokes access if all of the rules in the `dbsec.proxy_rule` table are not met.

Be careful when making the trigger or inserting rules into the `dbsec.proxy_rule` table because you may put the kibosh on *all* ability to log on to the database. To be certain that we don't do this, we use two filters in our trigger. The first filter evaluates if the user is to be limited at logon or not. The second filter does the credential check and either lets the session live or calls the `revoke_proxy` and `kill_session` procedures shown previously.

Before we create the trigger, we'll put some data in our `dbsec_proxy_rule_type` tables. Here are two examples of the INSERT statement:

```
SQL> INSERT INTO dbsec.proxy_rule_type
  2   VALUES (1,'IP_RANGE',1,SYSDATE,1,SYSDATE);
SQL> INSERT INTO dbsec.proxy_rule_type
  2   VALUES (2,'OS_USERNAME',1,SYSDATE,1,SYSDATE);
```

Now, we'll put some data into the `dbsec_contact` and `dbsec_system_user` tables; examples of INSERT statements to the `dbsec_contact` and `dbsec_system_user` tables follow:

```
SQL> INSERT INTO dbsec.contact
  2   VALUES
  3   ( 10, 1, 1,'Thornton','Billy','Bob','Red','Pizza'
  4   , 1, SYSDATE, 1, SYSDATE);
SQL> INSERT INTO dbsec.system_user
  2   VALUES
  3   ( 1,10,'thorntonbb',2,1
  4   , dbsec.utl_sec.hashed('thorntonbb','abc123','pizza','red')
  5   , 1, SYSDATE, 1, SYSDATE );
```

The following statements provide examples of INSERT statements to the `dbsec_proxy_rule` table:

```
SQL> INSERT INTO dbsec.proxy_rule
  2   VALUES ( 1, 1, 2, '10.118.194', 1, SYSDATE, 1, SYSDATE);
SQL> INSERT INTO dbsec.proxy_rule
  2   VALUES ( 3, 2, 2, 'oracle', 1, SYSDATE, 1, SYSDATE);
SQL> INSERT INTO dbsec.proxy_rule
  2   VALUES ( 4, 3, 2, 'proxy_dba', 1, SYSDATE, 1, SYSDATE);
```

Next, we query the tables to see what we have. This is an important step because the rules you set up can be a bit nebulous. If you don't get it right, you will either cut someone off or allow someone in when you shouldn't.

```
SQL> COLUMN system_user_name FORMAT A15
SQL> COLUMN proxy_rule_description FORMAT A20
SQL> COLUMN value FORMAT A20
SQL> SELECT    su.system_user_name
  2  ,          prt.proxy_rule_description
  3  ,          pr.value
  4  FROM       dbsec.system_user su
  5  JOIN       dbsec.proxy_rule pr
  6  ON         su.system_user_id = pr.system_user_id
  7  JOIN       dbsec.proxy_rule_type prt
  8  ON         pr.proxy_rule_type_id = prt.proxy_rule_type_id
  9  ORDER BY   su.system_user_name
 10  ,          prt.proxy_rule_description;
```

The query should return some set like this:

```
SYSTEM_USER_NAM PROXY_RULE_DESCRIPTI VALUE
--------------- -------------------- --------------------
fred            DB_USERNAME          proxy_dba
fred            IP_RANGE             10.118.194
fred            OS_USERNAME          oracle
fred            PROXY_USER           fred
fred            TIME_END             23:59:59
fred            TIME_START           01:00:00
thorntonbb      DB_USERNAME          proxy_dev
thorntonbb      IP_RANGE             10.118.194
thorntonbb      OS_USERNAME          oracle
thorntonbb      PROXY_USER           thorntonbb
thorntonbb      TIME_END             10:00:00
thorntonbb      TIME_START           06:00:00
```

According to our rules, we see that Fred and Billy Bob Thornton (thorntonbb) both have the proxy_dba super-role. We also see that Billy has the proxy_dev super-role, but he has access from 6 A.M. until 10 P.M.

We have to create the following trigger to enforce our proxy rules. It evaluates the users who log on against two tables. The first is our dbsec.system_user table. This allows us to only fire the trigger for specific users and prevents the lockout of users like sys and system. Then, it compares the user context against rules defined in the dbsec.proxy_rule table as follows:

```
SQL> CREATE OR REPLACE TRIGGER user_authorization
  2  AFTER LOGON ON DATABASE
  3  DECLARE
  4    lv_sid      NUMBER;
  5    lv_serial#  NUMBER;
```

```
 6    lv_now        VARCHAR2(50);
 7    lv_time       DATE;
 8    lv_db_user    VARCHAR2(50);
 9    lv_os_user    VARCHAR2(50);
10    lv_proxy_user VARCHAR2(50);
11    lv_ip_address VARCHAR2(50);
12    lv_counter1   NUMBER;
13    lv_counter2   NUMBER;
14  BEGIN
15    SELECT    COUNT(*)
16    INTO      lv_counter1
17    FROM      dbsec.system_user
18    WHERE     system_user_name = LOWER(SYS_CONTEXT('userenv','current_user'))
19    OR        system_user_name = LOWER(SYS_CONTEXT('userenv','proxy_user'));
20    IF lv_counter1 > 0 THEN
21  -----------------------------------------------------------------------
22  -- GET USERENV VALUES
23  -----------------------------------------------------------------------
24    SELECT    vs.sid
25    ,         vs.serial#
26    ,         LOWER(vs.username) db_user
27    ,         TO_CHAR(SYSDATE,'HH24:MI:SS' ) update_dt
28    ,         SYS_CONTEXT('userenv','ip_address') ip_address
29    ,         LOWER(SYS_CONTEXT('userenv','os_user')) os_user
30    ,         LOWER(SYS_CONTEXT('userenv','proxy_user')) proxy_user
31    ,         SYSDATE
32    INTO      lv_sid
33    ,         lv_serial#
34    ,         lv_db_user
35    ,         lv_now
36    ,         lv_ip_address
37    ,         lv_os_user
38    ,         lv_proxy_user
39    ,         lv_time
40    FROM      sys.v$process vp
41    JOIN      sys.v$session vs
42    ON        vp.addr = vs.paddr
43    AND       vs.audsid = USERENV('sessionid')
44    AND       vs.sid = USERENV('sid');
45
46    lv_ip_address := SUBSTR(lv_ip_address
47                            , 1
48                            , INSTR(lv_ip_address,'.',1,3) - 1);
```

There are many USERENV context values that you can pull from the Oracle session. You can create complex rules by simply adding more of them to the dbsec.proxy_rule table; however, you will want to make sure that you don't overdo it. Also see that we create a join from v$process to v$session. This lets us gather the sid and serial# values for our kill_session procedure. The following lines compare the values we collected previously to the dbsec.proxy_rule table:

```
49   -------------------------------------------------------------
50   -- EVALUATE AGAINST PROXY_RULE
51   -------------------------------------------------------------
52      WITH my_user AS
53      (SELECT   system_user_name
54      ,         proxy_rule_type_id
55      ,         value
56       FROM     dbsec.system_user su
57       JOIN     dbsec.proxy_rule pr
58       ON       su.system_user_id = pr.system_user_id)
59      , pivot_point AS
60      (SELECT   *
61       FROM     my_user
62       PIVOT    (MAX(value) value
63                 FOR (proxy_rule_type_id)
64                 IN ( 1 AS ip_range
65                    , 2 AS os_user
66                    , 3 AS db_user
67                    , 4 AS tod_start
68                    , 5 AS tod_end
69                    , 6 AS proxy_user)))
70      SELECT   COUNT(*)
71      INTO     lv_counter2
72      FROM     pivot_point pp
73      WHERE    db_user_value = lv_db_user
74      AND      lv_now BETWEEN tod_start_value AND tod_end_value
75      AND      proxy_user_value = lv_proxy_user
76      AND      os_user_value = lv_os_user
77      AND      lv_ip_address LIKE ip_range_value;
78
79      IF lv_proxy_user IS NOT NULL THEN
80        IF lv_counter2 = 0 THEN
81          INSERT
82          INTO     dbsec.logon VALUES ( lv_sid
83                                      , lv_serial#
84                                      , lv_db_user
85                                      , lv_proxy_user
86                                      , lv_os_user
87                                      , lv_ip_address
88                                      , 'failure'
89                                      , lv_time );
90        dbsec.utl_sec.revoke_proxy(lv_proxy_user, lv_db_user);
91        dbsec.utl_sec.kill_session(lv_sid, lv_serial#);
92        ELSE
93          INSERT
94          INTO     dbsec.logon
```

```
 95            VALUES
 96            ( lv_sid
 97            , lv_serial#
 98            , lv_db_user
 99            , lv_proxy_user
100            , lv_os_user
101            , lv_ip_address
102            ,'success'
103            , lv_time );
104        END IF;
105      END IF;
106    END IF;
107    COMMIT;
108  END;
109  /
```

Notice that we performed a pivot on lines 58 through 74. This enables us to flip the tuple values found in the dbsec.proxy_rule table so that we can use them in our WHERE clause filter later on. If the query returns a positive value, we allow the session to continue. If it returns a zero, the proxy rights are revoked on line 86 and the session is killed on line 87.

Now that we have a method of fine-grained access control, we attempt to log on as all three users:

```
SQL> CONNECT voightaj[proxy_dba]/abc123@pdb01;
Connected.
SQL> SHOW USER
USER is "PROXY_DBA"
SQL> CONNECT voightaj[proxy_dba]/abc123@pdb01;
Connected.
SQL> CONNECT fred[proxy_dba]/abc123@pdb01;
Connected.
SQL> CONNECT thorntonbb[proxy_dev]/abc123@pdb01;
Connected.
SQL> SELECT 1 FROM dual;
SELECT 1 FROM dual
*
ERROR at line 1:
ORA-03113: end-of-file on communication channel
Process ID: 17897
Session ID: 65 Serial number: 25985
```

See that Fred got inserted without any problems, but what about Billy? His location, super-role, and authentication parameters were perfect, but the logon trigger revoked his ability to connect to proxy_dev and killed his session.

One quick query on the time should help:

```
SQL> SELECT   TO_CHAR(SYSDATE,'HH24:MI:SS') AS now
  2  FROM   dual;
now
--------
23:01:56
```

Aha! Billy tried logging in when he shouldn't have. With this basic package, you have the ability to control authorization and access as precisely as you like. You can also greatly reduce the number of grants needed to maintain a system. In addition, your users never have more rights than the ability to create a session and proxy into a specific super-role. Moreover, super-roles can have rights directly granted to them without creating a spaghetti bowl of grants. They can also make named objects. Finally, your users (application or human) have a finite period to proxy into the super-roles. That means their accounts automatically revoke rights and you don't have to worry about remembering to revoke privileges any more.

Oracle's New Multitenant Architecture

We absolutely love Oracle's new security model. You have to license it separately from your regular database; however, it provides you with the ability to create virtual databases within a single container instance. In the past, customers who wanted their own database, instead of sharing a schema, were forced to create multihomed database instances. The major drawback to this approach is that all servers have a finite amount of RAM. If you're lucky, your server may have 512GB or 1TB.

This memory limitation meant that you could only spin so many instances per server, even with very expensive hardware. In many cases, an Oracle RAC cluster could only house 20 instances before using up all of the available memory. Furthermore, those instances were all starved of RAM. Lastly, some instances remained largely idle while others required much more system resources than they could acquire. It was frustrating, to say the least, and required data centers to spin hundreds or even thousands of servers that, for the most part, sat idle.

Enter virtual machines…

Many shops use virtual machines to increase the density of databases that can be applied to a single server. There's only one problem: you still have a finite amount of RAM. Oh! You now have an OS that needs resources on top of the Oracle instance. Yes, your servers report higher CPU utilization, but that's not necessarily a good thing. What's more, engineers tend to overutilize the servers with virtual machines, spinning more virtual machines than they should. Then, customers are out of luck when resources are needed, or when multiple machines all want resources at the same time. Instead, Oracle Multitenant Architecture allows you to spin many virtual databases and move them around easily between container instances. It is possible to place up to 100 instances on a single X-4 Exadata Machine with pluggable databases, but don't even think about it in a multihomed environment, because all of your instances will be so memory starved that it won't be worth your while.

Sanitizing SQL and PL/SQL

This section is about the use of bind variables and dbms_assert; it is not about wrapping your code. Refer to *Oracle Database 12c PL/SQL Programming* to learn how to wrap your code. We will start with bind variables and then move on to creating safe PL/SQL programs.

Bind Variables

You should know by now that bind variables are a much better choice than concatenating values in statements from a performance perspective. Another benefit of bind variables is that it is impossible to inject unwanted code into a bind variable. Within SQL, a bind variable looks something like this:

```
SQL> VARIABLE user_id NUMBER;
SQL> EXECUTE :user_id := 1;
BEGIN user_id := 1; END;
SQL> SELECT   system_user_name
  2  FROM      dbsec.system_user
  3  WHERE     system_user_id = :user_id;
SYSTEM_USER_NAM
---------------
Thorntonbb
```

In PL/SQL, bind variables look very similar:

```
SQL> SET SERVEROUTPUT ON
SQL> DECLARE
  2    lv_user_id   NUMBER := 1;
  3    lv_value     VARCHAR2(50);
  4  BEGIN
  5    EXECUTE IMMEDIATE 'SELECT system_user_name '
  6                      || 'FROM   dbsec.system_user '
  7                      || 'WHERE  system_user_id = :1 '
  7                         INTO lv_value
  8                         USING lv_user_id;
  9    dbms_output.put_line(lv_value);
 10  END;
SQL> /
Thorntonbb
```

In both cases, the bind variable has security benefits. You should opt for this method whenever possible; however, there are times when you must concatenate dynamic SQL with input parameter values. Whenever you do so, you must remember to sanitize the strings before executing a dynamic SQL statement. For that matter, it's just good practice to sanitize any string-related input with the dbms_assert package.

dbms_assert

The dbms_assert package comes to our rescue. It has seven functions and procedures, but one of them doesn't do any checking and is called the NOOP procedure. The other functions and procedures of the dbms_assert package are as follows:

- simple_sql_name   This function checks the input to make sure it starts with a letter, contains only the _, $, and # characters, and does not contain extra quoted characters like ' ' ' ' (you can do ' " ' ' " ').

- qualified_sql_name   This function is very similar to simple_function_name but allows for object names that are fully qualified with dot notation.

- schema_name   This function requires that the input value is a schema name.

- sql_object_name   This function requires that the input value is an existing object.

- enquote_name   This function encloses the input parameter in double quotes, unless they are already part of the input string. Then, it checks the entire string to make sure that all double quotes come in matching pairs.

- enquote_literal   This function is similar to enquote_name but it uses single quotes.

If you paid attention to the code in this chapter, you will have noticed that we used the `dbms_assert` package in our `utl_sec` program. You can double up checks, and we strongly suggest it where possible. For example, you could assess an input variable first with the `enquote_literal` function and then the `simple_sql_name` function for added security.

Supporting Scripts

The following programs and file are available on the McGraw-Hill Professional website to support this chapter:

- The `ch_08_compareme.sql` script and `englishWords.dat` file create the fuzzy comparison example.
- The `ch_08_utl_sec.sql` script creates the proxy user example.
- The `ch_08_bindvariables.sql` script creates the bind variable examples.

Summary

If you implement the principles presented in Chapter 7 and this chapter, you should be able to build more secure and stable environments for your users. What's more, you will know where to go for the source of security information. This is vital because receiving threat information too late or via some third party may put your systems at risk.

PART

IV

Applied Technologies

CHAPTER
9

dbms_scheduler Package

Purpose

The purpose of this chapter is to introduce you to Oracle's `dbms_scheduler` package and to give you practical knowledge regarding this excellent tool. Oracle introduced this program in its Oracle Database 10g release. At that time, its key benefits were its ability to start, stop, and reuse jobs. It represented a huge leap forward in job management. At least, it's a huge leap over the previous scheduling method, which combined the Linux or Unix `cron` utility and Oracle's `dbms_job` package.

The problem with writing one-off scripts is two-pronged. The first problem is the complexity involved in performing routine maintenance via shell programming scripts. Most administrators start by writing a few simple scripts to do a particular task. Then, they add several other tasks to complete a job. Their simple onesie-twosie scripts quickly balloon into 10, 20, or more files. Then, if that is not difficult enough, they must run the scripts in some order, providing restart ability, monitoring, and security. Before they know it, they have built an entire framework to support what should be a simple job.

The second problem is a jumble of overly complex scripts that exist because of the different levels and styles of programming. For example, while some administrators create tightly integrated code, others simply write something that *works*. Merging the two styles becomes difficult and over time, more expensive to support.

Oracle created its `dbms_scheduler` package as a complete framework to solve these problems. The `dbms_scheduler` package should empower administrators to spend more time getting work done, and less time creating the scripts to perform their jobs.

Advantages

As we stated in the previous section, administrators have different levels and styles of programming. Those who don't have good development skills create scripts that cost too much to support. These poorly coded scripts often have no start, stop, or restart functionality. These programs also don't report their status during execution because they only report success or failure when they complete. Moreover, when they do fail, they require extensive cleanup. The result means system and database administrators lose what could have been productive time to fixing problems created by the scripts. As a result, companies spend money and funding jobs to support these customer scripts, often referred to as spaghetti code.

The Oracle `dbms_scheduler` package represents a way to overcome the limitations of customized scripts. Over the years, Oracle has improved this package and it now represents a rich framework. The `dbms_scheduler` package lets you reduce your reliance on customized scripts.

You can do the following with the `dbms_scheduler` package:

- Create jobs based on events or time
- Create job groups
- Create/modify job chains
- Create jobs on remote databases
- Copy jobs
- Create job windows

- Watch job progress
- Watch job files
- Stop, start, pause, restart, and reset jobs
- E-mail job events

dbms_scheduler now makes it possible to create jobs that can do almost any task, locally or on remote database servers. You can now tune and refine legacy jobs that were extremely bulky and complicated. This reduces the maintenance workload for DBAs.

Disadvantages

It is difficult to come up with a list of disadvantages in version 12c. We did come up with a short list. For one, the dbms_scheduler tool has no GUI other than Oracle Enterprise Manager. However, if you are SQL savvy, a simple query against scheduler views renders adequate information about running jobs and completed jobs. We will show you how to do this later in the chapter.

Don't Re-write, Re-engineer What's Working

It is tempting to tear into your legacy code, slicing and dicing your way to database job nirvana; however, doing so often is impossible. What's more, replacing the code is a lot like the shrapnel predicament of the Iron Man comic book character. In that comic, Tony Stark gets shrapnel in his heart from a bomb. As a genius engineer, he devises a way to prevent the shrapnel from killing him. Unfortunately, the solution doesn't remove the shrapnel; it only keeps it at bay. That's because he'd die while trying to remove the shrapnel. In the process of engineering a suit to save his life, he becomes Iron Man.

As commercial DBAs, we're often in the same shrapnel predicament as Iron Man. The difference is that the unwanted and poorly written scripts take the place of the shrapnel, and our ongoing enterprise the role of the heart. It's possible that you may kill your day-to-day business system while attempting to remove the unwanted code.

Instead, evaluate the whole scenario. Focus on re-engineering only those parts of the code that can be improved to benefit your users; leave the rest of the code intact. Remember, you have both business customers *and* internal IT department customers. Cleaning up your code will increase database efficiency and have a positive effect on how your customers perceive the quality of your work. Moreover, your manager might recognize your accomplishments and provide you with rewards for excellence.

The cool part is that the dbms_scheduler package can help you to make improvements while reducing your overall maintenance load. We can see it now...you will go into your meeting bleary-eyed and clutching your coffee mug like you just finished a Herculean task. Your manager and business customers will be impressed. Then, you will go back to your office with a grin, knowing that you reduced the amount of work by being smarter instead of by working harder.

We agree that chaining and complex scheduling of jobs can be a bit overwhelming at first. In addition, it would be nice to have a good GUI that allowed the creation of complex jobs or schedules. The `dbms_scheduler` package also has the following limitations and rules:

- Only the `sys` user can perform scheduled actions on the `sys` schema.
- Some `dbms_scheduler` procedures accept single jobs or strings of jobs separated by commas. The scheduler will kill future iterations of jobs if it encounters errors within the programs.
- The scheduler assumes that stipulated objects exist and are valid. If they do not exist or are not valid, the job will fail and log that status to system tables. In future releases, it would be helpful to have the scheduler check the validity of jobs before allowing them to be scheduled or chained. At this time, you must check them yourself.

Overview
This chapter covers the following topics related to the `dbms_scheduler` package:

- Date intervals
- Scheduler views
- Creating chained jobs
- Creating clustered jobs
- Job management
- Job security

While some of these topics are routine, their application most definitely is not. We will show you how you can dramatically speed up tasks like rebuilding indexes or moving large amounts of data via the scheduler. We are also excited to introduce you to the benefits of flash storage.

Date Intervals
At first glance, your head may spin when you look at the `dbms_scheduler` date format. This is understandable. It covers at least ten pages in *Oracle Database PL/SQL Packages and Types Reference 12c Release*. An exhaustive discussion on all the possibilities might consume an entire chapter, which is beyond the scope of this book. Instead, we will provide you with the basic rules in the following examples. It suffices us to say that the `dbms_scheduler` package can provide you with nearly any data combination you desire.

Immediate Jobs
Our first example shows you how to run a job immediately and clean up the job after completion. We like to refer to this method as a run-me-now job:

```
SQL> DECLARE
  2    lv_job varchar2(30) :=
  3      'MYJOB' || to_char ( sysdate, 'DDMMYYYYHHMISS' );
  4  BEGIN
  5    dbms_scheduler.create_job(
```

```
  6        job_name => lv_job
  7      , job_type => 'PLSQL_BLOCK'
  8      , job_action => ' begin null; end; '
  9      , enabled => true
 10      , auto_drop => true );
 11   END;
 12   /
/
```

In this example, we do not call the `repeat_interval` parameter or `end_date` parameter. By default, they are left null. This signifies to Oracle that the job is a one-time task. Notice that the `enabled` and `auto_drop` parameters are set to `true`. These parameters tell Oracle to automatically start the job and drop it when it completes.

Simple Intervals

Our second example is a little more complicated. It has `start_date`, `repeat_interval`, and `end_date` parameters. It does not combine multiple schedules and is considered a simple repeatable job. First, we determine a schedule. We create the `repeat_interval` with a limited list for brevity, as shown here (with a shortened list of holidays):

```
SQL> BEGIN
  2    dbms_scheduler.create_schedule(
  3        schedule_name => 'company_holiday'
  4      , repeat_interval =>
  5        'FREQ=YEARLY;BYDATE=0101,0120,0217,0526,1225');
  6   END;
  7   /
```

Note that we stipulate a schedule name and give a `repeat_interval`. The interval format can become quite complex. In this case, we tell Oracle to repeat the `company_holiday` jobs each year on New Year's Day, Martin Luther King, Jr. Day, Washington's Birthday, Memorial Day, and Christmas (naturally, these holidays vary by year and don't always fall on the same days).

Built-in Intervals

Oracle has several built-in schedules that represent year, month, week, day, hour, minute, and second. In the following example, we create a heartbeat `repeat_interval` that runs every minute:

```
SQL> BEGIN
  2    dbms_scheduler.create_schedule(
  3        schedule_name => 'security_heartbeat'
  4      , repeat_interval => 'FREQ=MINUTELY');
  5   END;
  6   /
```

Observe that we simply put the word `MINUTELY` in the frequency parameter. The following are the possible predefined frequencies:

```
FREQ="YEARLY"|"MONTHLY"|"WEEKLY"|"DAILY"|"HOURLY"|"MINUTELY"|"SECONDLY"
```

For most users, this list is sufficient and no additional explanations are necessary; however, your company may need to run jobs on a specific schedule, as described next.

Combined Custom Intervals

Assume that your company needs a job scheduled at the end of each quarter and during the next four blue moons. The example is somewhat absurd, but it proves a point. You discover that the blue moons will occur on July 31, 2015; January 31, 2018; March 31, 2018; and October 31, 2020. From our previous holiday example, we can easily create the blue moon schedule like so:

```
SQL> BEGIN
  2    dbms_scheduler.create_schedule(
  3        schedule_name => 'blue_moons'
  4      , repeat_interval =>
  5          'FREQ=YEARLY;BYDATE=20150731,20180131,20180331,20200831');
  6  END;
  7  /
```

Notice that we extended the BYDATE format from our simple intervals example. The accepted format is [YYYYMMDD]. When we stipulate the year, the job is only run at that date. Now, we need to create a frequency that repeats once at the end of each quarter. We will use the widely accepted values of March 31, June 30, September 30, and December 31. We name this schedule something simple like quarterly_end so we can reuse it elsewhere. We create the next portion of our custom schedule like so:

```
SQL> BEGIN
  2    dbms_scheduler.create_schedule(
  3        schedule_name => 'quarterly_end'
  4      , repeat_interval => 'FREQ=YEARLY;BYDATE=0331,0630,0930,1231');
  5  END;
  6  /
```

Finally, we create a custom repeat interval based on the previous two customizations. It is important to realize that we are not actually running anything on the blue_moons and quarterly_end intervals. Instead, we use them to do the following buildup, named combined_001:

```
SQL> BEGIN
  2    dbms_scheduler.create_schedule(
  3        schedule_name => 'combined_001'
  4      , repeat_interval => 'FREQ=blue_moons;include=quarterly_end');
  5  END;
  6  /
/
```

Note that our repeat_interval phrase contains the blue_moons schedule, and that it uses the include keyword to add the quarterly_end schedule. This syntax begs the question, "What if I want to have multiple custom intervals?" We have the answer! This statement allows for a comma-delimited list. Adding a three-interval schedule is as easy as this:

```
SQL> BEGIN
  2    dbms_scheduler.create_schedule(
  3        schedule_name => 'combined_02'
  4      , repeat_interval =>
  5          'FREQ=MINUTELY;include=quarterly_end,blue_moons');
```

```
6  END;
7  /
```

Dropping schedules is as simple as making them. You can perform a simple SELECT statement against the dba_schedule_schedules view to see what schedules exist in your database. If you wanted to drop the BLUE_MOONS schedule, you would simply issue the following statement:

```
SQL> COLUMN schedule_name FORMAT a45;
SQL> SELECT schedule_name FROM dba_scheduler_schedules;
```

It displays:

```
SCHEDULE_NAME
---------------------------------------------
BSLN_MAINTAIN_STATS_SCHED
PMO_DEFERRED_GIDX_MAINT_SCHED
FILE_WATCHER_SCHEDULE
DAILY_PURGE_SCHEDULE
... omitted for brevity ...
```

You can then drop the schedule like this:

```
SQL> BEGIN
2     dbms_scheduler.drop_schedule('BLUE_MOONS');
3  END;
4  /
```

You can see from these examples that the scheduler can accept myriad custom options. You rarely may have to create schedules like BLUE_MOON, but you now have the expertise to do so.

dbms_scheduler View

Oracle provides an extensive list of views to help you monitor and view the status of running and completed jobs. The main CDB, DBA, ALL, and USER views you will interact with are

- *_scheduler_chains
- *_scheduler_chain_rules
- *_scheduler_chain_steps
- *_scheduler_credentials
- *_scheduler_db_dests
- *_scheduler_dests
- *_scheduler_file_watchers
- *_scheduler_groups
- *_scheduler_group_members
- *_scheduler_jobs
- *_scheduler_job_args
- *_scheduler_job_dests
- *_scheduler_job_log
- *_scheduler_job_run_details
- *_scheduler_notifications
- *_scheduler_programs
- *_scheduler_program_args
- *_scheduler_remote_jobstate
- *_scheduler_running_chains
- *_scheduler_running_jobs
- *_scheduler_schedules

The asterisks are placeholders for one of several categories of views. You still have the CDB, DBA, ALL, and USER prefixes. The following query returns all schedules for the current container:

```
SQL>   COLUMN owner FORMAT a15
SQL>   COLUMN schedule_name FORMAT a30
SQL>   COLUMN schedule_type FORMAT a15
SQL>   COLUMN repeat_interval FORMAT a60
SQL> SELECT   owner
  2  ,         schedule_name
  3  ,         schedule_type
  4  ,         repeat_interval
  5  FROM      dba_scheduler_schedules;
```

This returns the following:

```
OWNER             SCHEDULE_NAME                  SCHEDULE_TYPE
--------------    ------------------------------ ---------------
SYS               COMBINED_02                    CALENDAR
SYS               QUARTERLY_END                  CALENDAR
SYS               SECURITY_HEARTBEAT             CALENDAR
SYS               COMPANY_HOLIDAYS               CALENDAR
SYS               SIMPLE_QUARTERLY_END           CALENDAR
SYS               BLUE_MOONS                     CALENDAR
REPEAT_INTERVAL
------------------------------------------------------------
FREQ=MINUTELY;include=quarterly_end,blue_moons
FREQ=YEARLY;BYDATE=0331,0630,0930,1231
FREQ=MINUTELY
FREQ=YEARLY;BYDATE=0101,0120,0217,0526,1225
FREQ=YEARLY;BYDATE=0331,0630,0930,1231
FREQ=YEARLY;BYDATE=20150731,20180131,20180331,20230831
```

See the schedules we just created? This is a nifty view that will help you see all of the schedules in your database. We found ourselves asking, "How does the scheduler work with pluggable databases?" A Google search returned very little, so we tested a bit and found out that you need to either connect directly to the pluggable database or alter your session by setting the current container, if you are in the container instance. We do not have room in this book to go over every scheduler view; however, we will discuss the CDB, DBA, ALL, and USER views that we use most commonly:

- *_scheduler_jobs
- *_scheduler_running_jobs
- *_scheduler_job_run_details

*_scheduler_jobs

The *_scheduler_jobs view contains only current job information. If you create an auto-drop job, you might be quick enough to query this table and view information about that job; however, that information is removed as soon as the database issues the dbms_scheduler.drop_job procedure at the end of the job run. A quick look at this table shows a plethora of information. The following sections list a few of the interesting columns.

destination_name
In this column, Oracle shows the HOST:PORT where the remote job is to be run. Be sure to stipulate the port if you don't use the default, 1521.

instance_id and instance_stickiness
Single-node databases have information in these columns; however, these values only have meaning in an Oracle RAC environment. For example, many administrators have large extract, transform, and load (ETL) jobs that involve moving, transforming, and rebuilding indexes and configuring rights. These jobs are both I/O and CPU intensive. The instance_stickiness parameter allows a job to stay on a particular node. That way, all of the nodes in a cluster take a somewhat-equal share of the workload.

It may be tempting to pick the easy way out and schedule one massive serial job that takes advantage of only a single node. After all, you can kick the job off at night. Unfortunately, this may represent a considerable sacrifice on the part of the business, which might be able to make much better decisions if the data were fresh.

If you had a three-node Oracle RAC cluster and had permission to produce a large network and system load, you might be able to refresh business-critical data in very short bursts throughout the day instead of taking up a large amount of bandwidth and time early in the morning. For example, we were required to create a job that audited database links across hundreds of instances in a large corporation. Our initial attempt did not make use of the scheduler. Each instance was queried as the system looped through its massive list. If an instance was down for maintenance, the procedure had to time-out before moving on. The result was a very slow-running program that took hours to complete.

The amount of time the job took was not acceptable because links that were dynamically created and dropped were not being caught. We solved this conundrum by creating a dynamic PL/SQL block that could be scheduled against all of the remote databases simultaneously. After we rewrote the job, it took only 2 minutes to complete, and because each job represented an independent session with implied commits, we didn't have to wait for databases that timed out because of downtime.

Job Priority
This column indicates the priority of a job in relation to all others within the database instance. The value ranges from 1–5, with 1 being the first picked during job execution.

Job Type
This column indicates the type of job. Valid values are PLSQL_BLOCK, stored_procedure, executable, chain, external_script, sql_script, and backup_script.

Max Failures, Runs, Run Duration
These columns represent the maximum number of failures the schedule will encounter before cancelling the job, the maximum number of times a job can be run, and the maximum amount of time a job can take to complete.

Restartable
This column displays whether or not a job is restartable.

*_scheduler_running_jobs

This view holds information about jobs that are in process. Information is removed as soon as the job is completed. Interesting columns include `detached`, `session_id`, `running_instance`, `resource_consumer_group`, `elapsed_time`, and `cpu_used`.

detached

The `detached` parameter tells Oracle if the job is running remotely and if Oracle should wait around for a job to complete. Jobs that are scheduled with this parameter must also use the `dbms_scheduler.end_detached_run` command to inform Oracle that they are complete.

session_id

The `session_id` column holds both the `PID` and `SID` for the session.

running_instance

The `running_instance` column holds the ID of the Oracle node. If this is a stand-alone installation, the number will always be 1.

resource_consumer_group

The `resource_consumer_group` column is very interesting. If you haven't read up on resource groups, we suggest that you do so in the *Oracle Database PL/SQL Packages and Type Reference*. Then, always insist that your developers write programs that go as fast and hard as they can. Control the resources these jobs use via resource groups instead of asking developers to write slow code.

elapsed_time

The `elapsed_time` column holds the total amount of time a job has taken.

cpu_used

The `cpu_used` column holds the total CPU time consumed by the job. This data may or may not be available depending on the OS and hardware.

*_scheduler_job_run_details

This view is very much like `*_scheduler_running_jobs` but has additional columns, including `additional_info`, `error#`, `errors`, `output`, and `status`. These columns help you troubleshoot failed jobs or view output of the job, depending on the log level stipulated via the `dbms_scheduler.logging_off`, `dbms_scheduler.logging_runs`, `dbms_scheduler.logging_failed_runs`, and `dbms_scheduler.logging_full` job classes.

We will show you how the information in the `*_scheduler_job_run_details` view can help you troubleshoot runtime errors. First, we'll make a procedure that we know will break when we pass in specific parameters. We are looking for this error:

```
ORA-01476: DIVISOR IS EQUAL TO ZERO
```

The following procedure shows you how to generate the error:

```
SQL> CREATE OR REPLACE PROCEDURE break_me
  2  ( pi_numerator    IN    NUMBER
```

```
 3   , pi_denominator IN      NUMBER
 4   , po_quotient        OUT NUMBER) AS
 5     lv_quotient NUMBER;
 6   BEGIN
 7     lv_quotient := pi_numerator / pi_denominator;
 8     po_quotient := lv_quotient;
 9   END;
10   /
```

This is an easy error to create. We simply pass a zero value in the denominator. Next, we make a job that will successfully run:

```
SQL> DECLARE
  2     lv_job VARCHAR2(30)  := 'MY_JOB'
  3                            || TO_CHAR(SYSDATE,'DDMMYYYYHHMISS');
  4   BEGIN
  5     dbms_scheduler.create_job(
  6       job_name     => lv_job
  7     , job_type     => 'PLSQL_BLOCK'
  8     , job_action   => ' declare lv_quotient number; begin break_me '
  9                       || ' ( 1, 1, lv_quotient ); end; '
 10     , enabled      => true
 11     , auto_drop    => true);
 12   END;
 13   /
```

Now, we run the procedure again with a zero denominator parameter:

```
SQL> DECLARE
  2     lv_job VARCHAR2(30)  := 'MY_JOB'
  3                            || TO_CHAR(SYSDATE,'DDMMYYYYHHMISS');
  4   BEGIN
  5     dbms_scheduler.create_job(
  6       job_name     => lv_job
  7     , job_type     => 'PLSQL_BLOCK'
  8     , job_action   => ' declare lv_quotient number; begin break_me '
  9                       || ' ( 1, 0, lv_quotient ); end; '
 10     , enabled      => true
 11     , auto_drop    => true);
 12   END;
 13   /
```

Observe that the job creation procedure successfully completes; however, the job itself failed, as you will see from the following query:

```
SQL>   COLUMN job_name FORMAT a25
SQL>   COLUMN status FORMAT a10
SQL>   COLUMN error# FORMAT 9999999999
SQL>   COLUMN instance_id FORMAT 9999999999
SQL>   COLUMN session_id FORMAT a10
SQL>   COLUMN cpu_used FORMAT a10
SQL>   COLUMN additional_info FORMAT a40
```

```
SQL> SELECT    job_name
  2  ,          status
  3  ,          error#
  4  ,          instance_id
  5  ,          session_id
  6  ,          cpu_used
  7  ,          additional_info
  8  FROM       dba_scheduler_job_run_details
  9  WHERE      job_name like 'MY_JOB%';
```

It displays:

```
JOB_NAME                  STATUS        ERROR# INSTANCE_ID SESSION_ID CPU_USED
------------------- ----------- -------- ---------- --------- --------------
MY_JOB17032014060713      SUCCEEDED          0           1 23,381    +000
MY_JOB17032014060803      FAILED          1476           1 23,395    +000


ADDITIONAL_INFO
------------------------------------
(NULL)
ORA-01476: divisor is equal to zero
ORA-06512: at "SYS.BREAK_ME", line 10
ORA-06512: at line 1
```

Notice that the data contained in the errors and additional_info columns provides you with crucial troubleshooting information that can help you figure out why a job failed. You may notice that the additional_info column stays empty, depending on the level of logging that you stipulate. If you set the logging level, local-external jobs will begin populating this column; however, if you want information from remote-external jobs you must call dbms_scheduler .end_detached_run_program to fill in that field.

Chained and Clustered Jobs

If you are like most database programmers, you will get frustrated when you create your first cluster or chained job, primarily because there are many little pieces that must be created—both with the correct syntax and in the right order. It is also critical that you create these kinds of jobs in clear steps. You must make sure to be very disciplined and stop at each logical point and test, test, test…before moving on. Otherwise, we might find you mumbling to yourself while pulling your hair out, staring zombie-like at a computer screen. Remember, there is nothing more frustrating than trying to troubleshoot multiple programs at the same time, especially if you don't know which program(s) caused the error.

Clustered jobs run several programs at the same time. For example, you may find yourself rebuilding indexes in a large data warehouse system. Instead of rebuilding indexes in serial, you can create a clustered job that spins the rebuild of all indexes by table. On the other hand, chained jobs are serial. They require a previous program to complete or fail before moving on to the next

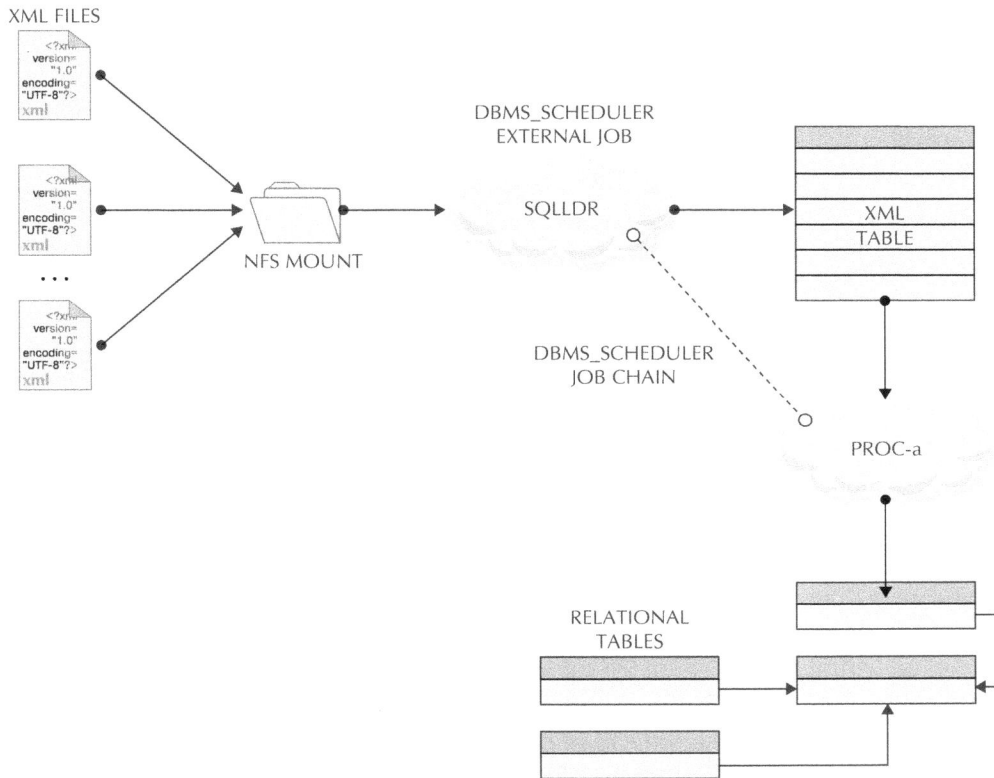

FIGURE 9-1. *Moving XML data into the database*

program in your chain. The example depicted in Figure 9-1 shows you how to put together a chained job that moves XML data from a networked folder to relational tables within the database.

As you can see, two processes are required from the database server:

■ Pick up XML-formatted data and load it into the database in a way that can be consumed easily by database users.

■ Move the data into relational tables that are better suited for data mining.

It may be tempting for you to write your own framework and import processes to move the XML data to relational tables. However, this effort has the potential of consuming your resources and possibly requiring several additional engineers for an extended period of time. Instead of going down that path, let us suggest a better way.

First, the Oracle RDBMS is fully compliant with XML. You don't need to create key-value tables with a parent key and BLOB/CLOB columns. Doing so will just complicate your effort and add extra processes. Rather than do that, create an object table of Oracle's XMLTYPE, like so:

```
SQL> CREATE TABLE test OF xmltype;
```

This table will accept any well-formed XML message. What's more, if you add a primary key value in your XML records, you can join against them via the extractvalue SQL function. Our XML message looks like the following:

```
<?xml version = '1.0'?><CONTACTS>
  <CONTACT>
    <CONTACT_ID>1</CONTACT_ID>
    <GIVEN_NAME_1>Thaddeus</GIVEN_NAME_1>
    <GIVEN_NAME_2>Jace</GIVEN_NAME_2>
    <FAMILY_NAME>Hay</FAMILY_NAME>
    <DOB>29-nov-1995</DOB>
    <EMAIL>thaddeus.j.hay@dontsend.com</EMAIL>
    <PHONE_TYPE>HOME</PHONE_TYPE>
    <PHONE_CODE_CTRY>+1</PHONE_CODE_CTRY>
    <PHONE_CODE_AREA>311</PHONE_CODE_AREA>
    <PHONE_CODE_DIAL>555-4661</PHONE_CODE_DIAL>
    <GENDER>M</GENDER>
  </CONTACT>
</CONTACTS>
```

We easily pull out the XML values using the SQL extractvalue function. In addition, we can use the SQL MERGE statement to automatically filter out the insertion of possible duplicate values and update existing values if we use the <CONTACT_ID> key.

The MERGE statement has some basic parts that you should understand. If you are already familiar with MERGE, then this will be a good review. We split the MERGE statement into three major parts to keep it simple for those of you who have not seen this statement yet. First, the MERGE statement header consists of the mandatory keywords MERGE and INTO (see Figure 9-2). It is possible to merge into a view as well as a table, so long as dependencies are met.

The second and mandatory section contains most of the logic behind MERGE statements (see Figure 9-3). It is crucial that you get the USING and ON sections right. Be sure your joins do not cause unwanted Cartesian products.

Lastly, the UPDATE, INSERT, and ERROR clauses allow you to both update and insert within the same DML statement (see Figure 9-4). This will save you a lot of CPU, memory, and time. What's more, the MERGE statement is highly tuned and acts more like a CREATE TABLE AS statement than a standard INSERT statement.

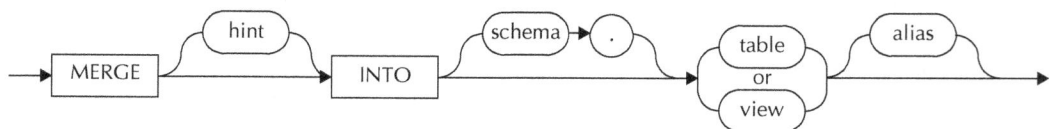

FIGURE 9-2. MERGE header clause

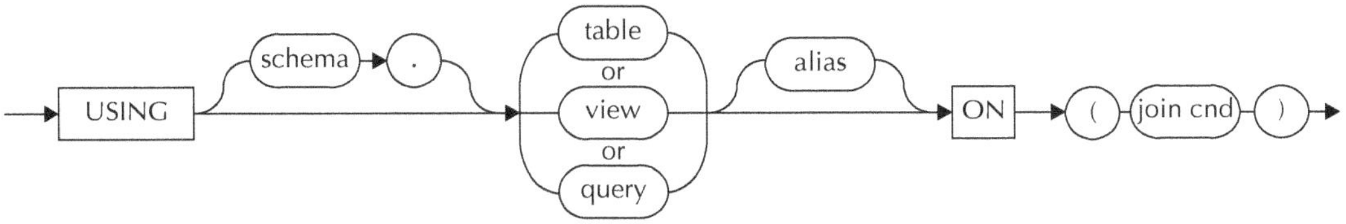

FIGURE 9-3. *MERGE join clause*

FIGURE 9-4. *UPDATE/INSERT/ERROR clause*

You can easily interact with XML within Oracle SQL and PL/SQL because of built-in functions like extractvalue, like so:

```
SQL> CREATE OR REPLACE PROCEDURE load_person AS
  2  BEGIN
  3    MERGE INTO person p
  4    USING (
  5    WITH extraction AS
  6    ( SELECT TO_NUMBER(extractvalue(
  7                 sys_nc_rowinfo$
  8               ,'/CONTACTS/CONTACT/CONTACT_ID' )) contact_id
  9    ,         extractvalue(
 10                 sys_nc_rowinfo$
 11               ,'/CONTACTS/CONTACT/GIVEN_NAME_1' ) given_name_1
 12    ,         extractvalue(
 13                 sys_nc_rowinfo$
 14               ,'/CONTACTS/CONTACT/GIVEN_NAME_2' ) given_name_2
 15    ,         extractvalue(
 16                 sys_nc_rowinfo$
 17               ,'/CONTACTS/CONTACT/FAMILY_NAME' ) family_name
 18    ,         extractvalue(
 19                 sys_nc_rowinfo$
 20               ,'/CONTACTS/CONTACT/DOB' ) dob
 21    ,         extractvalue(
 22                 sys_nc_rowinfo$
 23               ,'/CONTACTS/CONTACT/PHONE_CODE_CTRY' ) phone_code_ctry
 24    ,         extractvalue(
 25                 sys_nc_rowinfo$
 26               ,'/CONTACTS/CONTACT/PHONE_CODE_AREA' ) phone_code_area
 27    ,         extractvalue(
```

```
28                    sys_nc_rowinfo$
29                    ,'/CONTACTS/CONTACT/PHONE_CODE_DIAL' ) phone_code_dial
30       ,        extractvalue(
31                    sys_nc_rowinfo$
32                    ,'/CONTACTS/CONTACT/EMAIL' ) email
33       ,        extractvalue(SYS_NC_ROWINFO$
34                    ,'/CONTACTS/CONTACT/GENDER') gender
35       FROM     admjmh.test)
36       SELECT   TO_NUMBER(contact_id) contact_id
37       ,        given_name_1
38       ,        given_name_2
39       ,        family_name
40       ,        dob
41       ,        phone_code_ctry
42       ,        phone_code_area
43       ,        phone_code_dial
44       ,        email
45       ,        gender
46       FROM     extraction e) e
... continued below ...
```

Other XML built-in functions include the ability to use XQuery to intelligently parse through XML tables to perform full-text searches. In this case, we simply need the ability to treat the XML object as a table and join on the various <CONTACT_ID> values. We do so in the following join clause:

```
47       ON (p.contact_id = e.contact_id)
... continued below ...
```

Within the UPDATE clause, we set the non-join columns of the person table to the values within each XML record, like so:

```
48       WHEN MATCHED THEN
49       UPDATE
50       SET  given_name_1 = e.given_name_1
51       ,    given_name_2 = e.given_name_2
52       ,    family_name  = e.family_name
53       ,    dob = e.dob
54       ,    phone_code_ctry = e.phone_code_ctry
55       ,    phone_code_area = e.phone_code_area
56       ,    phone_code_dial = e.phone_code_dial
57       ,    email = e.email
58       ,    gender = e.gender
... continued below ...
```

Finally, if the values are not found in the person table, then an INSERT is performed. This ensures that the program does not create duplicate values if the contact_id value remains unique. We enforce data integrity by placing a unique key on the person.contact_id column:

```
59       WHEN NOT MATCHED THEN
60       INSERT
61       VALUES
62       ( e.contact_id
```

```
63      , e.given_name_1
64      , e.given_name_2
65      , e.family_name
66      , e.dob
67      , e.phone_code_ctry
68      , e.phone_code_area
69      , e.phone_code_dial
70      , e.email
71      , e.gender);
72   END;
73   /
```

The next several sections of code are more complicated. They must be completed in a particular order. It helps to think of the following definitions in sequential order:

- *Programs* are little robots; they are the minions that do your bidding.
- *Chains* group all of your programs together.
- *Chain steps* reference programs and their parameters.
- *Chain rules* determine what happens when programs succeed or fail.
- *Jobs* wrap all of the components together and can be triggered based on database or operating system events.

We start creating our chained job by making the credentials we need to interact with the database server's operating system:

```
SQL>  BEGIN
  2      sys.dbms_credential.create_credential(
  3        username => 'oracle'
  4      , password => 'changeme'
  5      , database_role => 'SYSDBA'
  6      , comments => 'Stored credentials for ingestion of xml samples'
  8      , enabled => true
  9      , credential_name => '"INGEST_XML_CREDENTIAL"');
 10   END;
 11   /
```

You can see that this step is straightforward. Credentials allow you to store sensitive information, such as usernames and passwords, within the database. They enable the database to spin shadow OS sessions such as Unix shells and Windows command prompts.

Next we create the two programs that will do our bidding. We start with the Unix executable program:

```
SQL> BEGIN
  2      dbms_scheduler.create_program(
  3        program_name => 'IMPDP_XML'
  4      , program_action =>
  5          '/u01/app/oracle/admin/A454/dpdump/person_xml/test.sh'
  6      , program_type => 'EXECUTABLE'
  7      , number_of_arguments => 0
  8      , comments => NULL
```

```
 9    , enabled => TRUE);
10  END;
11  /
```

You must make sure that the OS user stipulated in your credential has rights to execute the `test.sh` script. In this case, we use the Oracle user, and it has Unix 750 permissions. That means only the Oracle user or members of its `oinstall` group can interact with files in the `person_xml` folder. Also ensure that the database user has the following rights at a minimum:

- Create job
- Create external job
- Manage scheduler

The `test.sh` file contains the following entries:

```
#!/bin/bash
export ORACLE_BASE=/u01/app/oracle;
export ORACLE_HOME=$ORACLE_BASE/product/12.1.0/dbhome_1;
export ORACLE_SID=A454;
export ORACLE_BASE=/u01/app/oracle;
export PATH=$PATH:$ORACLE_HOME/bin;
time sqlldr username/password@pdb01 /u01/app/oracle/admin/A454/dpdump/person_
xml/test.ctl direct=true parallel=true skip_index_maintenance=true
```

Note that we call the `test.ctl` control file in the script. Its contents are simple and look like this:

```
LOAD DATA
INFILE '/u01/app/oracle/admin/A454/dpdump/person_xml/filelist.dat'
APPEND INTO admjmh.test
  xmltype(XMLDATA) (
    filename filler CHAR(120)
  , xmldata lobfile (filename) TERMINATED BY EOF)
```

Within the control file, we tell SQLLDR which files to process and how to interact with them. We create the `filelist.dat` file by performing a simple command like `ls *.xml > filelist.dat`. It is vital that you test your scripts now. You do so by scheduling a simple run-me-now job that calls the `impdp_xml` program. We did so by performing the following at a SQL*Plus prompt:

```
SQL> BEGIN
  2    dbms_scheduler.create_job(
  3      job_name => '"TEST_JOB"'
  4    , program_name => '"IMPDP_XML"'
  5    , start_date => NULL
  6    , repeat_interval => NULL
  7    , end_date => NULL
  8    , enabled => FALSE
  9    , auto_drop => TRUE
```

```
10        , comments => ''
11        , job_style => 'REGULAR'
12        , credential_name => 'INGEST_XML_CREDENTIAL');
13
14     dbms_scheduler.set_attribute(
15        name => '"TEST_JOB"'
16        , attribute => 'store_output'
17        , value => TRUE);
18
19     dbms_scheduler.set_attribute(
20        name => '"TEST_JOB"'
21        , attribute => 'logging_level'
22        , value => DBMS_SCHEDULER.LOGGING_OFF);
23
24     dbms_scheduler.enable(
25        name => '"TEST_JOB"');
26  END;
27  /
```

Then, we issued the following query against the dba_scheduler_job_run_details table to view the results of our one-time job:

```
SQL>   COLUMN job_name FORMAT a10
SQL>   COLUMN status FORMAT a10
SQL>   COLUMN output FORMAT a60SQL> SELECT    job_name
  2  ,          status
  3  ,          output
  4  FROM       dba_scheduler_job_run_details
  5  WHERE      owner = 'CHANGEME'
  6  AND        job_name LIKE '%TEST%';
```

It prints the following:

```
JOB_NAME    STATUS     OUTPUT

---------- ---------- ------------------------------------------------------------

TEST_JOB    SUCCEEDED  SQL*Loader: Release 12.1.0.1.0 - Production on ...

                       Copyright (c) 1982, 2013, Oracle and/or its affiliates.

Path used:      Direct

Load completed - logical record count 7.

Table ADMJMH.TEST:

7 Rows successfully loaded.
```

The merge_person program runs a stored procedure that pulls information from the XMLTYPE table and puts that data in relational tables. We create the program and test it like we did the first:

```
SQL> BEGIN
  2    dbms_scheduler.create_program(
  3      program_name => 'MERGE_PERSON'
  4    , program_action => 'LOAD_PERSON'
  5    , program_type => 'STORED_PROCEDURE'
  6    , number_of_arguments => 0
  7    , comments => 'A stored procedure writes to the person table.'
  8    , enabled => TRUE);
  9  END;
 10  /
```

Once the programs are in place, we create the chain as follows:

```
SQL> BEGIN
  2    dbms_scheduler.create_chain(
  3        comments => 'One chain to rule them all.'
  4      , chain_name => 'LOAD_XML');
  5    dbms_scheduler.enable(name=>'LOAD_XML');
  6  END;
  7  /
```

If you use SQL Developer, you can create chains, their steps, and rules with built-in wizards. You may want to use that method at first because you won't have to worry about syntax errors. We create chain steps in the following PL/SQL blocks:

```
SQL> BEGIN
  2    dbms_scheduler.define_chain_step(
  3        chain_name => '"LOAD_XML"'
  4      , step_name => '"XML_STAGE"'
  5      , program_name => '"IMPDP_XML"');
  6
  7    dbms_scheduler.alter_chain(
  8        chain_name => '"LOAD_XML"'
  9      , step_name => '"XML_STAGE"'
 10      , attribute => 'PAUSE'
 11      , value => false);
 12
 13    dbms_scheduler.alter_chain(
 14        chain_name => '"LOAD_XML"'
 15      , step_name => '"XML_STAGE"'
 16      , attribute => 'SKIP'
 17      , value => false);
 18
 19    dbms_scheduler.alter_chain(
 20        chain_name => '"LOAD_XML"'
 21      , step_name => '"XML_STAGE"'
 22      , attribute => 'RESTART_ON_FAILURE'
 23      , value => false);
```

```
24
25     dbms_scheduler.alter_chain(
26         chain_name => '"LOAD_XML"'
27       , step_name => '"XML_STAGE"'
28       , attribute => 'RESTART_ON_RECOVERY'
29       , value => false);
30
31     dbms_scheduler.alter_chain(
32         chain_name => '"LOAD_XML"'
33       , step_name => '"XML_STAGE"'
34       , attribute => 'CREDENTIAL_NAME'
35       , char_value => '"INGEST_XML_CREDENTIAL"');
36   END;
37   /
```

Whew! That was a lot of coding for a simple step. We created the chain (lines 2–7) and stipulated that the job could not be paused (lines 8–14), skipped (lines 15–21), or restarted (lines 22–28). We also gave this step our `ingest_xml_credential`, which allows Oracle to run the Unix shell script as the Oracle user.

The next block defines a chain rule. Think of chain rules as conditional gates that allow Oracle to continue to the next job or not. Valid options are `not_started`, `scheduled`, `running`, `paused`, `stalled`, `succeeded`, `completed`, `failed`, and `stopped`. There is only one other condition that chain rules can accept, and that is the `1=1` binary. We add this condition to the very first rule in our chain. It tells Oracle to automatically run through the initial gate, like so:

```
SQL> BEGIN
  2    dbms_scheduler.define_chain_rule(
  3        chain_name => '"LOAD_XML"'
  4      , comments => 'Starting test.sh'
  5      , rule_name  => '"START_XML_STAGE"'
  6      , condition => '1=1'
  7      , action => 'START XML_STAGE');
  8  END;
  9  /
```

Now for the next step we create the chain steps:

```
SQL> BEGIN
  2    dbms_scheduler.define_chain_step(
  3        chain_name => 'LOAD_XML"'
  4      , step_name => '"LOAD_PERSON_TABLE"'
  5      , program_name => '"MERGE_PERSON"');
  6
  7    dbms_scheduler.alter_chain(
  8        chain_name => '"LOAD_XML"'
  9      , step_name => '"LOAD_PERSON_TABLE"'
 10      , attribute => 'PAUSE'
 11      , value => false);
 12
 13    dbms_scheduler.alter_chain(
 14        chain_name => '"LOAD_XML"'
 15      , step_name => '"LOAD_PERSON_TABLE"'
```

```
16        , attribute => 'SKIP'
17        , value => false);
18
19    dbms_scheduler.alter_chain(
20        chain_name => '"LOAD_XML"'
21        , step_name => '"LOAD_PERSON_TABLE"'
22        , attribute => 'RESTART_ON_FAILURE'
23        , value => false);
24
25    dbms_scheduler.alter_chain(
26        chain_name => '"LOAD_XML"'
27        , step_name => '"LOAD_PERSON_TABLE"'
28        , attribute => 'RESTART_ON_RECOVERY'
29        , value => false);
30  END;
31  /
```

Like its sibling step, we told define_chain_rule that it could not pause, be skipped, or restarted. Note that we did not add a credential here. That's because we are already authenticated inside the database.

Our next set of rules is interesting, showing just how the "rule gates" work:

```
SQL> BEGIN
  2    dbms_scheduler.define_chain_rule(
  3        chain_name => '"LOAD_XML"'
  4        , comments => 'Start load_person procedure'
  5        , rule_name  => '"START_LOAD_PERSON_TABLE"'
  6        , condition => 'XML_STAGE SUCCEEDED'
  7        , action => 'START LOAD_PERSON_TABLE');
  8  END;
  9  /
```

Observe that the start_load_person_table rule only allows continuance if the xml_stage step succeeds. We're saying that we don't want to continue if the previous step fails. Next, we add a rule that stops our chain if the load_person_table step succeeds:

```
SQL> BEGIN
  2    dbms_scheduler.define_chain_rule(
  3        chain_name => '"LOAD_XML"'
  4        , comments => 'All done.'
  5        , rule_name  => '"FINISHED"'
  6        , condition => 'LOAD_PERSON_TABLE SUCCEEDED'
  7        , action => 'END');
  8  END;
  9  /
```

In the following block, we create a job that allows us to schedule the chain:

```
SQL> BEGIN
  2    dbms_scheduler.create_job(
  3        job_name => '"CHAIN_XML2PERSON"'
  4        , job_type => 'CHAIN'
```

```
 5        , job_action => '"LOAD_XML"'
 6        , number_of_arguments => 0
 7        , start_date =>
 8            TO_TIMESTAMP_TZ(
 9                '2014-03-29 11:30:36.000000000 AMERICA/DENVER'
10                ,'YYYY-MM-DD HH24:MI:SS.FF TZR')
11        , repeat_interval => 'FREQ=MINUTELY;INTERVAL=5'
12        , end_date => NULL
13        , enabled => FALSE
14        , auto_drop => FALSE
15        , comments => '');
16
17     dbms_scheduler.set_attribute(
18          name => '"CHAIN_XML2PERSON"'
19        , attribute => 'store_output'
20        , value => TRUE);
21
22     dbms_scheduler.set_attribute(
23          name => '"CHAIN_XML2PERSON"'
24        , attribute => 'job_priority'
25        , value => '1');
26
27     dbms_scheduler.set_attribute(
28          name => '"CHAIN_XML2PERSON"'
29        , attribute => 'logging_level'
30        , value => DBMS_SCHEDULER.LOGGING_FULL);
31
33     dbms_scheduler.enable('"CHAIN_XML2PERSON"');
34  END;
35  /
```

In this block, we named the job and told it that its job type is chain. This tells Oracle to look for the LOAD_XML chain as its JOB_ACTION input (lines 2–6). We also specified that the job is to run on a 5-minute increment (line 9), that it should store its output (lines 15–20), that it should run on the highest priority (lines 21–26), and finally to turn on all of its logging output (lines 27–33). Once all of this is done, Oracle will spin up every 5 minutes, load the XML messages found in the PERSON_XML folder, and then populate the person table from those XML messages. It will do so until you stop the job manually or it reaches an end date that you prescribe.

Job Management and Security

We stated earlier in this chapter that you cannot execute or manipulate jobs that belong to the SYS schema unless you are authenticated as that user. While this represents a slight drawback, the restriction is essential to the security of your system. That is because the SYS user owns, and thereby has access to, all of the objects in your database. You *must* do everything in your power to protect that account. It is also very likely that you have other accounts in your database that have elevated privileges. You must apply the same level of protection to these accounts as well.

In Chapter 7, we present a new security model. Implementing it will greatly reduce the risk of data breach and the amount of work you must do to audit and maintain user rights. If you haven't read Chapter 7, we strongly encourage you to do so. In our experience, database administrators who implement this model return to us with praise and thanks because their security workload is significantly reduced and simplified.

As for this section, you have already seen in previous sections many of the tasks related to the creation and alteration of jobs and chains, so in this section, we discuss how you can enable, disable, pause, and drop jobs.

The commands are straightforward. We will start with stopping and pausing jobs. To stop a job, issue the following statement:

```
SQL> BEGIN
  2    dbms_scheduler.stop_job(
  3        name=> '"test_job"'
  4        , force => TRUE);
  5  END;
  6  /
```

To stop a chain step, issue this PL/SQL block:

```
SQL> BEGIN
  2    dbms_scheduler.alter_running_chain(
  3        job_name => '"CHAINXML2PERSON"'
  4      , step_name => 'LOAD_PERSON_TABLE'
  5      , attribute => 'PAUSE BEFORE'
  6      , value => 'NOT_STARTED');
  7  END;
  8  /
```

Enabling and disabling jobs is just as straightforward. You do so by performing the following commands:

```
SQL> BEGIN
  2    dbms_scheduler.disable(name=>'"test_job"', force => TRUE);
  3  END;
  4  /
SQL> BEGIN
  2    dbms_scheduler.enable(name=>'"test_job"');
  3  END;
  4  /
```

Job maintenance really is that straightforward. One caveat: you will only be able to stop jobs or chains while they are running. If they aren't running, simply disable the job or chain. Doing so will prevent their next execution automatically.

Supporting Scripts

The following programs and file are available on the McGraw-Hill Professional website to support this chapter:

- The `ch_09_intervals.sql` program contains the code used to create the custom schedules.

- The `ch_09_breakme.sql` program contains the code used to create the simple run-me-now job.

- The `ch_09_xml_chained_job.sql` program contains the code used to create the chained job.

- The `person_xml.zip` file contains the simple XML files needed to import data in the chained job example.

- The `ch_09_performance_tests.sql` program contains the code used to create the `rental_item_fact` table and test the speed of index creation in serial and parallel.

All-Flash Endurance Test

It is a well-known fact that databases are growing at an alarming rate. In addition, database engineers are required to maintain more instances than ever before. In fact, larger companies employ entire teams of DBAs that must manage as many as 50 or 100 databases each. Because of growth like this, it is imperative that DBAs take full advantage of the scheduler, faster IO technology, and greater CPU capacity.

To illustrate the power of the scheduler and flash technology, we bulk loaded our `rental_item_fact` table with 10,000,000 rows of data. Then, we used the scheduler to simultaneously kick off the rebuild of all six indexes on that table; the following illustration shows the elapsed time to rebuild indexes. We were pleasantly surprised when the combination of HP servers and Fusion-io flash allowed us to rebuild all six indexes in less than 36 seconds. In comparison, older SaS arrays, without the use of parallel rebuilding, took 3 hours, 16 minutes, and 30 seconds. In parallel, the SaS array took 11 minutes and 35 seconds.

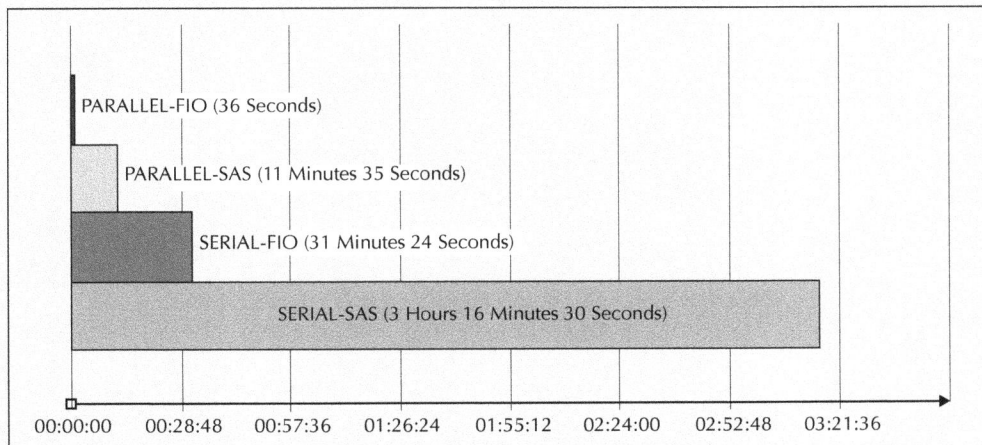

Summary

You should now feel comfortable creating complex schedules and jobs. Your ability to do so will help you drastically reduce the complexity and time that it takes to do everyday tasks like rebuilding indexes or moving data between systems or schemas. We focus on these kinds of tasks in Chapters 5, 6, and 10. You may want to pay special attention to Chapter 10 because it shows you how to use PL/SQL to help you tune and extend the life of your systems.

CHAPTER
10

Optimizing Using PL/SQL

Purpose

The purpose of this chapter is to introduce you to performance tuning concepts using PL/SQL as a statistics-gathering platform. Within an Oracle database there are many objects that provide differing levels of information which, if gathered and properly analyzed, can help to optimize areas such as indexing, data modeling, table structure, and SQL statements. For example, when using dbms_scheduler, as shown in Chapter 9, maintenance tasks become less frequent, or even better automated, and available database resources are more fully utilized through parallelizing dbms_scheduler jobs.

To help you better understand, think of statistics gathering on the database for performance optimization as being similar to trying to figure out the gas mileage on your car under different driving conditions. There may be several different types of driving for which you would be interested in gathering information, such as city driving, highway driving, and rush-hour driving. The first, tried-and-true method for gas-mileage calculations is to fill up your gas tank, reset the trip odometer, drive the car as you normally would for a few days, fill up again, and calculate the gas mileage by dividing the trip odometer by the number of gallons required to fill up again. This is a very ambiguous way of estimating fuel economy, in that you are averaging the amount of city, highway, and rush-hour fuel economies together. Another, more accurate method of calculating gas mileage is to fill up each time you change driving types; for example, right before you start driving on a highway, fill up your tank and reset the trip odometer, and then when you leave the highway, immediately fill up again and record your fuel economy in the same way as before.

An even more accurate method to calculate gas mileage in different conditions would be if you had a device in your car that could accurately measure the amount of gas in the tank down to the ounce at any point in time, whether you are driving or not, and could record the fuel level and mileage whenever you start different driving conditions. Using this method, when you are driving around town you would be recording those miles and fuel consumption only as in-town driving, and the same would happen for highway and rush-hour driving. This method would give you a much better sense of how your car is going to perform under different driving types. Also, with this method it would be much easier to factor in other conditions, such as weather, tire pressure, and other factors that affect gas mileage, and be able to reasonably forecast how much fuel you would use under different driving conditions.

Most of us know that driving down the highway at 65 MPH increases fuel economy as compared to driving through a subdivision, but by how much? If we used the second or third method, we could determine with a reasonable amount of certainty how much more efficient the highway trip would be than driving the same course through stop-and-go traffic in the city. Database optimization takes the same approach and can help you determine where resources can be used more efficiently.

The first method of database optimization is to use transaction times to determine what is most effective. This is a very common method and can be very effective, although limited. A second method is to measure statistics within a single session for a set of queries to obtain a decent determination of performance. (We address that method in this chapter.) The third method is to gather information on all sessions, at specific intervals, and then analyze the performance of different database users under load conditions. Typically, the information is gathered by Oracle's reporting tools, such as Automatic Workload Repository (AWR) and Automatic Database Diagnostic Monitor (ADDM), and if it is not gathered correctly, this method becomes very resource intensive. At the end of this chapter, you will have the necessary tools to answer questions such as, "What are the differences in IO between a full table scan, a B-tree index scan, and a bitmap index scan?"

Advantages

There are many advantages to optimizing the performance of the database, especially with the potentially very high cost of licensing cores. As the database uses its resources more efficiently, the financial cost for its operation goes down. As operations become more efficient, maintenance tasks can be made simpler through automation, and the total cost of running the database becomes lower as well.

Another advantage is that by understanding how different schemas/users are using the resources on the database, you can more efficiently place the users into resource groups to help control resource usage, rather than having a user throttle their performance through inefficient coding, or having some database detrimentally affect the performance of others.

Disadvantages

We all can understand the disadvantages of not conducting performance tuning, such as requiring more resources, including servers, CPU, and storage. The main disadvantage of performance tuning is labor costs to test and implement changes. If you are starting a database from scratch, there are several advantages in designing the data model and table structures correctly. But there is an opportunity cost to every action. As you make decisions about changing or developing a database, you need to be aware of what is being given up to achieve a performance goal and place that cost into your decision process.

Also, as you optimize a database, remember that the process for keeping the database optimized requires constant effort, unless you build automation into the process. There may come a time when it is easier and cheaper just to throw more hardware at the database to have it perform at the needed level, but generally, if a database is optimized properly, you can greatly reduce the costs of operation and ownership.

Overview

In this chapter, we use a star schema and billions of rows of data to mock up a realistic data warehouse environment. We purposefully created this large data set to discover how fast our all-flash storage was and to give you pragmatic examples. Our test environment consists of two Oracle RAC nodes with the following configuration:

- HP DL-380 Rev 8 Servers with 32 hyper-threaded, physical cores
- 256GB RAM per node
- 2TB SaS Internal Disk Array
- 10 Gigabit/sec Public NIC
- 40 Gigabit/sec Private Infiniband Mellanox NIC
- Mellanox Infiniband Switch
- Fusion-io ION 12.8TB Midrange, SAN Appliance

Before we continue, we want to stress the importance of logical thinking in tuning exercises. If you're unfamiliar with the scientific method, the basic steps are as follows:

1. Make an observation that contains a question to be answered.
2. Create educated guesses, called theories, that answer your question(s).
3. Create measures that will help you determine if your theories are accurate.
4. Test your theories. Your experiments should include both proofs and disproofs of your theories.
5. Analyze the results of your tests.
6. Make appropriate changes.
7. Repeat.

Be sensitive to your test results. We cannot overstate the impact of an "it depends" and "question everything" approach to the scientific method. Careful consideration of facts will usually lead to success, but the path to failure is paved with "you should always do" principles. If you follow this approach, you will soon discover that your questions have multiple solutions. It is up to you to determine which solution fits your short- and long-term goals. By the end of this chapter, you should be able to approach any tuning task in a scientific manner, producing quick, efficient, and repeatable results.

This chapter covers the following concepts related to optimizing performance using PL/SQL:

- Current Oracle optimization platforms
- v$_ views available for performance tuning
- Gathering statistics
- Statistics-gathering package design
- Analyzing a data model

Current Optimization Platforms

As mentioned earlier, Oracle already has performance-tuning platforms that you may have access to. Automatic Workload Repository (AWR) is one with which many DBAs are familiar. AWR contains operational statistics, along with setting and other usage information on the database. AWR compiles using aggregated (a default of 1 hour) statistics of database-resource usage and waits. Another optimization platform, Automatic Database Diagnostic Monitor (ADDM), tells a DBA about the activities that the database is spending the most time on, then dives down to the root cause of the issue and tries to report the cause of an issue rather than just the symptoms. Another source of information on database performance is Active Session History (ASH). This is a snapshot of what active sessions are doing once per second and is stored in v$_ views.

v$* Views for Performance Tuning

There are many v$_ views that offer insight into database performance; some that are beneficial for performance tuning are

- ■ v$sqlarea
- ■ v$sql
- ■ v$mystat
- ■ v$sesstat
- ■ v$sysstat
- ■ v$active_session_history

Many of the v$_ views require access to higher levels of licensing, and may incur additional licensing costs.

Two of the previously mentioned views that can provide insight into current performance are v$mystat and v$sesstat. v$mystat is very useful in showing what resources the current session has consumed to that point in time. This includes parallel sessions that the master session created. After a parallel session ends, the resource usage of that session accrues to the master session's statistics. Because of how the session accrues, v$mystat can be one of the most useful views for helping with performance tuning for data models or SQL statements. You need to gather statistics after the parallel session ends. A different view, v$sesstat, shows the same statistics as v$mystat, but for all active sessions on the database. The statistics that are available appear in the name column of v$statname. For definitions of what the statistics measure, please consult the Oracle documentation.

Gathering Statistics

In gathering statistics for performance tuning, you need to clearly define what is happening over a set period of time for a given statistics-gathering session. A statistics-gathering session is a time period over which you gather statistics on the current session, and during which you record resource usage for later consumption and analysis. The types of operations upon which you can gather information are UPDATE, INSERT, DELETE, and SELECT statements, DDL statements (such as CREATE TABLE AS SELECT [CTAS]), or even a PL/SQL block. Knowing the consumed resources during the statistics-gathering session is essential to determining how to improve the performance of the database, the data model, and any individual SQL statements that are running on the database, if necessary.

Oracle Database 12c (12.1.0) gathers over 850 data points. Each data point holds a different value based on the question you're trying to answer. However, the vast number of statistical data points can overwhelm analysts. We suggest that you craft your statistics gathering to focus on those data points that are most important to your key objectives.

Beyond the data points you collect, it's important that you know how frequently to collect them. The more often you gather them, the more precise your viewpoint of the health of the database. Unfortunately, gathering them too often can hamper how your database performs. The trick for you is to find a balance of how often and how widely you sample your database. For example, you could choose to sample every five to ten seconds and look at a narrow set of users, or you could sample less often across your entire database. It is really up to you. Bear in mind, real-time sampling requires a considerable amount of resources.

Statistics-Gathering Package

You can gather statistics for any SELECT, INSERT, UPDATE, DELETE, CREATE TABLE AS (CTAS), or PL/SQL block. We refer to the gathering process as *snapping* because you must take a quick snapshot before query execution and after. We wrapped a simplified version of our real-time statistics package to make it easier for you to begin.

There are four important tasks that you must complete in order to make the statistics you gather useful to an analyst:

- Customize the number of statistics to be gathered.

- Identify database resource usage during a succinct time frame.

- Make statistics available for future consumption.

- Optimize the organization of data for maximum query ability and interoperability with tools like Microsoft Excel and Business Intelligence Suites.

The first task is easy. We create a toggle table to hold all of the stats that a particular version of Oracle gathers. You have to change this per database version because each major release collects slightly different statistics. To create this table, run the following blocks as sys or system:

```
SQL> CREATE TABLE stat_toggle_control AS
  2    SELECT   statistic# AS stat_toggle_control_id
  3    ,        NAME AS stat_name
  4    ,        'N' AS collect_this_stat
  5    FROM     v$statname;
```

Notice that we set a literal of "N" for the collect_this_stat column. This toggles all statistics-gathering processes off in our stat_snap package, described later on in this chapter. If you want to gather a particular statistical point, set its collect_this_stat flag to "Y."

Next we create a global temporary table to hold the statistics. You can build a regular table if you want, but we find the global temporary table very convenient because it only holds information related to the session that is logged in. This is handy when you are gathering statistics on multiple sessions at the same time. Run the following block to create the stat_collection table:

```
SQL> CREATE GLOBAL TEMPORARY TABLE stat_collection
  2  ( snap_name    VARCHAR2(4000)
  3  , stat_name    VARCHAR2(128)
  4  , start_snap   NUMBER
  5  , end_snap     NUMBER)
  6  ON COMMIT PRESERVE ROWS;
```

We purposefully refrain from normalizing this data to make it easier to use in tools like Microsoft Excel and Business Intelligence tools. The table holds the actual statistics consumed, and they're stored by collecting before and after values. We create a secondary view that subtracts the start_snap from the end_snap values because global temporary tables don't support virtual columns.

Create the view by running the following block:

```
SQL> CREATE OR REPLACE VIEW stat_collection_vw AS
  2      SELECT    sc.*
  3      ,         end_snap - start_snap stat_diff
  4      FROM      stat_collection sc;
```

Now that we have a way to toggle which stats we want to use and we have a place to hold them, we build a simple package that can gather stats for us. The package holds five procedures. We detail them in the following list:

- **start_snap** This procedure gathers the statistics that we chose (SET collect_this_stat = 'Y') for performance analysis in stat_toggle_control and inserts the statistics into the stat_collection table. The procedure's user-supplied argument uniquely identifies the statistics-gathering session.

- **end_snap** This procedure regathers the statistics that the start_snap procedure gathered and updates the end_snap column in the stat_collection table with the latest values for the statistics-gathering session.

- **clear_snap** This procedure cleans up the stat_collection table (via TRUNCATE) in case we need to start our statistics-gathering session over.

- **print_snap** This is a dbms_output.put_line procedure to print the gathered statistics.

- **table_snap** A CREATE TABLE AS SELECT procedure to create a snapshot of the stat_collection table makes statistics available for future consumption.

To begin, we create our package spec:

```
SQL> CREATE OR REPLACE PACKAGE stat_snap AS
  2      PROCEDURE start_snap(snap_session IN VARCHAR2);
  3      PROCEDURE end_snap(snap_session IN VARCHAR2);
  4      PROCEDURE clear_snap;
  5      PROCEDURE print_snap;
  6      PROCEDURE table_snap (snap_session IN VARCHAR2);
  7  END stat_snap;
  8  /
```

For the package body to compile correctly, the user that compiles the package needs the following GRANT from SYSDBA:

```
SQL> GRANT SELECT ON v_$mystat TO <compiling_username>;
```

Next we build the body of the package:

```
SQL> CREATE OR REPLACE PACKAGE BODY start_snap AS
  2      PROCEDURE start_snap(snap_session IN VARCHAR2) IS
  3        lv_name  VARCHAR2(4000) := snap_session;
  4      BEGIN
```

```
 5      MERGE INTO stat_collection a
 6      USING (SELECT   lv_name AS query_name
 7             ,         stat_name
 8             ,         value
 9             FROM      stat_toggle_control stc INNER JOIN v$mystat ms
10             ON        stc.stat_toggle_control_id = ms.statistic#
11             AND       stc.collect_this_stat = 'Y' ) b
12      ON   (a.stat_name = b.stat_name
13      AND   a.snap_name = b.query_name)
14      WHEN MATCHED THEN
15        UPDATE SET a.start_snap = b.value
16      WHEN NOT MATCHED THEN
17        INSERT (snap_name, stat_name, start_snap)
18        VALUES (b.query_name, b.stat_name, b.value);
19      COMMIT;
20    END start_snap;
```

Observe that we uniquely identify the snap window via the `snap_session` input parameter. It accepts a variable character, so you can put just about anything in it; however, you should choose something that will make sense to your enterprise users. The `snap_session` value is stored in the `stat_collection.snap_name` column. We use a MERGE statement rather than an INSERT statement so that our end_snap values are updated instead of collecting extra rows of data. This is very helpful because running stats across a large database can result in tens of millions of rows if you do not merge the data.

The next block of code is the `end_snap` procedure; run it as follows:

```
22      PROCEDURE end_snap (snap_session IN VARCHAR2) IS
23        lv_name   VARCHAR2(256) := snap_session;
24      BEGIN
25        MERGE INTO stat_collection a
26        USING (SELECT   lv_name AS snap_name
27               ,         stat_name
28               ,         value AS stat_value
29               FROM      stat_toggle_control stc INNER JOIN v$mystat ms
30               ON        stc.rts_toggle_control_id = ms.statistic#
31               AND       rtc.collect_this_stat = 'Y' ) B
32        ON   (a.stat_name = b.stat_name
33        AND   a.snap_name = b.snap_name)
34        WHEN MATCHED THEN
35        UPDATE SET a.end_snap = b.stat_value;
36        COMMIT;
37      END end_snap;
```

In the end_snap procedure, we pass in the same `snap_name` as we did in the `start_snap` procedure. The `snap_name` drives the update of the `stat_collection` table.

The following block creates the `clear_snap` procedure. It empties the `stat_collection` table for all previous collection processes. You only have to use this procedure if you are gathering multiple snaps per session. You would do so if you wanted to compare two or more SQL statements that you were trying to tune. You do not need to run `clear_snap` if you are starting a new session because the global temporary table is session dependent and any new session you create will automatically have an empty `stat_collection` table.

```
39   PROCEDURE clear_snap IS
40   BEGIN
41     EXECUTE IMMEDIATE 'TRUNCATE TABLE stat_collection';
42   END clear_snap;
```

The `print_snap` procedure prints to the screen, via the `dbms_output.put_line` command, the resources consumed. It is created via the following block:

```
44   PROCEDURE print_snap IS
45     CURSOR collection_cur IS
46       SELECT * FROM RTS_COLLECTION_VW;
47   BEGIN
48     FOR i IN collection_cur LOOP
49       dbms_output.put_line(i.snap_name||' -- '||
50                            i.stat_name||': '||i.stat_diff);
51     END LOOP;
52   END print_snap;
```

Make sure you turn on your SQL*Plus SERVEROUTPUT or you won't see the results. If you want to collect the output, you can spool the output to a `.csv` or `.txt` file.

The last procedure dynamically creates tables that store all of the results from our snapped sessions. Create the procedure by issuing the following block:

```
54   PROCEDURE table_snap(snap_session IN VARCHAR2) IS
55     lv_date   VARCHAR2(30)  := TO_CHAR(SYSDATE, 'YYYYMMDDHH24MISS');
56     lv_name   VARCHAR2(4000) := snap_session;
57   BEGIN
58     EXECUTE IMMEDIATE 'CREATE TABLE '|| lv_name ||
59                       '_' || lv_date ||
60                       ' AS SELECT * FROM stat_collection_vw');
61   END table_snap;
62 END stat_snap;
63 /
```

Analyzing a Data Model

We used the `video_store` star schema tables in our analysis. Our goal is to optimize the speed and query ability of the data. Let's begin by gathering some baseline statistics. We will create several versions of the tables so we can mimic various scenarios. For example, we change the compression, partitioning, indexing, and PCTFREE values; however, we keep the parallel degree at 50 on all tests to maximize our performance test.

You must perform the following steps to gather stats in each set of queries:

1. Execute the `stat_snap.start_snap` command.

2. Run a query or PL/SQL block.

3. Execute the `stat_snap.end_snap` command.

In our tests, we will gather only the *physical reads* total IO requests, *physical reads* total bytes, and *logical reads* total IO requests. You must set the `collect_this_stat` flag to "Y" in order for the `stat_snap` package to gather any statistical points. You do so as follows:

```
SQL> UPDATE stat_toggle_control
  2  SET    collect_this_stat = 'Y'
  3  WHERE  UPPER(stat_name) IN UPPER('CONSISTENT GETS'
  4                                  ,'CPU USED BY THIS SESSION'
  5                                  ,'EFFECTIVE IO TIME'
  6                                  ,'INDEX FETCH BY KEY'
  7                                  ,'NUMBER OF IO READS ISSUED'
  8                                  ,'PHYSICAL READ IO REQUESTS'
  9                                  ,'PHYSICAL READ TOTAL BYTES'
 10                                  ,'SESSION LOGICAL READS');
```

This list is quite small but it is sufficient for illustrating the process you must follow to gather statistics that are pragmatic. All of our tests employ a `rental_item_fact` table that contains 3 billion rows, a `customer_dim` table that contains 5 million rows, and a `product_dim` table that contains 239,000 rows.

We run five tests total. Each will use six queries but point at five different table arrangements. We purposefully created very large tables to represent a realistic data warehouse environment. You can create these tables from our `video_store` creation scripts, available on the publisher's website, but you may want to shrink the data size.

The following tables describe the five table arrangements. Scenario 1 has the least amount of database modification, as shown in Table 10-1.

Scenario 2, shown in Table 10-2, sets the PCTFREE value to zero. This maximizes the amount of rows that can be placed in your database blocks. It is a good practice in some data warehouse cases, but should be used with caution. This scenario also creates standard B-tree indexes on the primary key and foreign key columns.

	rental_item_fact	product_dim	customer_dim
Compression	OLTP	OLTP	OLTP
PCTFREE	10	10	10
Index	None	None	None
Degree of Parallel	50	50	50
Partitioning	None	None	None

TABLE 10-1.   *Scenario 1*

	rental_item_fact	product_dim	customer_dim
Compression	OLTP	OLTP	OLTP
PCTFREE	0	0	0
Index	B-tree index on `date_key`, `product_key`, and `customer_key`	Primary key on `product_key`	Primary key on `customer_key`
Degree of Parallel	50	50	50
Partitioning	None	None	None

TABLE 10-2. *Scenario 2*

Scenario 3, shown in Table 10-3, uses the same B-tree indexes, table compression, and PCTFREE, but this scenario partitions all three tables based on the `date_key`, `product_key`, and `customer_key` ranges. We make very small changes to our scenarios to simplify our analysis. This is a good practice because too many changes will muddy the results.

Scenario 4, shown in Table 10-4, changes the index types to bitmap and reorganizes the data by ordering it on insert.

Scenario 5 in Table 10-5 changes the structure a little bit more. This time, we want to see the difference between a BITMAP index and a BITMAP JOIN index.

	rental_item_fact	product_dim	customer_dim
Compression	OLTP	OLTP	OLTP
PCTFREE	0	0	0
Index	B-tree index on `date_key`, `product_key`, and `customer_key`	Primary key on `product_key`	Primary key on `customer_key`
Degree of Parallel	50	50	50
Partitioning	`PARTITION BY RANGE (date_key) INTERVAL (100) (PARTITION p1 VALUES LESS THAN (20040500))`	`PARTITION BY RANGE (product_key) INTERVAL (50000) (PARTITION p1 VALUES LESS THAN (1))`	`PARTITION BY RANGE (customer_key) INTERVAL 100000) (PARTITION p1 VALUES LESS THAN (1))`

TABLE 10-3. *Scenario 3*

	rental_item_fact	product_dim	customer_dim
Compression	OLTP	OLTP	OLTP
PCTFREE	0	0	0
Index	Bitmap indexes on date_key, product_key, and customer_key columns	Primary key on product_key	Primary key on customer_key
Degree of Parallel	50	50	50
Partitioning	`PARTITION BY RANGE (date_key) INTERVAL (100) (PARTITION p1 VALUES LESS THAN (20040500))`	`PARTITION BY RANGE (product_key) INTERVAL (50000) (PARTITION p1 VALUES LESS THAN (1))`	`PARTITION BY RANGE (customer_key) INTERVAL 100000) (PARTITION p1 VALUES LESS THAN (1))`
Order By	date_key, product_key, customer_key	product_key	customer_key

TABLE 10-4. *Scenario 4*

	rental_item_fact	product_dim	customer_dim
Compression	OLTP	OLTP	OLTP
PCTFREE	0	0	0
Index	Bitmap join index for star schema	Primary key on product_key	Primary key on customer_key
Degree of Parallel	50	50	50
Partitioning	`PARTITION BY RANGE (date_key) INTERVAL (100) (PARTITION p1 VALUES LESS THAN (20040500))`	`PARTITION BY RANGE (product_key) INTERVAL (50000) (PARTITION p1 VALUES LESS THAN (1))`	`PARTITION BY RANGE (customer_key) INTERVAL 100000) (PARTITION p1 VALUES LESS THAN (1))`
Order By	date_key, product_key, customer_key	product_key	customer_key

TABLE 10-5. *Scenario 5*

In testing, we need to run the types of queries that commonly run against the data. We then optimize the table structure to produce optimal performance for reporting. We're not concerned about the effects that the table structure has on writing to tables, or maintaining indexes, because we are just optimizing read performance. We know that most reports use predicate filtering, so a large number of our tests will use predicate filtering as well. Many of the queries need aggregations for specific subsets of the data, so our queries should also use aggregate functions, mostly sums. To meet these requirements, we use the six queries introduced next.

Query 1 does a simple full scan of the video_store.rental_item_fact table:

```
SQL> SELECT COUNT(*)
  2  FROM    video_store.rental_item_fact;
```

Query 2 displays a count of the net sales by product_genre and address_region columns during December 2012:

```
SQL> SELECT      product_genre
  2  ,           address_region
  3  ,           SUM(sale_net)
  4  FROM        video_store.rental_item_fact rif INNER JOIN
  5              video_store.product_dim pd
  6  ON          rif.product_key = pd.product_key INNER JOIN
  7              video_store.customer_dim cd
  8  ON          cd.customer_key = rif.customer_key INNER JOIN
  9              video_store.date_dim_vs dd
 10  ON          rif.date_key = dd.date_key
 11  WHERE       date_curr
 12              BETWEEN TO_DATE('20121201','YYYYMMDD')
 13              AND     TO_DATE('20121231','YYYYMMDD')
 14  GROUP BY address_region
 15  ,           product_genre;
```

Query 3 displays a pivot of aggregate sales by address_region for the period between 2005 and 2014:

```
SQL> WITH alpha AS
  2  (SELECT     cd.address_region
  3  ,           dd.date_year
  4  ,           SUM(rif.sale_net) AS sale_net
  5  FROM        video_store.rental_item_fact rif INNER JOIN
  6              video_store.customer_dim cd
  7  ON          rif.customer_key = cd.customer_key INNER JOIN
  8              video_store.date_dim_vs dd
  9  ON          rif.date_key = dd.date_key
 10  GROUP BY cd.address_region
 11  ,           dd.date_year)
 12  SELECT      *
 13  FROM        alpha
 14  PIVOT       (MAX(sale_net) FOR(DATE_YEAR) IN (2005, 2006, 2007, 2008, 2009
 15                                  ,2010, 2011, 2012, 2013, 2014))
 16  ORDER BY address_region;
```

Query 4 lists sales for a specific customer and orders the results by the `product_genre` of the sales for a single region:

```
SQL> SELECT    pd.product_genre
  2  ,          SUM(rif.sale_net) AS sales_net
  3  FROM       video_store.rental_item_fact rif INNER JOIN
  4             video_store.customer_dim cd
  5  ON         rif.customer_key = cd.customer_key INNER JOIN
  6             video_store.product_dim pd
  7  ON         pd.product_key = rif.product_key
  8  WHERE      cd.address_region = 'ID'
  9  GROUP BY pd.product_genre;
```

Query 5 lists the buying habits of males by `date_key` during January 2013:

```
SQL> SELECT    cd.name_full
  2  ,          pd.product_title
  3  ,          pd.product_genre
  4  ,          TO_DATE(rif.date_key,'YYYYMMDD') AS purchase_date
  5  ,          rif.sale_price
  6  FROM       video_store.rental_item_fact rif INNER JOIN
  7             video_store.customer_dim cd
  8  ON         rif.customer_key = cd.customer_key INNER JOIN
  9             video_store.product_dim pd
 10  ON         rif.product_key = pd.product_key
 11  WHERE      cd.name_full = 'DEAN AVERY MONTGOMERY'
 12  ORDER BY rif.date_key;
```

Query 6 lists buying habits of males by `product_rating` during January 2013:

```
SQL> SELECT    pd.product_rating
  2  ,          cd.demographic_gender
  3  ,          dd.date_month_of_year
  4  ,          SUM(rif.product_price) product_price_daily_total
  5  ,          SUM(rif.product_cost) AS product_cost_daily_total
  6  ,          SUM(rif.sale_price) AS sale_price_daily_total
  7  ,          SUM(rif.sale_cost) AS sale_cost_daily_total
  8  ,          SUM(rif.sale_net) AS sale_net_daily_total
  9  FROM       video_store.rental_item_fact rif INNER JOIN
 10             video_store.product_dim pd
 11  ON         rif.product_key = pd.product_key INNER JOIN
 12             video_store.customer_dim cd
 13  ON         rif.customer_key = cd.customer_key INNER JOIN
 14             date_dim_vs dd
 15  ON         rif.date_key = dd.date_key
 16  WHERE      cd.demographic_gender = 'M'
 17  AND        dd.date_curr BETWEEN '01-JAN-2013' AND '31-JAN-2013'
 18  AND        rif.date_key BETWEEN 20130101 AND 20130131
 19  AND        product_rating IN ('PG','PG-13')
 20  GROUP BY pd.product_rating
 21  ,          cd.demographic_gender
```

```
22   ,           dd.date_month_of_year
23   ORDER BY pd.product_rating
24   ,           dd.date_month_of_year;
```

We now have all the tables built and the queries ready to use. We will now gather the statistics. We will gather two levels of statistics:

■ *Gather for each query individually.* Different types of queries help to optimize different types of reporting activity. If you run one type of query more often than others, then you can tune your table structures for the more frequently run query.

■ *Gather for all queries collectively.* We run more than one type of query. This means that sometimes a certain type of query performs better and another performs worse, but overall our performance times should average the lowest, using the least resources. If you know that you run one type of query three times more often than another, then your testing should include three types of that query. This may be difficult to determine if you build the system from scratch. You may have to make your best guess. Otherwise, a DBA or developer may know what types of queries to expect.

To start a statistics-gathering session, we need to call the `stat_snap.start_snap()` procedure and pass in a unique identifier for the statistics-gathering session, as shown next. We can also run statistics-gathering sessions inside of other statistics-gathering sessions, as you will see later. The parent gathering sessions include the overhead of gathering the statistics, but as we compare query performance against different table structures, the overhead is very close on all tests and shouldn't have a material impact on the resource usage.

```
SQL> EXECUTE stat_snap.start_snap('1 : ALL QUERIES');
SQL> EXECUTE stat_snap.start_snap('1 : RENTAL_ITEM COUNT');
SQL> SELECT   COUNT(*)
  2  FROM     video_store.rental_item_fact;
SQL> EXECUTE stat_snap.end_snap('1 : RENTAL_ITEM COUNT');
SQL> EXECUTE
  2    stat_snap.start_snap('1 : VIDEO GENRE BY STATE, DEC 2012');
SQL> SELECT   product_genre
  2  ,         address_region
  3  ,         SUM(sale_net)
  4  FROM     video_store.rental_item_fact rif INNER JOIN
  5           video_store.product_dim pd
  6  ON       rif.product_key = pd.product_key INNER JOIN
  7           video_store.customer_dim cd
  8  ON       cd.customer_key = rif.customer_key INNER JOIN
  9           video_store.date_dim_vs dd
 10  ON       rif.date_key = dd.date_key
 11  WHERE    date_curr BETWEEN TO_DATE('20121201','YYYYMMDD')
 12                    AND     TO_DATE('20121231','YYYYMMDD')
 13  GROUP BY address_region, product_genre;
SQL> EXECUTE
  2    stat_snap.end_snap('1 : VIDEO GENRE BY STATE, DEC 2012');
...  <ALL OTHER QUERIES>
SQL> EXECUTE
  2    stat_snap.start_snap('1 : MALE BUYING HABITS BY GENRE');
```

```
...  <query 6> ...
SQL> EXECUTE
  2    stat_snap.end_snap('1 : MALE BUYING HABITS BY GENRE');
SQL> EXECUTE
  2    stat_snap.end_snap('1 : ALL QUERIES');
```

We nested all of the queries inside a single snap named, '1: ALL QUERIES.' Then we issued each of our six queries in their own snap. We used the '1:' prefix to indicate scenario 1 and the '2:' prefix to indicate scenario 2, and so on. This uniquely identifies all of our query executions and specifically points out differences between each scenario.

Let's look at the results of running the queries against different tables for the statistics that we gathered. Several queries are described from our tests. The results for Query 1 show how the statistics change for each of our scenarios in Table 10-6. Our goal is to strike a balance between the resources used and the return time of the query.

It appears that scenario 4 used the least amount of resources in every category that we tracked. What's more, it returns in a fraction of the time that the others do. With stats like these, you can prove that one scheme is better or worse than another.

Now let's look at the results for Query 2, shown in Table 10-7. Notice the differences between these two kinds of queries. Query 1 is a simple count(*). It is used to fully scan the rental_item_fact. Query 2 represents a heavy-hitting but realistic data warehouse query. This time, the B-tree indexes consume the most resources and wall time.

Compare the number of session logical reads to the number of physical read total I/O requests. The physical read total I/O requests is more than 100 times higher for scenario 2, which is due to many single block reads from the B-tree indexes in the fact table.

The next three queries take advantage of partition pruning, which significantly lowers resources used such as physical read total bytes and wall time. Each partition in the rental_item_fact table is created for every 100 days worth of records. Each partition in the product_dim table is created for every 50,000 product_id values. Finally, each partition in

	Consistent Gets	CPU Used by This Session (seconds)	DB Time (seconds)	Physical Read Total Bytes (MB)	Physical Read Total IO Requests	Query Time	Session Logical Reads
Test scenario 1: Query 1	21,541,023	133	1,345	167,952	168,770	0:00:27	21,541,064
Test scenario 2: Query 1	19,302,753	118	1,238	150,507	151,303	0:00:25	19,302,790
Test scenario 3: Query 1	15,983,834	102	965	124,844	126,060	0:00:19	15,983,873
Test scenario 4: Query 1	68,161	4	12	446	7,994	0:00:01	68,198
Test scenario 5: Query 1	4,491,848	46	298	35,071	35,997	0:00:06	4,491,886

TABLE 10-6. *Query 1 Results*

	Consistent Gets	CPU Used by This Session (seconds)	DB Time (seconds)	Physical Read Total Bytes (MB)	Physical Read Total IO Requests	Query Time	Session Logical Reads
Test scenario 1: Query 2	21,921,192	401	2,895	169,616	171,269	0:00:29	21,921,231
Test scenario 2: Query 2	25,855,352	470	33,660	145,630	18,451,485	0:06:19	25,855,388
Test scenario 3: Query 2	464,189	51	619	2,580	5,174	0:00:06	464,225
Test scenario 4: Query 2	367,893	62	3,663	1,759	30,900	0:00:37	367,929
Test scenario 5: Query 2	366,699	42	626	1,833	2,602	0:00:06	366,735

TABLE 10-7. *Query 2 Results*

the `customer_dim` table is created for every 100,000 customers. These ranges are not set in stone. In fact, a rigorous set of tests should be run against partitioning by itself.

Query 3 is the most aggressive of the six because it did a general aggregation of all the rows in the `rental_item_fact` table. The results are shown in Table 10-8.

Notice that the quickest query time came from our unmodified tables. That query happens to be the most resource expensive. The reason it returned so quickly is that Oracle does not have any serial indexes to get in the way. It is free to utilize all 50 parallel sessions in an effort to return the rows as quickly as possible. Also see that this query used the most *consistent gets*, *physical reads*, and *logical reads*. This might be okay if that's what your goal is; however, you may not be able to justify so much resource use on a 49-second advantage.

The results of Query 4 are shown in Table 10-9. In test scenario 4, the query time is only one second off between table structures 4 and 5. See that the logical reads were very close as well. Recall that scenario 4 has bitmap indexes and the rows are ordered.

	Consistent Gets	CPU Used by This Session (seconds)	DB Time (seconds)	Physical Read Total Bytes (MB)	Physical Read Total IO Requests	Query Time	Session Logical Reads
Test scenario 1: Query 3	21,762,999	9,488	22,868	240,970	465,892	0:03:47	21,763,044
Test scenario 2: Query 3	19,603,775	4,555	10,963	152,000	153,547	0:04:48	19,603,813
Test scenario 3: Query 3	16,282,246	11,178	33,941	126,339	128,485	0:05:37	16,282,282
Test scenario 4: Query 3	4,789,956	8,516	28,011	36,565	38,339	0:04:37	4,789,994
Test scenario 5: Query 3	4,789,880	8,542	27,808	36,564	38,192	0:04:36	4,789,918

TABLE 10-8. *Query 3 Results*

	Consistent Gets	CPU Used by This Session (seconds)	DB Time (seconds)	Physical Read Total Bytes (MB)	Physical Read Total IO Requests	Query Time	Session Logical Reads
Test scenario 1: Query 4	21,920,575	522	2,788	169,616	171,270	0:00:28	21,920,614
Test scenario 2: Query 4	19,633,026	518	2,532	152,022	153,662	0:00:27	19,633,065
Test scenario 3: Query 4	16,310,727	491	2,261	126,337	128,305	0:00:23	16,310,768
Test scenario 4: Query 4	4,818,457	196	864	36,564	38,197	0:00:10	4,818,495
Test scenario 5: Query 4	4,818,456	204	829	36,564	38,192	0:00:09	4,818,494

TABLE 10-9. *Query 4 Results*

We made a very small change between test scenarios 4 and 5. The test scenario 5 uses a BITMAP JOIN index. These are created when you add more than one column to the CREATE BITMAP INDEX command. The results of Query 5 are found in Table 10-10.

Observe that the query time went up slightly, two seconds on the BITMAP index and four seconds on the BITMAP JOIN index; however, the costs in logical reads and consistent gets were down considerably. This may justify the use of one index type over the other. It depends on your goal.

	Consistent Gets	CPU Used by This Session (seconds)	DB Time (seconds)	Physical Read Total Bytes (MB)	Physical Read Total IO Requests	Query Time	Session Logical Reads
Test scenario 1: Query 5	21,771,006	359	3,293	169,616	171,269	0:00:37	21,771,049
Test scenario 2: Query 5	19,504,722	347	2,868	152,000	153,547	0:00:30	19,504,767
Test scenario 3: Query 5	16,180,046	334	2,401	126,337	128,299	0:00:27	16,180,089
Test scenario 4: Query 5	4,687,793	132	948	36,564	38,192	0:00:12	4,687,837
Test scenario 5: Query 5	4,687,798	131	1,054	36,564	38,192	0:00:13	4,687,840

TABLE 10-10. *Query 5 Results*

	Consistent Gets	CPU Used by This Session (seconds)	DB Time (seconds)	Physical Read Total Bytes (MB)	Physical Read Total IO Requests	Query Time	Session Logical Reads
Test scenario 1: Query 6	21,920,796	257	3,110	169,616	171,274	0:00:31	21,920,832
Test scenario 2: Query 6	25,696,352	532	31,993	121,693	15,576,688	0:08:13	25,696,393
Test scenario 3: Query 6	468,111	19	531	2,555	3,434	0:00:06	468,151
Test scenario 4: Query 6	369,772	16	326	1,767	3,094	0:00:04	369,811
Test scenario 5: Query 6	152,932	41	488	626	42,726	0:00:05	152,971

TABLE 10-11. *Query 6 Results*

Our final test scenario uses our sixth query. Remember that it is the one that is trying to discover the buying habits of males by product rating through the month of January 2013. This test is very similar to 4 and 5, but it represents a very realistic business question. Table 10-11 details the results of our test.

The only noticeable difference in this set is the halving of consistent gets and logical reads when we use the BITMAP JOIN index. This evidence may be more ammo for a decision to implement bitmap joins over bitmap indexes.

Table 10-12 provides a summary of all the statistics gathered. This overview may shed more light on the solution that should be used.

	Consistent Gets	CPU Used by This Session (seconds)	DB Time (seconds)	Physical Read Total Bytes (MB)	Physical Read Total IO Requests	Query Time	Session Logical Reads
Test scenario 1	130,839,181	11,161	36,299	1,087,385	1,319,746	0:06:19	130,847,375
Test scenario 2	129,597,456	6,540	83,255	873,853	34,640,233	0:20:01	129,605,658
Test scenario 3	65,690,609	12,175	40,719	508,991	519,757	0:06:58	65,698,829
Test scenario 4	15,103,488	8,926	33,824	113,665	156,716	0:05:40	15,111,685
Test scenario 5	19,309,070	9,007	31,103	147,222	195,901	0:05:15	19,317,294

TABLE 10-12. *Summary of Query Results*

We restate the setup in the following list to remind you what each one entailed:

- **Test 1** No indexes and no partitioning
- **Test 2** B-tree indexes, partitioning, no ordering of data during creation
- **Test 3** B-tree indexes, partitioning, ordering of data during creation
- **Test 4** Bitmap indexes, partitioning, ordering of data during creation
- **Test 5** Bitmap join indexes, partitioning, ordering of data during creation
- **Test 6** Specific query pushed through the battery of tests

Here are some of our brief observations:

- **Consistent Gets** The no index strategy cost a little less than the B-tree index strategy; however, the bitmap join index had a large advantage over the bitmap index.
- **CPU** The no index and bitmap index strategies used the most CPU. B-tree indexes used the least CPU resources.
- **DB Time** The B-tree indexes had the largest time. The bitmap join and no index strategy used pretty much the same time.
- **Physical Reads** The no index scenario outweighed all of the other index scenarios and eclipsed the bitmap scenarios by around 10 times.
- **Physical IO Requests** The B-tree index scenario dwarfed all other index scenarios, requesting around 30 times more than the no index scenario, and nearly 70 times that of the bitmap indexes.
- **Query Time** The no index and bitmap index scenarios were very similar. The B-tree index scenario took considerably more time.
- **Logical Reads** The no index and B-tree scenarios used about the same resources until the data was ordered on input. The bitmap index scenarios used nearly the same resources.

We were amazed at the kind of response times we got out of our small two-node Oracle RAC cluster. We believe that the all-flash IO subsystem empowered this extremely fast test system. We also found that the IO subsystem required us to make significant changes to the multiblock read count.

We observed that PCTFREE, partition pruning, and data ordering had significant performance benefits. Scenario 3 used more CPU than scenario 1, when we considered the overall DB time. Scenarios 4 and 5 showed that adding the ORDER BY clause during data population makes a significant difference in the resources used later by queries. Finally, the B-tree indexes in scenario 3 produced the highest number of IO requests.

Current Optimization Platforms

Oracle has a nifty, built-in, performance-tuning platform that you may have access to. The first tool in this platform is the Automatic Workload Repository (AWR). AWR contains operational statistics along with information on performance-based parameters and database usage statistics. AWR results are aggregated on the hour.

The second tool is its Automatic Database Diagnostic Monitor (ADDM). This tool informs the DBA about the activities that use the most database resources. Its beginning pages are summarizations that can be drilled into by clicking report hyperlinks. The details found in the subreports try to report the cause of an issue rather than merely showing symptoms.

The third tool is its Active Session History (ASH) report. It holds a historical report of database usage across all active sessions in one-second intervals. We find all three of these tools very helpful in our tuning and architectural efforts; however, their tendency to deliver averages found over larger periods of time requires us to use packages like `stat_snap`.

Supporting Scripts

The following programs are available on the McGraw-Hill Professional website to support this chapter:

- The `utl_file_append.sql` program lets you see how to append data to an existing file with the `utl_file` package's `put_line` procedure.
- The `sql_snap_tbls.sql` code creates the tables and view.
- The `sql_snap_pkg.sql` script contains the code for the package that is run to gather statistics. In that package, there are three procedures: `start_snap()` grabs statistics from v$mystat table; `end_snap()` grabs the statistics from the v$mystat table; and the procedure merges them into the `stat_collection` table.

Summary

You now have the ability to independently conduct statistics gathering, testing, and performance tuning with PL/SQL and to determine what works best for your database. Statistics gathering no longer is like filling up at the gas station once a week and looking at an average gas mileage; instead, you can very pointedly figure out the performance of your database under specific circumstances. If asked how an index impacts performance on the database, you can now give specific numbers about the performance impacts, including the resources for maintenance. Using concepts like statistics analysis and parallel operation using `dbms_scheduler`, you can now make informed decisions and significant performance improvement.

CHAPTER
11

External Procedures

Purpose

This chapter shows you how to create and deploy external procedures, and how to configure and use the heterogeneous service agent. The steps include configuration of the Oracle `listener.ora` and `tnsnames.ora` network configuration files. A sample C program is provided in the text and online to implement the external procedure for your specific platform.

Advantages

External procedures let you write external C or C-callable libraries to support business applications. C or C-callable libraries reside on the server tier, and their location and privileges must be defined within the `env` variable of the Oracle `listener.ora` file.

Disadvantages

The biggest disadvantage of external procedures is that the logic is separate from the database. That separation can pose a set of potential security risks.

While you should carefully review the logic of the C and C-callable libraries before you deploy them because they can pose a security risk, you also need to carefully manage them to ensure their behavior doesn't change.

You should also take precautions to use a separate schema for the PL/SQL wrappers that access the external libraries. The separate schema lets you easily manage the deployed wrappers and library references.

Overview

External routines are delivered in Oracle Database 12c through external procedures. They enable the database to communicate with external applications through PL/SQL. While it is nontrivial to configure the database to support them, external procedures provide a critical feature.

This chapter covers the following topics about external procedures. The chapter assumes you are reading it sequentially. It also assumes you have read the preceding ten chapters.

- Introducing external procedures
- Working with external procedures
- Troubleshooting external procedures

The introduction to this book provides scripts that create a user account and data model, and then seed the data model. You need to run them before working through the examples in the chapter.

Introducing External Procedures

External routines provide the ability to communicate between the database and external programs written in C, C++, COBOL, FORTRAN, PL/1, Visual Basic, and Java. There is one caveat: the language must be callable from C. While the surgeon general has not provided a warning, other languages can present different challenges than does PL/SQL. This chapter focuses on implementations of C and Java libraries as external routines.

Development teams may want to isolate programming logic from the database. External routines are the natural solution. They are ideal for computation-intensive programs, providing an interface between external data sources and the database. Unlike stand-alone Oracle Pro*C programs, external routines are callable from PL/SQL.

You will work with a C shared library in this chapter. The C example has been made as small and narrow in scope as possible to conserve space while you focus on PL/SQL programming.

External routines leverage the Oracle Net Services transport layer. You will need to work through a number of architectural and configuration issues to run the basic samples. It is helpful if you have some formal background in C, but it is not necessary. This chapter is important because PL/SQL programmers can be expected to explain the process to C and Java programmers. You will also write the PL/SQL library definitions, which become the gateways to these libraries. These are often called *PL/SQL wrappers*.

NOTE
The related Oracle documentation for this chapter is spread far and wide. The key configuration references are Appendix A in the Oracle Database Advanced Application Developer's Guide, *Chapter 4 in the* Oracle Database Heterogeneous Connectivity User's Guide, *and Chapter 13 in the* Oracle Database Net Services Administrator's Guide.

You will next learn how to implement external procedures.

Working with External Procedures

As discussed, external procedures enable you to communicate through PL/SQL with external programs. The external programs can call back to an Oracle database using the Oracle Call Interface (OCI). They can also communicate with external databases such as Sybase, IBM DB2, and Microsoft SQL Server. External procedures are ideal to work with external applications. External applications can use other databases or file systems as data repositories. Moreover, any combination of these is supported.

You will now learn about the architecture for external procedures. Then you will learn the setup issues for Oracle Networking and the heterogeneous service agent. When you have learned how to configure your environment, you will then work with building and accessing C and Java libraries from PL/SQL.

Defining the extproc Architecture

Oracle built an extensible architecture for external procedures. It is flexible to support any programming language that is callable by the C programming language. For example, you can call a C++ program using the `extern` command in C. However, callbacks into the database by the external programming languages are limited to those supported by OCI. OCI supports C, C++, COBOL, FORTRAN, PL/1, Visual Basic, and Java.

Whatever programming language you choose to implement must support building a shared library. Likewise, the platform must support shared libraries. Shared libraries, also called dynamic link libraries (DLLs), are code modules that can be leveraged by your program. Java shared libraries are called libunits. When you access shared libraries from PL/SQL, the libraries are loaded dynamically at runtime as external procedures. By default, each Remote Procedure Call uses a discrete and dedicated `extproc` agent to access the shared library. Alternatively, you can configure a multithreaded agent through the Oracle Heterogeneous Services. If you do so, you can share the `extproc` agent among any number of database sessions.

External procedures use the PL/SQL library definition to exchange data between the PL/SQL runtime engine and shared libraries. The PL/SQL library definition acts as a wrapper to the shared library. It defines the external call specification and maps PL/SQL data types to native-language equivalents. The map between data types is used to translate data types when exchanging information. Figure 11-1 illustrates the external procedure architecture.

A call to a PL/SQL wrapper translates types. Then, the wrapper sends a signal across Oracle Net Services. Oracle Net Services receives the signal and spawns or forks an `extproc` agent process. It is the `extproc` agent that accesses the shared library. The `extproc` agent forks a Remote Procedure Call (RPC) to the shared library. The shared library result is returned to the `extproc` agent by the RPC. The `extproc` agent then returns the result to the PL/SQL wrapper. Next, the PL/SQL wrapper receives and translates the data types from the local language to the native PL/SQL data types. Ultimately, the PL/SQL wrapper returns the value to the calling PL/SQL program.

As you can see from Figure 11-1, there are two potential failure points to dynamic execution. The decision diamonds in the process flowchart qualify potential failure points. Both failure points

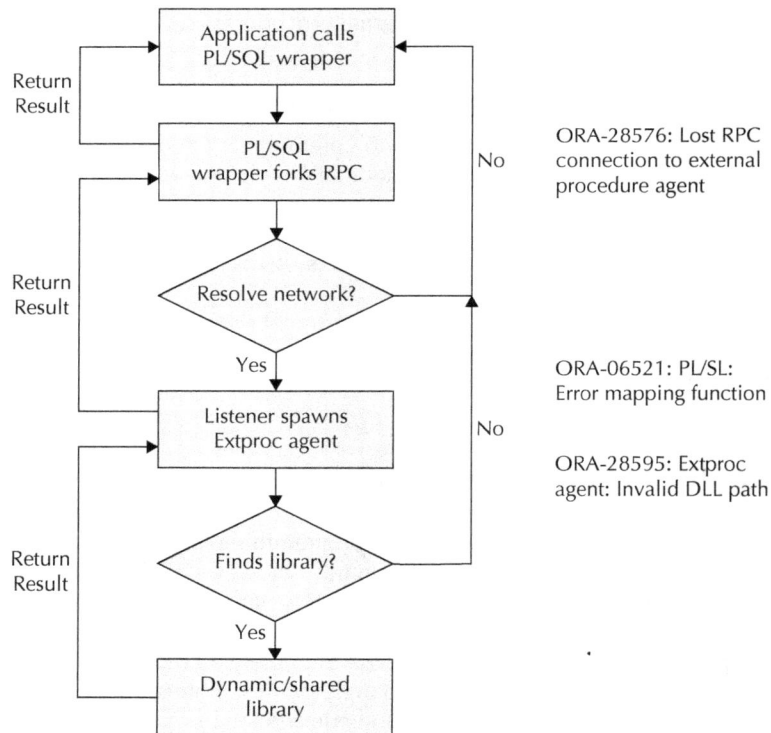

FIGURE 11-1. *External procedure architecture*

are linked to the listener. The second failure point can also be missing libraries in the defined locations.

One failure point exists when a separate `extproc` agent listener is either not configured or incorrectly configured. The other failure point arises in two possible cases. One case is when the `extproc` listener fails to resolve the connection. Another case is when a physical shared library is not found where defined in the PL/SQL library definition.

Configuring the heterogeneous multithreaded agent is complex. However, it enables you to share a single `extproc` agent among multiple database sessions. Benefits of this implementation are a reduction in resources required to dynamically fork `extproc` agents. The default behavior of external procedures is to fork a new `extproc` agent for each external procedure call. The default works, but consumes too many resources too frequently. When you have many sessions using external libraries, you should use a multithreaded `extproc` agent. Figure 11-2 shows how a multithreaded `extproc` agent works.

As shown in the diagram, multiple database sessions can connect through the heterogeneous multithreaded `extproc` agent, which fits into the `extproc` agent niche in Figure 11-1. Once the signal arrives at the agent, the monitor thread puts the connection into a FIFO (First In, First Out) queue. The monitor thread maintains load-balancing information; using that information, the monitor thread passes the connection to the first available dispatcher thread, which puts the request into another FIFO queue. Task threads read the dispatcher FIFO queues and process requests. Each task thread sends the result back to the requesting session. You will discover more about the multithreaded agent later in this chapter.

Now that you have developed an understanding of the basic architecture of external procedures, the next section will show you how to set up and configure Oracle Net Services to support external procedures.

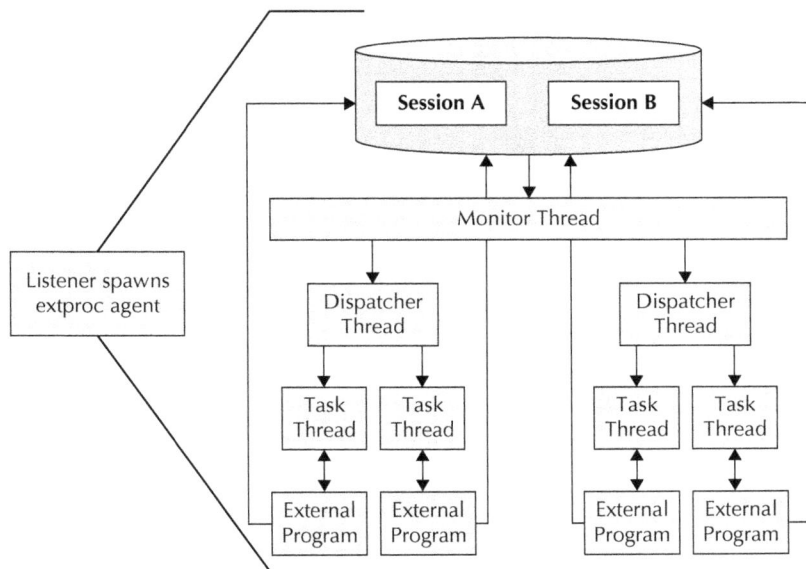

FIGURE 11-2. *Multithreaded agent architecture*

Defining extproc Oracle Net Services Configuration

External procedures use Oracle Net Services to fork or link signals to the extproc agent. As discussed, the extproc agent can be the default stand-alone unit or a multithreaded extproc agent. Unfortunately, configuring your listener.ora and tnsnames.ora files is a manual process.

The standard listener built by the Net Configuration Assistant on installation does not provide a complete extproc agent listener. The Net Configuration Assistant likewise does not provide an automated way to create an extproc agent listener. The standard listener includes an extproc handler service in the standard listener. This is not adequate for implementing the extproc agent. You must set up an exclusive listener for external procedures.

As a PL/SQL developer, configuring Oracle Net Services may not be something you do often. It is also possible your DBA may be unfamiliar with the nuances required to support extproc agents. This section provides the steps required to configure Oracle Net Services to support extproc agents.

The listener.ora file can be found in one of two locations. It can be found in the directory pointed to by the $TNS_ADMIN environment variable. Alternatively, the default location is in the $ORACLE_HOME/network/admin directory. The standard listener.ora file contains two entries: one is the LISTENER and the other is the SID_LIST_LISTENER.

The LISTENER describes an address list or set of address lists. Addresses consist of a protocol definition and a key value, or else a protocol definition, a hostname, and a port number. The generalized Oracle Database 12c standard fresh install LISTENER entry in the listener.ora file follows:

```
LISTENER =
  (DESCRIPTION_LIST =
    (DESCRIPTION =
      (ADDRESS_LIST =
        (ADDRESS = (PROTOCOL = IPC)
                   (KEY = EXTPROC1521)
        )
      )
      (ADDRESS_LIST =
        (ADDRESS = (PROTOCOL = TCP)
                   (HOST = <host_name>.<domain_name>)
                   (PORT = 1521)
        )
      )
    )
  )
```

The standard listener.ora file has a problem supporting the extproc agent. The problem is that the listener has two ADDRESS_LIST parameters using different protocols. The first listens for Internal Procedure Calls (IPCs). The second listens for TCP messages, like RPCs. This is the principal reason why a separate listener is required for extproc IPC calls.

NOTE
Oracle Database 12c lists the KEY value as
EXTPROC<listener_port>, whereas previously, only
EXTPROC was listed.

The SID_LIST_LISTENER, the second entry in the standard listener.ora file, contains the SID description. The Oracle Database 12c standard SID_DESC is defined by the SID_NAME, ORACLE_HOME, and PROGRAM parameter definitions. The SID_NAME parameter is defined as PLSExtProc, which is used as the extproc identifier. The ORACLE_HOME parameter defines the Oracle home directory. Finally, the PROGRAM parameter defines the extproc agent as the program. The Oracle Database 12c standard SID_LIST_LISTENER entry in the listener.ora file follows:

```
-- Available online as listener1.ora
SID_LIST_LISTENER =
  (SID_LIST =
    (SID_DESC =
      (SID_NAME = PLSExtProc)
      (ORACLE_HOME = <oracle_home_directory)
      (PROGRAM = extproc)
    )
  )
```

The standard SID_LIST_LISTENER is another mix of two purposes in one definition. The SID_NAME and PROGRAM parameters are there to support the extproc agent signals. The ORACLE_HOME parameter is provided for both the TCP listener and extproc IPC services. These two services run under a single standard listener, although they really are suited to separate listeners. The clincher is that *external procedures require their own listener*.

NOTE
Oracle provides the preceding caveat for the extproc listener in Appendix A of the Oracle Database Advanced Application Developer's Guide, Release 12c.

The standard listener.ora file works in tandem with the standard tnsnames.ora file. The listener.ora and tnsnames.ora files are used by Oracle Net Services. The standard tnsnames.ora file provides two service names. One is CODE, which replaces the standard listener to the database for IPC communication. The other is EXTPROC_CONNECTION_DATA, which maps to the extproc agent. The following is an example of the standard tnsnames.ora file:

```
-- Available online as part of tnsnames1.ora
CODE =
  (DESCRIPTION =
    (ADDRESS = (PROTOCOL = TCP)
               (HOST = <host_name>.<domain_name>)
               (PORT = 1521)
    )
    (CONNECT_DATA =
      (SERVER = DEDICATED)
      (SERVICE_NAME = <database_sid>)
    )
  )

EXTPROC_CONNECTION_DATA =
  (DESCRIPTION =
```

```
(ADDRESS_LIST =
  (ADDRESS = (PROTOCOL = IPC)
             (KEY = EXTPROC1521)
  )
)
(CONNECT_DATA =
  (SID = CLRExtProc)
  (PRESENTATION = RO)
)
)
```

The `tnsnames.ora` service names provide connection aliases that enable users and programs to connect to the listener. The service names resolve requests for connections by matching the `tnsnames.ora` ADDRESS parameter to the address in a running listener. Then they use the CONNECTION_DATA parameters to connect a database or agent. The `extproc` agent is not the only agent supported by Oracle Database 12c. You can define any number of heterogeneous servers that enable communication between Oracle and other databases.

On any case-insensitive system, these files resolve `extproc` across Oracle Net Services. They fail on a case-sensitive system. The KEY parameter in the `listener.ora` file is lowercase, while the KEY value in the `tnsnames.ora` file is uppercase. The two will fail to resolve. You can see if your system contains the error by using the `tnsping` utility.

For example, run `tnsping` with the following:

```
$ tnsping EXTPROC_CONNECTION_DATA
```

If you get the following, everything is correctly configured:

```
TNS Ping Utility for Linux: Version 12.1.0.1.0 - Production on 31-MAR-2014
Copyright (c) 1997, 2013, Oracle.  All rights reserved.
Used parameter files:
/u01/oracle/product/12.1.0/dbhome_1/network/admin/sqlnet.ora
Used TNSNAMES adapter to resolve the alias
Attempting to contact (DESCRIPTION = (ADDRESS_LIST = (ADDRESS = (PROTOCOL =
IPC)(KEY = EXTPROC1521))) (CONNECT_DATA = (SID = CLRExtProc) (PRESENTATION = RO)))
OK (0 msec)
```

If you get a TNS-12541 error when using `tnsping`, a mismatch likely exists between the ADDRESS parameter values in the `listener.ora` and `tnsnames.ora` files.

Before you are introduced to working files, you need to learn about the PROGRAM and ENV parameters in `listener.ora` files. The PROGRAM parameter must specify a valid executable in the $ORACLE_HOME/bin directory. The program can access only libraries found in the $ORACLE_HOME/lib directory by default. You can change the default by doing any of the following:

- Define EXTPROC_DLLS to enable loading of shared libraries. You have three choices for using EXTPROC_DLLS. They are shown in Table 11-1.
- Define the $LD_LIBRARY_PATH for the `extproc` agent.
- Define the $PATH for the `extproc` agent.
- Define the $APL_ENV_FILE to specify a set of environment variables for the external `extproc` agent.

Syntax	Description	Security Level
DLL:DLL	Allows the extproc agent to load any of the specified shared libraries located in the $ORACLE_HOME/lib directory.	Medium
ONLY:DLL:DLL	Allows extproc to run any entered DLLs from specified directories.	High (Recommended)
ANY	Allows extproc to load any DLL. It disables DLL checking.	Low

TABLE 11-1.   *Options for EXTPROC_DLLS*

The following listener.ora file separates the two listeners. It also defines an external library that you will work with later in the chapter. You can use it as an example to build your own listener.ora file.

```
LISTENER =
  (DESCRIPTION_LIST =
    (DESCRIPTION =
      (ADDRESS_LIST =
        (ADDRESS = (PROTOCOL = TCP)
                   (HOST = <host_name>.<domain_name>)
                   (PORT = 1521)
        )
      )
    )
  )

SID_LIST_LISTENER =
  (SID_LIST =
    (SID_DESC =
      (SID_NAME = <database_name>)
      (ORACLE_HOME = <oracle_home_directory>)
    )
  )

CALLOUT_LISTENER =
  (DESCRIPTION_LIST =
    (DESCRIPTION =
      (ADDRESS_LIST =
        (ADDRESS = (PROTOCOL = IPC)
                   (KEY = extproc)
        )
      )
    )
  )

SID_LIST_CALLOUT_LISTENER =
```

```
(SID_LIST =
  (SID_DESC =
    (SID_NAME = PLSExtProc)
    (ORACLE_HOME = <oracle_home_directory>)
    (PROGRAM = extproc)
    (ENV = "EXTPROC_DLLS=ONLY:
            <oracle_home_directory>/customlib/writestr1.so
            ,LD_LIBRARY_PATH=<oracle_home_directory>/lib")
  )
)
```

The sample `listener.ora` file has a standard `LISTENER` TCP listener on port 1521. You should note that the IPC `ADDRESS` information has been removed from the standard listener. The sample file also has a standard `SID_LIST_LISTENER`. You should notice that the `SID_NAME` parameter value is no longer `PLSExtProc`, which was used for the `extproc` agent. It uses the database name. You should also notice that the `PROGRAM` parameter and value are no longer in the `SID_LIST_LISTENER`.

The second address was removed from the standard listener and put in a separate listener, and the `CALLOUT_LISTENER` ICP listener uses a `KEY` value of `extproc`. As a result of this change, the `SID_NAME` parameter has a value of `PLSExtProc` and it should map to a case-sensitive equivalent `SID` parameter value in the `tnsnames.ora` service name. Also, the `PROGRAM` parameter is there with a new `ENV` parameter. The `ENV` parameter provides the recommended security implementation that allows access to only a specified library and the `LD_LIBRARY_PATH` for the external procedure.

The new `listener.ora` requires a new `tnsnames.ora` file. The following file works with the new `listener.ora` previously covered:

```
CODE =
  (DESCRIPTION =
    (ADDRESS = (PROTOCOL = TCP)
               (HOST = <host_name>.<domain_name>)
               (PORT = 1521)
    )
    (CONNECT_DATA =
      (SERVER = DEDICATED)
      (SERVICE_NAME = CODE)
    )
  )

EXTPROC_CONNECTION_DATA =
  (DESCRIPTION =
    (ADDRESS_LIST =
      (ADDRESS = (PROTOCOL = IPC)
                 (KEY = extproc)
      )
    )
    (CONNECT_DATA =
      (SID = PLSExtProc)
      (PRESENTATION = RO)
    )
  )
```

The sample `tnsnames.ora` file has a `CODE` alias that uses an `ADDRESS` pointing to the database and a `CONNECT_DATA` parameter supporting a dedicated connection. The `CONNECT_DATA` parameter `SERVER` has a dedicated value, which means a dedicated server connection. The sample file also has an `EXTPROC_CONNECTION_DATA` alias that uses a single `ADDRESS` to an IPC and `CONNECT_DATA` to the `extproc SID`.

You now have working `listener.ora` and `tnsnames.ora` files. You will need to shut down the listener services, copy the files into the new locations, and restart the listener. The following are the steps to take to replace the listener, by platform.

Windows:

■ As the `oracle` user, source your environment, navigate to your system services, and shut down the listener.

■ Copy the original `listener.ora` and `tnsnames.ora` files in the `%ORACLE_HOME%\network\admin` directory to `listener.ora.orig` and `tnsnames.ora.orig`.

■ Copy the new `listener2.ora` and `tnsnames2.ora` files into the `%ORACLE_HOME%\network\admin` directory and rename them as `listener.ora` and `tnsnames.ora`, respectively.

■ As the `oracle` user, source your environment, navigate to your system services, and start up the listener. In Windows, you will need to rebuild the original service and build a new service for the second listener.

■ Verify that you have two listener processes running by using the Task Manager. You will find the running services under the Processes tab.

Unix:

■ As the `oracle` user, source your environment and shut down the listener. You can use the following on a generic demonstration database:

$ lsnrctl stop LISTENER

■ Copy the original `listener.ora` and `tnsnames.ora` files in the `$ORACLE_HOME/network/admin` directory to `listener.ora.orig` and `tnsnames.ora.orig`.

■ Copy the new `listener2.ora` and `tnsnames2.ora` files into the `$ORACLE_HOME/network/admin` directory and rename them as `listener.ora` and `tnsnames.ora`, respectively.

■ As the `oracle` user, source your environment and start up the listener and `extproc` agent listener. You can use the following syntax, based on a generic demonstration database:

```
$ lsnrctl start LISTENER
$ lsnrctl start CALLOUT_LISTENER
```

■ Verify that you have two listener processes running by using the `ps` utility, as shown:

```
$ ps -ef | grep -v grep | grep tnslsnr
```

At this point, you should have a `LISTENER` for the database and a `CALLOUT_LISTENER` for the `extproc` agent. You should also have a background process running for the `extproc` agent. In Microsoft Windows, you can check with the Task Manager for an `extprocPLSExtProc` process. In Unix, you can use the `ps` utility to find it.

Assuming you have successfully started the two listeners, you need to confirm whether or not the IPC listener can communicate to the `extproc` agent. There are two steps to validating whether or not the IPC listener is working. After sourcing your environment files, you should first use the `tnsping` utility as you did earlier in the chapter to test the network connection. You will use the `EXTPROC_CONNECTION_DATA` alias to check connectivity. Run `tnsping` with the following:

```
$ tnsping EXTPROC_CONNECTION_DATA
```

If you get the following, everything is correctly configured:

```
TNS Ping Utility for Linux: Version 12.1.0.1.0 - Production on 31-MAR-2014
Copyright (c) 1997, 2013, Oracle.  All rights reserved.
Used parameter files:
/u01/oracle/product/12.1.0/dbhome_1/network/admin/sqlnet.ora
```

If you get a `TNS-12541` error when using `tnsping`, the likelihood is that there is a mismatch between the `ADDRESS` parameter values in the `listener.ora` and `tnsnames.ora` files. Please check if there is a typo in either the `listener.ora` file or `tnsnames.ora` file. You must resolve any `TNS-12541` error before continuing with the examples in the chapter.

Assuming you have successfully used the `tnsping` utility, the second step is to attempt to connect to the `extproc` agent TNS alias. Use this to attempt to connect to the `extproc` agent TNS alias:

```
$ sqlplus c##plsql/password@EXTPROC_CONNECTION_DATA
```

It should always fail. You should get the following output:

```
SQL*Plus: Release 12.1.0.1.0 Production on Tue Apr 1 00:02:53 2014
Copyright (c) 1982, 2013, Oracle.  All rights reserved.
ERROR:
ORA-28547: connection to server failed, probable Net8 admin error
```

This is the correct behavior, but sometimes you may get an `ORA-28546` error. It is actually telling you that the SQL*Plus connection is rejected by the `extproc` agent. For you to receive this message, the connection attempted to start and was rejected.

You have now learned how to configure your listener to support the `extproc` agent. The next section will demonstrate an alternative to spawning a dedicated `extproc` agent for each database session.

Defining the Multithreaded External Procedure Agent

As discussed in the review of the external procedure architecture, configuring the heterogeneous multithreaded agent is complex. However, it enables you to share a single `extproc` agent among multiple database sessions. Implementing a multithreaded external procedure agent reduces resources required to dynamically fork `extproc` agents.

The default behavior of external procedures is to fork a new `extproc` agent for each external procedure call. As mentioned, this default works, but consumes too many resources too frequently. When you have many sessions using external libraries, you should use a multithreaded `extproc` agent. This section will show you how to configure and use the multithreaded `extproc` agent.

Before you begin to learn how to configure the multithreaded external procedure agent, there are three things to note about it:

- The external library must be thread-safe.
- The agent process, the database server, and the listener process must be on the same host.
- The agent process must run from the same database instance that issues the external procedure call.

When using the multithreaded external procedure agent, you must start the agent separately from the database. The multithreaded external procedure agent is an implementation of Oracle Heterogeneous Connectivity Services. The `agtctl` executable to start and manage sessions is the Agent Control utility. You will find it in the `$ORACLE_HOME/hs/admin` directory.

If you attempt to use this tool without setting either the `$AGTCTL_ADMIN` or `$TNS_ADMIN` environment variable, you will generate the following error message:

```
$ agtctl

AGTCTL: Release 11.1.0.6.0 - Production on Wed Aug 22 07:57:24 2007

Copyright (c) 1982, 2007, Oracle.  All rights reserved.

ORA-28591: agent control utility: unable to access parameter file
ORA-28591: agent control utility: unable to access parameter file
```

It is recommended that you set the `$AGTCTL_ADMIN` environment variable to point to the `$ORACLE_HOME/hs/admin` directory. Any environment variables configured in the `ENV` parameter within your `extproc` listener must be in the sourced environment of the Oracle user when running `agtctl`.

The `agtctl` utility has two interfaces. One is the single-line command mode, and the other is the `agtctl` shell mode. There is no GUI to the `agtctl` utility. There is no text configuration file for this utility. It maintains parameter values in the `$ORACLE_HOME/hs/admin/initagt.dat` control file, which is a binary file maintained by the `agtctl` utility. Before you run the `agtctl` utility, the file will not exist. Table 11-2 provides a synopsis of the command structure.

There are six initialization parameters. All have default behaviors that can be overridden by using the `agtctl set` command. Table 11-3 provides the initialization parameters and their default values and descriptions.

You will now configure the `extproc` multithreaded agent using the `agtctl` shell mode. The following steps will enable 100 sessions and four dispatchers before starting the `extproc` multithreaded agent:

```
AGTCTL> set agent_sid CALLOUT_LISTENER
AGTCTL> set max_dispatchers 4
AGTCTL> set max_sessions 100
AGTCTL> show max_dispatchers
4
AGTCTL> show max_sessions
100
AGTCTL> startup extproc
```

Command Syntax	Description
delete *agent_sid*	Deletes an *agent_sid* entry.
exit	Exits the agtctl file.
help	Displays available commands.
set *parameter_name* param_value	Sets a configuration parameter.
show *parameter_name*	Shows a parameter's value.
shutdown *agent_sid*	Shuts down an *agent_sid* multithreaded agent.
startup *agent_sid*	Starts an *agent_sid* multithreaded agent.
unset *parameter_name* param_value	Unsets a configuration parameter.

TABLE 11-2. *Commands for the* agtctl *Utility*

Parameter	Default Value	Description
Listener_address	(ADDRESS_LIST = (ADDRESS = (PROTOCOL = IPC) (KEY = PNPKEY)) (ADDRESS = (PROTOCOL = IPC) (KEY= <oracle_sid>) (ADDRESS = (PROTOCOL = TCP) (HOST = 127.0.0.1) (PORT = 1521)))	Address list for the agent controller listener. The <oracle_sid> value is the <service_name> parameter in the tnsnames.ora entry for the database.
max_dispatchers	1	Maximum number of dispatchers.
max_sessions	5	Maximum number of sessions.
max_task_threads	2	Maximum number of threads.
shutdown_address	(ADDRESS_LIST = (ADDRESS = (PROTOCOL = IPC) (KEY = extproc)))	Address on which agtctl listens for shutdown instruction.
tcp_dispatchers	0	Number of dispatchers listening on TCP. All other dispatchers listen on IPC.

TABLE 11-3. *Initialization Parameters for the* agtctl *Utility*

In Unix, you can use the `ps` utility to see the multithreaded external procedure agent. The Task Manager in Microsoft Windows will also let you see the process. Here is the Unix command:

```
$ ps -ef | grep -v grep | grep extprocCALLOUT
```

The output from this command is

```
oracle    4635    1  0 18:41 ?   00:00:01 extprocCALLOUT_LISTENER -mt
```

You can now shut down the multithreaded external procedure agent by using the `shutdown` command. The `shutdown` command without an argument acts like a shutdown of the database, which means it allows transactions in progress to complete. The `shutdown immediate` command will cause in-progress external procedure calls to abort. This is the `immediate` command:

```
AGTCTL> shutdown immediate
```

When you start the `extproc` multithreaded agent, all new external procedure calls will route through the multithreaded agent. However, any calls previously started with dynamic stand-alone `extproc` agents will continue to completion.

When you shut down the `extproc` multithreaded agent, it stops taking new requests. This means all processing transactions should complete normally unless you stop the agent with the `immediate` clause. The `immediate` clause forces all running threads to stop. After you shut down the multithreaded agent, the external procedure monitoring thread rejects new calls. Dynamic `extproc` agents are then spawned for any new external procedure calls.

You have now learned how to start, configure, and stop the multithreaded external procedure agent. You have seen how you can seamlessly move between dedicated dynamic `extproc` sessions and a background multithreaded agent. The next section will demonstrate how you create an external C shared library.

Working with a C Shared Library

As we discussed when we covered the `extproc` architecture, Oracle built an extensible architecture for external procedures. It is flexible to support any programming language that is callable by the C programming language. For example, you can call a C++ program using the `extern` command in C. You could call another C program from the shared library. It could then call back into the database. The second C program would use embedded SQL to access data. Using embedded SQL requires use of the Oracle Pro*C precompiler and the Oracle Call Interface (OCI). Both the Pro*C precompiler and OCI tools require a solid working knowledge of C or C++. There are many books on C or C++, but we'd recommend you start with *C++ Primer Plus*, Sixth Edition, by Stephen Prata. You should also check the *Oracle Call Interface Programmer's Guide*, *Oracle C++ Call Interface Programmer's Guide*, and *Pro*C/C++ Programmer's Guide*.

Defining the C Shared Library

You will now define a simple C shared library. You will use the following C program as a DLL or shared library. The structure of this program has been chosen to avoid having to introduce you to the extensive details of Oracle Pro*C precompiler and OCI functionality. You will need to have a C compiler installed on your platform to compile this example.

Compiling a C program has several nuances. A C compiler does several things. It preprocesses the source code by breaking it down into tokens while validating syntax. Then, it compiles the program into assembly programming code and uses an assembler to create object code. After creating the object code, the compiler then links other object code into the program to create a stand-alone program unit.

The following program includes standard library header files but does not link libraries:

```c
/* Include standard IO. */
#include <stdio.h>

/* Declare a writestr function. */
void writestr(char *path, char *message)
{
  /* Declare a FILE variable. */
  FILE *file_name;

  /* Open the file in write-only mode. */
  file_name = fopen(path,"w");

  /* Write to file the message received. */
  fprintf(file_name,"%s\n",message);

  /* Close the file. */
  fclose(file_name);
}
```

The program includes the `stdio.h` file, which is called a header file. `stdio.h` contains the definitions required to do basic IO operations in C programs. The `#include <stdio.h>` statement tells the C precompiler to include the contents of the `/usr/include/stdio.h` file in the program. The program writes a new file with a string message passed by an actual parameter to the library.

It should be noted that the `writestr1.c` program does not have a `main()` function. A `main()` function is required for a stand-alone C program. This program can be used only as a DLL or shared library.

If you attempt a generic compilation of a library file that lacks a `main()` function, it will raise an error. For example, if `writestr1.c` were a stand-alone program, you would compile it into object code like this:

```
$ cc -o writestr.o writestr1.c
```

This will raise an error because there is no `main()` function in the program. The error message follows:

```
/usr/lib/gcc-lib/i386-redhat-linux7/2.96/../../../crt1.o(.text+0x18):
In function
'_start':
: undefined reference to 'main'
collect2: ld returned 1 exit status
```

It is assumed that you have a C or C++ IDE if you are working on the Microsoft Windows platform. Since each IDE works a bit differently, you will have to understand how to use your IDE to compile the program as a DLL.

If you are working on Unix, you live in the command-line world. The following examples illustrate the two methods for creating a C shared library in Unix. The first example works on the Sun Microsystems C compiler. The second example is the most common approach and supported on Linux.

Unix C compiler that supports the –G option:

```
cc -G -o writestr1.so writestr1.c
```

Unix C compiler that supports the –shared option:

```
cc -shared -o writestr1.so writestr1.c
  - OR -
gcc -shared -o writestr1.so writestr1.c
  - OR, a combination of -
gcc -c -Wall -Werror -fpic writestr1.c
gcc -shared -o writestr1.so writestr1.o
```

TIP
If you are using IBM AIX and the IBM C compiler, you need to ensure that you have a symbolic link named cc that points to xlc. The IBM C compiler will attempt to include proprietary libraries that are not referenced in the sample program. It will not attempt to include those libraries when the calling executable is a symbolic cc.

You should now have a C shared library. Now, you or your DBA should create a custom library directory off your $ORACLE_HOME. Please name it **customlib** if you want to be consistent with the examples in this chapter. You should ensure the permissions for the directory are read, write, and execute for owner and read and execute for group and user.

If you are not the DBA but a member of the DBA group, copying the file and executing it will work. If you are not in the DBA group, please have your DBA change the group ownership of the file to the DBA group. It will not prevent you from executing the shared library, but it is a check-in mechanism. Any files not in the DBA group would be considered development or stage program units.

You have now created a DLL/shared library and positioned it where a database external procedure can call it. Next, you will define the PL/SQL library definition and wrapper.

Defining and Calling the PL/SQL Library Wrapper

You have configured your network; learned how to start, configure, and shut down a multithreaded and stand-alone `extproc` agent; and created a C DLL or shared library. Now you need to define a PL/SQL library definition and wrapper so that you can pass information from the database to your C program.

PL/SQL Library Definition

The first step is to define the external library in the database. You do this after you have decided where to place your library. $ORACLE_HOME/customlib is used for the C external procedure example. As discussed, using a custom library requires configuration of the EXTPROC_DLLS value in the ENV parameter. The ENV parameter is found in the listener.ora file. Alternatively, you can put your libraries in the $ORACLE_HOME/bin directory or $ORACLE_HOME/lib directory and not configure the EXTPROC_DLLS value. If you have customized where you place your libraries, please synchronize the directory path for the library with your listener.ora file.

The PL/SQL library prototype is

```
CREATE [OR REPLACE] LIBRARY <library_name> AS | IS
'<file_specification>'
AGENT '<agent_dblink>';
/
```

The create_library1.sql and create_library2.sql files use Dynamic Native SQL (DNS) to build the library creation DLL. This was done to simplify your submission of a directory path. The command is provided in the comments section for the programs and noted in the following:

```
CREATE OR REPLACE LIBRARY library_write_string AS
'<oracle_home_directory>/<custom_library>/<file_name>.<file_ext>';
/
```

The PL/SQL library role defines the name of the library and the physical location where the library will be found. There is no validation of whether or not the file is physically located where you have specified. The library name is the access point for your PL/SQL wrapper. You will now learn about the PL/SQL library wrapper.

PL/SQL Library Wrapper

The principal role of the PL/SQL library wrapper is to define an interface between the database and the external procedure. The interface defines how the formal parameters map between PL/SQL and C data types. It also defines any context and the location of the external procedure or library. When you create a PL/SQL library wrapper, there is no check whether or not the shared library is in the directory. You need to have a management process to ensure check-in and version control.

Oracle provides additional derived types to support OCI. The columns of Table 11-4 show the source of data types. Table 11-4 also shows you the default conversion type. Table 11-4 maps PL/SQL and C data types.

In your small writestr1.c example, data types are converted only from PL/SQL to C, but the library definition supports bidirectional conversions. The bidirectional support is independent of the external shared library. Whether the external C library returns data or not, the PL/SQL library wrapper has defined it as bidirectional.

PL/SQL	Native C		Oracle	Default
BINARY_INTEGER BOOLEAN PLS_INTEGER	[UNSIGNED] CHAR [UNSIGNED] SHORT [UNSIGNED] INT [UNSIGNED] LONG		SB1, SB2, SB4 UB1, UB2, UB4 SIZE_T	INT
NATURAL NATURALN POSITIVE POSITIVEN SIGNTYPE	[UNSIGNED] CHAR [UNSIGNED] SHORT [UNSIGNED] INT [UNSIGNED] LONG		SB1, SB2, SB4 UB1, UB2, UB4 SIZE_T	[UNSIGNED] INT
FLOAT REAL	FLOAT			FLOAT
DOUBLE PRECISION	DOUBLE			DOUBLE
CHAR CHARACTER LONG NCHAR NVARCHAR2 ROWID VARCHAR VARCHAR2			STRING OCISTRING	STRING
LONG RAW RAW			RAW OCIRAW	RAW
BFILE BLOB CLOB NCLOB			OCILOBLOCATOR	OCILOBLOCATOR
NUMBER DEC DECIMAL INT INTEGER NUMERIC SMALLINT			OCINUMBER	OCINUMBER
DATE			OCIDATE	OCIDATE
TIMESTAMP TIMESTAMP WITH TIME ZONE TIMESTAMP WITH LOCAL TIME ZONE			OCIDATETIME	OCIDATETIME

(*continued*)

TABLE 11-4. *Mapping PL/SQL Data Types to C*

PL/SQL	Native C	Oracle	Default
INTERVAL DAY TO SECOND INTERVAL YEAR TO MONTH		OCIINTERVAL	OCIINTERVAL
Composite Object Types: ADTs		Dvoid	dvoid
Composite Object Types: Collections (VARRAYS, NESTED TABLES)		OCICOLL	OCICOLL

TABLE 11-4. *Mapping PL/SQL Data Types to C*

There are some differences beyond mapping between PL/SQL and C data types. They are qualified here:

- A variable can be NULL in PL/SQL, but there is no equivalent of a null value in C. When a variable can be NULL, you must use another variable to notify that a variable is null or not. This second variable is known as an indicator. You use OCI_IND_NULL and OCI_IND_NOTNULL to check whether the indicator variable is null or not. The indicator value is passed by value unless you override that behavior and pass by reference. An advanced consideration for an indicator variable is that it can have a type descriptor object (TDO) for composite objects and collections.

- Both C and PL/SQL need to know the length of character strings when they are exchanged. This is problematic because there is no standard means of determining the length of RAW or STRING parameter types. You can use the LENGTH or MAXLEN functions to determine the length of a formal parameter. It is important to note that LENGTH is passed into the external procedure by value when the mode is IN. It is passed by reference when using mode OUT.

- CHARSETID and CHARSETFORM are subject to globalization complexity if the extproc agent database is running in a different database. The calling database NLS_LANG and NLS_CHAR values are the expected values for the extproc agent. If this is not the case for the extproc agent, you need to use the OCI attribute names to set these for the program. The OCI attributes are OCI_ATTR_CHARSET_ID and OCI_ATTR_CHARSET_FORM. Both CHARSETID and CHARSETFORM are passed by value for IN mode and by reference for OUT mode.

The generalized format for creating a C library wrapper procedure is noted here:

```
CREATE [OR REPLACE] PROCEDURE name [parameter_list]
AS EXTERNAL
LIBRARY_NAME library_name
```

```
NAME "<external_library_name>"
AGENT IN [parameter_list]
WITH CONTEXT
PARAMETER [parameter_list];
```

It is important to note that the `external_library_name` is case sensitive when the operating system supports case sensitivity. Even while working on Microsoft Windows, you should always treat it as case sensitive. Good PL/SQL coding habits can make your life simpler when you change work environments. You can find complete examples of the C library wrapper at the McGraw-Hill Professional website. They're in the `create_library1.sql` and `create_library2.sql` files for this chapter.

When you define the parameter lists for a PL/SQL wrapper, positional order is not important. The PL/SQL wrapper relates them by name.

Objects present a unique case with the normally implicit `SELF`. In PL/SQL, you do not have to manage an object type's `SELF` member function, because it is implicitly managed. The problem is that the `SELF` reference is a parameter in the formal parameter list. The external C program requires the PL/SQL external procedure wrapper to define a complete formal parameter list. This means that it must formally define `SELF`. You pass an object to an external procedure by using the `WITH CONTEXT` clause when you define the object type. The following example illustrates defining an external object type:

```
SQL> CREATE OR REPLACE TYPE BODY object_library_sample AS
  2   MEMBER FUNCTION get_tea_temperature
  3   RETURN NUMBER
  4   AS LANGUAGE C
  5   NAME "tea_temp"
  6   WITH CONTEXT
  7   PARAMETERS
  8   ( CONTEXT
  9   , SELF
 10   , SELF INDICATOR STRUCT
 11   , SELF TDO
 12   , RETURN INDICATOR);
 13   END;
 14   /
```

Another rule applies to passing variables by reference to an external procedure. You must append the `BY REFERENCE` phrase to all variables passed by reference.

The `AGENT IN` clause allows runtime identification of the external agent program. This is an advanced feature. It is useful when you have more than one external agent running or configured. An example that would benefit from this type of PL/SQL wrapper is an environment with multiple external applications. Making the external agent a dynamic component gives you more flexibility. You can then use stored objects to make dynamic calls to different external application libraries.

You are now ready to create your PL/SQL external procedure wrapper. The sample program to build the PL/SQL wrapper follows:

```
SQL> CREATE OR REPLACE PROCEDURE write_string
  2   ( path       VARCHAR2
  3   , message    VARCHAR2) AS EXTERNAL
  4   LIBRARY library_write_string
  5   NAME "writestr"
```

```
6  PARAMETERS
7  ( path      STRING
8  , message   STRING);
9  /
```

The PL/SQL external procedure wrapper publishes the external library. It creates a data dictionary entry for a library named `library_write_string`. You should note that it qualifies the name of the external procedure without the `*.so` suffix (or on Microsoft Windows platforms, `*.dll`). The suffix is automatically post-pended. If it were included in the definition of the NAME value, the `extproc` agent would look for `writestr1.so.so` and fail.

You have learned how to define and configure a PL/SQL wrapper. Previously, you learned how to do all network plumbing, library coding, and agent configuration. It is now time to see if it was done correctly.

If you are working in Unix, use the `writestr1.c` file from the McGraw-Hill Professional website. However, if you are working in Microsoft Windows, change the first argument to the `write_string` procedure. It should change from `/tmp/file.txt` to `C:\TEMP\FILE.TXT`. You can now execute the external procedure by invoking the PL/SQL wrapper, as shown in the following code:

```
SQL> BEGIN
  2    write_string('/tmp/file.txt','Hello World!');
  3  END;
  4  /
```

When the procedure completes successfully, you can then open the file in the Unix `/tmp` directory or Microsoft Windows `C:\TEMP` directory. Rerunning the program will create a new file of the same name and rewrite the same string. If you're wondering why the file is replaced, it's because the `fopen` function in C opens a new file and thereby replaces any existing file using the same name. If the file is in the `/tmp` or `C:\TEMP` directory, only the file's date stamp will appear to change.

There are some restrictions when working with external procedures:

- You should not use global variables, because they are not thread-safe.
- You should not use external static variables, because they are not thread-safe.
- You can use this feature only on platforms that support DLLs or shared libraries.
- You can use only programming languages callable from the C programming language.
- You must use objects when you want to pass cursor or record variables to an external procedure.
- You cannot use a DB_LINK in the LIBRARY clause of a PL/SQL wrapper declaration.
- You can pass a maximum of 128 parameters. If you have FLOAT and DOUBLE data types, they count for two parameters.

You have completed everything required to configure and set up a C DLL or shared library. If everything worked, please accept our congratulations. However, if something failed, you can go straight to the following troubleshooting section, which will help you to troubleshoot the most common problems.

Troubleshooting External Procedures

This section covers some known errors and their fixes. When external procedures fail, typically the cause is either of two issues. The first potential issue to evaluate is whether the listener, shared library, or environment has been configured incorrectly. The previous sections covered all the components and how they fit together, so you should have a solid foundation for troubleshooting this issue. The second potential issue to evaluate is whether the definition of the external program differs from the PL/SQL wrapper. This typically happens when data types are incorrectly mapped. Each class of problem is described in the two subsections that follow.

Configuration of the Listener or Environment

There are four general problems with network connectivity. They are noted here with the typical error messages and explanations.

Listener ENV Parameter Is Incorrect

As previously discussed in the section "Defining extproc Oracle Net Services Configuration," the following error will be raised when the ENV variable is incorrectly configured:

```
BEGIN
*
ERROR at line 1:
ORA-06520: PL/SQL: Error loading external library
ORA-06522: /u01/oracle/product/12.1.0/dbhome_1/lib/writestr1.so:
cannot open shared object file: No such file or directory
ORA-06512: at "PLSQL.WRITE_STRING", line 1
ORA-06512: at line 4
```

If you receive this error, you have experienced either of two types of failures. One is that the library is not in the directory you have designated, is named differently, or is case sensitive. Another is that you have made an error in configuring the ENV parameter in your `listener.ora` file.

File Path Problem

If the file path is not in the directory you have designated in the ENV value, correcting the file path should resolve the problem. If the file path is missing a component or is not consistent in case with the PL/SQL wrapper NAME parameter value or EXTPROC_DLLS value, synchronizing all three entries will fix it.

If the file path is in the directory and all three locations mentioned are matched in spelling and case, the problem is in the listener ENV variable. Two areas can cause the problem: a bad EXTPROC_DLLS or a bad $LD_LIBRARY_PATH entry. There is a third potential error: the $APL_ENV_FILE value. This third error is typically a problem only when you have positioned the extproc agent in another Oracle home.

EXTPROC_DLLS Value Problem

You need to check the ENV variable in CALLOUT_LISTENER. The general rule is that you should have an entry for EXTPROC_DLLS and LD_LIBRARY_PATH in the ENV value. EXTPROC_DLLS should specify an equal sign, the word ONLY, a colon, and the shared libraries you want to use or a list of shared libraries separated by a colon. Alternatively, you can choose to leave out the ONLY qualifier and provide the name of a shared library or list of shared libraries separated by a colon. If you leave the ONLY qualifier out, you have not restricted the IPC listener to only those libraries. It is recommended by Oracle that you use ONLY to narrow the privileges of the listener.

You also need to check whether the shared libraries have a fully qualified path statement, and check the file name and extension to make sure they are accurate. Likewise, the LD_LIBRARY_PATH should at a minimum specify the fully qualified path to the $ORACLE_HOME/lib directory. If your libraries require other libraries, you would use the LD_LIBRARY_PATH reference. When you have more than the one library in the LD_LIBRARY_PATH, you use a set of fully qualified path statements separated by a colon.

If you would like to see this error, you can do the following:

1. Rename the shared library path in the PL/SQL wrapper. You would do this by rerunning the create_library1.sql script with an incorrect path statement.

2. Rerun the anonymous block PL/SQL call to the write_string procedure.

NOTE
If you test for this type of error, don't forget to fix everything before you move on to the rest of the chapter.

The extproc Listener Is Incorrectly Configured or Not Running

As discussed in the earlier section "Defining extproc Oracle Net Services Configuration," the following error will be raised if the extproc listener is not running or is not configured properly:

```
BEGIN
*
ERROR at line 1:
ORA-28576: lost RPC connection to external procedure agent
ORA-06512: at "PLSQL.WRITE_STRING", line 1
ORA-06512: at line 4
```

If you receive this error, the extproc listener is not running or the KEY parameter values don't match in both listener.ora and tnsnames.ora files. You need to verify the setup of your listener.ora and tnsnames.ora files, as described in "Defining extproc Oracle Net Services Configuration."

If you would like to see this error, you can do the following:

1. Shut down the CALLOUT_LISTENER.

2. Alter the KEY parameter value in the listener.ora file so that it no longer agrees with the tnsnames.ora file.

3. Start up the CALLOUT_LISTENER.

4. Rerun the anonymous-block PL/SQL call to the write_string procedure.

NOTE
If you do this test, do not forget to fix everything before you move on to the rest of the chapter.

There Is No Separate extproc Listener
As discussed in connection with the `extproc` Oracle Net Services configuration, the following error will be raised when these three conditions are met:

■ The correct environment is defined in the `extproc` listener.

■ There is no separate `extproc` listener.

■ The `extproc` agent is attempting to access the DLL or shared library in any directory other than `$ORACLE_HOME/bin` or `$ORACLE_HOME/lib`.

```
BEGIN
*
ERROR at line 1:
ORA-28595: Extproc agent : Invalid DLL Path
ORA-06522: h§n¶h§n¶
```

If you receive this error, the three conditions are met, since you have configured a perfect ENV variable in the standard single `LISTENER`. You now need to do one of two things. You can migrate the `extproc` agent listener to a separate listener. This is described in the section "Defining extproc Oracle Net Services Configuration." Alternatively, you can abandon the custom library directory and put the external libraries in the `$ORACLE_HOME/lib` directory.

If you would like to see this error, you can do the following:

1. Shut down the `CALLOUT_LISTENER`.

2. Using the online `listener1.ora` and `tnsnames2.ora` files, replace your `listener .ora` and `tnsnames.ora`, respectively. Do not forget to configure these files. You need to provide full path statements that match your system for them to work. Do not forget to make a copy of your modified files so that you can restore them.

3. Start up the `CALLOUT_LISTENER`.

4. Rerun the anonymous block PL/SQL call to the `write_string` procedure.

NOTE
Like the early error management test, don't forget to fix everything before you move on to the balance of the chapter.

PL/SQL Wrapper Defined NAME Value Is Incorrect
As discussed in the section "Defining and Calling the PL/SQL Library Wrapper," the following error will be raised if the NAME variable is incorrectly entered:

```
BEGIN
*
ERROR at line 1:
ORA-06521: PL/SQL: Error mapping function
ORA-06522: /u01/oracle/product/12.1.0/dbhome_1/lib/libagtsh.so:
undefined symbol: writestr1.so
ORA-06512: at "PLSQL.WRITE_STRING", line 1
ORA-06512: at line 3
```

If you receive this error, you need to check the NAME variable in the PL/SQL external library definition. The ORA-06522 error returns the file name of the object that cannot be found. It is unclear from the error if it was looking for the writestr1.so file in the $ORACLE_HOME/lib directory. Actually, it first looked in the designated custom library directory, then in the $ORACLE_HOME/lib directory. It could not find the writestr1.so.so file. Defining the NAME parameter of the external procedure with the file name and suffix can cause the problem. It should always be only the file name. The extproc agent implicitly appends .so or .DLL, depending on the platform.

NOTE
The extproc agent always searches the ENV defined directories first and the $ORACLE_HOME/lib last. Anytime the DLL or shared library name fails to match the value in the PL/SQL library definition, the ORA-06522 error will return the $ORACLE_HOME/lib directory.

If you encounter this error and verify everything is working, shut down your extproc listener. Use the ps utility to find the running extprocPLSExtProc agent. If it is running after you shut down the listener, it should not be running. Use the kill utility to end it. Then restart your extproc listener. This eliminates the conflict with the preserved state in the extproc agent.

If you would like to see this error, you can do the following:

1. Rename the writestr.so shared library file.
2. Rerun the anonymous block PL/SQL call to the write_string procedure.

NOTE
Again, don't forget to fix everything if you try to replicate the error.

The LD_LIBRARY_PATH should at a minimum specify the fully qualified path to the $ORACLE_HOME/lib directory. If you use the default location for your shared library, you can exclude it.

Configuration of the Shared Library or PL/SQL Library Wrapper

As you built the shared external library file and PL/SQL wrapper, you probably noticed that the formal parameter types mapped correctly. When they do not map correctly, you will lose the RPC connection and generate the following error message:

```
BEGIN
*
ERROR at line 1:
ORA-28576: lost RPC connection to external procedure agent
ORA-06512: at "PLSQL.WRITE_STRING", line 1
ORA-06512: at line 4
```

If you receive this error, the PL/SQL library is defining a mapping relationship that cannot be implicitly cast. This error is raised when you try to fork an external library with actual parameters that do not implicitly cast to the formal parameters of the library.

NOTE
Actually, implicit casting is a big nightmare. If you run into an implicit cast, you will not get an error during the call to the external procedure. You will likely get bad data from your program, and it may take a while to sort out why. Ensuring the external library types match the definition in the PL/SQL wrapper is a configuration management issue. You will save yourself countless hours of frustration and lost productivity if you create a check-in process that ensures external library definitions agree with PL/SQL library definitions.

If you would like to see this error, you can do the following:

1. Create a `writestr2.so` shared library from the online `writestr2.c` file.
2. Shut down the `CALLOUT_LISTENER`.
3. Use the online `listener3.ora` and `tnsnames3.ora` files to replace your `listener.ora` and `tnsnames.ora` files, respectively. Do not forget to configure these files. You need to provide full path statements that match your system for them to work.
4. Start up the `CALLOUT_LISTENER`.
5. Run the online `create_library2.sql` file to build the PL/SQL external procedure wrapper.
6. Rerun the anonymous block PL/SQL call to the `write_string` procedure.

NOTE
As a final reminder, when you see how an error occurs, fix those things before you move on to implementation.

Supporting Files

The following files are available on the McGraw-Hill Professional website to support this chapter:

- The `create_library1.sql` and `create_library2.sql` files use Dynamic Native SQL (DNS) to build the library creation DLL.
- `listener1.ora`, `listener2.ora`, and `listener3.ora` are example files that support dividing the TCP and ICP listener behaviors. The `listener1.ora` file provides a working example of a single TCP/ICP listener. The `listener2.ora` file provides a working example of a listener with separate TCP and ICP listener behaviors. The `listener3.ora` file shows a multiple-path library.

■ The `writestr1.c` and `writestr2.c` files hold the same source C file, and it simply writes a string to the file system. The two files are provided for mirrored examples because simply providing instructions to copy and rename one file seemed impractical.

■ `tnsnames1.ora`, `tnsnames2.ora`, and `tnsnames3.ora` are example files that support dividing the TCP and ICP listener behaviors.

Summary
You should now have an understanding of how to implement and deploy external procedures. With these skills, you can build robust external library solutions in C or any C-callable programming language.

CHAPTER
12

In-Memory Column Store

Purpose

In this chapter, you will learn how to implement Oracle's new In-Memory Column Store (IMCS). Oracle released this feature in its database version 12.1.0.2. The feature is easy enough to implement; however, its inner workings are not so easy to understand. What's more, it is vital that you understand the architecture because misuse or misconfiguration of the feature can be disastrous to your database instance.

The IMCS product uses the System Global Area (SGA). It is very tempting to configure IMCS so that it takes up too much of your SGA. Naturally, if this is done, your instance will have difficulty running. However, if you are careful, IMCS can be a great boon to your performance efforts. Some of the great features in the IMCS feature set are

- Its ability to store tables, materialized views, and partitions
- Its ability to assign differing levels of priority to columns and tables
- Its ability to compress and distribute data

IMCS provides the Oracle database with a broader in-memory processing ability, similar to SAP HANA (High-Performance Analytic Appliance) and Microsoft SQL Server 2014, and it supports columnar compression, which greatly improves query times even when tables become wider.

The Oracle TimesTen In-Memory Database product is similar to IMCS but does not allow for columnar compression at this time. The main difference is that TimesTen places the entire database in memory, versus allowing you to place pieces in memory, as IMCS does. We feel that both products have their place in nearly any enterprise. You use the IMCS product to speed up queries in normal Oracle ORDBMSs, while you use TimesTen to accelerate the entire database.

This chapter does not exhaust the topics surrounding IMCS; however, it will give you an enhanced understanding of IMCS and enable you to implement this new feature.

Advantages

The new IMCS provides better control over which tables stay in memory. You can reduce IO costs if you know how to use IMCS effectively. Before IMCS, we used multiple buffer caches so that the least used caches would age blocks out slower. Unfortunately, there wasn't a good way to mark a table to keep it in memory, and the available solutions left you contending with the cost of row-based reads. The new IMCS also lets a processor scan orders of magnitude more rows per second than it can in a row-based in-memory store.

Disadvantages

IMCS requires you to pay careful attention to table and partition priorities. It's the only way to ensure the right tables stay in memory. In some cases, we observed that late materialization, operations on compressed data, and column-oriented joins didn't perform well. GV$SESSTAT statistics showed these weakness in the execution plans that decompress data and use hash joins.

Overview

This chapter focuses on the following:

- In-memory setup and configuration
- In-memory options and syntax
- Query performance
- DML performance

We recommend that you cover the topics in series if you're planning to test code in your system. The sections stand independently if you want to skip around to check how to do one or more tasks separately.

In-Memory Setup and Configuration

IMCS requires that you use Oracle Database 12c, version 12.1.0.2 or greater. IMCS also requires that you configure the SGA by allocating memory for it. The configuration steps are covered in the following "Database Parameter Settings" and "Tablespace Settings" subsections.

Database Parameter Settings

There are four settings available at the database level: `inmemory_size`, `inmemory_force`, `inmemory_clause_default`, and `inmemory_query`. Changing `inmemory_size` requires a database restart, while the other parameters can be modified any time.

To get started using the IMCS, you need to allocate memory to it in the SGA by setting the `inmemory_size` parameter to something greater than zero. To do this, issue `alter system set inmemory_size=16G scope=spfile;`. You need to restart the database after issuing this command. Make sure your `pfile` is backed up before doing this. We had to re-create a test database because of this. There are some dependencies that aren't documented well by Oracle. The `sga_target` parameter must be bigger than the `inmemory_size` parameter by at least several gigabytes. This is because the `inmemory_size` parameter takes memory from the default buffer cache. We also had to set the `sga_target` size equal to the `sga_max_size` parameter, because otherwise it wouldn't be created large enough to include the `inmemory_size` parameter and the startup would fail. If the `sga_target` parameter isn't big enough to handle the extra memory allocated to the in-memory area, the database won't restart.

NOTE
A simple way to remember what settings are required on startup is that `memory_target`, `sga_target`, and `inmemory size` are critical.

We highly recommend testing this new feature out on a database that you can lose that has the same amount of memory as the production database you'll be implementing it with. To save yourself some headache, we'll cover everything you need to do to ensure you can recover the database you're testing on. Before running any of these commands in SQL*Plus, you should run CREATE PFILE FROM SPFILE;. This will be used to recover the parameters if they aren't working. Make sure you know where this is. It's usually in $ORACLE_HOME/dbs/init[instance name].ora. In our testing we used the following parameter settings:

```
SQL> ALTER SYSTEM SET SGA_MAX_SIZE = 100G SCOPE=SPFILE;
SQL> ALTER SYSTEM SET SGA_TARGET = 100G SCOPE=SPFILE;
SQL> ALTER SYSTEM SET MEMORY_MAX_TARGET=144G SCOPE=SPFILE;
SQL> ALTER SYSTEM SET MEMORY_TARGET=128G SCOPE=SPFILE;
SQL> ALTER SYSTEM SET INMEMORY_SIZE=80G SCOPE=SPFILE;
```

Once they're set, shut down and restart the database. If the database throws an error stating that it can't allocate memory or that one parameter does not take into account another parameter, the way to get the database back up and running is to tell the database where to get the backup pfile you just made by running

```
startup pfile='[ORACLE_HOME]/dbs/initA12102.ora';
```

Once started again, you need to run

```
SQL> CREATE spfile FROM pfile;
```

It restores the spfile from the backup. Sometimes you can run into issues with this type of configuration. During one test, we needed to restart our database more than 30 times.

We recommend making sure that it will start up by setting the inmemory_size parameter as follows:

```
inmemory_size = 0
```

Once that is working, you can find the upper limit of the inmemory_size parameter before beginning your test. We allocated the maximum amount of memory available because we wanted to fit the entire rental_item_fact table into memory for comparison during the performance tests.

If you're running a CDB, the inmemory_size parameter must be set for the CDB, and each PDB inherits the inmemory_size parameter value. This means a single PDB can use up the entire IMCS. You can set the inmemory_size parameter for a PDB to a size smaller than the same inmemory_size parameter for the CDB or any value up to the limit of the IMCS. To see the current setting for the inmemory_size parameter value, you can run

```
SHOW PARAMETER INMEMORY_SIZE
```

Or you can use the following query:

```
SQL> SELECT    *
  2  FROM      V$SGA_DYNAMIC_COMPONENTS
  3  WHERE     COMPONENT = ' In-memory Pool ';
```

If USER_SPECIFIED_SIZE is set to zero, then no tables will be kept in memory.

Oracle documentation says you can force the use of the IMCS for all tables by setting the inmemory_force parameter to ON. Setting this parameter to OFF disables the use of the IMCS for all tables, and leaving it at DEFAULT lets you decide which tables will be populated. Oracle can throw an error when trying to set this parameter to ON. It throws an ORA-00096 error, which means you have an invalid value set for the inmemory_force parameter.

Changing this parameter doesn't require a restart. Oracle loads the same tables into the IMCS that it does on startup when changed from OFF to DEFAULT.

The default inmemory clause that is applied to all new tables can be changed at the database level by setting the inmemory_clause_default parameter to a valid in-memory clause. The default is the empty string, which is the same as adding ' NO INMEMORY '. If this parameter starts with inmemory, then all new tables will be set to use the inmemory feature. It also means they inherit the inmemory clause defaults for those unspecified inmemory attributes.

So, you can issue the following command to override Oracle's default compression for inmemory tables:

```
SQL> ALTER SYSTEM
  2  SET INMEMORY_CLAUSE_DEFAULT = ' INMEMORY MEMCOMPRESS FOR CAPACITY LOW ';
```

Although this will override Oracle's default compression for in-memory tables, it will leave the defaults for priority and distribution, which we'll discuss later. Excluding the inmemory keyword while specifying the other in-memory attributes will make those attributes the default for the database for any table that is marked inmemory at creation time, whether in the DDL or by tablespace or database default.

The following command overrides the default compression for inmemory tables:

```
SQL> ALTER SYSTEM
  2  SET INMEMORY_CLAUSE_DEFAULT = 'MEMCOMPRESS FOR CAPACITY HIGH';
```

To allow the database to query the in-memory tables, the inmemory_query parameter needs to be set to ENABLE, and is enabled by default. Setting this to DISABLE will leave all tables in memory, but all query execution plans will only be allowed to use the buffer cache. This setting is probably only useful for test purposes. Changing it does not require a database restart.

Tablespace Settings

Now that you've set all the system parameters, you can set a default in-memory clause for each tablespace. We should note that tables in the system and sysaux tablespaces cannot be put in the IMCS. The default for a tablespace is NO INMEMORY, so each table or partition must be explicitly set to use the IMCS. We will only refer to tables for the rest of the chapter, because materialized views use the same syntax and mechanisms. You can use the following statement to alter a tablespace for default IMCS:

```
SQL> ALTER TABLESPACE FIO_DATA DEFAULT INMEMORY;
```

This will make all tables created on this tablespace use the inmemory option with the defaults set by the inmemory_default_clause system parameter. Changing the default to INMEMORY MEMCOMPRESS FOR CAPACITY HIGH will override the default compression setting while still using the other default settings.

In-Memory Options and Syntax

To add a table to the IMCS, you need to issue the inmemory clause in a CREATE or ALTER DDL statement. The syntax is the same for both. The three other options for compression, priority, and distribution can be specified, but just using inmemory will use the defaults. To put the rental_item_fact table in memory, you would use the following statement.

```
SQL> ALTER TABLE rental_item_fact INMEMORY;
```

This statement takes as long as any other DDL statement, because all it does is change the table definition in the data dictionary. The data is loaded asynchronously by another process. If the `rental_item_fact` table is interval partitioned on the `date_key` column by month, you can put some partitions in memory, each of them with a different priority. This can be managed automatically using jobs that run daily. The most recent year's data can be put in memory by evaluating the partitions dynamically, as in the following script. For this month, it will be executing

```
ALTER TABLE RENTAL_ITEM_FACT MODIFY PARTITION FOR (20140501) INMEMORY;
```

This can also be wrapped in a procedure and called from a daily job:

```
SQL> DECLARE
  2     lv_options   VARCHAR(255);
  3     lv_partition VARCHAR(10);
  4  BEGIN
  5     FOR I IN 0 .. 23 LOOP
  6        lv_options := CASE
  7                         WHEN I < 12 THEN
  8                           'INMEMORY'
  9                         ELSE
 10                           'NO INMEMORY'
 11                         END;
 12        lv_partition := TO_CHAR(ADD_MONTHS(SYSDATE,i),'YYYYMMDD');
 13        EXECUTE IMMEDIATE
 14          'ALTER TABLE RENTAL_ITEM_FACT ' ||
 15          'MODIFY PARTITION FOR ('|| lv_partition ||') '||
 16           lv_options;
 17     END LOOP;
 18  END;
 19  /
```

This feature allows a DBA or engineer exact control over what stays in memory and what has to be fetched from disk. You can use three columns to read all the in-memory settings from the data dictionary, `inmemory_priority`, `inmemory_compression`, and `inmemory_distribute`, which are found in the `*_tables` and `*_tab_partitions` system views. Just like other partition attributes, only the `*_tab_partitions` views contain data about partitioned tables. To see what tables or partitions are actually in the IMCS and to see their status, you can query the `gv$im_segments` view. It lists all segments that are loaded or are being loaded into memory with statistics such as the segment size on disk, the segment size in memory, and how many bytes haven't been populated.

When using the `IMPDP` command (discussed in Chapter 6), there are some new transform options that you can use to change how the in-memory options are handled. `TRANSFORM=INMEMORY=y` will leave the `inmemory` clause as is. `TRANSFORM=INMEMORY=n` will exclude the `inmemory` clause for all objects. You can also use the `TRANSFORM=INMEMORY_CLAUSE:[INMEMORY STRING]` to change the `inmemory` clause for all objects being imported. This is useful for changing column compression or disabling the in-memory option when importing to another database, such as a development instance with less memory.

Priority

To give the current partition for the `rental_item_fact` table, you specify the priority for memory by using another `ALTER` statement:

```
SQL> ALTER TABLE rental_item_fact
  2    MODIFY PARTITION FOR (20140501)
  3    inmemory priority critical;
```

This loads the partition before others, and it can have a positive impact on the database because most queries use the recent partitions most frequently. There are five priorities: NONE, LOW, MEDIUM, HIGH, and CRITICAL. Tables are loaded first starting with CRITICAL and each successive priority is loaded if there is enough memory. Tables with the lowest priority that can't all be fit into memory can be shuffled in and out of memory as determined by Oracle. If you have a 20GB in-memory area and CRITICAL priority tables use 10GB, HIGH priority tables use 8GB, and MEDIUM priority tables use 5GB, if available; then Oracle will determine which MEDIUM priority segments will be loaded into memory. When we first marked `rental_item_fact` for in-memory use, Oracle gave it the default priority of NONE. Tables with a priority of NONE will not be loaded in memory on startup. They will only be loaded after their first full scan. All other priorities are loaded into memory on startup, given that there is enough memory to hold them all. DDL statements on tables with a priority other than NONE will not return until the changes are recorded in the IMCS. If there is no space in the IMCS, then INSERT and UPDATE statements will commit without their changes being completely reflected, which causes those rows to be retrieved from disk.

When loading tables into memory, Oracle could only handle about 500 Mbps because all 32 processors were running at 97 percent. This should be a background process on startup and shouldn't affect queries, other than the fact that they won't be able to use the IMCS until the data they need is loaded. You can see the status of this process using the GV$IM_SEGMENTS and GV$IM_USER_SEGMENTS views and their V$ equivalents. There are other GV$ and V$ views that give very detailed information, all of which start with IM_.

Distribution

The distribution option gives some control over how in-memory segments are distributed across a RAC database. There are only two possible choices: AUTO DISTRIBUTE and DUPLICATE. These are mutually exclusive and only apply when using a RAC database.

AUTO DISTRIBUTE is the default and allows Oracle to determine whether to distribute a table across instances or duplicate it on every instance. Large tables are distributed based on query and access patterns, while smaller tables can be distributed or duplicated across nodes.

DUPLICATE forces duplication of the table across all instances. We couldn't test either of these options when we used a RAC setup because Oracle threw errors saying that the option is only available on Oracle-engineered RAC systems. The database wouldn't even start up on a RAC One Node if the `inmemory_size` parameter was greater than zero. When it did start up, we couldn't mark any table for in-memory use, even if the IMCS was not allocated.

Compression

Oracle lets you determine which compression to use per table and even for each partition and column. This is the only setting you can choose for individual columns. As you've seen, you do this by using MEMCOMPRESS followed by the compression type. There are four different compression

Compression Type	Description
BASIC	These tables are not compressed at all, and can result in taking up a large amount of memory.
FOR QUERY	Default compression. Best for combination of fast queries and upkeep with large amounts of DML.
FOR CAPACITY [LOW]	Balanced compression. Performed poorly in query tests, but handled DML well.
FOR CAPACITY HIGH	Best compression. Takes the longest to load, but did very well for warehouse-type queries. Handled 20 percent less DML.

TABLE 12-1. *Compression Types*

types: BASIC, FOR QUERY, FOR CAPACITY [LOW], and FOR CAPACITY HIGH (see Table 12-1). BASIC compression really means no compression and generally results in an in-memory size bigger than compressed tables on disk. These tables, partitions, or columns will not be compressed. There is no advantage to using this option—it uses more memory and results in slower queries because less data fits in memory. Using this option resulted in query times that were indistinguishable from FOR QUERY when the entire table fit in memory. FOR QUERY is Oracle's default and results in the best performance for queries, but not by much. Data is compressed to maximize throughput on reads, but this option sacrifices memory usage. FOR CAPACITY and FOR CAPACITY LOW are the same compression; specifying LOW is optional. This is supposed to be a balanced setting for optimum memory usage and query performance, but our tests showed that it performed the worst of all the compression algorithms for data warehouse–type queries. FOR CAPACITY HIGH compresses the data the most, and in our tests was as fast as or faster than the FOR CAPACITY compression level and was right on par with FOR QUERY with more consistency in query time measured by the standard deviation.

When specifying which columns to hold in memory, you can also set compression for each of them individually:

```
SQL> ALTER TABLE rental_item_fact
  2    INMEMORY PRIORITY HIGH MEMCOMPRESS FOR CAPACITY HIGH
  3    INMEMORY MEMCOMPRESS FOR QUERY (date_key, sale_net)
  4    INMEMORY MEMCOMPRESS FOR CAPACITY(product_key, product_quantity)
  5    INMEMORY MEMCOMPRESS FOR CAPACITY HIGH(customer_key, sale_price)
  6    NO INMEMORY (load_date);
```

The first in-memory clause specifies the priority, distribution, and default compression for the table. The second in-memory clause compresses the date_key and sale_net columns optimally for reads. The third clause specifies that product_key and product_quantity will use CAPACITY LOW compression. The fourth clause is actually unnecessary, as all columns not specified otherwise will still be put in memory with the table's default compression. The no in-memory clause specifies that those columns should not be used in the IMCS. Selecting columns marked NO INMEMORY will cause Oracle to get the table from disk, so columns that are only selected rarely should be marked NO INMEMORY. The optimizer's estimated cost of reading a table from disk has been anywhere between 2 times and 100 times the cost of reading in-memory columns for some of the tests we've done.

When you have already explicitly set the compression for a column and you run another statement that leaves it out, it will keep its previous specification. This means that if you set a column to NO INMEMORY and then you leave it out, it will not receive the default compression specification; it will remain as NO INMEMORY. We tested this with the rental_item_fact table and put only sale_price in memory because its type was NUMBER and had 39,024 distinct values. Then we added product_cost because it had the same data type with 43,968 distinct values, which we expected to compress to the same size. Table 12-2 shows the in-memory sizes of the tables at different compression levels.

If you specify a column more than once, Oracle throws the error ORA-64360, which means only one inmemory clause can be specified for each column. Specifying column compression can only be done when altering a table and is not allowed on partitions. Any attempt will throw an ORA-64350 error. If you want to specify column compression and which partitions will be in memory, you need to first set the columns. Anything not specified is set to DEFAULT, which gets its compression specification from each partition that you leave in memory. The pseudo-column ROWID is always included. We checked this by querying for the minimum and maximum ROWIDs on the rental_item_fact table when it was in memory. There was no activity on the disk.

The GV$IM_COLUMN_LEVEL view has information on what compression setting is used for each column. This is updated instantly when a CREATE or ALTER statement is run. It thereby acts like a supplement to the dictionary views for columns. If all columns in a table use the default, they do not appear in this view. If a table excludes a column or uses a different compression for one or more columns, then all of its columns will be listed in the view. The granularity of this view, which is one row per column per table, explains why the ORA-64350 error is thrown.

	NO INMEMORY (Bytes on Disk)	QUERY (Inmemory Size, Numbers in MB)	CAPACITY (Inmemory Size, Numbers in MB)	CAPACITY HIGH (Inmemory Size, Numbers in MB)	BASIC (Inmemory Size, Numbers in MB)
customer_dim	2,008.0	257.4	207.4	58.4	1,607.4
date_dim	160.0	22.5	22.5	22.5	22.5
product_dim	48.0	24.8	13.8	11.8	26.8
rental_item_fact	35,872.0	9,013.0	6,801.0	2,412.0	*63,690.3

*This test didn't fit completely in memory.

TABLE 12-2. *Comparative Statistics*

Query Performance

We ran five tests to measure the performance of the different compression algorithms. These tests used the same queries as in Chapter 10. The best-performing tables were copied into the 12.1.0.2 instance, which was running as a stand-alone instance because the beta does not support RAC with the in-memory option on systems not engineered by Oracle. This instance was allocated 128GB of RAM, with 80GB of that dedicated to the IMCS, and all 32 processors. The speed to the Fusion ION Accelerator was half the RAC instance and topped out at 3.8 Gbps.

We used a bigfile tablespace on the Fusion ION Accelerator disks, which isn't available on generic Linux or Unix servers.

```
SQL> CREATE bigfile TABLESPACE fio_data
  2    DATAFILE '+DATA/A12102/DATAFILE/fio_data'
  3    SIZE 500G AUTOEXTEND ON NEXT 10G MAXSIZE 4T
  4    DEFAULT COMPRESS FOR oltp NO INMEMORY NOLOGGING
  5    EXTENT MANAGEMENT LOCAL AUTOALLOCATE SEGMENT
  6    SPACE MANAGEMENT AUTO;
```

We also used a bigfile temporary tablespace on the same Fusion ION Accelerator disks:

```
SQL> CREATE bigfile TEMPORARY TABLESPACE fio_temp
  2    TEMPFILE '+DATA/A12102/DATAFILE/fio_temp' SIZE 1024G
  3    AUTOEXTEND ON NEXT 10G MAXSIZE 2048G;
```

The video_store user was created with both of those new tablespaces as default:

```
SQL> CREATE USER video_store IDENTIFIED BY fiooral2
  2    DEFAULT TABLESPACE fio_data
  3    TEMPORARY TABLESPACE fio_temp
  4    QUOTA UNLIMITED ON fio_data;
```

Compression Stats

The first test we ran was a baseline with none of the tables in memory. The structure of the tables we used never changed during the test. They were the same as those in Test 4 of Chapter 10, including their partitions and indexes. This is to ensure that we are comparing the best query performance from disk with the performance of the IMCS using different compression algorithms. The other four tests used the four different compression settings for all four tables in the model. BASIC had no advantage over NO INMEMORY. This is because rental_item_fact couldn't fit in memory. To give you an idea, rental_item_fact created with no compression was 189GB on disk. When we first created it, it was 147GB with advanced compression. That went down to 36GB (we had to check this to make sure it was accurate) if the table was re-created with an ORDER BY clause. Because BASIC decompresses the data in memory, we would have needed an IMCS of around 210GB, so only those partitions with high and critical priority fit completely in memory. The partitions with a priority of medium and low showed up in the GV$IM_SEGMENTS but never finished loading, while those with a priority of none were never marked to load. Even though this should have used up 80GB in the IMCS, we were only able to get 65GB in memory. This is probably due to another area in the IMCS that's used for temporary decompression for queries, as we'll see later. Oracle hasn't published any guidelines yet on how big that reserved area is so that DBAs can better plan for their IMCS size, so some trial and error may be necessary.

You'll notice that the different algorithms performed differently depending on the table. CAPACITY didn't make near as much of a difference with rental_item_fact and customer_dim as CAPACITY HIGH did, but CAPACITY HIGH did not compress product_dim much more than CAPACITY. The date_dim table had partitions that were too small for the compression to matter, as they were always the same size in memory. The smallest segment size in memory was 1.25MB, which appears to be the size of a columnar unit used for in-memory storage. It is interesting to note that the compression achieved with CAPACITY HIGH brought the average row size in memory to 6.28 bits per row for all 11 columns.

Obviously, the compression capabilities are pretty impressive, but how do they impact performance and how long do they take to load into memory? To automate the tests, we included code that altered the tables to NO INMEMORY and then to the compression we were testing. Then we queried the GV$IM_SEGMENTS view to wait for all the data to be loaded. It took anywhere from 10 seconds to 2 minutes to start, but generally just under 1 minute before we could see the Fusion ION Accelerator disks being read. The only way to make this immediate was to run a full table query like

```
SQL> SELECT /*+ full(rif) */ COUNT(*)
  2  FROM   rental_item_fact rif;
```

QUERY, CAPACITY, and CAPACITY HIGH could each read in data at around 500 Mbps from disk, compressed or not. The processors ran between 95 percent and 100 percent capacity for around two minutes for QUERY and CAPACITY. CAPACITY HIGH ran at the same capacity for about 3 minutes and 30 seconds, but had a total memory usage of 28 percent of QUERY. BASIC loaded in just over 30 seconds. Remember, these are reading and compressing 189GB of uncompressed data or 36GB of advanced compressed data.

Every time we ran the tests, we gathered the in-memory table size, and the size was always exactly the same for each compression algorithm. We copied the tables with different partitioning and ordering and compressed those to see if they would get the same in-memory compression... and they didn't. The customer_dim table was smaller on disk and in memory by up to 13 percent. The rental_item_fact table was bigger on disk and in-memory by up to 10 percent. Every compression algorithm, including BASIC, exhibited this behavior, and it appears that the smaller you can get a table on disk, the smaller it will be in memory.

Queries

We ran six queries against the data ten different times, because the first time we ran them there were some unexpected inconsistencies in query times and statistics gathered that caused us to wonder if they were really just anomalies. The queries are the same ones used in Chapter 10. We'll go over how each of them performed and point out any interesting statistics that we gathered using the method in Chapter 10. We can do that because the method is flexible enough to include some extra statistics, like memory usage of the IMCS found in the gv$im_segments view. It only takes a little extra work to accomplish. We added a single pivot query on the stats data, and it gave us everything we wanted to know. Well, everything, except the execution plans. Remember that our baseline queries are probably exceptionally fast because of the disk speeds we were able to achieve; however, because of these quick query times from disk, it makes the in-memory stats even more impressive.

	NO INMEMORY	QUERY	CAPACITY	CAPACITY HIGH	BASIC
All queries	85.47	63.68	70.02	63.25	88.29
Query 1	0.2	1.29	4.77	1.79	0.44
Query 2	1.95	1.68	1.85	1.56	2.39
Query 3	66.94	55.09	55.43	55.19	64.84
Query 4	11.38	1.58	3.39	1.96	9.52
Query 5	0.82	0.22	0.28	0.25	0.21
Query 6	1.16	0.78	0.94	0.82	0.84

TABLE 12-3. *Average Seconds per Query*

The server we tested on had DDR3 1600-MHz RAM, which isn't exceptionally fast, so commodity servers should be able to get comparable speeds when using the IMCS. Tables 12-3 and 12-4 contain comparative speeds for our six test queries.

Query 1

The first query was a simple COUNT(*) from the rental_item_fact table. This is the only query that was faster than the IMCS. For both NO INMEMORY and BASIC compression, the execution plan used a bitmap index fast full scan on the date_key column, which was right around 1GB in size. The other three compressions used a TABLE ACCESS INMEMORY FULL access plan. NO INMEMORY and BASIC both used around 66,000 consistent gets, while the others were very uniform at 3,600 consistent gets from cache. This type of behavior is pretty consistent across queries. Tables stored in the IMCS don't use as many gets as other tables. The real anomaly here is

	NO INMEMORY	QUERY	CAPACITY	CAPACITY HIGH	BASIC
All queries	7.720	9.386	9.892	4.506	20.509
Query 1	0.017	0.019	0.010	0.009	0.018
Query 2	0.035	0.102	0.143	0.013	1.728
Query 3	4.854	0.497	0.172	0.117	4.577
Query 4	0.061	0.049	0.031	0.018	0.269
Query 5	0.017	0.030	0.011	0.009	0.022
Query 6	0.035	0.050	0.041	0.022	0.022

TABLE 12-4. *Standard Deviation per Query*

that CAPACITY took more than three times as long as QUERY and CAPACITY HIGH but with a very small standard deviation. This is one of the reasons we ran the tests ten times.

Table 12-5 shows CPU usage and explains why CAPACITY was so much slower, but not why so much more CPU was used. The only other statistic that is somewhat different is "IM scan CUs columns decompressed," which tells us how much decompression work had to be done before Oracle could actually scan the data. This value only changes when scanning CAPACITY and CAPACITY HIGH compressed tables, and was 17,928 and 22,618 columnar units, respectively. For now, there must be something about the CAPACITY compression algorithm that makes it slower. You'll notice that CAPACITY was never faster than CAPACITY HIGH in our tests, which does not agree with what Oracle has in their documentation.

Query 2
The next query found the sum of sales for each product genre by customer's state for December 2012, which requires a filter on the date_key column and complete joins to the product_dim and customer_dim tables. All compression algorithms returned relatively quickly. CAPACITY HIGH had lower CPU usage than CAPACITY and was slightly lower than QUERY. The more impressive stat is that the standard deviation for CPU usage and DB time for CAPACITY HIGH was lower than CAPACITY and QUERY, as seen in Tables 12-4 and 12-5, which show CPU and database time, respectively. The effect of this can be seen in Table 12-3 where the total query time had 10 percent of the deviation compared to the other in-memory queries.

	NO INMEMORY	QUERY	CAPACITY	CAPACITY HIGH	BASIC
All queries	230938 (436.9)	180920 (828.7)	197931 (3442.4)	184424 (380.9)	218832 (1854.7)
Query 1	5423 (30.3)	3528 (3.8)	14005 (62.8)	5089 (14.4)	5373 (21.3)
Query 2	3692 (21)	3413 (291.4)	3830 (200.5)	3242 (22.7)	3612 (271.5)
Query 3	202134 (771.6)	169460 (150)	170597 (196.2)	170168 (124.3)	188478 (444.5)
Query 4	17602 (156.4)	3931 (7)	9296 (97.3)	5118 (7.8)	21034 (178.9)
Query 5	585 (23.7)	31 (5.1)	128 (14.2)	60 (8.6)	29 (5.8)
Query 6	1209 (16.4)	640 (18.4)	1034 (23.4)	810 (28.2)	768 (37.3)

TABLE 12-5.   *Summary Comparisons, CPU Used, Average by Standard Deviation*

Query 3

The third query was one of the most interesting. It used all the data in `rental_item_fact` to do a pivot for sales by year by customer's state, with the years making up the column headers. To do this pivot required an inline view. We tested the speed of that query, and Oracle returned in 22 seconds from disk, which included `BASIC` compression, but it took 2 minutes and 45 seconds to return when `rental_item_fact` was in memory for all other compressions. The execution plan for this madness was 86 steps and included the materialization of two temp tables, a `UNION ALL`, and several scans of the same bitmap indexes. The execution plan for the 22-second query was 30 steps shorter and excluded the `UNION ALL` operation.

While Oracle says that adding this option should be seamless and speed everything up, we didn't see that setting the option sped everything up. It appeared that the optimizer chose a poor plan. If there is the need to do some tuning, you can use optimizer hints. For now, there are four hints that can be used. `INMEMORY` and `NO_INMEMORY` do what you'd expect and require a table alias as a parameter just like the `FULL` hint if there are more than two tables in the query. The two other hints available are `INMEMORY_PRUNING` and `NO_INMEMORY_PRUNING`, which also require a table alias. The only documentation on this is that they allow or disallow pruning of in-memory queries. There is a statistic called "IM scan segments minmax eligible" that indicates the number of segments that could be used to prune a query using minimum and maximum values for a column, which are calculated during compression.

When running the actual pivot query, however, all our tests used the same execution plan, which was only 28 steps. With the `QUERY`, `CAPACITY`, and `CAPACITY HIGH` compressions all taking very close to the same amount of time, it appears that if the overhead of decompressing a compression unit is low relative to the rest of the work, then all three perform about the same.

Query 4

The fourth query returned the sum of sales for every product genre in a single state with no date constraints. This required a filter on the `customer_dim` table using a full table scan and then a lookup of rows in `rental_item_fact`, which were then grouped by product genre. When we looked at the statistics for this query, there was not anything very interesting or unexpected, so we looked at the execution plans for one of the last tests run. All five tests had the exact same plans with differing costs. The cost of reading `rental_item_fact` increased slightly with higher compressions, but not in relation to the compression ratios. The optimizer did a relatively good job at estimating the cost of reading `rental_item_fact` and took into account how much of it was in memory for the `BASIC` compression query. So what took our baseline query so long to execute? The optimizer guessed it needed to read through 44GB of data whether it was in memory, on disk, or split between both. The connection to the Fusion ION tops out at just over 3.8 GB/second. Simple arithmetic reveals that it would take 11.57 seconds at that speed, so it must have used blocks left over in the buffer cache to return the query as fast as it did. The cost of doing the joins was estimated to be almost nothing compared to the cost of reading in the data, and that is confirmed by the fact that the query returned as fast as it could read the data off the disks. That explains our baseline, but what about the in-memory queries?

This query allows us to find how many GB/second Oracle can effectively scan through using the IMCS. Every system is different, but this test shows that this one server could effectively scan through over 27 GB/second with `QUERY` compression and 22 GB/second with `CAPACITY HIGH` compression. Like we've seen before, `CAPACITY` was inexplicably slow. These speeds are 5 to 7 times faster than reading from the Fusion ION, which is already pretty impressive. However, that's not the case. The optimizer figured 44GB for a full table in-memory scan, but in practice, Oracle used the column store, so it only read the data it needed and then decompressed it. The stats confirm this. The baseline query read in 36GB with 4.8 million logical reads, while the in-memory queries read in one block and had over 4,700 logical reads. The one block is interesting because it was actually only reading one row every time. The statistic "IM scan rows" had one more row than "IM scan rows valid" and explains this, though it's unclear why exactly one row would be invalid for every compression algorithm. This is one reason why Oracle might go to disk to get some data, even if its table or partition is in memory.

Query 5

The fifth query selected the title, sale price, and date of each rental for a single customer. The execution plan for the baseline query used the bitmap indexes in a join filter from the customer_ dim table to the rental_item_fact table. The in-memory queries also used the bitmap indexes, but they were able to scan customer_dim much faster. It was the only table they scanned because the "IM scan rows" statistic was only at 5 million. When joining to product_dim, it had the list of keys it needed from rental_item_fact, so it was able to access them directly in memory. The query time doesn't give an accurate picture of how much easier it was for the database to complete the query in memory, partly due to the fact that the times we're reporting include the time it took to output the results and execution plan with AUTOTRACE turned on.

Query 6

The sixth query was all about filtering. It returned five different sums from rental_item_fact where male customers purchased a PG or PG-13 rental in January 2013, and it grouped by those same columns to return two rows. The time for this query also understates how much less work the database did for the in-memory queries. The difference between the figures in Table 12-6 can possibly be used as a rough proxy for determining how expensive it is for Oracle to decompress

	NO INMEMORY	QUERY	CAPACITY	CAPACITY HIGH	BASIC
All queries	832695 (74327.3)	614554 (89766.9)	661014 (97236.2)	608015 (42985.4)	808307 (206266.4)
Query 1	5956 (55.1)	5759 (61.9)	23269 (73.2)	8245 (38.1)	5900 (63.6)
Query 2	16479 (287.9)	13286 (1220)	14811 (1370.6)	12080 (63.6)	20050 (16989.9)
Query 3	672070 (48745.7)	551086 (4819.5)	554460 (1715.9)	552232 (1135.9)	624797 (46226.2)
Query 4	113300 (557.1)	13796 (479.3)	31946 (332.8)	17578 (176.9)	69708 (2232.8)
Query 5	6793 (119)	350 (36.5)	634 (30.3)	477 (31.3)	300 (47)
Query 6	8750 (118.3)	3560 (226.2)	4955 (77.3)	3954 (185.3)	4790 (253.7)

TABLE 12-6. *Database Time, Average by Standard Deviation*

data based on the differences between the CPU used for the in-memory queries. As long as your database isn't running at capacity, the difference should be negligible.

DML Performance

This section discusses the performance of DML statements, like the INSERT, UPDATE, and DELETE statements. DML statements perform differently than queries because they lock rows.

Test Setup

To test the performance of the IMCS and how it responds to high loads, we used Dominic Giles' SwingBench utility, available at http://dominicgiles.com/swingbench.html. The utility includes some tutorials on how to install and test the OrderEntry schema. We generated about 120GB of data for testing, which is just under two times what the IMCS would hold and one and a half times the size of the IMCS, because we wanted to make sure that all of the tables used for querying would fit in memory. SwingBench creates 11 standard tables, and we marked all of them for in-memory use except the logon table, which is only inserted into when using SwingBench's standard settings. You'll want to set up the SSH credentials as well so that you can benchmark the CPU and IO stats. You'll need to run the SwingBench utility to set it up. Make sure you know where the configuration file is saved.

While there's a lot that you can do to automate the testing, all you really need to do is install the OrderEntry schema and then run tests on it. SwingBench comes with a CharBench command-line interface that we used for testing because it has a nice tabular output that can be captured for later analysis. The command we used to run CharBench was from an automated_ test_scripts directory we created inside SwingBench:

```
../bin/charbench -c ~/swingbench/automated_test_scripts/swingconfig.xml \
-u SOE_120 -p fiooral2 -dt thin -cs //10.50.241.101:2483/A12102 -uc 200 -ld 10 \
-intermax 0 -intermin 0 -max 0 -min 0 \
-r ~/swingbench/automated_test_scripts/test_results/OE_NO_INMEMORY.xml \
-rr 1 -rt 00:10 -stats full -bs 00:00 -be 00:10 \
-v tpm,tps,users,cpu,disk,trans,errs,resp,vresp -f -a \
&>OE_NO_INMEMORY-results.txt
```

A description of all the options used is available by running charbench -help. We used the other server that was part of the RAC cluster in the other chapters to run these options so that any overhead of tracking results from the test didn't interfere with the test itself. The output captured is tab separated and is easily imported into Excel or a database after some cleanup using the following from the test results directory:

```
for i in *.txt
do
  grep -R '^[0-9]' $i | sed -e "s/^/$i\t/" > results.tab
done
```

Make sure you use a sufficient number of users to generate the targeted load on the database, but not so many that all of them can't log on. We were only able to get about 1,300 dedicated connections even though we set the max processes to 5,000 in an effort to load test with 2,000 users. When all of our requested users couldn't log on, the results were inaccurate and the tests ran multiple times longer than they should have.

To make sure that we tested the performance of the in-memory options and not the server's ability to write to log files, we restarted the database in `noarchivelog` mode and created four 5GB log files on the Fusion ION Accelerator disks and dropped the previous log files. In between every test, we killed all hanging sessions for the user and got a new log file and flushed any active log files:

```
SQL> BEGIN
  2    FOR i IN (SELECT    *
  3              FROM      gv$session
  4              WHERE     username = UPPER('SOE_120')) LOOP
  5      BEGIN
  6        EXECUTE IMMEDIATE 'ALTER SYSTEM KILL SESSION '''||
  7          i.sid||', '||i.serial#||'''';
  8        EXCEPTION WHEN OTHERS THEN NULL;
  9      END;
 10    END LOOP;
 11  END;
 12  /
SQL> ALTER SYSTEM SWITCH logfile;
SQL> ALTER SYSTEM checkpoint;
```

To automate the tests, we used some bash scripting to make changes to the database using SQL*Plus and several SQL scripts and to run the `CharBench` tests.

Supporting Scripts

The following files are available on the McGraw-Hill Professional website to support this chapter:

■ The `queries.sql` script file runs all the queries.

■ The `dml_statements.sql` script file runs the sample INSERT, UPDATE, and DELETE statements.

Test Results

We ran several tests and took the averages after the first minute. We found that 200 concurrent users had better transactions per second than 500 or 1,000 users, and the test was enough to use all available CPU cycles. Table 12-7 shows some of the more important statistics that we gathered during our testing with 200 users and no wait times between transactions.

	Baseline	Query	Capacity	Capacity High
Avg. Transactions Per Minute	573,054	272,686	276,049	211,178
Avg. Transactions Per Second	9,543	4,545	4,587	3,514
Avg. Response in Milliseconds	15	27	27	35

TABLE 12-7. *Average Transactions per Time Interval*

We were quite surprised and frustrated that we couldn't get the in-memory tables to do as many transactions as Oracle could without the in-memory option, even though the buffer cache was only 12GB. In order to figure out why, we did a little digging in the code used to generate the load, which is wrapped up in a package called orderentry. The cost of doing an index scan versus using the in-memory tables was quite surprising.

You should recall that we are testing on some very fast disks and that even though we didn't show a speedup in transactional processing, databases using a SAN or other storage that is slower may benefit from putting tables in memory. We would have liked to have a SAN for testing to show the differences and get some more information about where the IMCS helps. This will raise the question of whether more memory or faster disks will increase the throughput and lifespan of your current hardware.

Table 12-8 shows the cost estimate differences between performing an index scan and using the in-memory tables.

In every case that Oracle could use an index, it did. We just forced the optimizer to estimate the cost using a NO_INDEX hint for some of the queries that it ran. We were particularly interested in the orders and order_items tables because the Order Products transactions were the slowest for the in-memory queries. We went through all queries and DML statements in the package and found only one place where code needed to be changed. It turns out that there is a part of a query in an inline view that looks like the following:

```
SQL> SELECT    order_id
  2  ,          customer_id
  3  FROM       orders
  4  WHERE      order_status <= 4
  5  AND        rownum < 10;
```

The problem with this is that there isn't an index on the order_status column, which doesn't seem to cause any issues with the performance of the benchmarks, but it causes a huge issue when putting the tables in memory. The cost of doing a full table scan on orders is estimated to be 2 because Oracle knows it's only fetching nine rows at most. The cost of 1,250 comes from having to decompress the entire table. This appears to be an issue in the implementation because Oracle has to decompress the entire table, not just one column, and apparently can't scan just the one column while compressed until it gets its nine rows and then decompresses the matching order_id and customer_id rows. We got the tests to run slightly faster by changing the code to include a NO_INMEMORY hint, but it really just needed an index added.

One temptation you might face is to get rid of all non-unique indexes to speed up inserts and updates. This would be a very poor choice, as Table 12-8 shows, because columns in the IMCS are still not as fast as an index lookup on a single value. All indexes that are required for transactional processing need to remain in place. The only indexes that might be dropped are those that are used to help improve large queries, such as indexes that the data warehouse might run periodically to update data in their ETL processes.

One thing you'll notice as transactions are run against in-memory tables is that the bytes_not_populated value in gv$im_segments will fluctuate. This is the result of the IMCS marking rows as invalid when they're updated or deleted or needing to bring inserted rows in memory. During our testing, the value of bytes_not_populated for the customers table never got over 1GB, but that's quite high considering that the table was only 10GB when we started testing. Generally, this was around 100–200MB and would return to zero within about a minute as long as the IMCS had enough room to fit the updated values. This is where the priority settings might

Index/Table	NO INMEMORY Cost	FOR QUERY Cost
address_cust_ix	6	5576
inv_product_ix	3	8
order_pk	4	7307
ord_customer_ix	6	7933
order_items_pk	6	15616
inventory_pk	3	14
cust_func_lower_name_ix	19	5564
ord_warehouse_ix	104	1815
ORDERS Table	2	1250

TABLE 12-8. *Comparison of Index Scan to Index In-Memory*

not be followed. If a CRITICAL priority table got a bunch of data that the IMCS didn't have room for, we never saw tables with a lower priority get moved out to make room. CAPACITY compression did the best at keeping the BYTES_NOT_POPULATED down when transactions were being run, but was only marginally better than QUERY and CAPACITY HIGH. You can't get inconsistent data, but because updating the IMCS can be asynchronous, you may not be able to use in-memory tables to prune queries. This is why transactional indexes need to stay in place. They update synchronously and can be relied on to have the same data that the underlying table has. Also, the IMCS only keeps data in memory that is in the underlying table, so functional indexes still have their place when doing lookups that will return only a few rows or when the computation is relatively expensive.

Summary
By now, you should be very familiar with the new In-Memory Column Store. While it isn't a silver bullet, it does what it's designed to do well. With the skills you acquired in this chapter, you can diagnose in-memory issues and build robust analytical and reporting solutions.

APPENDIX

Oracle Database
Java Primer

This appendix is a basic primer on Java that covers how you use the Java Database Connectivity (JDBC) model to access an Oracle database. It provides PL/SQL developers supporting reference to work through examples found in Chapters 1, 2, and 4. This appendix covers the following:

- Java and JDBC architecture
- Configuring the Java and Oracle environment
- Java programming language primer
- Testing a client-side or thin-driver JDBC connection
- Accessing scalar variables
- Writing and accessing large objects

Java and JDBC Architecture

Java is an object-oriented programming language (OOPL) that is portable across platforms. This means you can write one program and then run it on Linux, Unix, or Microsoft Windows operating systems. Java accomplishes this by compiling the programs into Java byte code. Byte code, also known as byte streams, runs inside virtual machines that are known as Java Virtual Machines (JVMs).

Virtual machines create self-contained environments. JVM environments are interfaces between Java byte code and operating system services. JVMs run on all major operating systems. JVMs are written in the C/C++ programming language and compiled individually for each platform. Java programs run inside the JVM with all the rights and privileges granted to the JVM by the operating system. The java.policy and java.security files set permissions for how all Java programs run inside a JVM.

Java provides networking libraries that let you pass messages between different JVMs. Messages communicate between JVMs through sockets. A socket is built between two ephemeral ports—one where it sends the message and another where it listens for incoming messages. Java communicates with databases by using the JDBC libraries. Java also lets you build Java Servlets— known as JServlets. JServlets let you handle URL requests, like an Apache HTTP Server. Commercial Oracle databases also allow you to write and deploy Java programs in the database. You write PL/SQL programs as interfaces to these internally stored libraries. The interfaces are known as PL/SQL wrappers.

Similar permissions to those found in the java.policy and java.security files for external programs are also found in the Oracle database. These policy files enable or restrict how Java programs work inside the Oracle database. You configure these policy files by using the functions and procedures found in the dbms_java package. Changes to these configuration files require you to connect using the sysdba role.

Oracle provides three JDBC drivers: the client-side or thin driver, the Oracle Call Interface (OCI) or thick driver, and the server-side internal driver. The drivers have specific roles that govern how Java works with the database. The OCI and server-side internal drivers support Java stored inside the database. The OCI can also support external programs resident on a server with an

Oracle server or client installation. The client-side or thin driver acts independently of a local Oracle database or client installation. The thin driver lets you connect remotely to the Oracle instance through the Oracle listener. The listener transfers the incoming request to the database and opens a connection to it.

Configuring and verifying that your Java programs can connect to the database are critical to deploying the technology. You cannot connect without setting appropriate PATH and CLASSPATH environment variables. The next section discusses how to configure and test your Java installation by connecting to the Oracle database instance.

Configuring the Oracle Java Environment

The Oracle database ships with the necessary libraries to create and run Java programs. Oracle Database 12c ships with the Oracle JDBC libraries for Java 1.4, 5, and 6. You should note Sun changed the version naming convention with Java 1.5, making it Java 5 and so forth.

You need to set your PATH and CLASSPATH variables to work with the Java programming language. You can configure Java many ways because there are many ways to deploy your Java SDK. While you can install a separate Java SDK for external Java programs, you'll need to use the Java SDK shipped with the Oracle database for locally stored programs. The following assumes you're using the Java 6 or Java 7 SDK from the Oracle database, and provides syntax for the Microsoft Windows, Linux, and Unix platforms.

Windows

```
C:> set PATH=%PATH%;C:%ORACLE_HOME%\jdk\bin
C:> set CLASSPATH=%CLASSPATH%;C:%ORACLE_HOME%\jdbc\lib\ojdbc7.jar
```

Unix

```
# export PATH=$PATH:/<mount>/$ORACLE_HOME/jdk/bin
# export CLASSPATH=$CLASSPATH:/<mount>/$ORACLE_HOME/jdbc/lib/ojdbc7.jar
```

You should now be able to test basic Java programs. Source files are native Java files before compilation. They are written as plain text files and adhere to the syntax rules of the Java programming language. Class files are compiled Java source files, and they are stored in Java byte code or compressed formats such as Java archive (JAR) files.

You can find a nice Java tutorial at http://docs.oracle.com/javase/tutorial/index.html. This appendix is a short version to get you up and running with Java programs. There are two executables that you'll need to compile and run Java programs:

- **javac**   Compiles your text file Java programs into Java byte code
- **java**   Runs your compiled Java byte code programs

The file naming convention in Java is case sensitive, and you should ensure you name files in a manner consistent with the web-based code example files. If you attempt to compile a Java file when the file name and class name are different, you'll receive an error. Also, the file extension for Java programs is always a lowercase .java.

Microsoft Windows Presents Challenges to Java

Microsoft Windows is a case-insensitive operating system, while Linux and Unix are case sensitive. The case matters when you create files in Windows. You can change the case of a file name by using the RENAME command.

The file name's case can differ from the case provided as an argument to the javac program on the Windows platform. For example, a WriteReadCLOB.java file can be compiled as a WriteReadCLOB.class without raising an error. However, the case for the class file name must match exactly with the name defining the class in the source code. When it doesn't, you'll get the following error when you attempt to compile the Java source code:

```
C:\JavaDev>javac WriteReadCLOB.java
WriteReadCLOB.java:32: class WriteReadCLOB is public, should be declared
in a file named WriteReadCLOB.java
public class WriteReadCLOB extends JFrame {
            ^
1 error
```

There is another nuance you need to understand. No compilation errors are raised when the file name matches the case of the internal source but the name differs as an argument to the javac executable. This generates a runtime error:

```
C:\JavaDev>java WriteReadCLOB
Exception in thread "main" java.lang.NoClassDefFoundError: WriteReadCLOB
(wrong name: WriteReadCLOB)
    at java.lang.ClassLoader.defineClass1(Native Method)
    at java.lang.ClassLoader.defineClass(ClassLoader.java:620)
    at java.security.SecureClassLoader.defineClass(SecureClassLoader.
java:124)
    at java.net.URLClassLoader.defineClass(URLClassLoader.java:260)
    at java.net.URLClassLoader.access$000(URLClassLoader.java:56)
    at java.net.URLClassLoader$1.run(URLClassLoader.java:195)
    at java.security.AccessController.doPrivileged(Native Method)
    at java.net.URLClassLoader.findClass(URLClassLoader.java:188)
    at java.lang.ClassLoader.loadClass(ClassLoader.java:306)
    at sun.misc.Launcher$AppClassLoader.loadClass(Launcher.java:276)
    at java.lang.ClassLoader.loadClass(ClassLoader.java:251)
    at java.lang.ClassLoader.loadClassInternal(ClassLoader.java:319)
```

The solution is twofold. First, always remember to name the files the same as the source file class name. Second, always compile a class using the same case as the source file class name.

The `javac` executable compiles text files into Java byte code. Compiled code is known as Java class files. The JVM interprets Java class files at runtime by using the `java` executable.

Java uses a `main()` method to start a program from the command line. The `main()` method acts as the launching pad for the program when calling it from the `java` executable. You can only use classes without a `main()` method as class instances inside other Java class files.

The smallest footprint for a Java program is a Java class with only a `main()` method definition. The following illustrates a basic program. It defines a class that contains only a `main()` method. The `main()` method calls a static method to print a string to standard output. This program lets you check whether you have correctly configured your Java environment:

```
public class HelloWorld {
  public static void main(String args[]) {
    System.out.println("Hello World."); }}
```

Assuming you're at the command line in the same directory as the Java program, use the following syntax to compile the file:

```
javac HelloWorld.java
```

You may then execute the Java program class file:

```
java HelloWorld
```

If it executes successfully, you will see the following output:

```
Hello World.
```

You have now configured and verified your Java environment. The next section provides a whirlwind tour of the Java programming language.

Java Programming Language Primer

The Java programming language was originally developed to support embedded devices. The embedded device language Oak was renamed Java in the early 1990s. Java is an object-oriented programming language. This means that the basic programming unit is known as an *object* or *class*. The programming language also shares many syntax rules with the C++ programming language.

Java Basics

The language defines a class by specifying four items. The first item is an optional access modifier, which can be `public`, `protected`, `private`, or *default*. The compiler assumes a *default* access modifier when one is not provided. The second item is a reserved word `class`. The third is a case-sensitive class name. The fourth is an implementation inside curly braces. Curly braces designate your coding blocks—class, condition if-then-else, loop, method, etc. The generic prototype of a class is

```
[public | protected | private] class class_name [extends parent_class] {}
```

Access modifiers determine who can execute a copy of the class. Table A-1 lists the access modifiers. You use access modifiers to qualify classes, variables, and methods. Classes can

Access Modifier	Access from Same Class	Access from Same Package	Access from Subclass	Access from Another Package
public	✓	✓	✓	✓
protected	✓	✓	✓	
(default)	✓	✓		
private	✓			

TABLE A-1. *Access Modifiers*

contain variable definitions, declarations, nested classes (known as inner classes), and methods. You should also organize your Java classes into packages. Packages act like database user accounts, and access modifiers act like grants to users. Packages provide libraries of related classes that work cooperatively to solve business problems.

The extends clause is optional in your code. You extend the base *Object* class by default. Java is a single-root node object hierarchy, and the *Object* class is the topmost class file. All classes inherit the base behaviors of the *Object* class. Classes that extend the behavior of a child node of the *Object* class inherit all behaviors of their parent class, as well as of the parent class antecedents up to and including the *Object* class.

Interfaces are also optional. *Interfaces* specify methods that classes must implement. They let you define a general set of behaviors for a set of classes.

Packages are directories where you place your code before creating libraries. *Libraries* are known as Java archive (JAR) files. You assign directories before the class definition, using a prototype like

```
package company_name.directory_name.subdirectory_name;
```

For example, a company name of plsql and package name of fileio would look like the folder structure in Figure A-1. After you define your library of Java classes, you can use the jar executable to create a Java archive. You can then use the code in the Java archive file by referencing it in your CLASSPATH environment variable.

The package command must be the first program in your class file. It is followed by any importing commands. You import other classes that you use inside your class implementation. The following prototype imports a *Component* class from the awt package of the rt.jar Java archive:

```
import java.awt.Component;
```

FIGURE A-1. *Package hierarchy for* FileIO.jar

There was no reference to the `rt.jar` file when you set the `CLASSPATH` earlier. None is required because the Java compiler and runtime executables know where the file is located and it is built into the compiler configuration.

You can define attributes and methods in your class implementation. The naming rules differ from the convention. The rules are that a variable or method name (also known as an identifier) can include characters, digits, underscores, and dollar signs. Variable names cannot use any of the reserved words found in Table A-2.

You also define variables by specifying a valid type followed by a name or identifier. Java has eight primitive types, which are listed and described in Table A-3. These types qualify characters, numbers, and Boolean true and false values. Any class in your `CLASSPATH` source may also define a variable type, such as `java.lang.String`.

After you define a variable, you assign it a value. This can be done with a string or numeric literal or with an instance of a class. Class instances are more often known as object instances, and they are runtime containers of class definitions. You create a runtime class container by "initializing" a copy of the class. You declare a variable when you both define and assign a value on the same statement line. Examples of declaring variables are

```
boolean my_boolean = true;                     // Declare a Boolean.
byte my_byte = 1;                              // Declare a byte.
float my_float = 3000F;                        // Declare a float.
String string = new String("My New String"); // Declare a class instance.
```

Two forward slashes (//) designate a single-line comment. The /* starts a multiple-line comment that is ended by the */. Single-line comments are easy but can be problematic when you have a closing curly brace that is at the end of the line. It will comment out the closing curly brace and leave your block open. You should check to make sure you don't open your code block by commenting out closing curly braces.

Variable definitions and declarations can only be made inside code block curly braces. Declaring variables also lets you call methods of the current class or referenced classes. You can designate variables as static or instance variables. A *static* variable is known as a class variable

abstract	continue	Float	new	switch
assert	default	Goto	package	synchronized
boolean	do	If	private	this
break	double	Implements	protected	throw
byte	else	Import	public	throws
case	enum	Instanceof	return	transient
catch	extends	Int	short	try
char	for	interface	static	void
class	final	long	strictfp	volatile
const	finally	native	super	while

TABLE A-2. *Java Reserved Word List*

Name	Range	Size
char	The `char` data type is a single 16-bit Unicode character. It has a minimum value of `'\u0000'` (or 0) and a maximum value of `'\uffff'` (or 65,535).	16-bit unsigned
boolean	The `boolean` data type has only two possible values: `true` and `false`.	Unpublished
byte	The `byte` data type is an 8-bit signed two's complement integer. It has a minimum value of –128 and a maximum value of 127.	8-bit signed
int	The `int` data type is a 32-bit signed two's complement integer. It has a minimum value of –2,147,483,648 and a maximum value of 2,147,483,647.	32-bit signed
double	The `double` data type is a double-precision 64-bit IEEE 754 floating point number. It has a negative range between –1.7976931348623157E + 308 to –4.9E – 324; and it has a positive range between 1.4E – 45 to 1.7976931348623157E + 308.	64-bit IEEE 754
float	The `float` data type is a single-precision 32-bit IEEE 754 floating point number. It has a negative range between –3.4028235E + 38 to –1.4E – 45; and it has a positive range between 1.4E – 45 to 3.4028235E + 38.	32-bit IEEE 754
long	The `long` data type is a 64-bit signed two's complement integer. It has a minimum value of –9,223,372,036,854,775,808 and a maximum value of 9,223,372,036,854,775,807.	64-bit signed
short	The `short` data type is a 16-bit signed two's complement integer. It has a minimum value of –32,768 and a maximum value of 32,767.	16-bit signed

TABLE A-3. *Java Primitive Data Types*

and is assigned a value at compile time. *Instance* variables are known as runtime variables and have no value until you instantiate a runtime class instance. Examples of writing and using each are in the sample code of this appendix.

Coding logic, like if-then-else statements and loops, reside in methods. Methods are functions or subroutines in class files. Two methods have special rules. The first is the main() method, which is used to run a class from the command line. It is the externally executable access to your program. The main() method from the HelloWorld.java class shows you how to implement a class file that is callable from the command line. It prints a string to the standard output device.

The second special method is the constructor method, which must have the exact case-sensitive name as the enclosing file. You don't need to provide a constructor method when you want to use the default constructor because the compiler generates one when none is provided in the source file. Default constructors take no formal parameters. However, if you implement a class with an overriding constructor, the compiler no longer automatically creates a default constructor. After adding any constructor method, you must implement a constructor with no formal parameters when required. The following shows the default constructor built for the `HelloWorld.java` file:

```
public HelloWorld() {};
```

Java Assignment Operators

Assignment is straightforward when you assign the contents of one variable to another variable of the same type. You do it with the equal symbol (=). It is not straightforward when you're assigning a different type, because that involves a casting operation. *Casting* is taking the value in one data type and moving it to another data type.

You can cast any primitive to a more precise primitive because nothing is lost. On the other hand, you must explicitly state your intent when you cast a more precise primitive to a less precise data type. This explicit acknowledgement ensures that developers know that they are intentionally sacrificing precision. An example of this is found in the following code snippet:

```
int i;
float f = 30001.4F;
i = (int) f;
```

The first line defines a variable `i`, and its initial value is null. The second line assigns a real number (designated by the trailing `F`) to the variable `f`. The third line takes the real number and explicitly casts it as an *Integer*. This is known as downcasting. You *downcast* when you assign a value from a more precise data type to a less precise one. The assignment tells the program to discard the right side of the decimal and assign the left side to the *Integer* variable.

You can also downcast *Object* types. Downcasting an object instance actually makes the behavior more general. An example of downcasting a *String* to an *Object* is

```
String s = new String("Hello");
Object o = (Object) s;
```

This section has covered Java basics. The next section covers how to make conditional decisions and repeat operations until conditions are met.

Java Conditional and Iterative Structures

You have if-then-else and switch statements in Java. The if statement may include curly braces that define operating scope. Curly braces are necessary when the code block is more than a single statement. You may exclude curly braces when the code block is a single statement. The following provides an example that uses curly braces with single-statement code blocks:

```
if (someVariable == 0) {
  statement1; }
else if (someVariable == 1) {
  statement2; }
else {
  statement3; }
```

The if statement performs a comparison operation. Comparisons can be tricky when you forget to use two equal symbols and substitute a single equal statement. A single equal symbol performs an assignment and does not raise a compilation error. Unfortunately, these types of errors only manifest themselves during program runtime. You can also compare inequalities by using the less than, less than or equal to, and other operators.

NOTE
The comparison operator is a little thing if you write more Java than PL/SQL but a big thing when the opposite is true. PL/SQL uses the equal symbol for comparisons.

TIP
Always consider using curly braces to delimit code blocks. They save you time debugging when modifying code, which can add statements in conditional blocks.

Java `switch` statements work like those in C++ and C#. Unlike PL/SQL `CASE` statements, `switch` statements experience fall-through without `break` statements in each case. *Fall-through* is the principle of finding a match and then executing everything from that point forward until you encounter a `break` statement. You can use a `char` or `int` variable for a simple `switch` statement and use any Boolean expression for a searched case. The following illustrates a simple `switch` statement using an `int` variable:

```
int someVariable = 2;
switch (someVariable) {
  case 1:
    statement1;
    break;
  case 2:
    statement2;
    break;
  default:
    statement3;
    break; }
```

Iterative statements are loops. You have the do-while, for, and while loops in the Java programming language. The do-while loop doesn't set an entrance barrier and runs until the exit criterion is met at the bottom of the loop. Both of the other loops set an entrance barrier and run until the exit criterion is met at the top of the loop. Figure A-2 shows the flowcharts for these loop structures.

You should note that you can use a logical AND (`&&`) to make the criterion the result of two criteria. Likewise, you can use a logical OR (`||`) to make the criterion the result of one of two criteria. The following example checks for real numbers not between 6 and 7:

```
if ((variableOne < 6) && (variableOne > 7))
```

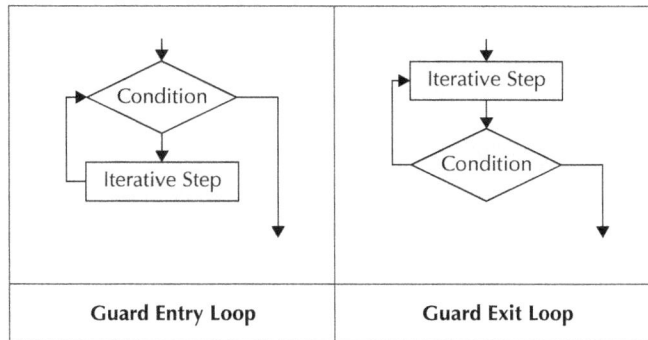

FIGURE A-2. *Iterative control flow diagrams*

The do-while Loop

The do-while loop guarantees that your loop runs *once* before checking the criterion. The criterion is generally a variable set prior to the beginning of the loop. This is known as a *gate on exit* loop. The `while` statement follows the closing curly brace and requires a semicolon because it is a statement. The general syntax is

```
do {
   repeatingStatement;
} while (someVariable == 0);
```

The while Loop

The while loop checks for a condition on entry. Like the do-while loop, the while loop also relies on a variable set before the loop. This is known as a *gate on entry* loop. Unlike the do-while loop, the `while` statement is not followed by a semicolon because it is followed by the code block designated by curly braces. The general syntax is

```
while(someVariable == 0) {
   repeatingStatement;
}
```

The for Loop

The for loop behaves differently than the while loop because the evaluation variable is set in the statement. This is another variation of gate on entry loops. The criterion of a for loop is defined by a numeric variable, limit, and incrementing or decrementing value. The general syntax is

```
for (int i; i < someValue; i++) {
   repeatingStatement;
}
```

The `i++` is a post-operation unary operator, and it adds 1 to the value of the number after performing that line's action. A pre-operation unary operator is defined by `--i`, and it decrements the variable before performing that line's action. The double pluses are for incrementing, while double minuses are for decrementing. They are interchangeable as pre- or post-operation unary operators.

Java Method Definitions

You define subroutines in Java as methods. They can be static or instance methods. Static methods have the ability of being called without instantiating a class, whereas you must instantiate a class for an instance method. You should assign access modifiers to method definitions. The *default* access method is assigned when you don't explicitly assign an access modifier. The downside of the *default* modifier is that the method can't be subclassed by another class.

TIP
The default method is ideal when you want to prevent subclassing a method that has tightly coupled dependencies.

The following prototype defines a `private static` method:

```
private static String someMethod(String someFormalParameter) {
  String someString =  new String("some string literal");
  someStatement;
  return someString; }
```

The following prototype defines a `public` non-static or instance method:

```
public String someMethod(String someFormalParameter) {
  String someString =  new String("some string literal");
  someStatement;
  return someString; }
```

You can execute a static method without instantiating an object instance. The excerpt from the `WriteReadCLOB.java` program demonstrates a static call (using basic Network Input and Output, or NIO):

```
clobText = FileIO.openFile(FileIO.findFile(this));
```

While this uses NIO, you can also use NIO2 with Java 7. We've opted to use NIO in this example because it's more frequently used at the time of writing.

The static method lets you open a file chooser. It passes the `this` operator as an actual parameter. The static method returns the contents of a character file as a Java `String`.

Calling an instance method is always a two-step process. First, you create an instance or a copy of the other class as a variable in your current class file. Creating an instance of a class is also known as *instantiating* a class. After you create an instance of the class, you can then call an instance method by appending the class method using a period. The example from the `WriteReadCLOB.java` file creates a variable of the `DataConnectionPane` class and names it `message`:

```
private DataConnectionPane message = new DataConnectionPane();
```

Later in the same program, a call is made to an instance method of the instantiated class:

```
host = message.getHost();
```

There are also varied means of chaining methods and return types, but they're beyond the scope of this primer. However, the basic rule is that *the object return type from a method provides a class instance, and you can then append any instance method to it.*

Java try-catch Blocks

The `try-catch` block is a mechanism to manage error handling. You place statements in the `try` block that may fail on an external resource. Then you place code to catch, report, and log errors in the `catch` block. You also have the `finally` block, and you put code in it that you want executed whether the `try` block failed or not. The following is a prototype for the `try-catch-finally` block:

```
try {
  resource_statement; }
catch (Exception e) {
  exception_handling_statement; }
finally {
  always_process_statement; }
```

You are required to use a `try-catch` block when calling a class method that throws an exception. If you're unaware that one is required, the Java compiler will throw an exception when you try to compile your code without the `try-catch` block and one is required.

This section has reviewed the basics of using the Java programming language. Broader tutorials are found at the http://docs.oracle.com/javase/tutorial/ web page. The next section demonstrates how to verify a connection to an Oracle database. Subsequent sections work with various data types, like scalar variables and large objects.

Testing a Client-Side or Thin-Driver JDBC Connection

Oracle Database 11*g* introduces a significant change to how JDBC connections work. You no longer connect directly to the database beginning with the `ojdbc6.jar` library. You connect through the new database collection pool using Java 6 or 7. This change means that every program you had working in Java 5 must be rewritten to work in your new Oracle Database 12*c* instance. Alternatively, you may continue to use the `ojdbc6.jar` file that is also provided in the Oracle Database 12*c* instance.

Import packages for the Oracle JDBC implementation are found in Table A-4. The Oracle `ojdbc6.jar` library and forward adds the *OracleDataSource* class and deletes the *DriverManager* class. You should consider using the new connection pool to better utilize database resources.

The examples in this appendix connect through the new connection pool. If you would like to connect directly, please see the "Comparative JDBC Syntax" sidebar.

Package Import Statements	Description
`import java.sql.*;`	Standard JDBC packages.
`import java.math.*;`	The *BigDecimal* and *BigInteger* classes.
`import oracle.jdbc.*;`	Oracle extensions to JDBC.
`import oracle.jdbc.pool.*;`	*OracleDataSource* class used to connect through the Oracle Database 11*g* connection pool, using the `ojdbc6.jar` libraries.
`import oracle.sql.*;`	Oracle type extensions.

TABLE A-4. *Package JDBC Import Statements*

Comparative JDBC Syntax

You can connect directly to the Oracle Database 12*c* database by using the `ojdbc6.jar` or `ojdbc7.jar` libraries. You need to put one of the older Java archives in your `CLASSPATH` environment variable. If you have two JDBC Java archives in your `CLASSPATH` environment, the *DatabaseMetaData* class uses the driver information from the first Java archive in the `CLASSPATH`. The following code lets you connect directly to the database:

```
// Load Oracle JDBC driver.
DriverManager.registerDriver(new oracle.jdbc.driver.OracleDriver());

// Define connection.
Connection conn = DriverManager.getConnection("jdbc:oracle:thin:@" +
                  host + ":" + port + ":" + database, user, password);
```

The new syntax works with Oracle 11*g* and forward and supports a connection pool. It instantiates an *OracleDataSource* instance and then sets the URL, user, and password for the connections, as shown here:

```
// Set the Pooled Connection Source.
OracleDataSource ods = new OracleDataSource();
String url = "jdbc:oracle:thin:@//" + host + ":" + port + "/" + db;
ods.setURL(url);
ods.setUser(user);
ods.setPassword(passwd)

// Define connection.
Connection conn = ods.getConnection();
```

If you look closely at the difference between the connections, the old syntax uses the @ symbol to resolve through the TNS alias (found in the `tnsnames.ora` file). The new syntax resolves through a URL listening on the same port as the Oracle Database 12*c* database listener.

You must choose which syntax works best for your purposes. Migrating to the new connection pool requires fixing all data abstraction layers that communicate directly with the database.

The following Java program lets you test your JDBC connection. It collects input arguments to connect to an Oracle instance when you run it. The program queries a string literal from the dual table. You provide the following input parameters when you run the program:

```
----------------------------------------------------------------
Enter User [UID/PASSWD]: <userid>/<passwd>
Enter Host Name: <hostname.domain_name>
Enter Port Name: <listener_port>
Enter Database Name: <tns_alias>
```

Appendix A of *Oracle Database 12c PL/SQL Programming* explains what the tns_alias is and how it resolves connections to the database instance. The readEntry() method is also available in the FileIO.java class as a static method if you'd like to leverage a preexisting command-line interface. You would call the method like

```
String commandInput = FileIO.readEntry();
```

You can use this class file to connect to any Oracle database through the Oracle listener:

```java
// Class imports.
import java.io.IOException;
import java.sql.Connection;
import java.sql.DatabaseMetaData;
import java.sql.ResultSet;
import java.sql.ResultSetMetaData;
import java.sql.SQLException;
import java.sql.Statement;

// Oracle class imports.
import oracle.jdbc.driver.OracleDriver;
import oracle.jdbc.pool.OracleDataSource;
// ------------------------------------------------------------------/
public class HelloWorldThin {
  // Define a static class String variable.
  private static String user;

  // ------------------------------------------------------------------/
  private static void printLine() {
    printLine(null); }
  // ------------------------------------------------------------------/
  private static void printLine(String s) {
    if (s != null) {
      System.out.println(s); }

    // Print line.
    System.out.print  ("----------------------------------------");
    System.out.println("----------------------------------------"); }
  // ------------------------------------------------------------------/
  private static String readEntry() {
    try {

      // Define method variables.
      int c;
      StringBuffer buffer = new StringBuffer();
```

```java
      // Read first character.
      c = System.in.read();

      // Read remaining characters.
      while (c != '\n' && c != -1) {
        buffer.append((char) c);
        c = System.in.read(); }

      // Return buffer.
      return buffer.toString().trim(); }
    catch (IOException e) {
      return null; }}
// ----------------------------------------------------------------/
public static void main(String args[]) throws SQLException, IOException {
  // Define method variables.
  boolean debug = false;
  int slashIndex;
  String userIn;
  String password;
  String host;
  String port;
  String database;
  String debugString = new String("DEBUG");

  // Print line.
  printLine();

  // Verify and print debug mode.
  if (args.length > 0) {
    if (args[0].toUpperCase().equals(debugString)) {
      debug = true;
      printLine("Debug mode is enabled."); }
    else {
      for (int i = 0;i < args.length;i++) {
        System.out.println("Incorrect argument(s): [" + args[i] + "]"); }

      // Print line and message.
      printLine();
      printLine("Valid case insensitive argument is: DEBUG."); }}

  // Prompt, read, and capture credentials.
  System.out.print("Enter User [UID/PASSWD]: ");

  // Read input.
  userIn = readEntry();

  // Parse and check for token between user name and password.
  slashIndex = userIn.indexOf("/");
  if (slashIndex != -1) {
    user = userIn.substring(0, slashIndex);
    password = userIn.substring(slashIndex + 1); }
  else {
    user = userIn;
    System.out.print("Enter Password: ");
    password = readEntry(); }
```

```
// Prompt, read, and capture host name.
System.out.print("Enter Host Name: ");
host = readEntry();

// Prompt, read, and capture port number.
System.out.print("Enter Port Number: ");
port = readEntry();

// Prompt, read, and capture database name.
System.out.print("Enter Database Name: ");
database = readEntry();

// Print line and message.
printLine("Connecting to the database ...");
printLine("jdbc:oracle:oci8:@" +
          host + ":" + port + ":" + database + "," +
          user + "," + password);

// Attempt database connection.
try {
  // Set the Pooled Connection Source
  OracleDataSource ods = new OracleDataSource();
  String url = "jdbc:oracle:thin:@//" + host + ":" + port + "/" + db;
  ods.setURL(url);
  ods.setUser(user);
  ods.setPassword(passwd);

  // Define connection.
  Connection conn = ods.getConnection();

  // Signal connection.
  printLine("Connected.");

  // Define metadata object and print message.
  DatabaseMetaData dmd = conn.getMetaData();
  printLine("Driver Version: [" + dmd.getDriverVersion() + "]\n" +
            "Driver Name:    [" + dmd.getDriverName() + "]");

  // Create and execute statement.
  Statement stmt = conn.createStatement();
  ResultSet rset = stmt.executeQuery("SELECT 'Hello World.' FROM dual");

  // Read row returns.
  while (rset.next()) {
    printLine(rset.getString(1)); }

  // Close result set.
  rset.close();
  stmt.close();
  conn.close();

  // Print line and message.
  printLine("The JDBC Connection worked."); }
catch (SQLException e) {
  if (debug) {
```

```
      e.printStackTrace();
      printLine(); }
   else {
     if (e.getSQLState() == null) {
       System.out.println(
         new SQLException("Oracle Thin Client Net8 Connection Error.",
                 "ORA-" + e.getErrorCode() +
                 ": Incorrect Net8 thin client arguments:\n\n" +
                 "  host name       [" + host + "]\n" +
                 "  port number     [" + port + "]\n" +
                 "  database name [" + database + "]\n",
                 e.getErrorCode()).getSQLState()); }
     else {
       // Trim the postpended "\n".
       printLine(e.getMessage().substring(0,e.getMessage().length() - 1)); }}

   // Print line and message.
   printLine("The JDBC Connection failed."); }}}
```

Before introducing the program, you saw the program output to collect arguments. The balance of the output is shown next:

```
Connecting to the database ...
------------------------------------------------------------------
jdbc:oracle:oci8:@<hostname.domain_name>:<port>:<sid>,<uid>,<passwd>
------------------------------------------------------------------
Connected.
------------------------------------------------------------------
Driver Version: [11.1.0.0.0-Alpha]
Driver Name:    [Oracle JDBC driver]
------------------------------------------------------------------
Hello World.
------------------------------------------------------------------
The JDBC Connection worked.
------------------------------------------------------------------
```

NOTE
You should check the management of the ORA-17002 error in the SQL connection catch block. It can be very useful when writing Java programs that use distributed architectures like Enterprise JavaBeans (EJBs).

Java Classes Stored in the Oracle Database
Internally stored Java class files require you to configure the env parameter in your listener.ora file. You will need to set the LD_LIBRARY_PATH in the listener.ora file. You set it by providing the canonical path to the generic Oracle libraries in the lib and jdbc/lib directories of the Oracle home. Appendix A of *Oracle Database 12c PL/SQL Programming* contains detailed steps to set up your listener.ora file.

Your setup is incomplete or incorrect if you encounter any error messages or console printing errors. You'll need to revisit the instructions and troubleshoot the problem.

Accessing Scalar Variables

Java Swing applications let you build nice testing tools to verify data sets returned by your J2EE or J3EE beans. The `JTable` works well with scalar type variables, but does not work well with large objects. Binary Large Objects (BLOBs) and Character Large Objects (CLOBs) are displayed in a single line. LONG data types display in `JTable` classes like BLOB and CLOB types. Character File (CFILE) and Binary File (BFILE) large objects simply can't be displayed in a `JTable`.

When you run the `QueryTable.java` program, you're presented with a tabbed dialog box to enter database connection information. Figure A-3 shows how the dialog looks. You should enter your hostname with a fully qualified domain name in the Host tab. Enter the listening port number for the Oracle database in the Port tab. Enter the TNS alias, discussed in Appendix A of the *Oracle Database 12c PL/SQL Programming*, in the Database tab. You should then enter the user account name in the UserID tab and the password in the Password tab.

You can modify the query to work with any table using the `DataTablePane.class` library file. The class allows you to enter any valid table name. Table A-5 lists three constants that change the number of tabs displayed. An operating system prompt is provided in all cases with a Windows default value.

After you are prompted for the connection string components, you will be prompted for the table name, as shown in Figure A-4. Later in this appendix there is a variation of this interface that uses all five columns.

This program only displays dates, strings, and numbers in the `JTable`. If you want to also work with CLOB data types, you can borrow that feature from the `WriteReadCLOB.java` file later in this appendix. Other data types don't work well with the *JTable*, and you should consider alternative solutions. Figure A-5 shows the returned data after some manipulation of column widths.

FIGURE A-3.   *Database connection input dialog*

Constant Names	Constant Uses
TABLE_COLUMN_ALL	You use this constant to instantiate a tabbed pane with only a prompt for the table name. Use this when you want to return all columns from a table.
TABLE_AND_COLUMN	You use this constant to instantiate a tabbed pane with a prompt for table and column. Use this when you want to return all rows of a column.
TABLE_COLUMN_KEY	You use this constant to instantiate a tabbed pane with a prompt for table, column, primary key column name, and primary key column value. Use this when you want to return only a filtered set of rows of a column.

TABLE A-5. *Static Constants for the* DataTablePane.java *Class*

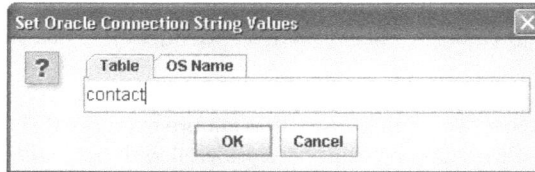

FIGURE A-4. *Database query input dialog*

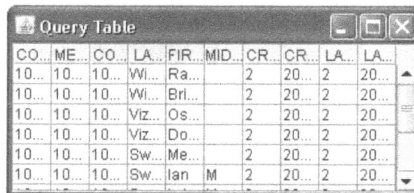

FIGURE A-5. QueryTable.java *display*

The `QueryTable.java` program shows how you retrieve, format, and display scalar types. It displays the results in a `JTable`. The program imports individual classes so you can see all the dependencies. The program follows:

```java
// Java Application class imports.
import java.awt.Component;
import java.awt.Dimension;
import java.awt.image.BufferedImage;
import java.awt.GridLayout;
import javax.swing.JFrame;
import javax.swing.JOptionPane;
import javax.swing.JPanel;
import javax.swing.JScrollPane;
import javax.swing.JTable;
import javax.swing.table.DefaultTableModel;
import javax.swing.table.TableCellRenderer;
import javax.swing.table.TableColumn;
import javax.swing.table.TableModel;

// Generic JDBC imports.
import java.sql.Clob;
import java.sql.Connection;
import java.sql.DatabaseMetaData;
import java.sql.DriverManager;
import java.sql.ResultSet;
import java.sql.ResultSetMetaData;
import java.sql.SQLException;
import java.sql.Statement;

// Oracle class imports.
import oracle.jdbc.driver.OracleDriver;
import oracle.jdbc.pool.OracleDataSource;

// Include book libraries (available at publisher's website).
import plsql.fileio.FileIO;
import plsql.jdbc.DataConnectionPane;
import plsql.jdbc.DataTablePane;
// -----------------------------------------------------------------/
public class QueryTable extends JFrame {
  // Define database connections.
  private String host;
  private String port;
  private String dbname;
  private String userid;
  private String passwd;

  // Define query variables.
  private String tableName;

  // Define data connection pane.
  private DataConnectionPane message = new DataConnectionPane();
  private DataTablePane table = new DataTablePane(DataTablePane.TABLE_COLUMN_ALL);

  // Construct the class.
  public QueryTable (String s) {
    super(s);
```

```java
    // Get database connection values or exit.
    if (JOptionPane.showConfirmDialog(this,message
        ,"Set Oracle Connection String Values"
        ,JOptionPane.OK_CANCEL_OPTION) == 0) {

      // Set class connection variables.
      host = message.getHost();
      port = message.getPort();
      dbname = message.getDatabase();
      userid = message.getUserID();
      passwd = message.getPassword();

      // Print connection to console (debugging tool).
      message.getConnection();

      // Collect query parameters.
      if (JOptionPane.showConfirmDialog(this,table
          ,"Set Oracle Connection String Values"
          ,JOptionPane.OK_CANCEL_OPTION) == 0) {

        // Set class query variables.
        tableName = table.getTableName();

      // Create a JPanel for data display.
      ManageTable panel = new ManageTable();

      // Configure the JPanel.
      panel.setOpaque(true);
      setContentPane(panel);

      // Configure the JFrame.
      setDefaultCloseOperation(JFrame.EXIT_ON_CLOSE);
      setLocation(100,100);
      pack();
      setVisible(true); }
    else
      System.exit(1); }
// ------------------------------------------------------------------/
private class ManageTable extends JPanel {
  // Define target table and query row size variable.
  private String target = tableName;
  private int querySize = 0;

  // Define containers.
  private Object[][] data = getQuery(host,port,dbname,userid,passwd,target);
  private Object[][] cells = getData();
  private Object[] columns = getColumnHeaders();

  // Define display variables.
  private JTable table = new JTable(cells,columns);
  private JScrollPane scrollPane;
  private TableModel tableModel;
  // ------------------------------------------------------------------/
  public ManageTable () {
    super(new GridLayout(1,0));
```

```
   decorate(300,100); }
// ----------------------------------------------------------------/
private String[] getColumnHeaders() {
  // Size container, copy column headers, and return data.
  String[] headers = new String[data[0].length];
  for (int i = 0;i < data[0].length;i++)
    headers[i] = (String) data[0][i];
  return headers; }
// ----------------------------------------------------------------/
private Object[][] getData() {
  // Size container, copy cells, and return data.
  Object[][] cells = new Object[querySize][];
  for (int i = 0;i < querySize;i++) {
    cells[i] = new Object[data[i + 1].length];
    for (int j = 0;j < data[i + 1].length;j++)
      cells[i][j] = data[i + 1][j]; }
  return cells; }
// ----------------------------------------------------------------/
private void decorate (int width, int height) {
  // Configure JPanel.
  setSize(width,height);

  // Configure and initialize JTable.
  table.setPreferredScrollableViewportSize(new Dimension(width,height));
  table.setFillsViewportHeight(true);
  initColumns(table);

  // Assign JScrollPane.
  scrollPane = new JScrollPane(table);
  add(scrollPane); }
// ----------------------------------------------------------------/
private void initColumns(JTable table) {
  // Initialize cell width.
  int headerWidth = 0;
  int cellWidth = 0;

  // Define display variables.
  Component component = null;
  TableColumn tableColumn = null;
  TableCellRenderer headerRenderer =
    table.getTableHeader().getDefaultRenderer();

  // Initialize TableModel class.
  tableModel = table.getModel();

  // Initialize columns.
  for (int i = 0;i < table.getColumnCount();i++)
    tableColumn = table.getColumnModel().getColumn(i); }
// ----------------------------------------------------------------/
private Object[][] getQuery(String host,String port,String dbname
                          ,String user,String pswd,String table) {
  // Define return type container.
  Object[][] dataset = null;
  String[] datatype = null;

  try {
```

```java
   // Load driver, initialize connection, metadata, and statement..
   OracleDataSource ods = new OracleDataSource();
   String url = "jdbc:oracle:thin:@//"+host+":"+port+"/"+dbname;
   ods.setURL(url);
   ods.setUser(userid);
   ods.setPassword(passwd);
   Connection conn = ods.getConnection();
   DatabaseMetaData dmd = conn.getMetaData();
   Statement stmt = conn.createStatement();

   // Declare result set, initialize dataset, and close result set.
   ResultSet rset = stmt.executeQuery("SELECT COUNT(*) FROM " + table);
   while (rset.next())
     dataset = new Object[rset.getInt(1) + 1][];
   rset.close();

   // Reusing result set and get result set metadata.
   rset = stmt.executeQuery("SELECT * FROM " + table);
   ResultSetMetaData rsmd = rset.getMetaData();

   // Declare row counter.
   int row = 0;

   // Assign array sizes.
   dataset[row] = new Object[rsmd.getColumnCount()];
   datatype = new String[rsmd.getColumnCount()];

   // Assign column labels and types.
   for (int col = 0;col < rsmd.getColumnCount();col++) {
     dataset[row][col] = rsmd.getColumnName(col + 1);
     datatype[col] = rsmd.getColumnTypeName(col + 1); }

   // Size nested arrays and assign column values for rows.
   while (rset.next()) {
     dataset[++row] = new Object[rsmd.getColumnCount()];
     for (int col = 0;col < rsmd.getColumnCount();col++) {
       if (datatype[col] == "DATE")
         dataset[row][col] = rset.getDate(col + 1);
       else if (datatype[col] == "NUMBER")
         dataset[row][col] = rset.getLong(col + 1);
       else if (datatype[col] == "VARCHAR2")
         dataset[row][col] = rset.getString(col + 1); }}

   // Set query return size.
   querySize = row;

   // Close resources.
   rset.close();
   stmt.close();
   conn.close();

   // Return data.
   return dataset; }
 catch (SQLException e) {
   // Check for and return connection error or SQL error.
   if (e.getSQLState() == null) {
```

```
     System.out.println(
       new SQLException("Oracle Thin Client Net8 Connection Error.",
                        "ORA-" + e.getErrorCode() +
                        ": Incorrect Net8 thin client arguments:\n\n" +
                        "  host name     [" + host + "]\n" +
                        "  port number   [" + port + "]\n" +
                        "  database name [" + dbname + "]\n"
                        , e.getErrorCode()).getSQLState());
       return dataset; }
     else {
       System.out.println(e.getMessage());
       return dataset; }}}}
  // ----------------------------------------------------------------/
  public static void main(String[] args) {
  // Define window.
  QueryTable frame = new QueryTable("Query Table"); }}
```

The `getQuery()` method contains the JDBC component. The method actually processes two queries. The first query counts the number of rows, and the second selects all columns from those rows. The while loop reads the rows, and the nested for loop reads the columns. An if statement processes DATE, VARCHAR2, and NUMBER data types. All other data types are ignored.

There are two alternatives using PL/SQL to read scalar data types. You can read one row at a time, or a group of rows. You can use a system reference cursor or a series of scalar arrays to return a set of rows.

This section has shown you how to access scalar variables and display them in a Java application. The next section explores how to query and manage large objects.

Writing and Accessing Large Objects

Java also can access large objects. Oracle supports Binary Large Objects (BLOBs), Character Large Objects (CLOBs), National Character Large Objects (NCLOBs), Binary Files (BFILEs), and Character Files (CFILEs). These types are generically known as LOBs or Large Objects. LOB columns are not stored inline with other data in a row. Only a reference is stored inline for LOBs. The reference points to where the LOB is stored. BLOB, CLOB, and NCLOB data columns are stored inside the database. BFILE and CFILE data types are stored externally in the file system. These columns cannot be indexed and are the principal subject of Chapter 10 in *Oracle Database 12c PL/SQL Programming*.

NOTE
You cannot use the DISTINCT function with a SELECT clause that returns a CFILE or BFILE column. If you attempt it, you will return an ORA-00932 error. This is raised because these LOB types cannot be indexed or sorted by the database.

The inline reference is alternatively called a descriptor or locator. Both words really mean an external reference because they are stored externally from the row. The best qualification of when to use *descriptor* or *locator* is whether the LOB is internally stored in the database. Many choose to use *descriptor* when the object is inside the database and *locator* when it is external to the database.

The following two sections illustrate examples of writing and reading a CLOB to the database and reading a BFILE reference from the database.

Writing and Accessing a CLOB Column

The BLOB, CLOB, and NCLOB are internally stored structures. CLOB and NCLOB columns are frequently long character streams. BLOB columns often contain media (like PDF files) or images. This example works with reading a large character stream—the description of the items in the media store.

The WriteReadCLOB.java program depends on a CLOB column item_desc in the item table. The column can be null, empty, or populated when you run the program. Any previous data is replaced by what you load into the column. You can create and seed values by running the create_store.sql and seed_store.sql scripts found on the McGraw-Hill Professional website for this book.

> **NOTE**
> *The WriteReadCLOB class can hang if you have another transaction pending against the same row. You should commit any pending changes before running the WriteReadCLOB class.*

When you run the WriteReadCLOB.java program, you're presented with a tabbed dialog box to enter database connection information, as shown in Figure A-3 in the "Accessing Scalar Variables" section. You should enter your hostname with a fully qualified domain name in the Host tab. Enter the listening port number for the Oracle database in the Port tab, and enter the TNS alias, discussed in Appendix A in *Oracle Database 12c PL/SQL Programming*, in the Database tab. You should then enter the user account name in the UserID tab and the password in the Password tab.

After you enter the database connection information, the WriteReadCLOB.java program will present you with a file chooser. Navigate to where you have stored the LOTRFellowship .txt file and choose the file, as shown in Figure A-6. Click Open, and the program will read the file and pass its contents as a string to the insertClob() method, where it is written to the database. After successfully writing the file contents to the CLOB column, the program calls the getQuery() method to read the column.

You use the getClob() method of the *ResultSet* class to assign the column reference to your Java program. This opens a special thread to the database. Through the thread, you read the out-of-line stored CLOB using the getCharacterStream() method of the Clob class. The output is returned as an input stream, which you can then assign to a *Reader* class. After you have read the input stream, you need to check that the CLOB column is both not null and populated.

CLOB columns have three states—null, empty, and populated. You should only attempt to read a Clob instance once you know that it isn't null and contains data. Then, you read it using the read() method of the Reader class. The read() method is a pass-by-reference subroutine (see Chapters 3 and 8 of *Oracle Database 12c PL/SQL Programming* for more on types of subroutines). It reads the contents of the input stream into the buffer, returning the number of characters read or a –1. It raises an error when the stream is empty, which is why you check it first. The program also raises an error when you attempt to read beyond the length of the CLOB value.

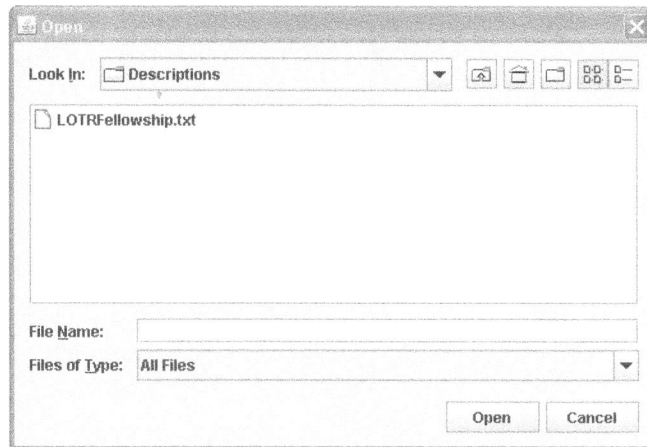

FIGURE A-6. *WriteReadCLOB.java file chooser display*

TIP
This program manages CLOB values that are larger than 4,000 characters but not large enough to collapse the memory of the JVM. Truly large files need to be read in chunks. You need to make sure that the total size of your buffer reads matches the length of the CLOB column. You can find the CLOB column length by using the DBMS_LOB.GETLENGTH() function before attempting to read it.

The WriteReadCLOB.java displays the CLOB column contents in a scrollable *JTextArea*. Figure A-7 displays the rendered results.

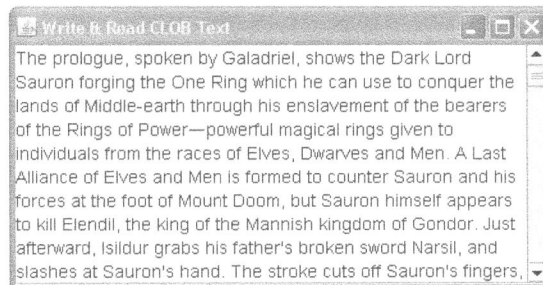

FIGURE A-7. *WriteReadCLOB.java display*

Leveraging Java Libraries

The `WriteReadCLOB.java` program uses a custom JAR file—`FileIO.jar`. You can download it from the publisher's website as a JAR file, or in its original source. The `FileIO.jar` file contains utilities for connecting across the network and a set of libraries for reading files on Microsoft Windows, Linux, or Unix systems. You can source this in your environment by adding it to your `CLASSPATH` environment variable. It follows the same rules as the `ojdbc6.jar` file covered earlier.

You can discover the contents of any Java archive by using the following command:

```
jar -tf GenericJavaArchive.jar
```

If you want to build your own `jar` files, you should check the online tutorial at http://docs.oracle.com/javase/tutorial/. One caveat: don't forget that each Java file must contain the

```
package path.subpath;
```

statement, which must be the first line in the file. While you can use the `jar` utility to build Java archives, any class without the correct `package` statement line is unrecognized by other files trying to reference it.

The following demonstrates how to read and display a `CLOB` column in a Java Swing application:

```
// Java Application class imports.
import java.awt.Dimension;
import java.awt.Font;
import java.awt.GridLayout;
import java.io.Reader;
import javax.swing.JFrame;
import javax.swing.JLabel;
import javax.swing.JOptionPane;
import javax.swing.JPanel;
import javax.swing.JScrollPane;
import javax.swing.JTextArea;

// Generic JDBC imports.
import java.sql.CallableStatement;
import java.sql.Clob;
import java.sql.Connection;
import java.sql.DatabaseMetaData;
import java.sql.ResultSet;
import java.sql.ResultSetMetaData;
import java.sql.SQLException;
import java.sql.Statement;

// Oracle JDBC import.
import oracle.jdbc.driver.OracleDriver;
import oracle.jdbc.pool.OracleDataSource;
```

```java
// Include book libraries (available at publisher's website).
import plsql.jdbc.DataConnectionPane;
import plsql.fileio.FileIO;
// -------------------------------------------------------------------/
public class WriteReadCLOB extends JFrame {
  // Define database connections.
  private String host;
  private String port;
  private String dbname;
  private String userid;
  private String passwd;

  // Define data connection pane.
  private DataConnectionPane message = new DataConnectionPane();

  // Construct the class.
  public WriteReadCLOB (String s) {
    super(s);

    // Get database connection values or exit.
    if (JOptionPane.showConfirmDialog(this,message
          ,"Set Oracle Connection String Values"
          ,JOptionPane.OK_CANCEL_OPTION) == 0) {

      // Set class connection variables.
      host = message.getHost();
      port = message.getPort();
      dbname = message.getDatabase();
      userid = message.getUserID();
      passwd = message.getPassword();

      // Print connection to console (debugging tool).
      message.getConnection();

      // Create a JPanel for data display.
      ManageCLOB panel = new ManageCLOB();

      // Configure the JPanel.
      panel.setOpaque(true);
      setContentPane(panel);

      // Configure the JFrame.
      setDefaultCloseOperation(JFrame.EXIT_ON_CLOSE);
      setLocation(100,100);
      pack();
      setVisible(true); }
    else
      System.exit(1); }
    // --------------------------------------------------------------/
    private class ManageCLOB extends JPanel {
      // Define display variables.
      private String clobText;
      private JScrollPane scrollPane;
      private JTextArea textArea;
      // --------------------------------------------------------------/
      public ManageCLOB () {
```

```
    // Set layout manager.
    super(new GridLayout(1,0));

    // Assign file read to String.
    clobText = FileIO.openFile(FileIO.findFile(this));

    // Insert record before querying it.
    if (clobText.length() > 0) {
      if (insertClob(host,port,dbname,userid,passwd,clobText))
        clobText = getQuery(host,port,dbname,userid,passwd); }
    else
      System.exit(2);

    // Construct text area and format it.
    textArea = new JTextArea(clobText);
    textArea.setEditable(false);
    textArea.setFont(new Font(Font.SANS_SERIF,Font.PLAIN,14));
    textArea.setLineWrap(true);
    textArea.setRows(10);
    textArea.setSize(400,100);
    textArea.setWrapStyleWord(true);

    // Put the image in container, and add label to panel.
    scrollPane = new JScrollPane(textArea);
    add(scrollPane); }
  // ----------------------------------------------------------/
  private Boolean insertClob(String host,String port,String dbname
                            ,String user,String pswd,String fileString) {
    try {
      // Set the Pooled Connection Source
      OracleDataSource ods = new OracleDataSource();
      String url = "jdbc:oracle:thin:@//"+host+":"+port+"/"+dbname;
      ods.setURL(url);
      ods.setUser(userid);
      ods.setPassword(passwd);

      // Define connection.
      Connection conn = ods.getConnection();

      // Create statement.
      CallableStatement stmt =
        conn.prepareCall("UPDATE item "+
                         "SET    item_desc = ? "+
                         "WHERE  item_title = "+
                         "'The Lord of the Rings - Fellowship of the Ring'"+
                         "AND    item_subtitle = 'Widescreen Edition'");

      // Set string into statement.
      stmt.setString(1,fileString);

      // Execute query.
      if (stmt.execute())
        conn.commit();

      // Close resources.
      stmt.close();
      conn.close();
```

```
      // Return CLOB as a String data type.
      return true; }
  catch (SQLException e) {
    if (e.getSQLState() == null) {
      System.out.println(
        new SQLException("Oracle Thin Client Net8 Connection Error.",
                         "ORA-" + e.getErrorCode() +
                         ": Incorrect Net8 thin client arguments:\n\n" +
                         "  host name      [" + host + "]\n" +
                         "  port number    [" + port + "]\n" +
                         "  database name  [" + dbname + "]\n"
                         , e.getErrorCode()).getSQLState());

      // Return an empty String on error.
      return false; }
    else {
      System.out.println(e.getMessage());

      // Return an empty String on error.
      return false; }}}
// -----------------------------------------------------------------/
private String getQuery(String host,String port,String dbname
                        ,String user,String pswd) {
  // Define method variables.
  char[] buffer;
  int count = 0;
  int length = 0;
  String data = null;
  String[] type;
  StringBuffer sb;

  try {
    // Set the Pooled Connection Source.
    OracleDataSource ods = new OracleDataSource();
    String url = "jdbc:oracle:thin:@//"+host+":"+port+"/"+dbname;
    ods.setURL(url);
    ods.setUser(userid);
    ods.setPassword(passwd);

    // Define connection.
    Connection conn = ods.getConnection();

    // Define metadata object.
    DatabaseMetaData dmd = conn.getMetaData();

    // Create statement.
    Statement stmt = conn.createStatement();

    // Execute query.
    ResultSet rset =
      stmt.executeQuery(
        "SELECT item_desc " +
        "FROM   item " +
        "WHERE  item_title = " +
        "'The Lord of the Rings - Fellowship of the Ring'"+
        "AND    item_subtitle = 'Widescreen Edition'");
```

```
    // Get the query metadata, size array, and assign column values.
    ResultSetMetaData rsmd = rset.getMetaData();
    type = new String[rsmd.getColumnCount()];
    for (int col = 0;col < rsmd.getColumnCount();col++)
      type[col] = rsmd.getColumnTypeName(col + 1);

    // Read rows and only CLOB data type columns.
    while (rset.next()) {
      for (int col = 0;col < rsmd.getColumnCount();col++) {
        if (type[col] == "CLOB") {
          // Assign result set to CLOB variable.
          Clob clob = rset.getClob(col + 1);

          // Check that it is not null and read the character stream.
          if (clob != null) {
            Reader is = clob.getCharacterStream();

            // Initialize local variables.
            sb = new StringBuffer();
            length = (int) clob.length();

            // Check CLOB is not empty.
            if (length > 0) {
              // Initialize control structures to read stream.
              buffer = new char[length];
              count = 0;

              // Read stream and append to StringBuffer.
              try {
                while ((count = is.read(buffer)) != -1)
                  sb.append(buffer);

                // Assign StringBuffer to String.
                data = new String(sb); }
              catch (Exception e) {} }
            else
              data = (String) null; }
          else
            data = (String) null; }
        else {
          data = (String) rset.getObject(col + 1); }}}

  // Close resources.
  rset.close();
  stmt.close();
  conn.close();

  // Return CLOB as a String data type.
  return data; }
catch (SQLException e) {
  if (e.getSQLState() == null) {
    System.out.println(
      new SQLException("Oracle Thin Client Net8 Connection Error.",
                       "ORA-" + e.getErrorCode() +
                       ": Incorrect Net8 thin client arguments:\n\n" +
                       "  host name       [" + host + "]\n" +
```

```
                          "  port number    [" + port + "]\n" +
                          "  database name  [" + dbname + "]\n"
                          , e.getErrorCode()).getSQLState());

          // Return an empty String on error.
          return data; }
        else {
          System.out.println(e.getMessage());
          return data; }}
        finally {
          if (data == null) System.exit(1); }}}
  // ------------------------------------------------------------/
  public static void main(String[] args) {
    // Define window.
    WriteReadCLOB frame = new WriteReadCLOB("Write & Read CLOB Text"); }}
```

The WriteReadCLOB.java program has demonstrated how to write and read a CLOB column from the database. The next section discusses how to use database references to read externally stored files.

Accessing a BFILE Column

Accessing an image stored in a BFILE requires you to understand how to process graphic images in Java Swing applications. The first example demonstrates how to read an image from the file system and display the image in a Swing application. The second shows how to read and translate the references to an external file into a canonical file name. Canonical file names are fully qualified file names that include an explicit path statement.

Reading and Displaying an Image

Reading files from the operating system is done by using an input stream. The ImageIO.read(new File(String *file_name*)) static method requires explicitly creating a File class and returns a BufferedImage instance. It hides the complexity of working with streams. You can also simplify the program by constructing an ImageIcon instance from a string, but this sometimes confuses maintenance programmers. The physical construction of a File class reference lets maintenance programmers know that the string maps to a physical file name. Figure A-8 shows how ReadImage.java renders the image.

FIGURE A-8. *ReadImage.java display*

File Dependency Error

The `ReadImage.java` file requires a valid `.gif`, `.jpg`, or `.png` file. You will raise the following exception when the file is not found:

```
Can't read input file!
Exception in thread "main" java.lang.NullPointerException
        at javax.swing.ImageIcon.<init>(ImageIcon.java:161)
        at ReadImage.<init>(ReadImage.java:43)
        at ReadImage.main(ReadImage.java:55)
```

The `read()` method of the *ImageIO* class also requires you to explicitly put a try-catch block in your code to handle any thrown `IOException`. After you read the file into a `BufferedImage`, you use it to build an instance of `ImageIcon` and then use it to build a `JLabel`. The `JLabel` is then added to the `JPanel` and rendered when the `JPanel` is added to a `JFrame` instance. The `ReadImage.java` file demonstrates these steps as shown:

```java
// Required imports.
import javax.swing.ImageIcon;
import javax.swing.JFrame;
import javax.swing.JLabel;
import javax.swing.JPanel;
import java.awt.GridLayout;
import java.awt.image.BufferedImage;
import java.io.IOException;
import java.io.File;
import javax.imageio.ImageIO;

// Include book libraries (available at publisher's website).
import plsql.fileio.FileIO;
// ----------------------------------------------------------------/
public class ReadImage extends JPanel {
  // Use to read and display BFILE image file.
  private BufferedImage image;
  private JLabel label;
  // ----------------------------------------------------------------/
  public ReadImage () {
    // Set layout manager.
    super(new GridLayout(1,0));

    // Read image file.
    try {
      image = ImageIO.read(FileIO.findFile(this)); }
    catch (IOException e) {
      System.out.println(e.getMessage()); }
```

```
        // Put the image into a container and add container to JPanel.
        label = new JLabel(new ImageIcon(image));
        add(label); }
    // --------------------------------------------------------------/
    public static void main(String[] args) {
        // Define window.
        JFrame frame = new JFrame("Read BFILE Image");

        // Define and configure panel.
        ReadImage panel = new ReadImage();
        panel.setOpaque(true);
        // Configure window and enable default close operation.
        frame.setContentPane(panel);
        frame.setDefaultCloseOperation(JFrame.EXIT_ON_CLOSE);
        frame.setLocation(100,100);
        frame.pack();
        frame.setVisible(true); }}
```

The static `main()` method creates a `JFrame` and decorates it with an instance of the `ReadImage` class. It launches a file chooser that lets you pick an image file to display. The `FileIO.jar` file contains the file chooser code.

This has demonstrated how to use Java to read and render an image file in a Java Swing application. The next section will demonstrate how to find the image by reading the locator reference in a `BFILE` column.

Reading and Displaying an Image by Using the Stored Reference

The inline reference for `BFILE` and `CFILE` columns contains a virtual directory and file name. This differs from the internal reference found in `BLOB`, `CLOB`, and `NCLOB` columns. You create virtual directories before you can insert a `BFILE` or `CFILE` column locator value. You insert the locator values by using the `CFILENAME` and `BFILENAME` functions. As qualified in Chapter 10 of *Oracle Database 12c PL/SQL Programming*, `BFILE` and `CFILE` data types are read-only types. They are read-only because you can only insert or update these columns with a new virtual directory or file name. There is also no way to write a new external file through the database unless you provide external libraries to do it. Likewise, there is also no Oracle utility that lets you read a canonical path directly. An available canonical path would let you prepend it to a file name and create a canonical file name.

Web applications overcome this limitation by configuring an alias and virtual directory in your HTTP server. You can use the Apache, Oracle HTTP Server, or Oracle WebLogic Server as the HTTP server. The alias maps to the database virtual path, and the virtual path maps to the database canonical path. Unfortunately, this type of architecture is tightly coupled, which means that when you change one, you must change the other.

Chapter 10 of *Oracle Database 12c PL/SQL Programming* contains a means to overcome this limitation. It extends the database catalog by adding the `get_directory_path` function to the `system` schema and granting access to it to the `video` schema. Then, it creates a `get_canonical_bfilename` function to the `PLSQL` schema. While these functions do not eliminate the tight coupling between the HTTP server and database, they do eliminate it for your programs interacting with the `PLSQL` schema.

Extending the Database Catalog

Virtual directories are created by the sys or system users and owned by the sys user. By default, system only has read permissions to the dba_directories view through the select_catalog_role. Roles limit the ability to directly access tables from PL/SQL programs.

In order to grant direct permissions in this case, you must first connect without a schema as the sysdba user. As the superuser, you can grant SELECT privilege on the dba_directories view to the system user, as noted:

```
SQL> CONNECT / as sysdba
Connected.
SQL> GRANT SELECT ON dba_directories TO system;
Grant succeeded.
```

After granting the permission, you can connect as the system user and run get_directory_path.sql to create the get_directory_path function. This extends the catalog behaviors, but you'll still need to grant permissions to the designated user scheme. You do this by granting EXECUTE permission on the get_directory_path function. The following grants that privilege to the PLSQL user:

```
SQL> GRANT EXECUTE ON get_directory_path TO plsql;
```

Reconnect as the video user and create a synonym to the get_directory_path() function. You can create a local copy of the get_canonical_bfile() function. The following syntax builds the synonym:

```
SQL> CREATE SYNONYM get_canonical_bfilename FOR system.get_directory_path;
```

Run the get_canonical_bfilename.sql script. It builds a local copy of the get_canonical_bfile() function. The function returns a canonical file name.

The ReadBFILE.java program depends on several things. It expects that you have compiled both the get_directory_path and get_canonical_path functions with their appropriate grants and synonyms. If you have not run these programs, you can find full instructions to run the create_store.sql and seed_store.sql scripts on the McGraw-Hill Professional website. Also, after running them you must create a virtual directory that points to where you will physically locate the files. Appendix A of *Oracle Database 12c PL/SQL Programming* demonstrates how to set up and grant permissions to a virtual directory.

You can test whether they're properly configured by running the following query on the respective platforms:

Windows

```
SELECT   get_canonical_bfilename('ITEM'
                                ,'ITEM_PHOTO'
                                ,'ITEM_TITLE'
                                ,'Star Wars I')
FROM     dual;
```

Unix

```
SELECT   get_canonical_bfilename('ITEM'
                                ,'ITEM_PHOTO'
                                ,'ITEM_TITLE'
                                ,'Star Wars I'
                                , 'LINUX')
FROM     dual;
```

You have correctly configured your environment when this SELECT statement returns the canonical file name. Reading the file is dependent on the correct file permissions.

The ReadBFILE.class uses the database connection input dialog, shown earlier in Figure A-3. After entering the connection data, you are prompted to enter the query data in the database query input dialog. Figure A-9 shows you that dialog.

Clicking OK displays a JFrame containing the poster for *Star Wars: Episode I – The Phantom Menace*. Figure A-10 displays the image by resolving the path through the database and avoids using an external virtual directory.

NOTE
The ReadBFILE.java class must run on the same physical machine as the database, and must have at least group read-only privileges to the canonical path or directory.

The ReadBFILE.java script uses a CallableStatement, not a Statement. Previous examples use Statement for preparsed SQL statements. You use a CallableStatement when you want to submit parameters to a SQL statement. This is also known as binding values.

A CallableStatement also lets you work with PL/SQL stored functions or procedures. This example uses an anonymous block to capture the canonical file name. It takes one output parameter from the CallableStatement. You map the output parameter by using the registerOutParameter() method from the CallableStatement. You map the input parameters by using the setString() method, but there are other methods that support different Oracle data types.

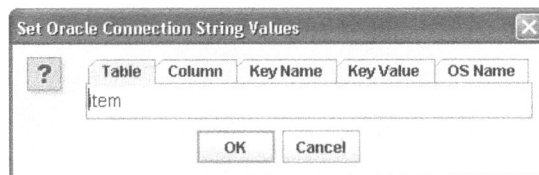

FIGURE A-9. *Database query input dialog*

FIGURE A-10. *ReadBFILE.java display*

TIP
Function and procedure calls should be made in an anonymous block program. Incorrect calls to stored functions and procedures inside a CallableStatement *instance can raise an* ORA-17033 *error. This is true using Java 5 or earlier, but Java 6 and Java 7 forward simply raise an NIO error.*

You also use the execute() method, not the executeQuery() method. OUT parameters can be captured by either name or positional reference. In this case, the OUT parameter uses positional reference. The program is

```java
// Required imports.
import java.awt.GridLayout;
import java.awt.image.BufferedImage;
import java.io.IOException;
import java.io.File;
import javax.imageio.ImageIO;
import javax.swing.ImageIcon;
import javax.swing.JFrame;
import javax.swing.JLabel;
import javax.swing.JOptionPane;
import javax.swing.JPanel;

// Generic JDBC imports.
import java.sql.CallableStatement;
import java.sql.Connection;
import java.sql.DatabaseMetaData;
import java.sql.DriverManager;
import java.sql.ResultSet;
import java.sql.ResultSetMetaData;
import java.sql.SQLException;
import java.sql.Types;
```

```java
// Oracle JDBC import.
import oracle.jdbc.driver.OracleDriver;
import oracle.jdbc.pool.OracleDataSource;

// Include book libraries (available at publisher's website).
import plsql.jdbc.DataConnectionPane;
import plsql.jdbc.DataTablePane;
// -----------------------------------------------------------------/
public class ReadBFILE extends JFrame {
  // Define database connections.
  private String host;
  private String port;
  private String dbname;
  private String userid;
  private String passwd;

  // Define query variables.
  private String tableName;
  private String columnName;
  private String keyColumnName;
  private String keyColumnValue;
  private String operatingSystem;

  // Define data connection and query panes.
  private DataConnectionPane message = new DataConnectionPane();
  private DataTablePane table = new DataTablePane(DataTablePane.TABLE_COLUMN_KEY);

  // Construct the class.
  public ReadBFILE (String s) {
    super(s);

    // Get database connection values or exit.
    if (JOptionPane.showConfirmDialog(this,message
          ,"Set Oracle Connection String Values"
          ,JOptionPane.OK_CANCEL_OPTION) == 0) {

      // Set class connection variables.
      host = message.getHost();
      port = message.getPort();
      dbname = message.getDatabase();
      userid = message.getUserID();
      passwd = message.getPassword();

      // Print connection to console (debugging tool).
      message.getConnection();

      // Collect query parameters.
      if (JOptionPane.showConfirmDialog(this,table
            ,"Set Oracle Connection String Values"
            ,JOptionPane.OK_CANCEL_OPTION) == 0) {

        // Set class query variables.
        tableName = table.getTableName();
        columnName = table.getColumnName();
        keyColumnName = table.getKeyColumnName();
```

```
            keyColumnValue = table.getKeyColumnValue();
            operatingSystem = table.getOperatingSystem();

             // Print table query variables.
            table.getTable(); }
          else
            System.exit(2);

          // Create a JPanel for data display.
          ManageBFILE panel = new ManageBFILE();

          // Configure the JPanel.
          panel.setOpaque(true);
          setContentPane(panel);

          // Configure the JFrame.
          setDefaultCloseOperation(JFrame.EXIT_ON_CLOSE);
          setLocation(100,100);
          pack();
          setVisible(true); }
        else
          System.exit(1); }
  // ------------------------------------------------------------------/
  private class ManageBFILE extends JPanel {
    // Use to read and display BFILE image file.
    private BufferedImage image;
    private JLabel label;
    private String canonicalFileName;
  // ------------------------------------------------------------------/
  public ManageBFILE () {

    // Set layout manager.
    super(new GridLayout(1,0));

    // Query the database and read canonical file name.
    canonicalFileName = getQuery(host,port,dbname,userid,passwd);

    try {
      image = ImageIO.read(new File(canonicalFileName)); }
    catch (IOException e) {
      System.out.println(e.getMessage());
      System.exit(3); }

    // Put the image into a container and add container to JPanel.
    label = new JLabel(new ImageIcon(image));
    add(label); }
  // ------------------------------------------------------------------/
  private String getQuery(String host,String port,String dbname
                         ,String user,String pswd) {

    // Define return variable.
    String data = null;

    try {
      // Set the Pooled Connection Source
      OracleDataSource ods = new OracleDataSource();
```

```
      String url = "jdbc:oracle:thin:@//"+host+":"+port+"/"+dbname;
      ods.setURL(url);
      ods.setUser(userid);
      ods.setPassword(passwd);

      // Define connection.
      Connection conn = ods.getConnection();

      // Create statement.
      CallableStatement stmt =
        conn.prepareCall("BEGIN " +
                          "  ? := get_canonical_bfilename(?,?,?,?,?);" +
                          "END;");

      // Register the OUT mode variable.
      stmt.registerOutParameter(1,Types.VARCHAR);

      // Register the IN mode variables.
      stmt.setString(2,tableName);
      stmt.setString(3,columnName);
      stmt.setString(4,keyColumnName);
      stmt.setString(5,keyColumnValue);
      stmt.setString(6,operatingSystem);

      // Execute query.
      if (stmt.execute());

      // Read rows and only CLOB data type columns.
      data = (String) stmt.getString(1);

      // Close resources.
      stmt.close();
      conn.close();

      // Return CLOB as a String data type.
      return data; }
  catch (SQLException e) {
    if (e.getSQLState() == null) {
      System.out.println(
        new SQLException("Oracle Thin Client Net8 Connection Error.",
                         "ORA-" + e.getErrorCode() +
                         ": Incorrect Net8 thin client arguments:\n\n" +
                         "  host name       [" + host + "]\n" +
                         "  port number     [" + port + "]\n" +
                         "  database name [" + dbname + "]\n"
                         , e.getErrorCode()).getSQLState());

      // Return an empty String on error.
      return data; }
    else { System.out.println("here");
      System.out.println(e.getMessage());

      // Return an empty String on error.
      return data; }}
    finally {
if (data == null) System.exit(1); }}}
```

```
// -----------------------------------------------------------/
public static void main(String[] args) {
  ReadBFILE frame = new ReadBFILE("Read BFILE Image"); }}
```

NOTE
Diagnostic information for your keyed inputs is printed to the command console when you run the ReadBFILE.class file.

This section has shown you how to read and display images stored on the file system. It has also demonstrated how you can leverage the Oracle Database 12c database to find and read canonical file names. The PL/SQL functions from Chapter 10 of *Oracle Database 12c PL/SQL Programming* show you how to extend the data catalog to deliver this functionality.

Supporting Scripts

The following programs are available on the McGraw-Hill Professional website to support this appendix:

- The HelloWorldThin.java program contains the basic connection code from this appendix.

- The QueryTable.java program contains the code that demonstrates reading tables from the Oracle database.

- The WriteReadCLOB.java program contains the code that shows you how to write a large string to a CLOB column and how to read the contents of a CLOB column to a large string.

- The ReadImage.java program contains the code to read an image file and display it inside a Java Swing application.

- The ReadBFILE.java program contains the code to read an image from a BFILE column and display it in a JOptionPane.

Summary

This appendix has reviewed the basics of working with Java and the JDBC. You have seen how to work with scalar and large objects. This appendix has provided coding examples to support how you'll write PL/SQL programming units to support external programming languages.

Index

Symbols

A

Join the Largest Tech Community in the World

Download the latest software, tools, and developer templates

Get exclusive access to hands-on trainings and workshops

Grow your professional network through the Oracle ACE Program

Publish your technical articles – and get paid to share your expertise

Join the Oracle Technology Network
Membership is free. Visit oracle.com/technetwork

@OracleOTN   facebook.com/OracleTechnologyNetwork

ORACLE®

Beta Test Oracle Software

Get a first look at our newest products—and help perfect them. You must meet the following criteria:

✔ **Licensed Oracle customer or Oracle PartnerNetwork member**

✔ **Oracle software expert**

✔ **Early adopter of Oracle products**

Please apply at: pdpm.oracle.com/BPO/userprofile

ORACLE®

If your interests match upcoming activities, we'll contact you. Profiles are kept on file for 12 months.

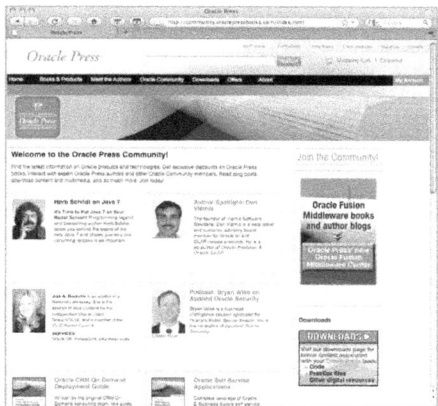

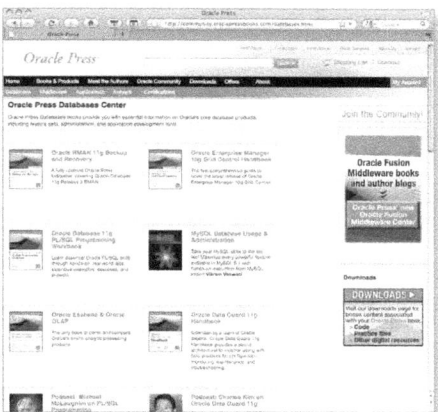

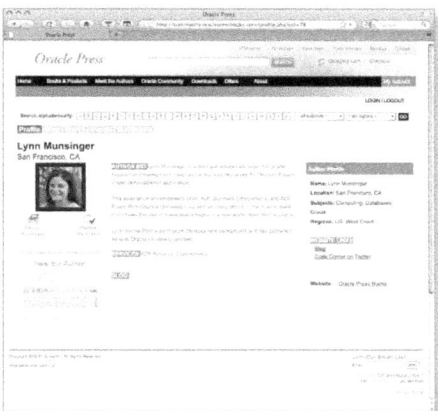

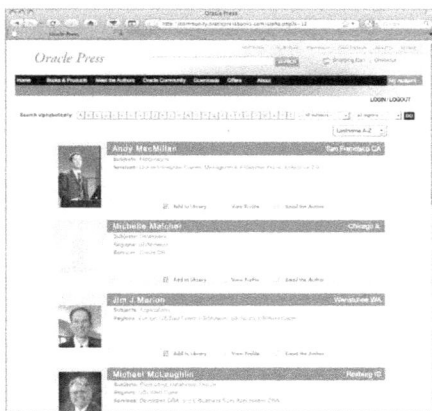

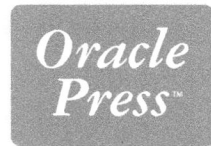

www.ingramcontent.com/pod-product-compliance
Lightning Source LLC
Chambersburg PA
CBHW080652220326
41598CB00033B/5179